The Castell of Love

A Critical Edition of Lord Berners's Romance

MEDIEVAL AND RENAISSANCE
TEXTS AND STUDIES

VOLUME 336

The Castell of Love

A Critical Edition of Lord Berners's Romance

Joyce Boro

ACMRS
(Arizona Center for Medieval and Renaissance Studies)
Tempe, Arizona
2007

*The publication of this volume has been greatly assisted by
a grant from the Program for Cultural Cooperation between
Spain's Ministry of Culture and United States Universities.*

Library of Congress Cataloging-in-Publication Data

Boro, Joyce Leslie.
  The castell of love : a critical edition of Lord Berners's romance / Joyce Boro.
    p. cm. -- (Medieval and Renaissance texts and studies ; v. 336)
  Includes bibliographical references.
  ISBN 978-0-86698-384-6 (alk. paper)
  1. San Pedro, Diego de, fl. 1500. Carcel de amor. 2. San Pedro, Diego de, fl.
1500--Criticism and interpretation. 3. San Pedro, Diego de, fl. 1500--Trans-
lations into English. 4. Berners, John Bourchier, Lord, 1466 or 7-1533. 5.
Translators--Great Britain--Biography. I. San Pedro, Diego de, fl. 1500. Carcel de amor. English. II. Title.

PQ6431.S4C333 2007
863'.2--dc22
                                                              2007029891

∞
This book is made to last.
It is set in Adobe Caslon Pro,
smyth-sewn and printed on acid-free paper
to library specifications.
Printed in the United States of America

TABLE OF CONTENTS

Acknowledgements

There are many people to whom I am indebted for their assistance over the course of writing this book, and I am delighted to have the opportunity to acknowledge them here. Helen Moore supervised this project in its earlier form as my D.Phil. thesis, and I am grateful for her encouragement and guidance. The astute comments, criticisms, and suggestions of my thesis examiners, Helen Cooper and James Carley, were essential to the transformation of the thesis into its present form. Helen Cooper sparked my interest in prose romance and was a formative influence in my thinking about Berners during tutorials and during her supervision of my M.Phil. thesis. I cannot thank her enough for her continued advice and extreme generosity over the years on all my research projects. James Carley has been a great source of support, reading and commenting on several drafts of this book and indulging me in many conversations about Berners and books. Douglas Gray is responsible for leading me to Berners when I was searching for a topic for my M.Phil. thesis, and I am grateful to him for numerous discussions over the years about Berners and medieval literature. A.S.G. Edwards first commented on my work as an anonymous reader for ACMRS. His insights at that stage and over the course of numerous subsequent conversations helped transform this into a much stronger book. The second reader for ACMRS, who has remained anonymous, also provided me with helpful comments, which I have integrated into this book. I would also like to acknowledge two of my undergraduate professors from McGill University, Dorothy Bray and Abbott Conway. They taught me to enjoy medieval literature, encouraged me to undertake postgraduate study at Oxford, and have maintained a keen interest in my work over the years. Alan Deyermond, Joseph Gwara, Marina Brownlee, and Barbara Weissberger also deserve a special mention for kindly providing me with unpublished materials, for being enthusiastic about my work, and for talking to me about San Pedro and the *novelas sentimentales*. I also owe a great debt to the friends and colleagues who have supported and encouraged me throughout the process of writing and revising this edition: Alexandra Gillespie, Anthony Bale, Michael Eberle-Sinatra, Martha Driver, Valerie Wayne, Don Beecher, Gail Scott, Robbie Schwartzwald, Paul Yachnin, Katherine Plowright, Kimberly Coles, Roger Dalrymple, Claire Loughlin-Chow, Jean Brink, Anna Marley, Frank DeMita, Sophie Beecher, Franco Pignoli, Helen Polychronakos, Jen Drouin, Denys

Landry, Lise Vautour, and the Norman family. My thanks also go to my research assistants, Josie Panzuto, and Katie Musgrave, and to Roy Rukkila and the staff at ACMRS for their patience and expert handling of my manuscript. My deepest thanks go to Julie Norman, who has held my hand through it all, and to whom I owe more than I could ever express.

I gratefully acknowledge the institutional and financial support from the following institutions: Université de Montréal, Fonds Québécois de la Recherche sur la Société et la Culture (FQRSC), Social Sciences and Humanities Research Council of Canada (SSHRC), the Overseas Research Students Awards Scheme, the University of Oxford, St Cross College, Wolfson College, and the Scatcherd European Travelling Fellowship Foundation. I would also like to thank the staff at the following libraries for their help and their willingness to put up with my often excessive requests for books: the Bodleian Library (especially the staff at Duke Humfrey's), the Taylor Institution, the British Library, the Folger Shakespeare Library, the Huntington Library, the Universidad de Salamanca, and the Biblioteca Nacional de España (Madrid).

Materials in some parts of this book appear in earlier forms in the following essays: "Lord Berners and His Books: A New Survey." *Huntington Library Quarterly*. Special Issue. Early Tudor Literature in Manuscript and Print. Ed. Alexandra Gillespie. 67 (2004): 236-50; and "'this rude laboure': Lord Berners's Translation Methods and Prose Style in *Castell of Love*." *Translation and Literature* 13 (2004): 1-23. I would like to thank the editors and publishers for allowing me to reprint them here.

Finally, I would like to thank my family, to whom this book is dedicated, for their unconditional love and support.

List of Abbreviations

adj.	adjective
adv.	adverb
B.L.	British Library
B.N.	Biblioteca Nacional de España (Madrid)
Bod.	Bodleian Library
Cárcel	*Cárcel de amor*
Castell	Castell of Love
CSP Ven.	*Calendar of state papers and manuscripts, relating to English affairs existing in the archives and collections of Venice, and in other libraries of northern Italy, 1202 – 1675.* Ed. Rawdon Brown, et al. 38 vols. London: Longman, Green, Longman, Roberts and Green, 1864-1940.
CSP Sp.	*Calendar of letters, despatches, and state papers, relating to the negotiations between England and Spain: preserved in the archives at Simancas and elsewhere.* Ed. G.A. Bergenroth, et al. 13 vols. London: Longman, Green, Longman and Roberts. 1862-1954.
DNB	*The Dictionary of National Biography.* CD-ROM. Oxford: Oxford University Press, 1995.
EETS	Early English Text Society
EETS ES	Early English Text Society, Extra Series
L&P	*Letters and papers, foreign and domestic of the reign of Henry VIII, preserved in the Public record office, the British museum, and elsewhere in England.* Ed. John S. Brewer. 21 Vols. 2nd edn. rev. J. Gardiner and R. H. Brodie. London: Her Majesty's Stationary Office, 1862-1932.
n.	noun
OED	*The Oxford English Dictionary.* http://dictionary.oed.com. Oxford: Oxford University Press.
prep.	preposition
STC	*A Short Title Catalogue of Books Printed in England, Scotland and Ireland, 1475-1640.* A. W. Pollard and G. R. Redgrave. 2nd edn. rev. W. A. Jacobs, F. S. Ferguson and Katherine R. Pantzer. 3 vols. London: Bibliographical Society, 1976-91.
v.	verb
vbl.	verbal

CONVENTIONS

The individual chapters of my edition of *Castell* are referred to by roman numerals followed by the page signature from the first edition of *Castell*.

All citations of *Castell* are from my edition.

There are many different spellings of the characters' names in the different languages and editions. I use the versions from the first English edition, i.e., Lereano, Laureola, Auctor, King Guallo, and Teseo.

There are many quotations from the continental versions of *Castell* throughout this book. Spanish quotations are from Carmen Parrilla's 1995 edition. For the French I use the second printed edition of 1526 (B.L. C.33.f.1). Italian quotations are from the first edition of 1514 (B.L. G.10100). The Italian and French are based on my transcription and have been slightly modernised: accents are provided, abbreviations are expanded, and the use of u/v and i/j have been regularised. Where the Spanish, Italian, and/or French are quoted, translations are always provided: I indicate the language by following the quotation with Sp for Spanish, It for Italian, or Fr for French in parenthesis, and follow that abbreviation with a translation. Where the two languages have the same translation, I provide only one translation, which is given after the letters following the final term. Translations are also always supplied after all other quotations of Spanish, French, and Italian texts.

All translations are my own, unless otherwise indicated. The main dictionaries I have used are as follows. For medieval Spanish translations I have had recourse to Martin Alonso, *Diccionario Medieval Español. Desde las Glosas Emilianenses y Silenses (s. X) hasta el siglo XV*, 2 vols. (Salamanca: Universidad Pontifica de Salamanca, 1986); and Robert Wyer, *The boke of Englysshe, and Spanysshe* (London: Wyer, 1554?) (*STC* 23010.5). Sixteenth-century French translations have been made with the use of Edmond Huguet, *Dictionnaire de la Langue Française du Seizième Siècle*, 8 vols. (Paris: Didier, 1925-1973); and Randle Cotgrave, *A Dictionarie of the French and English Tongues*, (London: Islip, 1611; rpt. with intro. by William S. Woods, Columbia, South Carolina: University of South Carolina Press, 1950). For Italian translations I have used *Grande Dizionario Della Lingua Italiana Moderna*, 5 vols. (Milan: Garzanti, 1996). Collins bilingual Spanish-English, French-English, and Italian-English dictionaries have also been used where necessary.

Introduction

1. John Bourchier, Lord Berners: Biography and Works

John Bourchier was born in Tharfield, Herefordshire in c.1467.[1] His father, Humphrey Bourchier, a Yorkist, was killed in the battle of Barnet in 1471, and so in 1474, John Bourchier succeeded his grandfather as second Baron Berners. His mother, Elizabeth, was the daughter and sole heir of Sir Fredrick Tilney. After Humphrey Bourchier's death she married (and outlived) Sir Thomas Howard, the second Duke of Norfolk (1430?–1485), establishing close ties between the families. The first Duke of Norfolk, John Howard, became Berners's guardian in 1475, and Berners married Howard's eldest daughter from his second marriage, Catherine.[2] The year of their wedding is unknown, although as early as 1481 Catherine Howard is referred to as "my Lady Barnes" in the Howard household books.[3] Berners and Catherine had two daughters, Mary and Jane (or Joan). Berners also had four illegitimate children with his mistress, Elizabeth Bakyn: James, Humphrey, George, and Ursula.[4] Berners's younger daughter and heiress, Jane

---

[1] John Bourchier, Lord Berners, *The Boke of Duke Huon of Burdeux*, ed. S. L. Lee. EETS ES 40, 41, 43, 50. (London: Trubner, 1882–1887), xl.; S. L. Lee, "Bourchier, John," *DNB*. CD-ROM. (Oxford: Oxford University Press), 1995.

[2] Dennis J. O'Brien, "Lord Berners's 'Huon of Burdeux': Its Cultural Context and its Language" (Ph.D. diss. Ohio State University. 1986), 34; idem, "Lord Berners's *Huon of Burdeux*: The Survival of Medieval Ideals in the Reign of Henry VIII," in *Medievalism in England*. Studies in Medievalism, ed. Leslie J. Workman, vol. 4. (Cambridge: Brewer, 1992), 36–44, 39; N. F. Blake, "Lord Berners: A Survey," *Medievalia et Humanistica* 2 (1971): 119–32, here 119. Berners's mother was married to Catherine's half-brother. Catherine outlived Berners, not dying until 12 March 1536, see George Edward Cokayne, *Complete Peerage of England Scotland Ireland Great Britain and the United Kingdom Extant, Extinct, or Dormant*, ed. Vicary Gibbs, vol. 1 (London, 1887) 2nd ed. (London: St Catherine Press, 1910; repr. Gloucester: Alan Sutton, 1987), 154.

[3] Anne Crawford ed., *The Household Books of John Howard, Duke of Norfolk, 1462–1471, 1481–1483*, vol. II (Gloucestershire: Sutton, 1992), 17.

[4] Nicholas Harris Nicolas, *Testamenta vetusta: Being Illustrations from Wills, of Manners, Customs, &c. as well as of the Descents and Possessions of Many Distinguished Families.*

(d. 1561), married Sir Edmund Knyvet, sergeant porter to Henry VIII.[5] They had one son, Thomas, who unsuccessfully tried to inherit the barony; it fell into abeyance until 1720.[6] Mary, who predeceased her father, married Alexander Unton of Wadley, and Ursula married Sir William Sherington—both were childless.[7]

Just as the dates of his marriage and births of his children are unknown, Berners's education also remains a mystery. It is unlikely, despite Anthony à Wood's claims, that he was educated at Balliol College, Oxford: Berners's name does not appear in the University registers.[8] Furthermore, the very detailed Howard household books, which do record the payment of university fees and maintenance for other young men in the early 1480s, do not mention Berners's tutelage.[9] It is likely that Wood mistook our John Bourchier for John Bourchier, the son of Lord FitzWarin.[10] Berners was well cared for by the Howards: numerous entries in their household books refer to provisions for the young ward.[11] No mention is made of a tutor for Berners, but we do know that Howard maintained a schoolmaster in his home long after his own children had outgrown the need for him, and this man may have been responsible for Berners's education.[12] On a naval mission to Scotland in 1481, Howard took fourteen secular French books with him, including many romances.[13] This suggests a larger collection left safely at

---

From the Reign of Henry the Second to the Accession of Queen Elizabeth, vol. 2 (London: Nichols & son, 1826), 657. In the list of pardons of 1509–10 he is pardoned as "John Barnes or Barneys, of Hevenyngham and Fynchyngfeld, Essex, esq., and Elizabeth his wife, late the wife of Robert Corbet, late of Asyngton, Suff., esq, 20 June" (*L&P*, I, 438 3m.16). This woman mentioned as his wife may have been the Elizabeth whom we know of as his mistress.

[5] It is believed that the signature E.K. in *Songs and Sonnets* belongs to Edmund Knyvet: see Emily Tennyson Bradley, "Edmund Knyvet," *DNB*, CD-ROM. (Oxford: Oxford University Press, 1995).

[6] Lee, "Bourchier, John." On the history of the barony see Cokayne, *Complete Peerage*, 154–9.

[7] Nicolas, *Testamenta vetusta*, 657.

[8] Anthony à Wood, *Athenae Oxonienses*, ed. Phillip Bliss, 3rd edn. (London: Rivington, 1813), 72.

[9] Crawford, *The Household Books*, II, 99, 147, 149, 300, 338, 341.

[10] Emden, A. B., *A Biographical Register of the University of Oxford to A.D. 1500* (London: Oxford University Press, 1957), 230.

[11] Crawford, *The Household Books*, II, 53, 95, 125, 146, 164, 200, 218, 318, 355, 402, 436, 440, 442, 449, 463.

[12] Crawford, *The Household Books*, xiv.

[13] The volumes are: *La destrucion de Troye, La Recuel des histoires troianes, Labre des batailes, Pontius, Sir Baudin conte de flandres, La Belle dame sans merci, Les Acusations de la dame, Le Myroir de la Mort, Le Jeu des Echecs, Le Jeu des Des, Le debat de la demoiselle et bon freres, Lamant rendu cordelier, Les d dessages,* and *Paris et Vienne*. Crawford, *The Household Books*, xix, and II, 277.

home, and this selection is possibly indicative of the type of literature to which Berners was exposed as a young man: romance, Trojan narratives, and other forms of courtly literature.

While Berners's personal life is not well documented, his public endeavours are. He was knighted at the age of 10 (on 17 January 1478) at the marriage of Richard, second son of Edward IV, and in 1484, he participated in an unsuccessful rebellion against Richard III on behalf of Henry, Earl of Richmond's supporters.[14] This act saw him opposing his former guardian and father-in-law: John Howard fought with Richard's army. As the result of this failed venture Berners was forced to flee to Brittany.[15] In 1492 he entered the service of Henry VII.[16] He helped quell the Perkin Warbeck rebellion in 1497,[17] frequently attended parliament,[18] and was one of the chief mourners at Henry VII's funeral.[19] Berners continued in royal service under Henry VIII. On 18 May 1509, Berners was nominated for the Order of the Garter by the Earl of Arundel, and on 23 April 1514, he was again nominated, this time by the Duke of Norfolk; both attempts proved unsuccessful.[20] During Henry VIII's reign, Berners continued to attend parliament and frequently acted as Justice of the Peace for Dorset, Herefordshire, and Surrey.[21] Berners formed part of the king's retinue on his journey to Calais in 1513 and also was present when the English army captured Terouenne on 22 August 1513.[22] It is believed that on returning from the Continent, Berners travelled to Scotland where he acted as marshal in Thomas Howard, Earl of Surrey's

---

[14] James P. Carley, "Bourchier, John, second Baron Berners (*c*.1467–1533)," *The Oxford Dictionary of National Biography*, ed. H. C. G. Matthew and Brian Harrison (Oxford: Oxford University Press, 2004).

[15] Berners, *The Boke of Duke Huon of Burdeux*, xl.

[16] Carley, "Bourchier, John, second Baron Berners (*c*.1467–1533)." See also *Calendar of Patent Rolls Preserved in the Public Record Office. Henry VII*, vol. II. A.D. 1494–1509. (London: H. M. S. O., 1916), 161, 326, 661.

[17] E. V. Utterson, ed., *Sir John Froissart's Chronicles of England, France [&c.] tr. by J. Bourchier, lord Berners. To which are added, a memoir of the translator, and a copious index*, 2 vols. (London: n.p., 1812), xiv.

[18] He was first summoned in October 1495, see Carley, "Bourchier, John, second Baron Berners (*c*.1467–1533)."

[19] *L&P*, I 20.

[20] *L&P*, I 37, 2838.

[21] Berners, *The Boke of Duke Huon of Burdeux*, xlii. For example, Berners was summoned to the Parliaments of 21 January 1510 and 4 February 1512 (*L&P*, I 205, 963). In November 1515, September 1518, January 1525, February 1526, and December 1528 he is named as a Commissioner of the peace for Surrey (*L&P*, II 1220, 4437; IV 1049 [16], 2002 [11] 5083 [11]). He fills the same post for Dorset in February 1524 (*L&P*, 137 [8]), and for Norfolk in March 1531 and December 1532 (*L&P*, V 166 [12], 1694 ii.).

[22] Berners, *The Boke of Duke Huon of Burdeux*, xli–xlii. On his presence at Terouenne see *L&P*, I 2051, 2053: 1, 2, 3, 4, 5, 6ii; I 2053 (1), 2218, 2413, 2480 i.44, ii.

army at the Battle of Flodden (September 1513).[23] Berners then acted as chamberlain to Princess Mary on the occasion of her marriage to Louis XII of France on 9 October 1514.[24] On 18 May 1514, Berners was awarded the prestigious position of Chancellor of the Exchequer, but he did not actually occupy the post until Sir Thomas Lovel's death in 1524.[25]

Ample travel opportunities presented themselves to Berners, and from April to December 1518 he accompanied Sir John Kite, the Archbishop of Armagh, on a diplomatic mission to Spain to forge an alliance between Henry and Charles V.[26] Unfortunately, Berners had to abstain from many conferences as he was plagued by gout, an illness that would continue to haunt him for the remainder of his life.[27] From Spain, Berners and Kite sent numerous letters to Cardinal Wolsey and Henry reporting on their meetings with Charles and his officials,[28] as well as epistles describing "daily triumphs, fighting at the bars, justs, and juga de kanes," pageants, processions, bull-fighting, and other festivities witnessed at the Spanish court.[29]

Despite Sidney Lee's assertions, Berners was not one of Henry's attendants at the Field of the Cloth of Gold.[30] Berners's signature appears on a letter from the Privy Council to Henry dated 13 June, from which it is clear that Berners is in England.[31] Berners's name does appear on the list of participants, but given that his signature appears on the letter from the Privy Council, it seems as though he was intended to travel to France in Henry's retinue and that his plans changed and he remained in England.[32]

---

[23] See Lee, "Bourchier, John"; Carley, "Bourchier, John, second Baron Berners (c.1467–1533)."

[24] L&P, I 3272, 3294, 3321, 3348 (3), 3355.

[25] L&P, IV 3540 (19), 3811. Berners's only recorded income for this post is the sum of 26l. 13s. 4d. received in Jan 1526. Presumably he earned this salary yearly, even though there is no record of the payments. L&P, IV 1939 (9).

[26] For details of this mission see L&P, I 4135, 4136, 4137, 3976; Berners, *The Boke of Duke Huon of Burdeux*, xli.

[27] His illness is mentioned in L&P, II 4383, 4440, 4629, 4660.

[28] L&P II 4160, 4161, 4164, 4165, 4228, 4313, 4342, 4436, 4590, 4658.

[29] L&P II 4282, 4342.

[30] Lee, "Bourchier, John"; Berners, *The Boke of Duke Huon of Burdeux*. Lee further asserts that on 2 July 1520 the Privy Council thanked Berners for his report of the meeting of the two monarchs, but in fact on that date Henry is thanked for the report and Berners is mentioned in relation to his accompanying visitors from France: see L&P, III 896.

[31] L&P, III 873.

[32] L&P, III 702–4; Berners is also mentioned in a document entitled "The appointment for the king and queene at Canterburie and so to Calias and Guynes to the meeting of the French king 1520" (Bod. MS Ashmole 1116, ff. 95r–99v). For a transcription see Joycelyne G. Russell, *The Field of the Cloth of Gold: Men and Manners in 1520* (London:

On 13 June 1520 he was an attendant to Princess Mary at Richmond,[33] and on 28 November 1520 he was appointed deputy of Calais, with the yearly salary of £100 for himself, and £104 for "spyall money."[34] Calais was an important territory in the context of trade, negotiation, and war with mainland Europe, and as a result, Berners's tasks combined mercantile, diplomatic, and military activities.[35] He was involved in affairs of commerce such as the Wool Staple,[36] and in June 1524, Berners was ordered to prepare a defence against a possible French attack.[37] He was responsible for conveying news from English informants in France to Henry and Wolsey on a regular basis; keeping them aware of all conflict—potential or actual—with France; informing them of any other news regarding the welfare of Calais and England; and communicating with Henry's ambassadors in France.[38] Spying and issues of national security were also part of his duties.[39] While the grandeur witnessed by Calais during the Field of the Cloth of Gold was never reproduced, as the centre of negotiations between England and the continent, Calais was the site of many magnificent conferences, treatises, and ceremonies.[40] The most splendid visit while Berners was Deputy was probably that of Henry and Anne Boleyn in October 1532. Other notable guests while Berners was Deputy were Wolsey in 1521, with whom Berners was in frequent contact, and Charles V in 1522, whom Berners had met four years previously in Spain.[41] Berners's tasks equally involved greeting, entertaining and ensuring the safe-passage of all officials and visitors who passed through the town on they way to, or from, England.[42]

Routledge and Kegan Paul, 1969), 191–204. It is believed that this document was prepared several months prior to the event, and so it further supports my hypothesis that Berners intended to, but never actually did, travel to France. See Russell, *The Field*, 194.

[33] *L&P*, III 873.

[34] *L&P*, III 1074.

[35] On Calais in general, see Muriel St Clare Byrne, ed., *The Lisle Letters* (Chicago and London: University of Chicago Press, 1981), 421–52; and George Amelius Crawshay Sandeman, *Calais under English Rule*, (Oxford: Basil Blackwell, 1908), 84ff. For examples of these different duties, see *L&P*, V 370v, 787, 1703 ii, 1708; III 2334.

[36] *L&P*, III 2777.

[37] *L&P*, IV 414.

[38] *L&P*, III 1141, 2376, 2802; IV 564, 1167, 2006, 2027, 2048, 2088, 2109, 2135, 2169, 2217, 2219, Appendix 26.

[39] Sandeman, *Calais under English Rule*, 45; *L&P*, III 2890, 3014; IV 1128, 1363, 1473, 1535, 1664, 1731, 1922, 2047.

[40] Sandeman, *Calais under English Rule*, 121–22.

[41] Berners, *The Boke of Duke Huon of Burdeux*, xlv; Sandeman, *Calais under English Rule*, 123.

[42] Ferrers was there in 1523, Bryan in 1522, and the Chancellor of Alençon and Lord Bevers in 1525: see *L&P*, III 428, 2837, 2973; IV 457, 999, 1000.

It was once believed that Berners remained Deputy of Calais from 1520 until his death in 1533, but it is clear that this period was interrupted by a dismissal from his post and a return to England.[43] In October 1526, Sir Robert Wingfield was appointed deputy of Calais and he performed that function until 27 March 1531, when Berners was reinstated.[44] Berners's name appears on various documents between 1526 and 1531 attesting to his presence in Britain, including Henry's divorce petition to Pope Clement VII of July 1530.[45] The reasons for Berners's removal from Calais are unknown. There is no evidence of misconduct or of an inability to adequately perform his duties. The dismissal could have been related to his large financial obligations to the king.[46] Steadily accumulating since 1511, his substantial debts to Henry may have caused him to fall out of favour.[47] On 26 November 1520, the Duke of Buckingham was sent to discuss Berners's debts with him and Berners's appointment as Deputy was made two days later suggesting a link between the two events.[48] The Deputy-ship may have been seen as a way of controlling Berners's spending, or of proving him with an income that would allow him to repay some debts. When the plan failed, Berners

---

[43] John McDill, "The Life of Lord Berners," *TLS* (17 April 1930): 336. The original belief is not completely far-fetched since in November 1526 and May 1527 men were still given grants to enter into Berners's retinue: see *L&P*, IV 2673 (3), 3142 (19). In addition, on 30 June 1527, Berners wrote to Wolsey regarding the wheat supply in Calais: see *L&P*, IV 3209.

[44] I. S. Leadam, "Sir Robert Wingfield," *DNB*. CD-ROM. (Oxford: Oxford University Press, 1995). See *L&P*, IV 2518, 2519 on Wingfield's appointment. On 12 August 1531 Berners's signature appears in the book of payments for the new fortifications of Calais, so by this point he must have been reinstated in his post: see *L&P*, V 370v.

[45] McDill, "The Life of Lord Berners," 336. Norfolk mentioned him as being in England in a letter to Wolsey dated 23 April 1528 (*L&P*, IV 4192). Berners was present and involved in land disputes regarding his property in Finchley in 1528 (*L&P*, IV 4442 [6]). His signature appears on various documents; including an Act of Parliament in November 1529 (*L&P*, IV 3087, 6044). On 11 April 1529 Berners wrote a letter to Cromwell, signed at Aschwelthrope (*L&P*, IV 5456). And in 1529 Berners was considered as a possible ambassador to Charles V (*L&P*, IV 5885). The divorce petition was signed on 13 July 1530 (*L&P*, IV 6513).

[46] McDill, "The Life of Lord Berners," 336.

[47] Berners, *The Boke of Duke Huon of Burdeux*, xlii. He was frequently recorded as owing Henry money. In December 1515 he is listed as owing 350*l*, and it is mentioned again in 1517 and 1518, *L&P*, III 1364, 3087, 4143. Berners's debts continued to be noted in December 1530: see *L&P*, IV 6216, 6792; V 1715. On 1 December 1532 Henry loaned Berners an additional £500:see *L&P*, V 1600.

[48] *L&P*, III 1070, 1074. In addition, Buckingham may have suggested an exchange of lands between himself and Berners following this meeting since an exchange occurred shortly thereafter. See, for example, *L&P*, III 1286, 1287, 1288 (7), 2027, 2169, 2218, 2730.

may have been recalled. Nevertheless, Berners's income was seriously reduced when he returned to England, allowing his debts to increase further. In 1527 Robert Viscount Fitzwater replaced Berners as Chancellor of the Exchequer and so until Berners was reinstated in Calais, his income solely consisted of rents on his lands.[49] Berners's financial situation became very important to Henry in March 1533, when he perceived Berners to be on his deathbed. He wrote the following to his officials in Calais: "As lord Berners, deputy of Calais, is dangerously ill, and much in our debt, we command you, in case of his decease, to arrest all his goods, either within his house, or within the town and marches, and keep them till we be satisfied."[50] The exact amount owed to Henry at this point is unknown, but £700 was still outstanding in June 1536.[51]

As soon as Berners died, Henry ordered his goods seized and appointed Arthur Plantagenet, viscount Lisle as Deputy of Calais.[52] The settlement of Berners's estate proved rather complicated, despite the fact that Berners left a detailed will (dated 3 March 1533 and proved 4 February 1534) and that two separate inventories were taken of his goods, dated 21 March 1533 and 17 March 1534.[53] Some lands and possessions are traceable but attempts to definitively locate his library have proved futile, even though his books are noted in both inventories.[54] The earlier inventory includes the following: "*Item* in the stoody $^{xx}_{iiij}$ [80] books vz oon of Latten & frenche."[55] The titles of the books are not given in this document nor do they appear in his will. The second inventory lists Berners's possessions and to whom they were distributed; but information about his library, however, is even less specific in this inventory than in the first: it states that in the pantry there is "a plain chest nailed up with certain books," valued at 18 1/2*d*.[56] These may be the same eighty books listed in the earlier document, but if they are, all it tells us is that the books remained in Calais a year after Berners's death—we still do not know what became of this chest.

---

[49] *L&P*, IV 3540 (19), 3811. His land holdings were significant, but would not have provided him with a very large income. See, for example, *L&P*, IV 3991 (15).

[50] This was actually dated 16 March 1533, the day of Berners's death: see *L&P*, VI 240.

[51] *L&P*, X 1257.

[52] *L&P*, VI 308; X 628–9.

[53] His will is in Nicolas, *Testamenta vetusta*, 657–59. On the first inventory, see Berners, *The Boke of Duke Huon of Burdeux*, xlvi; *L&P*, VI appendix 2. The second inventory is in *L&P*, VII 336. For details regarding some of the problems with his estate see *L&P*, VI 581; VII 213, 461, 474, 502–3, 522, 614, 627, 652, 686; X 270, 337, 765; XI 387, 466.

[54] On his lands see *L&P*, VI 241, 277; XV 852–3; and on his some of his goods see Byrne, *Lisle Letters*, I 441, 444, 451, letters 1–4, 6; II letter 148, 151, 152, 159, 160, 168, 171, 183–5, 191, 489; III letter 645; V letter 1260; VI 190, 191.

[55] *L&P*, VI appendix 2.

[56] *L&P*, VII 336.

Berners's books may have wound up in the possession of Elizabeth and Nicholas Carew.[57] As Elizabeth Carew was his niece, was involved in the composition of *Castell*, and was literate (she was known to have owned a copy of Lydgate's *Fall of Princes* [BL MS Sloane 4031]), it is not improbable that she should have inherited his books. [58] An inventory was taken of the Carews' possessions at Beddington in 1539, after Nicholas Carew's execution, which lists the contents of his library. The library included only one text that was specifically classified as English, an illuminated manuscript of Gower's *Confessio Amantis*. It also contained the following French works: *Lancelot*, two volumes of *Orosius*, the works of Alain Chartier, two volumes of selections from the *Chroniques* by Enguerran de Monstrelet, the *Chroniques de France*, Nicole Le Huen's translation of the *Peregrinatio in Terram Sanctam*, *Ordinaire des Chrétiens*, and most significantly, ten copies of Froissart's *Chroniques*.[59] There were four copies of volume one of Froissart, three of the second volume, two of the third, and an additional book with an unspecified volume number, "this one just possibly the English translation."[60] It is highly unlikely that anyone other than Berners, the translator of Froissart, would have amassed such a large collection of different editions of this work. [61] Moreover, the predominantly literary and historical collection suggests Berners's tastes. If these were Berners's books then the fact that he owned numerous copies of the work he was translating can shed additional light on his translation practices, indicating that he may have compared the different texts in order to select the best reading, which he would then translate. This is certainly not incongruous with my observations regarding his use of two different language versions of *Castell*, as described below.

Whilst we are unsure of how he translated *Chronicles*, it is certain that Berners began the task during his first stay in Calais, after the signing of the Treaty of Bruges (August 1521), and that he completed the first volume in 1522. On the title page and in the preface of the first edition, it states that the translation was made at the request of Henry VIII and the Tudor arms decorate the verso of the title page; the same coat of arms is used in Lydgate's *Troy Book*.[62] Pamela Neville-Sington posits that "[i]ts intention, like Christine de Pisan's *Fayttes of arms* and Lydgate's *Troy Book*, was to remind Englishmen that France was their

---

[57] James P. Carley, ed., *The Libraries of King Henry VIII*, Corpus of British Medieval Library Catalogues 7 (London: British Library in association with British Academy, 2000), liv.

[58] Carley, *The Libraries of King Henry VIII*, liv.

[59] Carley, "Bourchier, John, second Baron Berners (*c*.1467–1533)."; Carley, *The Libraries of King Henry VIII*, liv–lv, 294–96.

[60] Carley, *The Libraries of King Henry VIII*, 294.

[61] Cf. Carley, *The Libraries of King Henry VIII*, lv.

[62] It was printed by Richard Pynson on 28 January 1523 (*STC* 11396).

traditional enemy and to inspire its readers to feats of glory on the battlefield."[63] She observes that the publication of the first volume coincides with Henry's renewed claims of his rightful French inheritance, and she conjectures that "The Crown almost certainly delayed the publication of the second and final part, describing the close of the Hundred Years' War, to coincide with the signing of the peace treaty between England and France at the More, one of Wolsey's residences, on 30 August 1525."[64] The colophon of the second volume states its date of completion as 10 March 1525, but the date of publication is given as "the last day of August the yere of our lorde god. M. D. xxv [31 August 1525]," just one day after the signing of the peace treaty.[65] The first volume of the *Chronicles* was printed three times, and the second underwent two editions.[66] The *Chronicles* were frequently found in early modern libraries such as those of Nicholas Carew, Lord Lumley, and Sir Edward Dering.[67] Until recently it has been believed that Berners's work was preserved only in print; however, a manuscript fragment of 10 folios of his translation of Froissart's *Chronicles* has been recently indexed. The manuscript is housed at Keio University Library, Japan, and its provenance is unknown. A. S. G. Edwards dates it to the late sixteenth or early seventeenth century, and suggests that it may have been copied from a printed edition which is no longer extant.[68]

Berners's earliest translation was probably the romance, *The History of the moost noble and valyaunt knight, Arthur of Lytell Brytayne*, translated from the French *Artus de la Petite Bretagne*.[69] The French prose romance was first printed in 1493.[70] There are three extant, very similar, editions of *Arthur*: the first was

---

[63] Pamela Neville-Sington, "Press, Politics and Religion," in *The Cambridge History of the Book in Britain, Volume III, 1400–1557*, ed. Lotte Hellinga and J. B. Trapp (Cambridge: Cambridge University Press, 1999), 576–607, 585.

[64] Neville-Sington, "Press, Politics," 585.

[65] f. 319r (*STC* 11397).

[66] *STC* 11396–6.7 and *STC* 11397–7a.

[67] James Gardiner, "Nicholas Carew," *DNB*. CD-ROM. (Oxford: Oxford University Press, 1995); Carley, *The Libraries of King Henry VIII*, liv–lv, 294–6; Sears Reynolds Jayne and Francis R. Johnson, eds., *The Lumley Library. The Catalogue of 1609*, (London: Trustees of the British Museum, 1956), 154; Nati H. Krivatsy and Laetitia Yeandle, "Sir Edward Dering," *Private Libraries in Renaissance England* 1 (Binghampton: MRTS, 1992), 137–269, 266

[68] A. S. G. Edwards, "Lord Berners' Translation of Froissart's *Chronicle*, Fragment of a Manuscript Copy," in *Mostly British: Manuscripts and Early Printed Materials from Classical Rome to Renaissance England in the Collection of Keio University Library*, ed. Takami Matsuda (Tokyo: Keio University Press, 2001), 172–76, esp. 173, 175–76. There is a photocopy of this fragment at the B.L.

[69] Blake, "Lord Berners: A Survey," 130. Henceforth this romance will be referred to as *Arthur*.

[70] Carley, "Bourchier, John, second Baron Berners (*c*.1467–1533)."

printed in 1560 by William Copland for Robert Redborne; the second, also from 1560, names only Copland; and the third appeared in 1582, printed by Thomas East.[71] It is possible that there was an earlier edition of the romance as John Bale notes a copy of *Arthur* in a bookshop in his *Index Britanniae Scriptorum*.[72] *Arthur* was a popular romance: it is listed as a favourite romance in *The Complaynte of Scotland;*[73] and it is thought that *Arthur* influenced Spenser's *Faerie Queene*.[74] In his study of *Arthur* and *The Faerie Queene*, Edwin Greenlaw declares that it is "probably the greatest single influence to be traced in Spenser's poem," and Sarah Michie demonstrates that it is "a tale which offers more suggestive parallels to the narrative patterns of the *Faerie Queene* than any other one romance, save Ariosto's *Orlando Furioso*."[75] Michie notes an abundance of "corespondences in narrative sequence, incident, and descriptive detail" between the *Arthur* and *The Faerie Queene*, running all the way through Spenser's poem.[76]

Like *Arthur*, *Huon of Burdeux* is the translation of a French chivalric prose romance.[77] There is only one extant edition of *Huon*, which was printed by Thomas Purfoot in 1601. External evidence suggests that there were additional printings, probably amounting to three or four in total dating from 1515, c.1545–1558, 1570, and 1601.[78] *Huon* narrates the fantastic adventures of the eponymous character as he witnesses the marvellous and accomplishes the unexpected, often with the assistance of Oberon, the Fairy King. It was a very popular romance, owned by many such as Richard Brereton and the fictional Captain Cox. It was condemned by Edward Dering, and influenced later writers such as Spenser, Jonson, Marlowe, and Shakespeare.[79]

---

[71] *STC* 807–808. On bibliographical problems, see G. E. Mitchell, "The Sixteenth Century Editions of *Arthur of Little Britain*," *Revue Belge de Philologie et d'Histoire* 50 (1972): 793–95; and Joyce Boro, "Lord Berners and His Books: A New Survey," *Huntington Library Quarterly*, Special Issue, Early Tudor Literature in Manuscript and Print, ed. Alexandra Gillespie, 67 (2004): 236–50, here 237–39.

[72] John Bale, *Index Britanniae scriptorum quos ex variis bibliothecis non parvo labore collegit Ioannes Baleus*, ed. Reginald Lane Poole (Oxford: Clarendon Press, 1902), 184.

[73] F. J. Furnivall, ed., *Complaynte of Scotland* (London: Kegan Paul, Trench, Trübner, 1890), cxlv.

[74] Edwin A. Greenlaw, "Britomart at the House of Busirane," *Studies in Philology* 26 (1929): 117–30; Michie, "*The Faerie Queene*," 105–23.

[75] Greenlaw, "Britomart at the House," 124; Michie, "*The Faerie Queene*," 105.

[76] Michie, "*The Faerie Queene*," 107.

[77] Subsequent references to this romance will be to *Huon*.

[78] Joyce Boro, "The Textual History of *Huon of Burdeux*: A Reassessment of the Facts," *Notes and Queries* n.s. 48 (2001): 233–37; and Boro, "Lord Berners and His Books: A New Survey," 239–40.

[79] John W. Draper, "A Reference to *Huon* in Ben Jonson," *Modern Langauge Notes* 35 (1920): 439–40; Jefferson B. Fletcher, "*Huon of Burdeux* and *The Fairie Queene*," *JEGP* 2 (1899): 203–12; John R. MacArthur, "The Influence of *Huon of Burdeux* upon *The*

John Bale declares that Berners made translations from Italian, but we have no evidence to support such a statement. He was possibly mistakenly referring to Berners's two Spanish translations: *Castell* and *The Golden Book of Marcus Aurelius*;[80] although he indexes them separately. It is believed that *Castell* was composed in the late 1520s or early 1530s, before *Golden Book* but after *Huon, Arthur,* and *Chronicles. Castell* was first printed by Johan Turke in 1548?, and was reprinted shortly thereafter, in 1552?, by Robert Wyer for Richard Kele, and again in c.1555 by John Kynge.[81] The second and third editions are almost identical to Turke's except for minor textual variants, the addition of marginal notes, and the inclusion of four poems by Andrew Spigurnell, all of which will be discussed below.

Unlike Berners's *Froissart,* which was owned by many, or *Huon* and *Arthur,* whose influence is readily apparent in subsequent texts, I have found only three direct references to *Castell* and no evidence of its direct influence on later literature. Yet from these references we can conclude that *Castell* was known in late sixteenth-century England. The first mention of *Castell* occurs in Bale's *Index Britanniae Scriptorum,* wherein he notes that a copy of the romance was owned by William Hanleye.[82] Unfortunately not much more is known about Hanleye's library; in the *Index* "[h]e is cited a number of times, but always for recent or contemporary works."[83] The second mention of *Castell* occurs in a list of licentious books in *A briefe and necessary instruction* by J. More and revised by E. D., dated 1572 (*STC* 6679). J. P. Collier originally thought that E. D. was Edward Dyer, but archivists at the B. L. and the *STC* later identified him as Edward Dering.[84] In this work, Dering condemns romances for "their spiritual enchauntementes, in which they were bewytched [such as,] *Beuis* of Hampton, *Guy* of Warwike, *Arthur* of the round table, *Huon* of Burdeaux, *Oliuer* of the Castle, the foure sonnes

---

Fairie Queene," JEGP 4 (1902): 215–38; Ethel Seaton, "Marlowe's Light Reading," in *Elizabethan and Jacobean Studies Presented to Frank Percy Wilson,* ed. Herbert Davis and Helen Gardner (Oxford: Clarendon Press, 1959), 17–35; Muriel Kinney, "Possible Traces of *Huon de Bordeaux* in the English Ballad of Sir Aldingar," *Romanic Review* 1 (1910): 314–21.

[80] This text will henceforth be referred to as *Golden Boke.*

[81] Information on these editions is provided below. The colophon to the first edition names Johan Turke as the printer; however, the *STC* conjectures that Reginald Wolfe printed the text for Turke, while the electronic *STC* (http:// eureka.rlg.ac.uk/cgi-bin/ zgate2.prod) conjectures that Richard Field printed the text for Turke. Due to this lack of consensus, for simplicity's sake, I will refer to Turke as the printer of the first edition throughout this book.

[82] Bale, *Index Britanniae scriptorum,* 184.

[83] Bale, *Index Britanniae scriptorum,* xxv.

[84] J. P. Collier, *A Bibliographical and Critical Account of the Rarest Books in the English Language, Alphabetically Arranged,* vol. 1 (London: Joseph Lilly, 1865), 327; see the *STC* entry and B.L. catalogue entry (C. 53 aa 31).

of *Amond,* and a great many other such childish follye."[85] After listing many other volumes, Dering declares, "Yea some haue ben so impudent, as new borne *Moabites,* which wallow in their own vomit, and haue not bene a shamed to entitle their bookes, The Court of Venus, The Castle of Loue, and manye such other as shamelesse as these."[86] The positioning of *Castell* separate from *Huon* and the other romances seems to be due to its lack of supernatural elements as well as to its racy, "impudent" title. Interestingly, *Castell* is also separated from *Huon* in the description of Captain Cox's library in *Robert Laneham's Letter.* Cox's fictional library contents are divided into six sections: "matters of storie"; "Philosophy both morall and naturall"; "auncient playz"; a breviary; "a bunch of ballets & songs"; and almanacs.[87] The first, and by far the largest, category contains many of the same romances as those that Dering initially condemns, such as *Guy, Bevis, Huon, Arthur, Oliver,* and *Aymon,* as well as ballads and other fiction. *Castell,* however, is not included in this section, but is found the second category along with moral and philosophical works, jest books, fabliaux, and satires of women.

This positioning of *Castell* raises questions regarding how it was read: namely whether or not it was read as a romance, as a moral work, an advice manual, or satire of women. While *Castell* treats political themes and can be read as part of the woman debate, it is primarily a work of fiction. Yet the categories are not closely adhered to in Cox's list. For example, works which are more "philosophical" than *Castell* appear in the first section, such as *The Churl and the Bird,* which is an overtly moral poem; *The Seven Wise Masters,* which deals more explicitly with moral and political themes than *Castell;* and *The Wife Lapt in a Morels Skin,* which is explicitly about women. I would also have expected *Howeglass, The Sak full of Nuez,* and *Skogan* to be in the same group as *The Hundred Mery Tales, The Demaunded Joyous,* and *The Book of Riddels,* but the former three jestbooks are in the first group with the romances, and the latter are in the second with *Castell.* The separation may be arbitrary, but then again, the cumulative evidence provided by the two inventories suggests that *Castell* may not have been read in the same way as a traditional native romance. While there may be many inconsistencies in the categories, the grouping of romances together, separate from *Castell,* occurs in both inventories. This may be a result of *Castell*'s later date in publication, its more eloquent prose style, its Spanish influences, its interest in the psychology of love and women's position in amorous relationships, its focus on

---

[85] Edward Dering, *A briefe & necessary introduction* (London: Awdley, 1572) A2v.

[86] Dering, *A briefe & necessary,* A3r.

[87] Frederick J. Furnivall, *Captain Cox, his Ballads and Books; or Robert Laneham's Letter: Whearin part of the entertaunement untoo the Queen Majesty at Killingworth Castl, in Warwik Sheer in this Soomerz Progress. 1575. is signified, from a freend officer attendant in the court, unto hiz freend, a citizen and merchaunt of London* (London: Taylor for The Ballad Society, 1871), xii–xiv.

counsel and kingship, or its interest in epistolarity, to name but a few possibilities. It may have been read as a work of "Philosophy both morall and naturall," possibly as counsel literature or as epistolary instruction. It may also have been read as part of the woman debate, as it was in Spain. (These generic affiliations will be discussed below). The latter is suggested by Cox's categories and by Andrew Spigurnell's prologue, which focuses on the acceptable behaviour and reading material for women.

The colophon to *Golden Book* dates it to 10 March 1532. *Golden Book* is a translation of a French version of Antonio de Guevara's *Libro Aureo de Marco Aurelio*. The French translation used by Berners, probably made by René Berthault, appeared in Paris in 1531, thus providing a *terminus a quo* for Berners's translation.[88] The translation was undertaken at the request of Francis Bryan, Berners's nephew. It was a very popular book, first printed in 1535 by Thomas Berthelet, and it was reissued sixteen times by different printers up to 1586.[89] Berners's two Spanish translations differ in tone and content from his earlier three works. The latter, of French origin, are old-fashioned chivalric texts incorporating magic and marvels, and are written in an often clumsy, slightly dated prose style, comparable to William Caxton's romances. The Spanish texts, by contemporary authors, are more modern in style and content and exhibit a Humanist concern with rhetoric, eloquence, epistolarity, good kingship, and counsel. These changes in Berners's literary production and style could be a result of increased contact with younger family members upon his return to England from Calais in 1526: both were translated for his sister's (Margaret, Lady Bryan) children — *Golden Boke* for Francis Bryan, and *Castell* for Lady Elizabeth Carew. Both Bryan and Carew had close court connections and their taste most likely reflects current literary trends at the Henrican court. Bryan himself translated another work by Guevara.[90]

Bale attributes two additional texts to Berners in the *Index Britanniae Scriptorum* according to "ex testibus Calesiensibus."[91] The first, *Ite ad Vineam*, is likely to be a Latin religious drama. The second, *De officiis Calesianorum*, may be the text now known as *Ordinances for watch and ward of Calais*.[92]

---

[88] Carley, "Bourchier, John, second Baron Berners (*c*.1467–1533)."

[89] *STC* 12436–47.

[90] Bryan's translation is entitled *A dispraise of the life of a courtier*. It was printed by Grafton in 1548, *STC* 12431.

[91] Bale, *Index Britanniae scriptorum*,183–84. Trans. From the attestation of the people of Calais.

[92] Berners, *The Boke of Duke Huon of Burdeux*, 13–14; Nicolas, *Testamenta vetusta*, 140–62. This text is preserved in Cotton MS. Faustina E.VII, ff. 89–102v and it is printed in Byrne, *Lisle Letters*, II 659–69.

2. Castell of Love's European Sources

The first edition of Berners's Spanish source for *Castell*, Diego de San Pedro's *Cárcel de amor*, was issued by the *Quatro Compañeros Alemanes* in 1492.[93] Unsatisfied with *Cárcel's* conclusion, Nicolás Núñez supplied it with a new ending in the form of a continuation. When *Cárcel* was reprinted in 1496, Núñez's addition was appended and it was retained in all subsequent Spanish editions.[94] *Cárcel* was printed twenty-nine times in sixteenth-century Spain, but it was popular not only with Spanish audiences: in the 150 years following its initial publication it was translated into Catalan, Italian, French, English, and German. Given the geographical proximity of Catalonia and Castille, it is no surprise that the first translation of *Cárcel* was into Catalan in 1493. Bernardí Vallmanyà's Catalan edition of 1493 was based on the 1492 printing of *Cárcel*, and so does not contain Núñez's continuation.[95] Readers of the Italian, German, and English translations, however, were obliged to read the compound text.

Lelio Manfredi of Ferrara is credited with the Italian translation of *Cárcel*. The earliest extant edition of his *Carcer damore* (*Carcer*) was printed in Venice by Georgio de Rusconi in 1514.[96] Incredibly popular, this volume underwent at least ten subsequent editions.[97] Within ten years of its publication *Carcer* attracted the attention of its French neighbours, one of whom decided to translate Manfredi's translation. It is likely that the French translator was François d'Assy. Assy is not identified in the early prints; however, there are four extant manuscripts of the

---

[93] This printing partnership was based in Seville and was comprised of Paul of Cologne, Johann Pegnitzer of Nurenberg, Magnus Herbst of Fils, and Thomas Glockner.

[94] It was first printed in Burgos by Fadrique Alemán de Baslea in 1496.

[95] This edition is remarkable for the numerous woodcuts it contains. See Bernardí Vallmanyà, *Lo carcer de Amor* (Barcelona: Johann Rosenbach, 1493) (B.L. G.10225). Cf. S. Sanpere I. Miguel, "Lo *Carcer d'Amor* de Diego de San Pedro: Edición catalana de Rosembach (Barcelona 1493)," *Revista de Bibliografía Catalana* 2 (1902): 46–84.

[96] Extant copies include, B.L. G.10100; University of Pennsylvania Sc Sa 538 Ei 513m 1514.

[97] Subsequent editions, all published in Venice, are as follows: Rusconi, 1515, B.N. R–12477, B.L. 12470.b.4; Rusconi, 1518, B.L. 12770.aaa.17; unknown publisher, 1521, Bod. Mason L 43; unknown publisher, 1525, Bod. Don.f. 244; unknown publisher, 1525, B.L. 12490.b.5; Bindoni and Pasini, 1530, B.L. 12470.aa.18; Bindoni and Pasini, 1533, B.L. 12490.b.24; unknown publisher, 1537, Bod. Douce F 447 (2); Bindoni and Pasini, 1537, B.L. 1084.d.1C4, Folger PQ 4276 C7 1536; Bindoni and Pasini, 1546, B.L. 12490.b.25, University of Michigan; unknown publisher, 1561, unknown location. There are also copies of the 1525 editions at Harvard University (Sc Sa 535 Ei 513mf) and at the Huntington (370305): these editions have not been compared to the other extant editions of 1525, and so the edition(s) to which they correspond is unknown.

Prison d'Amour (Prison) and one names him as the translator.[98] Assy was secretary to Jean d'Albret, the King of Navarre, and is best known for his translation, also from Italian, of *Dialogue très élégant intitulé le Pérégrin.*[99] Assy's *Prison*, first printed in Paris in 1525, went through at least eight additional editions and circulated widely: both Berners and the second French translator, Gilles Corrozet, made use of it. Corrozet's *Prison* is a bilingual French-Spanish edition.[100] Corrozet was the first printer of his own work in Paris in 1552, and it was followed by at least eighteen subsequent editions, issued by various printers.[101] While *Cárcel* was at the height of its popularity in Spain, Italy, France, and England in the sixteenth century, it was not translated into German until the seventeenth century by Hans Ludwig von Kufstein. His "excellent, if sometimes free, translation," *Gefängnis der Lieb*, was first published in Leipzig in 1625 and was re-issued four more times.[102]

---

[98] François d'Assy is named as the translator in Bibliothèque Nationale (Paris) MS fr. 24382. The earliest extant manuscript is Phillipps 3631, dated c. 1520. It was sold at Sotheby's on 30 November 1971. For a bibliographic description see, Edward M. Wilson, "De l'amour de Leriano a Laureolle," Lot 524, in *Biblioteca Phillippica. Medieval Manusacripts: New Series: Part VI. Catalogue of Manuscripts on Papyrus, Vellum and Paper of the 7th Century to the 18th Century from the Celebrated Collection Formed by Sir Thomas Phillipps (1792–1872). Day of Sale Tuesday 30th November at Eleven O'Clock.* (London: Sotheby, 1971), 104–5. The beginning of MS Phillipps 3631 agrees with the printed version but there are differences in the later part of the text. Some changes are slight including the substitution of almost synonymous terms and altering the Latinate syntax in the manuscript. Larger changes include rewriting of three verse letters in prose, and the omission of Lereano's mother's *planctus*, Lereano's defence of women, and the translator's prologue. Wilson concludes, "The present manuscript [Phillipps] evidently represents the earlier version of François d'Assy's translation, subsequently revised before publication. There are three manuscripts of the text in the Bibliothèque Nationale and detailed comparison would be needed to establish the relationship of Phillipps 3631 with them." These three manuscripts are fr. 2150, fr. n.a. 7552, and fr. 24382. The French text was printed in 1525, 1526, 1527, 1528, 1533, 1581, 1583, and 1594. For details of these editions see Ivy A. Corfis, *Diego de San Pedro's Cárcel de amor, A Critical Edition* (London: Tamesis, 1987), 16.

[99] J. Balteau, "Assy, François d'," in *Dictionnaire de Biographie Française*, ed. J. Balteau et al. (Paris: Librarie Letouzey, 1939), 3: 1330. The Italian original is by Giacomo Caviceo, and Assy's translation was first printed by Galiot du Pré in Paris in 1527.

[100] On some differences between the two French versions see Corfis, *Diego de San Pedro's*, 64–66.

[101] It was printed by Gilles Corrozet in Paris in 1552, and reprinted ten times between 1552 and 1616. For a detailed catalogue of the editions see Corfis, *Diego de San Pedro's*, 39–47.

[102] Keith Whinnom, trans., *Prison of Love, c. 1492, Diego de San Pedro, Together with the Continuation, c. 1496 by Nicolas Núñez* (Edinburgh: Edinburgh University Press, 1979), ix; Gerhart Hoffmeister, "Diego de San Pedro und Hans Ludwig von Kufstein:

Nicolás Núñez's continuation to *Cárcel* is generally dismissed by critics as inferior and demeaning to San Pedro's masterpiece.[103] The only modern edition to include it with *Cárcel* is the most recent by Carmen Parrilla from 1995. However, as it was appended to all but the first Spanish edition of *Cárcel*, for most early Spanish readers it would have formed part of their textual experience of the work. Núñez's continuation, as we will see, functions as a commentary on, and rewriting of, San Pedro's work, as it profoundly alters *Cárcel*. Although the Spanish editions clearly demarcate Núñez's and San Pedro's works, Berners joins the two presenting them as an integral composition. Berners's inclusion of the continuation is the most obvious and most radical way that *Castell* differs from San Pedro's *Cárcel*.

Núñez's addition is a thematic and ideological rewriting of San Pedro's romance, which is executed through changes in attitudes towards, and the depiction of, Laureola.[104] *Cárcel* employs indirect narration and direct discourse, to further the plot and develop the characters, and as Parrilla and Sun-Me Yoon demonstrate, Laureola is transformed through the manipulation and alteration

---

über eine frühbarocke Bearbeitung der spanischen Liebesgeschichte *Cárcel de Amor*," *Arcadia* 6 (1971): 139–50.

[103] In addition to the continuation to *Cárcel*, Nicolás Núñez penned several *cancionero* poems, but nothing is known about his life. For his poems, see F. Foulché-Delbosc, ed., *Cancionero castillano del siglo XV* (Madrid: Bailly-Ballière, 1915), 2: 478–88. For attempts at, and problems related to, his biography and canon, see Alan Deyermond, "The Poetry of Nicolás Núñez," in *The Age of the Catholic Monarchs 1474–1516: Literary Studies in Memory of Keith Whinnom*, ed. Alan Deyermond and Ian Macpherson (Liverpool: Liverpool University Press, 1989), 25–36; Guillermo Diaz-Plaja, ed., *Historia general de las literaturas hispánicas* (Barcelona: Editorial Barna, 1953), 3: 878; Martín de Riqueur, *Historia de la literatura catalana* (Barcelona: Ariel, 1964), 3: 364; D. W. Pheeters, *El humanista español Alonso de Proasa* (Valencia: Castalia, 1961), 176–78. For critiques of the continuation see Keith Whinnom, "Nicolás Núñez's Continuation of the *Cárcel de Amor* (Burgos, 1496)," in *Studies in Spanish Literature of the Golden Age Presented to Edward M. Wilson*, ed. R. O. Jones (London: Tamesis, 1973), 359–360; Maria Luisa Indini, "Nicolás Núñez 'Traditore' di Diego de San Pedro," in *Miscellanea di studi romanzi offerta a Giuliano Gasca Queirazza per il suo 65 compleanno*, ed. Anna Cornagliotti et al. (Alessandria: Edizioni dell'Orso, 1988), 1: 489–504.

[104] Very few scholars focus on Núñez's text and the effect it has on San Pedro's. For the few who do so, see Indini, "Nicolás Núñez"; Carmen Parrilla, "'Acresentar lo que de suyo esta crescido': El cumplimento de Nicolas Núñez," in *Historias y ficciones: Coloquio sobre la litteratura del siglo XV*, ed. R. Beltran et al. (Valencia: University of Valencia Press, 1992), 241–56; Marcelino Menéndez y Pelayo, *Antología de poetas líricos castellanos* Edición Nacional, vol. 3 (Santander: Aldus S. A. de Artes Gráficas, 1944–1945), 173–74; Whinnom, "Nicolás Núñez's Continuation"; and Sun-Me Yoon, "La continuación de Nicolás Núñez a *Cárcel de amor*," *Dicenda* 10 (1991–1992): 327–43. Parrilla, Whinnom, and Yoon also note this change in Laureola.

of both these discursive levels.[105] In San Pedro's text Laureola's voice is often mediated through Auctor as he reports details of his interactions with her to Lereano or to us, the readers. Auctor often declares himself incapable of understanding her and has frequent recourse to brevity topoi to avoid describing her reactions. Even in her direct speech she holds back, fearful of compromising her position and revealing too much.[106] In the continuation, however, Auctor exhibits no doubts in his ability to understand and verbally define Laureola, and she is more loquacious as she defends herself and declares her feelings explicitly and unambiguously to Lereano and Auctor.[107] Moreover, Laureola's increased expressiveness, as she is given the space physically and verbally to express her sorrow and regret, reconfigures her as a pathetic figure: in reaction to Lereano's death she laments, rails, and cries so profusely that her tears wet her clothes and inhibit her speech.[108] The *letras* she wears in the dream vision reinforce her expressions of guilt, remorse and despair.[109] These public displays of emotion increase our understanding of her feelings and her situation and also our sympathy for her. Parrilla notes that Laureola's increased verbosity in the continuation, despite its reasoned structural form, aligns her with the typical loquacious woman, often derided in anti-feminist literature.[110] This is in line with a reading of Núñez as an anti-feminist rewriter of San Pedro's feminist text, defining feminism and anti-feminist as pro- or anti-woman within the terms of the fifteenth-century Spanish debate on women. Critics define San Pedro's *Cárcel* as a pro-woman text, due to the depiction of Laureola as a supremely virtuous object of devotion; the narrative focus on her feelings; the respect for her decision not to accept Lereano as her lover; and Lereano's speeches in defence of women.[111] Within the perimeters of the debate, these factors identify San Pedro's *Cárcel* and Núñez's continuation as fifteenth-century Spanish feminist and anti-feminist propaganda, respectively.

---

[105] Yoon, "La continuación de Nicolás Núñez," 329–30.

[106] Parrilla, "'Acresentar lo que de suyo,'" 246.

[107] Parrilla, "'Acresentar lo que de suyo,'" 246.

[108] See Chaps. LII, LX, LXII.

[109] Chap. LVI. For a definition of the *letra*, see Keith Whinnom, *La poesía amatoria de la época de los Reyes Católicos* (Durham: Durham University Press, 1981), 46.

[110] Parrilla, "'Acresentar lo que de suyo,'" 252–53.

[111] See Jacob Ornstein, "La misogonia y el profeminismo en la literatura castellana," *Revista de Filología Hispánica* 3 (1942): 219–32; Alan Deyermond, *Tradiciones y puntos de vista en la ficción sentimental* (México: Universidad Nacional Autónoma de México, 1993); Louise M. Haywood, "Female Voices in Spanish Sentimental Romances," *Journal of the Institute of Romance Studies* 4 (1996): 17–35; Antony Van Beysterveldt, "El amor caballeresco del *Amadís* y del *Tirante*," *Hispanic Review* 49 (1981): 407–25; idem, "La nueva teoría del amor en las novelas de Diego de San Pedro," *Cuadernos Hispanoamericanos* 349 (1979): 70–83.

In San Pedro's *Cárcel*, Laureola is portrayed as more than just the object of Lereano's affections; ample textual space is given to exploring her thoughts and emotions both through her epistles and through Lereano's and Auctor's attempts to decipher her oral and written messages. Similarly to Lereano, she is shown grappling with the contrasting pressures of personal desire and social demands, and her concern for her honour, which prevents her from heeding Lereano's requests is, in general, treated sympathetically. Lereano argues that women should be loved, respected, honoured, and pitied.[112] This is because the culturally accepted behavioural code prevents women from loving, and so they should not be blamed for not satisfying their lovers.[113] Basically, Laureola is not expected to requite her lover because to do so would signify a breach in her chastity, thus making her a less-than-perfect being, and as such, unworthy of Lereano's affection and devotion.[114] The most to which Lereano can aspire is to receive his lady's pity, not her love, and he implores her repeatedly for the former.[115] Thus when Lereano dies everyone laments his death, and pities him. No one in the text, with the exception of the misogynist Teseo, blames Laureola for his death. Even Lereano's mother holds Lereano's nature responsible for his condition, and does not blame Laureola.[116]

Readers are also discouraged from condemning Laureola, especially when they see how Lereano treats Teseo, who utters anti-feminist comments in an attempt to make Lereano stop loving Laureola.[117] Unfortunately, Teseo's words have the opposite effect, as Lereano will not tolerate that Laureola, nor any woman, be slandered. As a testament to his love for her, he uses the little breath he has left to refute the anti-feminist comments by making a long speech in defence of women, wherein he lists examples of virtuous women and reasons why women should be loved.[118] Shortly after his discourse, he dies with thoughts of Laureola foremost in his mind. Lereano is satisfied to die in order to preserve Laureola's honour. He does not hold her responsible for his death since social constraints prevent her from requiting his love, and because as a perfect lover in love with a perfect lady, he knows that it is both impossible and unrealistic to expect her to reciprocate his feelings. While Lereano is the one who dies, Laureola is equally pitiful. She is presented as a sympathetic character who is not culpable for the tragic outcome.

---

[112] Chaps. XLIII–XLV.

[113] Cf. Pamela Waley, "Love and Honour in the *Novelas sentimentales* of Diego de San Pedro and Juan de Flores," *Bulletin of Hispanic Studies* 43 (1966): 253–75; Haywood, "Female Voices"; Van Beysterveldt, "La nueva teoría".

[114] Cf. Yoon, "La continuación de Nicolás Núñez," 339.

[115] See for example, Chaps. XV, XXXIX.

[116] Chap. XLVII.

[117] Chap. XLII.

[118] Chaps. XLII–XLIV.

In this story that examines the interplay of love and honour and the conflicting norms that they imply, for Lereano and Laureola honour is deemed more important than love. Of course Lereano does not want to die and would much rather be united with Laureola, but he will not compromise her reputation. Similarly, Laureola will not risk her good name to satisfy him. The end is tragic, but readers are left feeling that the tragic outcome was inevitable.

Núñez, however, does not share the same feelings of resignation concerning the ending. In the prologue to his continuation he voices dismay at the conclusion of the tale.[119] He wishes that both Auctor and Lereano could see Laureola express grief and regret at Lereano's death, and so he uses the forum of the continuation to fulfil that desire. In the addition, Auctor returns to court to tell Laureola that she is to blame for Lereano's death, accusing her of cruelty and a lack of compassion. He tells her that she has stained her reputation and lineage since she was obliged to requite Lereano's love but failed to do so. While Laureola defends her behaviour, claiming that she acted only to preserve her honour, she divulges that she really did love Lereano and that she regrets his death. Her admissions of sorrow and love reconcile Auctor to her, as he can now believe that Lereano's death had a purpose. New feelings of compassion replace the fury he earlier felt towards her, and while the story does not end on a happy note, the grief that she predicts she will suffer for the rest of her days is comforting to Núñez's Auctor, who deems it to be just retribution for her cruel actions towards him and Lereano. Nevertheless, despite Auctor's impression, Lereano's death is not vindicated by the continuation. His death becomes an error in interpretation rather than a tragedy since the continuation shows that his suffering continues in the after-life, and that it served no purpose. In contrast, once the inner turmoil that Laureola has been suffering is made known, she appears more heroic.[120]

One of the innovations of San Pedro's *Cárcel* is the exploration of the female perspective.[121] Laureola has depth and is difficult to read, but in the continuation, as I alluded to above, the ambiguity of her persona is effaced through her verbose, confessional utterances. I additionally noted that this increased loquacity allies her to the stereotypical female of anti-feminist literature. The continuation also positions her within the cliché of *la belle dame sans mercy*, since she is presented as a woman in love who will not requite her lover. Despite her confession in the addition, in San Pedro's text we do not know whether or not Laureola

---

[119] For a translation of his prologue, see *Prison of Love*, trans. Whinnom, 83–84.

[120] Cf. Yoon, "La continuación de Nicolás Núñez," 335, 337.

[121] This is typical of the *novela sentimental* genre. See for example, Parrilla, "'Acre-sentar lo que de suyo,'" 245; Keith Whinnom, ed., *Obras Completas, II Cárcel de Amor*, Diego de San Pedro (Madrid: Clásicos Castalia, 1971), 66; Alan Deyermond, *Tradiciones y puntos de vista*; Barbara Weissberger, review of *Tradiciones y puntos de vista en la ficción sentimental*, by Alan Deyermond, *La Corónica* 24 (1996): 211–12.

loves Lereano.[122] Lereano is unsure. Auctor erroneously assumes that she must, but is acting as though she does not love in order to preserve her reputation. At the end of San Pedro's text, Auctor realises his error, entertaining the possibility that she may not have loved Lereano after all. The story ends with a lot of unanswered questions.[123] The uncertainty that remains regarding Laureola's emotions has been described by Barbara Weissberger as "a bypassing of the dialectics of desire . . . a particularly feminine 'act of victory'."[124] As Laureola never discloses her feelings, she circumnavigates the reductive positions that the love ideology would force her to inhabit, namely those of the passionate or pitiless woman, which, as many critics have shown, are not actually very different.[125] Because the continuation forces Laureola to participate in the amorous situation and "seeks to resolve an all-important question San Pedro chose to leave open: whether or not Laureola loves Leriano," Weissberger characterises it as "an overtly masculinist rewriting."[126]

The open-endedness regarding Laureola's emotions produces a feeling of discomfort in Núñez. Núñez projects his confusion and desire for resolution onto Auctor and redirects them in the form of anger towards Laureola. In the original text, Auctor's feelings are unstated. We know that Laureola's words and behaviour confused him and that he had difficulty trying to interpret them, and while Auctor was definitely on Lereano's side, trying to convince Laureola to love Lereano, he was not hostile toward her. This animosity that Auctor feels for Laureola is new to Núñez's text. Like Laureola, in the continuation he is made to

---

[122] While most readers agree that this is left open, some assert that Laureola's position is discernible. For instance, Bruce Wardropper asserts that Laureola does not love Lereano: see "El mundo sentimental de la *Cárcel de Amor*," *Revista de la Filología Española* 37 (1953): 168–95, here 183–92; Waley says she does love Lereano: see Waley, "Love and Honour," 253–75; and Lida de Malkiel writes that it is deliberately left ambiguous: see María Rosa Lida de Malkiel, *La originalidad artística de la Celestina* (Buenos Aires: Eudeba, 1962), 454.

[123] This situates it in the tradition of the *débats/questions d'amour*, as it asks: did Laureola love Lereano? Was Lereano's death justified?

[124] Barbara Weissberger, "Role-Reversal and Festivity in the Romances of Juan de Flores," *Journal of Hispanic Philology* 13 (1989): 197–213, here 208.

[125] Cf. Van Beysterveldt, "El amor caballeresco," 5; Elena Gascón Vera, "La ambegüedad en el concepto del amor y de la mujer en la prosa castellana del siglo XV," *Boletín de la Real Academia Española* 59 (1979): 119–55, here 122–29; Weissberger, Review; Weissberger, "Role Reversal and Festivity," 200; María Eugenia Lacarra, "Representaciones femininas en la poesía cortesana y en la narrativa sentimental del siglo XV," in *Breve historia feminista de la literatura española (en lengua castellana). II. La mujer en la literatura española: modos de representación. Desde la Edad Media hasta el siglo XVII*, ed. Iris M. Zavala (Madrid: Anthropos, 1995), 159–75, here 159.

[126] Weissberger, "Role-Reversal and Festivity," 208.

express definite opinions, and he is changed from a multidimensional character, who is difficult to interpret, into a univocal antagonistic force. In the continuation, Auctor takes the opposing position to Lereano's and Laureola's regarding the conflict of love and honour. He thinks that love and male desire ought to take precedence over female honour. Unlike Lereano, he does not believe that Laureola's feelings are important enough to warrant the sacrifice of Lereano's life. His voice pleads for a happy ending and he does not feel the need to question whether or not she loves Lereano. The concerns of San Pedro's text, such as the woman's feelings and her attitude towards her life, society, and lover, are ignored as Núñez rewrites the story propounding, and ascribing importance to, his own opinions, and causing Lereano and Laureola to recant their original views in favour of his own.

It is precisely because Núñez works within the same system as San Pedro, answering questions, filling in thematic voids, and rounding off the character sketches that San Pedro leaves open, that his conclusion easily permeates the gaps left in readers' minds. If he had written over details unconditionally asserted by San Pedro's text, asking his readers to erase what the original text claimed as fact, and replace it with the new information that he provided, they would have found it difficult to reconcile his text with San Pedro's, and the two compositions would have remained separate in their minds. But he does not go against what San Pedro asserted; instead he fills in the cracks, writing in between the lines of San Pedro's text, and so after reading his addition it is almost impossible to separate it from San Pedro's.[127] The two compositions merge, and it is only with great difficulty that the two Laureolas, the two Lereanos, and the two Auctors can be separated. Careful readers can revisit San Pedro's text, deleting Núñez's conclusion from their minds, in an attempt to confront the questions posed by San Pedro's text, but such an activity is not easy.

As noted above, in all the Spanish editions, both early and modern, Núñez's text is clearly demarcated from San Pedro's; however in Berners's English translation there is no indication that *Castell* has two Spanish authors.[128] In his prologue, Berners says that *Castell* is translated from Spanish but he names neither San Pedro nor Núñez as its author. Further, when Núñez refers to San Pedro at the end of his text, Berners omits this mention, as it would imply dual authorship. In Chap. LXII, Berners writes "at my owne poore mansion" (O7v) rather than the Spanish concluding words, which translate as "in Peñafiel (as San Pedro said) where I remain kissing the hands of your greatness." Berners also omits the explicit to San Pedro's text and Núñez's incipit and prologue, thus seamlessly joining the two texts. The original Spanish text ends as follows:

---

[127] Cf. Yoon, "La continuación de Nicolás Núñez," 328.
[128] Whinnom, "Nicolás Núñez's Continuation," 357–59, looks at the page layout of the transition from San Pedro's to Núñez's text in various editions.

sus onrras fueron conformes a su merecimiento, las quales acabadas, acordé
de partirme. Por cierto con mejor voluntad caminara para la otra vida que
para esta tierra; con sospiros caminé; con lágrimas partí; con gemidos ha-
blé; y con tales pasatienpos llegué aquí a Peñafiel, donde quedo besando las
manos de vuestra merced. (ed. Parrilla, 79)

[His obsequies were conformable to his deserving, the which, being finished, I decided to leave. Certainly, I had a greater desire to make my way
to to the other world than to venture forth in this land. With sighs I walked
along; with tears I left; with moans I spoke; and with such passtimes, I arrived here in Peñafiel, where I remain kising your lordship's hands.]

The text comes to a definite close and Núñez makes it clear that he is taking up
and adding to San Pedro's text. He begins:

Muy virtuosos señores:

Porque si, conosciendo mi poco saber, culpáredes mi atrevimiento en verme
poner en acrescentar lo que de suyo está crescido, quiero, si pudiere, con mi
descargo satisfazer lo que fize, ahunque mi intención me descarga.

Leyendo un día el tratado del no menos virtuoso que discreto de Diego de
San Pedro que fizo de *Cárcel de amor*, en la estoria Leriano y Laureola . . .
(ed. Parrilla, 83)

[Most virtuous lords, Since you know my meagre understanding, you may
condemn my temerity as you see me venture to extend what is already extensive, I would like, if I may, to excuse myself for what I did, although my
good intentions themselves absolve me.

As I was one day reading the treatise, by the no less virtuous than clever
Diego de San Pedro, called *The Castell of Love*, in the story of Lereano and
Laureola . . .]

The French text, Berners's other source, also has a definite ending, omitting the
last sentence from San Pedro's text and excluding the continuation:

La funeraille pompe et les honneurs siens au merite sien furent conformes.
Cy fine ce present livre intitule la prison D'amour de Leriano a Laureole.
(M8r)

[His funeral, pomp, and honours were equal to his deserving. Here ends
this present book, entitled The Prison of Love from Lereano to Laureola.]

In Berners's translation, despite the examples of the French and Spanish texts, he neglects to formally end San Pedro's, or formally begin Núñez's, text, including no indication that he is joining two separate compositions. He writes:

> Th*en* his obsequyes and buryals were done most honourably, accordyng to the deserdes of his vertues. & as for my selfe, with a better wyll I wolde have depertyd this lyfe then to have taryed on the yerth alyve. So with sighes I went my way, and depertyd wyth wepyng, and with lamentacion I sore complaynyde, and with suche thoughtes I wente to my lodgynge. And when I saw that the consentynge and desirynge of my deth could not remedy hym that was passyd . . . (Chap. XLVIII; M7v)

Rather than translate "llegué aquí a Peñafiel" (I arrived at Peñafiel) Berners writes "I wente to my lodgynge" so that the story can continue without interruption. He thus joins the two texts, effacing their independent origins. Not only does Berners choose to translate the continuation, but by obfuscating all evidence that *Castell* includes an original text and an addition, the interpretation of the English work is profoundly affected. In the English text, in contrast to San Pedro's *Cárcel*, Auctor is a good reader of Laureola. Despite all of her protestations, she really loves Lereano, and Auctor is astute enough to recognise that fact. Lereano and Auctor are experts at dissimulation, able to appear sympathetic to, and respectful of, Laureola and her views, when really they are annoyed and angry at her refusal to requite him. Laureola is a cruel and simple woman who refuses to acknowledge that she loves Lereano for fear of being betrayed. She is merely testing Lereano's faith and devotion to her, not believing he will really die from love. She is mean and foolish, and as a result Lereano dies and she is forced to live the remainder of her days in despair, unable to be with her lover. These characters and this story are not those written by San Pedro, they are Núñez's characters and Núñez's story, but they are those preferred, and presented, by Berners.

The most drastic alteration in the continuation is that made to Laureola's character. By circumscribing Laureola to a stereotypical role, and by blaming her and making her accept the blame for Lereano's death, her voice is obliterated. Furthermore, this profoundly alters the depiction of love in San Pedro's text. Laureola is no longer the superior, worshipped being, and dying for love is no longer the greatest honour that Lereano can attain. As Whinnom posits, "Whereas San Pedro displayed a perfect lover accepting without reproach his inevitable fate since he had attached his constant love to an unattainable object, Núñez insists on the pathos rather than the dignity of Lereano's death."[129] Also, Núñez blames Laureola rather than the complexities of the love ideology, which controlled her and Lereano's actions, and which could not be altered. By making

---

[129] Whinnom, "Nicolás Núñez's Continuation," 365.

Laureola love Lereano, Núñez refashions her as an imperfect woman, lacking in chastity, modesty, and moderation, and so according to the principles of love advanced by San Pedro, she is not worthy of Lereano's affections. This amorous ideology, wherein the perfect lover suffers (and expects to do nothing else) as a result of the superiority of the deified object of his affections, is absent from Núñez's continuation and Berners's translation. Núñez's theory is one wherein the man must play the role of the suffering lover about to die for his love, only to capture the woman, who is also playing a role, pretending that she does not love only to test the man's affections. And she must requite him once she is confident that he truly loves her.

This change in the depiction of love and of the characters, on which the text's pro-woman position (partially) rests, causes this position to be negated. In Núñez's and Berners's texts, Laureola is transformed from a piteous individual into a mean, heartless woman, as she is reproached, and expresses responsibility, for Lereano's death. She is no longer deified: she ceases to fill the superior position typically occupied by women in the feminist literature of the medieval debate about women. Berners's translation reinforces Núñez's work, ratifying the changes he made to the original text, since, presented with two versions of the work, he consciously decided to translate the one with the addition, and furthermore, he deliberately effaced all evidence of his union of the two texts. By continuing the romance, and opting to translate the continuation, whether they intended to or not, Núñez and Berners negate the female. The final product is in conflict with the preoccupations of San Pedro's *Cárcel*. Through his decision seamlessly to include the continuation, Berners's translation supports the changes made by Núñez, providing English readers with a gendered rewriting of the *Cárcel* that can be neither detected nor undone.

While the continuation jars with the sensibilities of most modern readers, it is quite possible that its presence made San Pedro's text more palatable for his contemporaries. As Whinnom observes: "We simply cannot tell whether Nicolás Núñez rode to success on the back of San Pedro's best-seller and owed the major part of his apparent popularity to the sheer inertia of printing traditions, or whether the success of San Pedro's uncompromising narrative did not owe something to Núñez's modification of its ending."[130] Andrew Spigurnell's added English prologue, which appears in the second and third editions of *Castell* and which I will discuss below, evidences a reading similar to Núñez's as he condemns Laureola's treatment of Lereano. Assy's (the French translator's) interpretation of the text is unknown, but unlike Spigurnell who claimed *Castell* to be an unfit gift for a lady due to Laureola's negative example, Assy does dedicate his translation to an unnamed lady, as does Manfredi (the Italian translator). Even so, Núñez

---

[130] Whinnom, "Nicolás Núñez's Continuation," 359.

and Spigurnell were not alone in their reactions to Laureola. Other *novelas sentimentales* (this Spanish generic term is defined below) evoked similar responses in their readers and translators due to their vocalisation of feminist concerns. For instance, the Italian translator of San Pedro's *Arnalte y Lucenda* prefaces his translation with abuse of Lucenda for rejecting Arnalte (even though he was unworthy of her love) and implores all women to be kind to their lovers.[131] His title reinforces his hostility towards Lucenda: *Picciol trattato d'Arnalte e di Lucenda intitolato L'amante mal trattato dalla sua amorosa* (The little treatise of Arnalte and Lucenda, entitled the lover poorly treated by his beloved). Similarly, the Polish translator of *Grisel y Mirabella*, Bartosz Paprocki, a known anti-feminist, omits Breçayda's important speech wherein she argues that men are able to attack and subjugate women because they monopolise education and access to the written word.[132] In an important article, Weissberger explores how the *novelas* manage to evoke totally contrasting interpretations from different readers: the same *novela* can be read as a feminist or an anti-feminist work, depending on the reader's outlook and reading methodology. She shows that many *novelas* contain subversive, carnivalesque elements which invert authority and hierarchy and which would have been recognised as such by those opposed to traditional hegemony. Looking at Gradissa's reaction to *Fiammetta* in *Grimalte y Gradissa*, Weissberger suggests that female readers, in contrast to the reader-responses noted above, would neither have sympathised with Arnalte nor have condemned Lucenda, and analogously, they would have greeted Laureola's predicament sympathetically and without reproach.[133] According to Whinnom, differing interpretations of *Cárcel* hinge on the readers' perceptions of Laureola and their attitudes towards women. He posits that many readers, like Núñez, could not fathom the magnitude of Lereano's devotion, nor could they accept the "uncompromising feminism of San Pedro."[134] As a result, for these readers the text would have been incomprehensible without the addition. Yoon also proposes that the continuation would have made *Cárcel* more acceptable to its sixteenth-century reading public.[135] Berners's

---

[131] Bartolomeo Maraffi, *Picciol trattato d'Arnalte e di Lucenda intiolato L'amante mal trattato dalla sua amorosa.* (Lyon: Balthasar Arnoullet, 1555). This does not appear in the French or English translations of *Arnalte y Lucenda*.

[132] Elias Rivers, "A Sixteenth-Century Polish Translation of Flores' *Grisel y Mirabella*," *Bulletin of Hispanic Studies* 35 (1958): 34–37. The first edition dates from 1578.

[133] Weissberger, "Role-Reversal and Festivity,"199. In this *novela* when Gradissa's lover presents her with a copy of *Fiammetta*, hoping thereby to win her love, her reaction to the book is contrary to his expectations. She interprets Fiammetta's misfortune as a warning and refuses to heed her lover's requests unless he goes to Italy and successfully reconciles Fiammetta and her lover.

[134] Whinnom, "Nicolás Núñez's Continuation," 365.

[135] Yoon, "La continuación de Nicolás Núñez," 339.

translation is the most persuasive evidence that attests to a preference for *Cárcel* with the continuation. Whereas other readers were obliged to read the text in whatever form it was available to them — i.e. with the addition or not — Berners is unique in that he had two versions of *Cárcel*, one with, and the other without, the addition, and he deliberately included Núñez's text. This composite text may have suited his preferences, or he may have assumed that it would have the greater audience appeal. Judging by Spigurnell's reaction to Laureola, if Berners thought the latter, he was correct in his assumption.

3. Translation Methodology and Prose Style

This section synthesises the information provided in the notes to the edition of *Castell*. While the notes indicate specific instances of additions, omissions, alterations, mistranslations, and interesting uses of vocabulary, this section presents a more global picture of Berners's methodology and style. Berners adopted the unusual system of basing his translation on two sources, and I will begin by explaining how that policy worked in practice. My practical explication of how Berners used the Spanish and French sources in composing *Castell* will be followed by a discussion of the most prevalent tendencies in Berners's translation methods, looking at, sequentially, alterations, additions, omissions, and linguistic patterns. The final portion of the section will explore the use of rhetoric in *Castell*, with a focus on the rhetorical devices that are derived from Berners's French and Spanish sources.

In his prologue to *Castell of Love*, Lord Berners claims to have translated the romance "out of Spanyshe in to Englyshe" (A2r). This declaration is echoed by the title pages to all three early printed editions (1548?, 1552?, and c. 1555), which advertise the volume as "The Castell of Love, translated out of Spanishe in to Englyshe by Johan Bowrchier Knyght, Lorde Bernis" (A1r). While Berners maintains that he translated Diego de San Pedro's *Cárcel de amor* directly from Spanish, his assertion is not completely accurate, as his translation is marked by close verbal parallels to the French translation of San Pedro's text. Moreover, the French prologue differs completely from the Spanish, and Berners's prologue matches the French almost word-for-word, sharing no variant readings with the Spanish prologue. Part of Berners's *Castell*, however, is definitely translated directly from Spanish: it includes the Spanish continuation written by Nicolás Núñez, which was not included in any French translation prior to 1533, the year of Berners's death. The continuation is far from the only instance where Berners uses the Spanish original; traces of indebtedness to the Spanish text can be found throughout the entirety of *Castell*. My comparison of the three language versions (English, French, and Spanish) indicates that, in the English translation, many Spanish readings are retained and given priority over the French variants, demonstrating a reliance on the Spanish text, and that equally many French additions, omissions, and alterations are preserved by Berners, showing a dependence on that source. I have found that both sources were consistently important and instrumental in the translation process. It appears as though in composing the romance Berners had the Spanish and French versions of *Castell* open in front of him and he looked from one to the other, comparing and contrasting the two, in order to select which variant readings to include or omit, and to devise ways of combining his two sources to create an entirely new English text. The Spanish and French versions of the romance are very close, and so it is often impossible to ascertain which one Berners was using; yet the slight variants between the sources have allowed me to trace Berners's precise methods and to identify exactly where he uses each source. In this section, I will demonstrate that *Castell* is a translation of both a French and a Spanish version of the romance and that Berners used these two sources throughout the translation process. Berners's unusual practice of using two sources in two different languages for *Castell* has led to much critical confusion regarding his translation methods, and so through this exposition I will correct some factual inaccuracies and misconceptions regarding Berners's translation policy articulated by earlier scholars, such as Keith Whinnom, Ivy Corfis, and William Crane. Until now, no one has examined the entirety of *Castell* in relation to its sources, and so assertions regarding Berners's methods and his use of the two sources have ranged from totally inaccurate contentions to fortuitously hazarded guesses.

In the introduction to his modern English translation of *Cárcel de amor*, Keith Whinnom declares that Berners's *Castell* is indebted to both a French and a Spanish version of the romance. He notes that "on numerous occasions it seems probable that he [Berners] is translating from the not always accurate French rather than the Spanish," but that "nevertheless, Lord Berners did also have a full Spanish edition to hand, for his translation includes Nicolás Núñez's continuation."[136] Whinnom does not explain how Berners used the two texts, but concludes that Berners executed his translation using a bilingual French-Spanish edition of *Cárcel de amor*; however, as the first bilingual edition was not printed until 1552, such a hypothesis is implausible.[137] Likewise ignoring chronology, Ivy Corfis ascribes Berners's translation to c.1549, which is impossible given that he died in 1533.[138] Equally spuriously, she also claims that a second independent English translation was made in 1550.[139] She does not mention a French source, leaving readers to assume that *Castell* is purely a Spanish translation.

William Crane, *Castell*'s first modern scholar, came closest to understanding Berners's translation methods. In a letter to the *Times Literary Supplement*

---

[136] *Prison of Love*, trans. Whinnom, viii.

[137] *Prison of Love*, trans. Whinnom, viii.

[138] See above. Corfis, *Diego de San Pedro's*, 16 n. 2, 68.

[139] Corfis, *Diego de San Pedro's*, 16 n. 2.

in 1933, Crane observed that *Castell* had both a Spanish and a French source.[140] This letter was intended to correct the earlier letter to the same publication by G. W. Cottrell who, on the basis of an examination of the English and French prologues, asserted that *Castell*'s source must have been the French *Prison d'Amour*.[141] In 1934, and again in 1950, Crane expanded upon his prior observations.[142] He posited that Berners began *Castell* by using only the French version and gradually increased his dependence on the Spanish version until he stopped using the French text altogether. Crane advanced three possible explanations and two proofs for this translation methodology. The first reason offered is that Berners was not in possession of a Spanish version at the onset, and so drew on the French until the Spanish became available to him. Second, Berners did not know Spanish when he started working on *Castell* and became proficient in Spanish by comparing the Spanish source with the French, which he could read and understand with ease.[143] Or finally, that Berners had learned Spanish on his diplomatic mission to Spain in 1518, but had forgotten it in the intervening years and so was comparing the French to the Spanish in order to jog his memory and relearn the language.[144] Crane further suggested that once Berners acquired either the Spanish text or the linguistic competence necessary to understand it, he

---

[140] William G. Crane, "*Cárcel de Amor*," *TLS* (1 June 1933) 380.

[141] G. W. Cottrell, "*Cárcel de Amor*," *TLS* (27 April 1933) 295.

[142] William G. Crane, "Lord Berners's Translation of Diego de San Pedro's *Cárcel de Amor*," *PMLA* 49 (1934): 1032–35; and idem, *The Castle of Love, a Translation by John Bourchier*, Facs. (Gainesville: Scholars Facsimiles and Reprints, 1950), n.p. [viii–ix].

[143] The comparison of different language versions of a text was a common way of learning languages. See Crane, "Lord Berners's Translation," 1035. This is also attested to by the numerous parallel, bilingual editions which profess to have the purpose of language instruction, such as Juan de Flores's *Grisel y Mirabella*, San Pedro's *Arnalte y Lucenda*, and Corrozet's French-Spanish edition of *Castell*, referred to above. *Grisel y Mirabella* circulated in numerous multilingual editions: sixteen Italian-French editions appeared before the close of the sixteenth century; four Spanish-French editions appeared; one trilingual French-Italian-English edition was entered to Edward White in 1586; two quadrilingual Italian-Spanish-French-English editions were printed in each of 1556 and 1608, and a fifth edition was entered to Edward Aggas in 1588. See *STC*, 11092, 11092a, 11093, 11093.5. For information on all these editions see Joyce Boro, "A Source and Date for the Fragment of *Grisel y Mirabella* Found in the Binding of Emmanuel College 338.5.43," in *Transactions of the Cambridge Bibliographical Society* 12 (2003): 422–36. The Italian-English editions of *Arnalte y Lucenda* were prepared and translated by Claudius Hollyband and printed in 1575, 1597, and 1608 (*STC* 6758, 6759, 6760).

[144] From April to December 1518 Berners accompanied Sir John Kite, the Archbishop of Armagh, on a diplomatic mission to Spain to forge an alliance between Henry and Charles V. For details of this mission see *L&P*, I 4135, 4136, 4137, 3976; *L&P*, II 4160, 4161, 4164, 4165, 4228, 4282, 4313, 4342, 4383, 4436, 4440, 4590, 4629, 4658, 4660; Berners, *The Boke of Duke Huon of Burdeux*, xli.

abandoned the French text, relying exclusively on the Spanish. These hypotheses are plausible, but they do not withstand close scrutiny. Likewise, the two pieces of evidence that he advanced in support of his argument are untenable. Since the French prologue differs from the Spanish and Berners's prologue follows the French, and since Núñez's conclusion was available only in Spanish, Crane deduced that the beginning and end of *Castell* were translated exclusively and respectively from the French and Spanish. From these facts, he extrapolated his theory of a progressive change in language dependence. His observations regarding the exclusive uses of the French and Spanish for the prologue and conclusion are accurate, and I will return to this point below, but as Crane neglected to examine the body of the text, he failed to notice that these two instances of sole dependence are the exception rather than the rule. A line-by-line comparison of the English, Spanish, and French negates Crane's suppositions and reveals that Berners used both sources equally throughout his translation.

In order to show how this dual language dependence occurs all the way through *Castell*, I will begin by analysing three sentences from the romance taken from three different sections of the text. The first sentence is drawn from the first chapter of *Castell*; the second is from Chapter XXI, which is from the middle of the romance; and the third is from the final chapter of *Castell*. In determining the central and final chapters of the romance I am not including Núñez's addition in my calculations, as it is omitted from the French translation. I will then look at two additional phrases and several doublets from various points in the text. These additional examples have been chosen in order to illustrate some of the more creative ways whereby Berners combines his sources.

The first sentence of *Castell* reads as follows:

> After *the* warres done and finyshyd in my countrey, beynge in my poore mansion, in a mornyng whan the sonne illuminyd the earthe, in a shadow-yde darke valey, in the mountayne called Serua de Maren*us*, in the coun-trey of Masedonia, as I walkyd in a strayte way shadowyd *with* fayer trees sodenly I mette with a knight fyers and furious, whose presence was ferfull to regarde. (Chap. I; A3v)

The Spanish opening is:

> Después de hecha la guerra del año passado, veniendo a tener el invierno a mi pobre reposo, passando una mañana, quando ya el sol quería esclarescer la tierra, por unos valles hondos y escuros que se hazen en la Sierra Morena, vi salir a mi encuentro, por entre unos robledales do mi camino se hazía, un cavallero assí feroz de presencia como espantoso de vista. (ed. Parrilla, 4)

> [After last year's war was finished, I was returning to spend the winter in my poor abode. One morning, as the sun began to illuminate the earth, I was passing through the deep and shadowy valleys that are in the Sierra

Morena, I saw coming to meet me, from amongst the oak trees through which my path progressed, a knight as fierce in countenance as he was frightful to behold.]

And the corresponding French passage is as follows:

Depuis la guerre faicte & finee de l'an passe, venant tenir mon yuer et me reposer en mon povre repaire passant ung matin quant ia le soleil commencoit a esclairer & illuminer la terre par ung val umbreux et obscur qui est en la montaigne nommee la Surre de Morienne, situee ou pays de Macedoine, veis sallir & venir en mon encontre par ung estroit & boys de chesnes ou mon chemin s'adressoit ung chevalier non moins fereux et farouche de presence comme espoventable de veue. (B1r–v).

[After last year's war was done and finished, I was coming to spend the winter and to rest myself in my poor abode. One morning, as the sun had begun to light up and illuminate the earth, I was passing through a shadowy and dark valley, which is in the mountains named the Sierra Morena, situated in the country of Macedonia, I saw going and coming towards me, by a narrow oak forest through which my path progressed, a knight no less ferocious and fierce in countenance as he was fearful to behold.]

A comparison of these three citations reveals that the English doublets "done and finyshyd" and "fiers and furious" are derived from the French added doublets of "faicte & finee" and "fereux et farouche." The Spanish has the single terms "hecha" (done) and "feroz" (fierce). Berners specifies that the way taken is a "strayte" way, which is based on the French addition "ung estroit," and he also situates the narrative in Macedonia, following the French addition, "situee ou pays de Macedoine." Despite the translations of these French additions, Berners does not follow the French for the whole sentence. The French adds verbs to create the doublets "esclairer & illumoner" and "sallir et venir." The first doublet expands upon the Spanish "esclarecer"; Berners follows the Spanish and writes "illuminyd." Where the French reads "sallir et venir," the Spanish has "salir," which Berners translates with the single term "walkyd." Thus we can see that in this initial sentence Berners is combining his two sources, and not relying exclusively on either one.

In Chapter XXI the following line occurs:

Thus evyll Fortune, envyous of the welth & prosperite of Lereano, usyng againste hym her naturall chaungea[b]le condycion, she gave hym a torne whan she saw hym in his moste prosperite, whose mysfortune to behold was great passion, and constreyned the here[r]s to payne. (E8v)

This corresponds to the Spanish:

Como la mala fortuna enbidiosa de los bienes de Leriano usase con él de su natural condición, diole tal revés cuando le vido mayor en prosperidad; sus desdichas causavan pasión a quien las vio y combidan a pena a quien las oyé. (ed. Parrilla, 34)

[As evil Fortune, envious of Lereano's prosperity, acted against him according to her natural condition; she subjected him to such a reversal of fortune when she saw him in such prosperity. His misfortune caused pain in those who saw him and aroused pity in those who heard about it.]

And the French passage is:

Ainsi que malle fortune, envyeuse du bien & prosperite de Leriano, usant envers luy de sa naturelle condition, le voyant en son plus hault degre monte se declairant ennemye de la felicite, & estoit son malheur si tres grant qu'il causoit a tous pitie a chascun qui l'oyoit l'incitoit a passion. (F1v)

[Thus evil Fortune, envious of Lereano's happiness and prosperity, acted against him according to her natural condition; seeing him raised to his highest condition, she declared herself an enemy to felicity. And his misery was so intense that it led to pity in everyone, and aroused pain in those who heard of it.]

The paired nouns "welth & prosperite" in the English text are a translation of the French "bien & prosperite." The Spanish text has the single term "bienes." While Berners follows the French source with this addition, he does not translate the French "se declairant ennemye de la felicite," which replaces the Spanish, "diole tal reves": the English phrase "she gave hym a torne" is based on the Spanish. Moreover, the French text reverses the sequence of the Spanish terms "pasion" and "pena," writing first of "pitie" and then of "passion." Berners follows the Spanish with the terms in the order of "passion" and "payne." At the start of the line Berners is using the French, but he shifts to the Spanish for the remainder of the sentence.

Lereano's mother's lament in Chapter XLVII begins, "O Lereano! The myrth, comforte, rest and supporte of myne olde dayes!" (M5r). The Spanish *planctus* starts as follows: "¡O alegre descanso de mi vegez . . . !" ([ed. Parrilla, 77] O happy comfort [or rest] of my old age!); and the French translator writes, "O joyeulx confort de la mienne vieillesse!" ([M4r] O joyous comfort of my old age!). In the English translation four nouns are listed, while the French and Spanish each have one noun and one adjective. The English "myrth" is based on the adjectives "allegre" and "joyeulx"; the term "comforte" is based on the French "confort"; "rest" is derived from the Spanish "descanso," which means either "rest" or "comfort"; and the final term, "supporte," is added by Berners. In this short sentence, we see how Berners continues to blend his two sources, and by adding a term of his own invention he creates an entirely new English reading.

Close scrutiny reveals that sometimes Berners's translation of a word, phrase, or sentence is based exclusively on one source, and that at others it is derived from a combination of the two. Many paragraphs contain sentences from both sources, and in turn, many sentences contain clauses or words from both sources. In fact, some of the most linguistically interesting sentences occur when the two sources are fused to create a unique English reading, as in the above sentences and in the following examples. In Chap. XXI, in the phrase "with lyke seremonyes, how be it, they were not lyke in fame & honour" (F1v) Berners combines the French and Spanish terms in a manner similar to that seen in the final sentence examined above. The Spanish is "iguales en ceremonia aunque desiguales en fama" ([ed. Parrilla, 35] with equal ceremony, although they were unequal in honour) and the French is "mais non pas en louenge et renommee" ([F2v] but not [of equal value] in terms of laud and renown). The noun "seremoynes" occurs in the Spanish, but is omitted from the French. But Berners also retains the added French doublet, "louenge et renommee," translating it as "fame & honour." By taking "seremonyes" from the Spanish and "louenge et renommee" from the French, Berners combines his two sources, thus demonstrating, yet again, that he was using them both simultaneously.

Similarly in the phrase, "for *the* beautie and grace *that* is in women, the whiche is of suche excelence" (Chap. XLII; L1v), Berners translates the doublet, "beautie and grace," from the French "la beaulte & grace" (L1r) while the Spanish uses the single noun, "la hermosura" ([ed. Parrilla, 67] the beauty). The corresponding Spanish and French passages are as follows: "es por la hermosura que tienen, la qual es de tanta excellencia" (it is because of the beauty that they possess, which is of such excellence), and "est pour la beaulte & grace qu'elles ont, lesquelles sont de tant grant excellence" (it is because of the beauty and grace that they have, which are of such great excellence). After the added doublet, the French verb is conjugated in the third person plural in order to agree with the dual subject, "beaulte & grace": but even though Berners adds the doublet he neglects to accord the verb with the new plural subject, as does the French. The verbs, instead, are conjugated in the third person singular, following the Spanish. This shows that while Berners translates the doublet from the French, for the remainder of the sentence his eyes are on the Spanish text with its singular verbs.

The most widespread method of combining the sources is through the creation of doublets by translating one term from each source and joining them with the conjunction "and." For example, "thoughtes and trowbles" (Chap. XXXVIII; I8r) is based on a combination of "las congoxas" ([ed. Parrillla, 59] Sp, the thoughts) and "passions" ([I7r] passions, troubles); and "payne and adversite" (Chap. V; C3v) derives from joining "penar" ([ed. Parrillla, 15] to suffer) to "l'adversite" ([C4v] the adversity).

There are larger passages where Berners gives one language priority over the other. These, which I mentioned earlier in relation to Crane's argument, occur primarily at the very beginning and end of *Castell*. Berners's prologue to the text is a direct translation from the French. In the prologue, Berners follows almost all the alterations that the French makes to the Spanish, including additions and omissions. The opening of the English prologue is as follows:

> For the affeccyant, desyre, and obligacyon that I ame bownde in towardes your ryghte vertuous and good Lady, as well for the goodnes that it hath pleased you to shewe me [. . .] (A2r)

This is a direct translation of the French:

> Rememorant en quante servitude & obligatio*n* estoye envers toy tres ver-tueuse et tres prudente Dame, lye tenu & obstrainct po*ur* les graces et biens-faicts qu'il t'a plu m'octroyer[. . .] (A2r)

> [In remembrance of the servitude and obligation in which I am bound to you, most virtuous and most prudent Lady, I am tied, held and bound be-cause of the grace and good deeds which it has pleased you to grant me.]

And it has little in common with the Spanish:

> Ahunque me falta soffrimiento para callar, no me fallesce conoscimiento para ver quánto me estaría mejor preciarme de lo que callasse que arepen-tirme de lo que dixiese. (ed. Parrillla,3)

> [While I am lacking in the restraint needed to remain silent, I am not lack-ing in the knowledge to see how much better it would be for me to value myself for what I have not said, than to repent for having spoken.]

The same pattern occurs throughout the prologue, with Berners consistently giv-ing priority to the French variants. Berners probably chose to model his prologue on the French because being dedicated to, and in praise of, a female patron, the French prologue was well suited to his needs: Berners's *Castell* was dedicated to his niece, Elizabeth Carew. In contrast, the Spanish is dedicated to a knight and contains references to San Pedro's acquaintances and past compositions. Such material was irrelevant to the French translator and Berners, and so they do not follow it. This is the largest block of text in which Berners restricts himself to the French source.

The Spanish text is used exclusively by Berners from partway through Chap. XLVIII to the end of *Castell* (M7v–O8r). This portion of the text, which repre-sents Núñez's addition, was not translated into French prior to Berners's death, and so Berners had no choice but exclusively to use the Spanish. There are three additional chapters in which Berners largely ignores the French. These are Chaps. XXXV, XXXIX, and XLI, which the French translator versifies (H5v–H7v; K1r–K2v; and K2v–K4v). Despite the poetic form, in these chapters the French remains close to the Spanish, with the exception of slight changes in syntax and small additions and omissions in order to make the material fit the verse scheme. A comparison of the French and English texts shows that Berners never follows the syntactical alterations of the French. Moreover, of the numerous additions to and omissions from the French very few are preserved by Berners. In fact, in each of Chaps. XXXV and XLI there is only one instance where Berners may have been influenced by the French, and there are two occasions in Chap. XXXIX. These figures are surprisingly low, given that throughout *Castell* Berners seems to move freely between the two texts leading almost to one or two borrowings per sentence, rather than per chapter. Also, in each of these cases where it seems as though Berners may have used the French verse, it is possible that he made the changes independently of his French source. For example, in Chap. XXXV Berners writes "More surer it is to be belovyd for usynge of pitie and clemence" (H6r). Where the English has "pitie and clemence," the Spanish uses the single term "clemencia" (ed. Parrillla, 51), and the French employs the paired nouns "clemence et douleur" (H5v). The doublet "pitie and clemence" may be based on the French doublet, or Berners may have introduced the additional term, "pitie," of his own initiative, as he makes the same addition later in the chapter with no help from the French: he writes "O how frely delyveryd fro suche occasions are those prynces whose hartes are endeued with clemencye and pitie!" (H6v). In this sentence, the French has "clemence" (Hvr) and the Spanish "clemencia" (ed. Parrillla, 52). In Chap. XXXIX Berners translates the Spanish "ufano" (Parrilla 60) as "gloriouse" (K1r). "Pride," with its pejorative connotations, would have been a better translation, but it is possible that Berners was influenced by the French "glorieux" (K8v). Nonetheless, "gloriouse" is a valid translation of "ufano"; it is defined by the *OED* as "Boastful; ostentatious, fond of splendour; proud, haughty; vainglorious."[145] Later in the chapter, the English "syn ye wyll gyve no reward" (K2r) seems closer to the French "Puis donc a tant tu nyes grace" ([L1r] since that you so deny a reward) than to the Spanish "no niegues galardón" ([ed. Parrillla, 61] do not deny a reward). But despite the affinity of the French and English, Berners could have easily transformed the Spanish imperfect to a conditional construction without any assistance or inspiration from the French text. The unique instance in Chap. XLI where Berners may have used the French verse translation occurs when Berners translates "estrecho" ([ed. Parrillla, 62] the extremity) as "the perell" (K3r). This translation is probably based on the French "le peril" (L2v), but "perell" is a valid translation of "estrecho" and so we cannot be certain that the French was used. These few correspondences suggest that Berners possibly looked at the French verse, but that he relied almost entirely on the Spanish source for these three chapters: these instances may suggest that he used the French, but they are inconclusive. They do not vary significantly enough from the Spanish or from his own translation habits to provide definite

---

[145] *OED* 1.

proof. In any event, such a disproportionately small amount of French variants translated by Berners in these versified chapters, suggests that he was more comfortable working from the Spanish prose than the French verse. In fact, his practice of translating verse as prose in the remainder of the text, as with the verse mottos in Chaps. LII and LIV (N4v–N5v and N7v–N8v), lends further support to this hypothesis. In addition, even when he introduces what is poetry in the original as something which is "songe" to a "harpe," he provides a prose translation (Chap. LXII; O7r).

Not only are the final chapters, representing Núñez's continuation, the most extended portion of *Castell* based exclusively on a Spanish source, the translation and seamless appendage of these chapters is the most drastic alteration Berners makes to his sources. But equally notable are the more slight changes made throughout the translation, such as alterations in verb tense, grammatical person, and vocabulary. Regarding these types of variations it is difficult to ascertain whether or not the change was deliberate—whether it is an alteration or a mistranslation. In terms of the first kind of modification, a clear example of a mistranslation occurs in Chap. XXII where Berners changes a past tense Spanish verb to a present. The verbal phrase "quedaste satisfecho de su descargo" ([ed. Parrillla, 36] that you were satisfied of her innocence) becomes "now ye be well satysfied of her d[is]charge and ignorance" (F3r), but the present tense verb makes little sense in the context of the story. The subject of the verb is the king and the phrase is uttered by Lereano while trying to convince the monarch of Laureola's blamelessness. Since we know that the king is not satisfied of her innocence at the present time of the narrative—he is refusing to free Laureola from prison—this change is most likely an error. The entire Spanish sentence translates as "I think that by the trial you must have been satisfied of her innocence." The French would not have been the source of Berners's alteration as it retains the past tense verb: "ne te scauroit" (F4r). On many other occasions it is not possible to categorise the change as either a conscious, creative decision or as a mistake on Berners's part. A case in point is in Chap. LXII where the present subjunctive "si creyera hallar" ([ed. Parrilla, 103] if I thought to find) is translated as the past tense verbal phrase "therby thynkynge to have founde [happiness]" (O6v). (There is no corresponding French passage as this chapter is part of the continuation.) While in the Spanish Auctor is unsure if he will ever find happiness, in the English the possibility is no longer available to him: it remains locked in the past. Variations in verb tense increase in frequency towards the end of the text, which may indicate that without the French to help him Berners had difficulties in identifying the verb tense.

Closely related to changes in verb tense are alterations in grammatical person, under which category I am including changes in pronoun and subject. This is the most prevalent kind of error or alteration made by Berners. One modification of this type is in Chap. XXVIII, in Laureola's letter to Lereano. The sources for this sentence, "No sé, Leriano, qué te responda" (ed. Parrilla, 42), and "Je ne scay, Leriano, que te respondre" (G3v), both translate as "I do not know, Lere-ano, how to answer you." Berners, however, misunderstands the indirect pronoun "te" (you) used in both sources, and confuses it with the nominative pronoun "tu." He thus makes "you" rather than "I" the implied grammatical subject of the verb, writing "I can not tell the, Lereano, how to answer" (G3r). This makes little sense as Lereano has not asked Laureola for advice regarding his response, and it would be out of character for her to offer it to him, solicited or otherwise. Similarly, in Chap. XIII, Auctor asks "What shall I say?" (D4v), while the Span-ish reads, "Que dirás?" ([ed. Parrilla, 23] What will you say?) and the French has "Mais que diras tu?" ([D6r] But what will you say?). The context makes it clear that this is not supposed to be a self-reflexive question. In Ch XVI, Auctor con-cludes his speech with, "Therfore, her aunswere was shorte" (E2r). The sources all translate as "my answer was brief": the Spanish is "mi respuesta fue breve" (ed. Parrilla, 27) and the French is "Ma reponse fut brefve" (E2v). The pronoun "my" is the correct, sensible reading as Auctor is describing his own response and not commenting on Laureola's "aunswere."

There are some consistencies in alterations made in idiom, such as the re-peated substitution of "hand" as a singular noun for the plural "hands" in the sources in the context of kissing Laureola's hand(s).[146] For instance, Auctor's de-scription "So she toke me the letter, and kyst her hand" (Chap. XVI; E2r), is based on the Spanish "y despues de besalle las manos, recebí su carta" (ed. Parril-la,27), and the French "Et apres avoir baise ses mains, receu sa lettre" ([E2v] and after kissing her hands, I received her letter).[147] Unrelated, but equally consistent, is the translation of "parientes" (Sp) and "parents" (Fr) as "friends." In Chap. XXI Auctor describes the actions of 'Persyus' frendes' (F1v) but the sources refer to "sus parientes" (C7v) and "ses parens" (F2r–v). In XXII, Berners writes "his frendes" (F3r), while the sources mention "sus parientes" (C8v) and "siens pa-rens" (F4r). While the French term translates as "parents," the Spanish term can mean relatives, ancestors, family members, servants, or intimates. By repeatedly translating these terms as "friends," Berners places an emphasis on friendship rather than on familial relationships, which may be related to the value placed on friendship in Tudor discourse. There are two other types of additions that Ber-ners makes which are closely related to the latter alteration. He adds "Friend" repeatedly as a form of address used by Lereano and Auctor when speaking to each other, as in "Frende, for the love of God I pray the folow me and ayde me in this my great beisynes" (Chap. I; A8r), and "Frende, certaynly accordyng to my

---

[146] This also occurs in Chaps. XVIII (E4v), XXXVI (I2v), XXXVI (I3r), XXXVIII (I8r), LIX (O3r), and LX (O4v).

[147] For additional examples, see Chaps. XXIII (F4v), XXIX (G4v), XXXV (I1r), and XXXVIII (I7v).

naturall condycion I oughte to gyve the none aunswere" (Chap. I; A8v).[148] A corresponding term, such as "amigo" or "ami," is not present in either source. Berners also adds descriptive terms such as "his daughter" and "her father" to "Laureola" and "the king," emphasising their familial relationship.[149] It is possible that not only did Berners want to emphasise male friendship, but that he also wanted to highlight the kinship of Laureola and the king, to the exclusion of all other familial relationships. Thus, in order to stress the king's predicament, as he must choose between justice and his love for his daughter, Berners sought to eliminate other references to kinship that could detract from, or be compared to, that of Laureola and her father.

There are several types of omission that Berners makes consistently throughout the text. One involves the excision of all references to suicide. One of Auctor's wishes to die is excised. His statement, "Y assí me despido de más enojarte, lo que de la vida quería fazer" ([ed. Parrilla, 89] And so I take my leave, not troubling you any longer, wishing I could as easily take leave of my life), becomes "Thus I wyll leve any further to trouble the" (LIII; N4v).[150] And all mentions of Lereano's death as suicide are also omitted.[151] For instance, Berners writes, "So anone it was publyshed abrode, in the realme and in the courte how Lereano was lyke to dye" (Chap. XLII; K6r), but rather than "was lyke to dye," the Spanish and French translate as "was allowing himself to die." The Spanish line is, "Pues como por la corte y todo el reino se publicase que Leriano se dexava morir" (ed. Parrilla, 64); and the French, "Et quant fut publie par la court & par tout le royaulme que Leriano se laissoit mourir" (L5r). Auctor's musings regarding whether or not Lereano will go to heaven are equally omitted. In Ch LIII, Auctor states, "For now if thou knewyst the repentance of Laureola, thou woldest change the glory celestyall for thy lyfe temporal, for by thy deth thou hast lost thy desyre" (N4r). The sentence omits the Spanish phrase "si por dicha la tienes" ([ed. Parrilla, 88] if you have the chance [the good fortune] to attain salvation). This phrase occurs after "celestyall," and it serves to question whether or not Lereano has attained salvation. Moreover, the English "for by thy deth, thou hast lost thy desyre" replaces "que por darte la muerte perdiste" ([ed. Parrilla, 88] which you lost when you killed yourself). Moreover, in the following sentence, the Spanish

---

[148] There are further examples in Chaps. XLIII (K6v), XLVIII (M7v), LVII (N8v), LXI (O5r). Berners omits such a reference in Chap. LIII, where Auctor refers to Lereano as 'mi verdadero amigo' ([H4v] my true friend).

[149] These occur in Chaps. XIX (E6v), XXIV (F8r), XXVIII (G3v), XXIX (G5r), XXX (G7r), XXXII (H2r), XXXIV (H5r), XLI (K4r), LI (N3r), and LVII (O1v). He also once adds a reference to 'her uncle' in Chap. XXXVI (H8r).

[150] This is part of the continuation and so there is no French translation.

[151] For additional examples see Chaps. XLII (K6r), LV (N7r), and LVII (N8v; O1v).

"o si tan arrebatada no la tomaras, con tu vida" ([ed. Parrilla, 88] Oh, if you had not so rashly taken your life), is altered to "if thou haddest savyd thy lyfe" (N4r), omitting the mention of Lereano's death as suicide (Chap. LIII). Both these Spanish sentences cast doubt on whether or not Lereano was saved, and so by altering them Berners evades the issue. Such erasures are not surprising given the otherwise exemplary depiction of Lereano and the sinfulness of suicide. Lereano could hardly be advanced as the model perfect lover if he were damned as a result of his love. Berners was not alone in finding this paradoxical conflation of lover and sinner problematic: several critics, such as Bruno Damiani, Bruce Wardropper and Samuel Gili y Gaya, do not accept his death as a suicide, choosing rather to interpret it symbolically.[152]

Another strange omission is the exclusion of many Spanish doublets. For instance "batallas y conbates" ([ed. Parrilla, 36], battles and combats), becomes "bateyls" (Chap. XXII; F3r); "mudables o desatinados" ([ed. Parrilla, 37] change or become perplexed) becomes "swarvyd" (Chap. XXIII; F5r); "sinple y libre" ([ed. Parrilla, 38] simple and free [from prejudice]) becomes "symple" (Chap. XXIV; F6r); "cortesía y acatamiento" ([ed. Parrilla, 98] courtesy and respect) becomes "curtesye" (Chap. LVIII; O2v); and "rezio y dolorido" ([ed. Parrilla, 100] painful and dolorous) becomes "dolorous" (Chap. LX; O4v). As a reading of the text makes obvious, doublets occur with intense frequency: on any given page several can be found. The French translator is also very fond of this device and many English doublets are derived from the incorporation of French additions; however, San Pedro uses them infrequently. Given Berners's tendency to include French doublets and habitually to create his own, it is peculiar that in many of the rare instances where the Spanish has a doublet, it is omitted from the English.

There are additional discernible linguistic patterns, such as Berners's tendency to translate the Spanish and French verbs for "to say" or "to tell" as "to show." The use of "show" as synonymous for "say" or "tell" was an acceptable and widespread use of the verb in sixteenth-century English, but it is interesting that Berners uses it to the exclusion of the other verbs.[153] Sensory and cognitive verbs,

---

[152] Bruno Damiani, "The Didactic Intention of the *Cárcel de Amor*," *Hispanófila* 56 (1976): 29–43, here 37 n.31; Wardropper, "El mundo sentimental," 176; Samuel Gili Gaya, ed., *Cárcel de Amor* (Madrid: Espasa-Calpe, 1967), xii–iii. Others designate his death as suicide and discuss its implications on the romance and on the characterisation of Lereano. See Barbara Matulka, *The Novels of Juan de Flores and their European Diffusion* (New York: Columbia University Press, 1931), 34, 158; Otis H. Green, *España y la tradición occidental. El espíritu castellano el la literature desde el 'Cid' hasta Calderón*, 4 vols. (Madrid: Gredos, 1969) 3: 204–24; Lida de Malkiel, *La originalidad artistica*, 239 ff.

[153] *OED* V.23. See Chaps. I (A1r, B1v), II (B5r), IV (C1v), XIII (D4r, D5r), XIV (E1v), XVIII (E5v), XXIII (F4v), XXXI (G8r), XXXVI (H8r, H8v), XXXVIII (I7r), XLVI (M4v), LIII (N4r), and LVII (O1r). He uses 'say' as part of a doublet with 'show' in Chap. XLII (K6r): 'he sayd and shewyde'.

such as "to hear," "to see," "to think," and "to say" are often muddled or replace each other in the translations. For instance "seing" replaces "hearing" in Chap. II (B5r), and in the same chapter, the French "see" and Spanish "hear" are translated as "herest" (B6r). Likewise, in Chap. XXVI the Spanish and French translate as "neither to hear nor to know," but Berners writes "sene nor harde" (G1r).

There are several basic Spanish words which repeatedly cause problems for Berners. For instance, he twice mistranslates "calidad" (quality) as "heat," confusing "calidad" with "caliente" (heat) or "calor" (hot) (Chap. XI; D3r, and Chap. XVIII; E5v). Additionally, "esperar" (wait) is translated once as "breathed" (Chap. XVI; E1v) and once as "lokest" (Chap. XVII; E2r). In the former instance, Berners possibly confused "esperar" with "respirar," which means "breathed," and in the latter, he may have fallen into the trap of mistaking the verb for its *faux-ami* "espy." Likewise "consuelo" (comfort) is translated as "counsel" three times (Chap. XII; D4r and twice in Chap. XXVI; G1r). Berners is clearly mistaking "consuelo" for "consejo." In all these instances the French translates the Spanish correctly. The semantically related legal terms "juizio," "justicada," "juzgada," and "justiciar," which can all mean either "bring to justice" or "execute," are consistently translated as the former by Berners and the French translator, even though they are being used to mean "execute" (Chap. XXII; F3r, Chap. XXVI; G1r, Chap. XXX; G7r, Chap. XXXII; H2v, Chap. XXXVIII; I74). This may indicate that the two translators were unfamiliar with the complementary definition. There are other words which seem to cause problems for Berners at the beginning of the text, but are correctly translated towards the end. One such term is the noun "dicho" (fortune) which is mistaken for the past participle of the verb "to say" (which is also "dicho") even though the French correctly translates it (Chap. XIII; D4r). When the term reappears in Chaps. XIV (D6r) and XXVI (G1r), however, it is translated as "fortune." Likewise "colorada" (red or coloured) is problematic in Chap. XVIII (E3v), omitted in Chap. LIV (N5r), but accurately translated in Chap. LVI (N8r).[154]

Berners has an extensive vocabulary, often using words newly adopted into the English language. Many terms employed predate their first recorded usages in the *OED*. Some such terms are "affyrmacion" (Chap. XXIII), meaning an assertion or declaration (*OED* 4); "bleryd" (Chap. XLIX) in the context of to morally stain, or to defile (*OED* 2); "brayng" (Chap. XLII) used to denote a loud or harsh crying, or hoarse shouting (*OED* 1); "clowdy" (Chap. II) to describe something dim

---

[154] Some other terms which cause problems include 'adornavan' (Chap. I; B4r); 'subitamente' (Chap. I; B4r); 'ronca' (Chap. VII; C6v); 'memorial de su hazienda' (Chap. VII; C7r); 'desvio' (Chap. XII; D3v); 'esperiencia' (Chap. XV; D8r); 'asuelto' (Chap. XVII; E2v); the technical armoury terms in Chap. XIX (E7r); 'pequisar' (Chap. XXX; G7r); 'vía' (Chap. XLIII; K7r); 'fuercas' (Chap. XLIII; L2r); 'presunciones' (Chap. XLIV; L5r); and 'verter' (Chap. XLIV: L7r).

or obscure (*OED* 4c); "folyage" (Chap. LVI), meaning the representation of leaves used for decoration (*OED* 1); and "black more" (Ch II) or "blacke morion" (Ch I) as a name for a very dark-skinned person (*OED* 1).[155] Also, some terminology that Berners uses had only recently entered the English language. One such term is "inventor," used in Chap. XLV.[156] The term was innovative at this time, having been used first in 1509 by Barclay, and by More in 1513, and it is not documented with any frequency by the *OED* until the later half of the sixteenth century.

I already mentioned Berners's fondness for doublets and their derivation either from French, from a combination of French and Spanish terms, or created independently by him. While the French can be credited with a great many doublets, the Spanish text is the usual source of the numerous antitheses and parallelisms that run through the text. Berners does not preserve all instances of antitheses and parallelisms from his sources: regarding the latter, often a very small change is enough to ruin the device. For example, the Spanish "Si te parece que soy bien servido, tú lo juzga; si remedio e menester, tú lo vees" (ed. Parrilla, 11), becomes "Now judge thy self if I be wel served, if I have need of remedy *thou* seyst" (Chap. II; B7r). The Spanish parallelism is obvious to the sight as well as to the ear. The first half has slightly more syllables than the second, but both parts have the same verbal structure and syntax: they begin with "if," are followed by present tense verbal phrases of roughly the same length, and end with short clauses formed by a personal pronoun followed by a direct object pronoun and ending with a present tense verb. The English sentence also has two instances of "if," retains the same verbs as the Spanish, and has a pause in the middle, but the structure has been altered. In the first half, the verb "to judge," appearing in the short final clause in Spanish, is transposed to the beginning of the sentence and the verb "parece" has been omitted. In the second half of the sentence, the position of the final verb is retained but the direct object pronoun is omitted and there is no corresponding clause in the first half with which it can balance. The meaning of the Spanish is accurately conveyed, but the slight stylistic and structural changes disrupt the rhetorical device. Despite the omission or disruption of several parallelisms, it is still possible to say that they are characteristic of Berners's prose style, as a great many are preserved. One such example is: "Dolour turmenteth hym, passy*on* foloweth hym, dispaire destroieth him, deth manasheth hym, payne executeth hym, thoughtes waketh hym, desyre troubleth hym, hevynes *con*demneth hym, his fayth wyll not save hym" (Chap. V; C2v). This sentence is composed of eight parallel clauses, each composed of personal pronoun (subject), verb, personal pronoun (direct object). The final clause varies the structure, as it contains two verbs and the first is negated, which allows the rhetorical construction to lend emphasis to the thematic climax.

---

[155] For additional examples, see the glossary.

[156] In Chap. XLIII (L2r) he neglects to use the term, writing 'inventive persons' instead.

Most, but not all, Spanish antitheses are preserved. There are numerous examples of antitheses in *Castell*, especially in Auctor's discourse, as he tends to analyse his options and emotions through comparisons and oppositions. For instance in Chaps. XII and XIII (D3v–D5v), almost all the sentences are antithetical. More interesting are the cases of parallel antithesis, which also occur frequently in *Castell*. These are invariably derived from the Spanish. Some examples are: "men workyth, and fortune judgith" (Chap. XXIV; F6v), "Though myne arme fayle me to defende, yet my harte faylyth not to dye" (Chap. XXI; F1v), and "For more vertue it is to remedy them that be in tribulation, then to susteyne them that be in prosperite" (Chap. II; B7v). As a result of the abundance of parallelisms, antitheses, and parallel antitheses, the prose of *Castell* has a definite rhythm. For instance, in the following citation, almost all of the sentences contain one of these devices, creating a highly rhythmic effect:

> I pray the take for satisfaction not that I do, but that I desire. [antithesis] Of thy comyng hyther, I ame the cause. I ame he whome thou sawest led as a prisoner: bycause of the tribulacion that thou arte in thou knowest me not. [antithesis] Torne agayne to thy spirites and take rest and quyet judgement to th'entent thou mayst be ententyve to that I wyll say. Thy comyng was to remedy me, my wordes shall be to advertyse *thee*. [parallel antithesis] Who I ame, I shall shew the. [parallelism] (Chap. II; B4v)

Berners's parallelisms are not always perfect. He is less precise in the use of this device than San Pedro. While in the Spanish the parallel clauses have an equal, or very close to equal, number of syllables, in the English there is a greater discrepancy in the number of syllables and the balance of the device frequently rests more upon the similar structure of the clauses and the central pause.

While San Pedro's syntax is often Latinate, Berners refashions his source to conform to the norms of English grammar and syntax. San Pedro tends to postpone the verb, as in Latin prose, but Berners does not.[157] This tendency on Berners's behalf is partially responsible for the ruined parallelism discussed above. A reason why the parallelism was disrupted is because the postponed Spanish verb from the end of the first half of the sentence, "judge," was moved to the regular English position.

Rhetorical questions, brevity topoi, and hyperboles are also often found in *Castell*. Because the text is divided into extended monologues uttered by different characters and there is no dialogue, the characters are divested of the opportunity to interrogate each other directly, and so many questions are rhetorical in nature. Most of the rhetorical questions derive from the Spanish, although

---

[157] On this tendency see Keith Whinnom, "Diego de San Pedro's Stylistic Reform," *Bulletin of Hispanic Studies* 37 (1960): 1–15, here 2–3. He also discusses San Pedro's tendency to apply Latin rules to the use of the Spanish subjunctive.

some are added or omitted by Berners.[158] Brevity topoi are also frequently found in *Castell* and in San Pedro's text. Most instances are derived from Spanish, although Berners adds some of his own and omits a few as well.[159] Hyperboles likewise occur regularly. These are to be expected within Lereano's extreme discourse of love, but they are often used by Auctor, which is somewhat unexpected. Auctor emphasises with Lereano to such an extent that Lereano's pain becomes his own. This is especially apparent in his reactions of confusion and bewilderment to Laureola and her discourse. It would be impossible to note all instances of hyperbole in his speech, but one such example is, "But her wordes dyd put me in to suche passion, that who so hadde folowyd me by the trace of my wepynge myght well have found me out" (Chap. XXVII; G2v–G3r).[160] Occurring with less frequency, but equally remarkable are the proverbs, alliteration, polyptoton, anaphora, colour symbolism, allegory, personification, pleonasms, and metaphors that Berners includes.

Berners's prose style is varied and rhythmic, structured by, and ornamented with, rhetorical devices and imaginative, innovative vocabulary. The rhetorical devices used situate the text in a specifically Tudor context, as well as demonstrate Berners's indebtedness to earlier prose writers. As Norman Blake posits, "if Berners is the first to write modern English prose, it was only because many others before him had shown him the way."[161] Berners's fondness for doublets is shared by many late fifteenth- and early sixteenth-century writers including William Caxton and Thomas Elyot, both of whom employed the device to create specific rhetorical effects and to introduce loan words into their compositions.[162] Like Caxton and Elyot, Berners uses doublets for emphasis, and also often pairs a newer word with one that would be more familiar to his readers. For instance, the term "affyrmacion," which Berners is using in a novel way, is paired with the more common noun "wytnes" (Chap. XXIII; F5r); the Latinate term "temerous" is paired with the well-known English adjective "fearefull" (Chap. VI; C4r); and the expression "to put them downe," which Berners seems to be the first person to use to mean "to kill," is joined to "to slee them" (Chap. XXXV; H6v).

---

[158] Rhetorical questions are added to Chaps. XLVII (Mr6–M6v) and LVII (O1r).

[159] They occur in Chaps. XIII (D5v), XV (D8v), XVII (E3r), XXI (F1r, F2r–F2v), XXVI (G2r), XXX (G7v), XXXVII (I6r), XXXVIII (I7v), XLI (K4v), XLIV (L2r), and XLV (M3r). The brevity topos in the Spanish in Chap. XXXVI (I4v) is omitted, and the topoi in Chaps. XX (E8r) and XLV (L8r) are added by Berners.

[160] For additional examples of hyperboles, see Chaps. IX (C8v), XVI (D8v–Er1), XXI (F2r–F2v), XXXVI (H8r), XLII (K4v–K5r), and XLVIII (M7v).

[161] N. F. Blake, "Caxton and Courtly Style," *Essays and Studies* 21 (1968): 29–45, here 41.

[162] Blake, "Caxton and Courtly Style," 36; Anne Drury Hall, "Tudor Prose Style: English Humanists and the Problem of a Standard," *English Literary Renaissance* 7 (1977): 267–96, here 284ff.

Also in a manner analogous to Caxton and other Tudor translators, Berners's practice of close, direct translation enables him effortlessly to adopt many of the stylistic features of his originals.[163] Because these translators rendered their sources word for word, or clause for clause, it was almost inevitable that they should duplicate the style and some of the rhetorical effects of their originals. As I indicated above, many of the rhetorical devices in *Castell* derive from Berners's sources: the doublets largely from the French, and the antitheses and parallelisms from the Spanish. In his study of Thomas Malory's prose, P. J. C. Field observes, "Word-for-word translation allows the translators to preserve some remarkable subtle and complex patterns from Latin and French, in sharp contrast to the syntactic chaos which ensues when they interpolate passages of their own composition. Caxton and Berners are eminent examples of this."[164] The difference in style between Berners's translations and his original compositions, such as some of his prologues, has also been noted by Kenneth Oberembt, as well as by C.S. Lewis and R.W. Chambers, with the latter two expressing a definite preference for his translated over his original compositions.[165] Chambers condemns Berners specifically for his "trick of duplication or even triplication," which he employs with "maddening persistency," and he ascribes these stylistic blunders to Berners's failed attempts at eloquence.[166] Lewis also disapprovingly notes the "multiplication of synonyms" in Berners's prefaces.[167] While these twentieth-century scholars object to the use of doublets, there is no denying that it was a fashionable and popular device used with frequency by Berners and many of his contemporaries, including Caxton and Elyot. Parallelisms and antitheses enjoyed a similar vogue in the sixteenth century, and I will discuss them in the context of euphuism below.

Differences are similarly observable between Berners's earlier and later prose styles, with *Huon*, *Arthur*, and Froissart's *Chronicles* as examples of the former, and *Castell* and *Golden Book* (Berners's translation of Antonio de Guevara's *Libro Aureo de Marco Aurelio*) of the latter.[168] This change in style largely can be

---

[163] See Blake, "Caxton and Courtly Style," 35; P. J. C. Field, *Romance and Chronicle: A Study of Malory's Prose Style* (London: Barrie & Jenkins, 1971), 24; Samuel K. Workman, *Fifteenth Century Translation as an Influence on English Prose* (Princeton: Princeton University Press, 1940; repr. New York: Octagon, 1972), 10ff.

[164] Field, *Romance and Chronicle*, 24.

[165] Kenneth J. Oberembt, "Lord Berners's Translation of *Artus de la Petite Bretagne*," *Mediaevalia et Humanistica* 5 (1974): 191–99, here 196; R. W. Chambers, *On the Continuity of English Prose from Alfred to More and his School*, EETS 191 (London: Oxford University Press, 1952), cliv–v; C. S. Lewis, *English Literature in the Sixteenth Century (Excluding Drama)* (Oxford: Oxford University Press, 1954), 149.

[166] Chambers, *On the Continuity*, cliv, clv.

[167] Lewis, *English Literature in the Sixteenth Century*, 149.

[168] Cf. Lewis, *English Literature in the Sixteenth Century*, 150–55. He does not discuss *Castell*, but its stylistic similarities to *The Golden Boke of Marcus Aurelius* are indisputable.

ascribed to Berners's practice of duplicating the stylistic features of his originals, and there are significant differences between the French sources of his first three works in comparison with the sources of the later two Spanish texts. It must be noted, however, that Berners does not blindly emulate his originals. For instance, in his study of *Arthur,* Oberembt notes that despite Berners's general practice of word-for-word translation, Berners makes significant changes to the French *Artus*: Berners adds doublets; his dialogue is more formal; his diction is more elevated; and his use of subordinate and relative clauses transforms the parataxis of his source to hypotaxis.[169] This more complex sentence structure is typical of all of Berners's prose, and it is equally characteristic of Tudor prose in general.[170] The main difference between the style of Berners's Spanish and French sources is the abundance of rhetorical devices in the former, especially the use of parallelisms and antitheses which characterise the prose of *Castell* and *Golden Book.* As a result of these rhetorical features, earlier examinations of *Golden Book* and of its Spanish source have observed their affinities to euphuism.[171] In fact, Friedrich Landmann went so far as to situate the genesis of the stylistic tradition in Guevara's prose and its English translations. It is now accepted that there is no single source for euphuism, but rather that the rhetorical features by which it is typified were widely used by classical, medieval and early modern Latin writers, as well as by early modern English and continental vernacular authors.[172] Euphuism is characterised by the use of successive clauses of about the same length and form, linked through similarities of sound which can be created by a wide variety of rhetorical devices, including alliteration, homoioteleuton, anaphora, polyptoton, or basic word repetition.[173] Stylistic, rather than purely thematic, antithesis

---

[169] Oberembt, "Lord Berners's Translation," 194–99.

[170] Gert Ronberg, *A Way With Words: The Language of English Renaissance Literature* (London: Arnold, 1992), 101–2; Workman, *Fifteenth Century Translation,* 35, 56.

[171] Eduard Norden, *Die antike Kunstprosa vom VI. Jahrhundert vor Christi bis in die Zeit der Renaissance,* 2 vols. (Leipzig: Teubner, 1909); Friedrich Landmann, "Shakespeare and Euphuism. Euphues an Adaptation from Guevara," in *Transactions of the New Shakespeare Society,* offprint (London, 1882), 241–76.

[172] See Morris W. Croll, "The Sources of the Euphuistic Rhetoric," ed. R. J. Schoeck and J. Max Patrick, in *Style, Rhetoric, and Rhythm. Essays by Morris W. Croll,* ed. J. Max Patrick and Robert O. Evans et al. (Princeton: Princeton University Press, 1966), 241–95; William Ringler, "The Immediate Source of Euphuism," *PMLA* 53 (1938): 678–86; R. W. Zandvoort, "What is Euphuism?" in *Mélanges de Linguistique et de Philologie. Fernand Mossé In Memorium.* (Paris: Didier, 1959), 509–17; Ronberg, *A Way With Words,* 174–83. These critics all summarise the earlier arguments of Landmann, "Shakespeare and Euphuism"; Albert Feuillerat, *John Lyly, Contribution à l'Histoire de la Renaissance en Angleterre* (Cambridge: Cambridge University Press, 1910); and Norden, *Die antike Kunstprosa.*

[173] Croll, "The Sources," 242; Ringler, "The Immediate Source," 678; Ronberg, *A Way With Words,* 174.

is also often included in the definition.[174] These features are notable in *Castell*, as I indicated above, and it is possible to situate *Castell* within this stylistic trend.[175] Other rhetorical devices commonly used by Tudor writers appear with frequency in *Castell*, further emphasising its relationship to contemporary literary style. Some such examples are asyndeton, assonance, metaphor, hyperbole, metonymy, synecdoche, paradox, personification, rhetorical questions, and simile, some of which were noted earlier, and all of which are enumerated by Gert Ronberg in his list of the most commonly used rhetorical devices in Renaissance prose.[176]

All the stylistic features in *Castell* combine to create a linguistically sophisticated text, characterised by syntactical, rhetorical, and stylistic variation. These features also serve to highlight *Castell*'s affinities to contemporary stylistic norms and literary practices. Berners's use of parallelisms and antitheses, hypotactic sentences, doublets, and other rhetorical devices, aligns his text with the dominant Tudor prose styles. As I demonstrated above, many of these stylistic characteristics are the direct result of almost literal translation from *Castell*'s sources, but Berners also demonstrates a degree of autonomy as he adds, alters, and omits many rhetorical features. He is not a slavish translator: his work demonstrates a high level of skill, creativity, and understanding of his material. Despite Whinnom's dismissal of *Castell* as "disastrously bad ... grossly inaccurate ... [and] very frequently pure gibberish," Berners's translation *is* good.[177] Whinnom arrives at such a conclusion because he dismisses all (and even slight) alterations from the Spanish as mistranslations. This assumes, first, that the Spanish was Berners's only source, and second, that Berners was aiming to produce a direct, literal translation of the Spanish. As I have shown, neither of these assumptions is borne out by the facts. The Spanish is neither Berners's sole nor his main source: he uses the Spanish and French equally throughout his translation. Berners's translation is, at times, highly creative as he seeks to convey the sense rather than the exact structure of the Spanish. Moreover, he often combines his two sources creating a novel English reading. While he often translates his sources word-for-word, preserving their style and rhetorical effects, he does not always do so and there is no reason for us to believe that he intended to do so. He adds, alters, and omits rhetorical devices, and takes similar liberties with the content of his sources. *Castell* is more than a "rude laboure"; it is an accomplished translation. It successfully conveys both the narrative and the style of its two sources, and it does so in Berners's unique manner, accommodating Berners's thematic

---

[174] Croll, "The Sources," 243.

[175] Crane makes a similar observation: see William G. Crane, *Wit and Rhetoric in the Renaissance: The Formal Basis of Elizabethan Prose Style* (New York: Columbia University Press, 1937), 167.

[176] Ronberg, *A Way With Words*, 148–64.

[177] *Prison of Love*, trans. Whinnom, xxxiii–xxxiv.

and moral concerns, and reflecting early sixteenth-century linguistic, rhetorical and stylistic practices.

4. Genre: *Novela Sentimental* and Counsel Literature

Castell has an extensive repertoire of generic affiliations, maintaining dialogic and complex relationships with the genres of *novela sentimental, cancionero* lyric, epistolary fiction, and treatise as well as with the modal classifications of tragedy, romance, and parody. These taxonomies are not mutually exclusive and each plays an important role in *Castell*'s literary heritage, inception, and reception. In the following pages, by exploring these two of the dominant literary traditions which underlie the formation and immediate reception of *Castel—novela* and counsel literature—my aim is to show the complicated ways whereby *Castell* engages in dialogue with its literary inheritance and discursive environment. The *novela* is the genre to which the Spanish text has the closest affinities at the time of its creation and initial publication, while at the time of its translation Berners's *Castell* responds to, and partakes in, the tradition of counsel literature.

a) Novela Sentimental

Hispanists classify the Spanish source for *Castell, Cárcel de amor*, as a *novela sentimental* and have accordingly devoted much time and energy to defining that nomenclature. Their efforts have produced some stimulating, insightful criticism since as different generic attributes of the *novelas* are explored, new facets of the works are uncovered. There is no clear consensus, however, regarding which texts comprise the genre. Marcelino Menéndez y Pelayo, the first critic to differentiate the *novela* from the romance, proposes that there are thirteen *novelas*; Armando Durán examines six texts; seven and nine works are discussed by Marina Brownlee and Dinko Cvitanovic respectively; and in his bibliography of the *novela*, Keith Whinnom includes twenty-one "short, or comparatively short, love stories composed in Spain between 1440? and 1550."[178] For every work that

---

[178] See Marcélino Menéndez y Pelayo, *Orígenes de la novela*, 4 vols. (Madrid: Bally–Ballière, 1905–1915; repr. Edición Nacional, 4 vols., Santander: C.S.I.C., 1962); Armando Durán, *Estructura y técnicas de la novela sentimenal y caballeresca* (Madrid: Gredos, 1973); Marina Scordilis Brownlee, *The Severed Word: Ovid's* Heroides *and the Novela Sentimental* (Princeton: Princeton University Press, 1990); Dinko Cvitanovic, *La novela sentimental española*. (Madrid: Prensa Española, 1973); Keith Whinnom, *The Spanish Sentimental Romance 1440–1550: A Critical Bibliography* (London: Grant and Cutler, 1983), 5. The dates that Whinnom uses roughly correspond to the dates of composition of *Siervo libre de amor* (1439) and *Proceso de cartas* (1548). Until a short while ago, that these two works represented the temporal limits of the genre was an undisputed fact;

someone includes or expels from within the limits of the genre, their reasons or conclusions are invariably opposed by another individual. The five works which are generally agreed to form the nucleus of the genre are: *El Siervo libre de Amor* by Juan Rodríguez del Padrón; *Cárcel* and *Arnalte y Lucenda* by Diego de San Pedro; and *Grisel y Mirabella* and *Grimalte y Gradissa* by Juan de Flores. This short list is variably supplemented by some or all of the following texts depending on the critics' prerogative: *Tratado e despido a una dama de religión* by Fernando de la Torre; *Sátira de felice e infelice vida* by Dom Pedro de Portugal; *Triste deleitación* (Anon.); *Triunfo de amor* by Juan de Flores; *Repetición de amores* by Luis de Lucena; *Cárcel de amor* with Nicolás Núñez's continuation; *Tratado de amores* (Anon.); *La coronación de la señora Gracisla* (Anon.);[179] *Cuestión de Amor* (Anon.); *Penetencia de Amor* by Pedro Manuel Jiménez de Urrea; *Queja ante el dios de Amor* by Comendador Escrivá; *Cartas y coplas para requerir nuevos amores* (Anon.); *Veneris tribunal* by Ludovico Escrivá; *Tratado llamado Notable de Amor* by Juan de Cardona; and *Proceso de cartas de amores* and *Queja y aviso contra Amor* by Juan de Segura. The purpose of the following discussion is not to argue for or against the inclusion of any of the works enumerated above, neither is it to find the model *novela*, nor is it to arrive at a succinct one-sentence definition of the genre. Rather, I will explore some of the more interesting studies of the *novela* and use these differing critical approaches in order to gesture towards some of the literary attributes that *Cárcel / Castell* shares with several other texts classified as *novelas*, in order to gain a greater understanding of the text.

The term *novela sentimental* was first coined by Menéndez y Pelayo in order to differentiate this group of texts, dating from the mid-fifteenth to the mid-sixteenth century, from the chivalric romances. He explains that the main difference between the romance and the *novela* is the *novela*'s increased focus on emotion and love at the expense of chivalric action. He also claims that the new works respond to what he ambiguously terms "un concepto de la vida muy diverso" (Sp, a very different understanding of life).[180] He notes that the *novelas* are characterised by a mixture of chivalric and erotic elements, derived from a combination of their

---

however, recent articles by E. Michael Gerli and Marina Scordilis Brownlee have problematised their status as *novelas*: see E. Michael Gerli, "The Old French Source of *Siervo libre de amor*: Guillaume de Deguileville's *Le Rommant des trois pèlerinages*," in *Studies on the Spanish Sentimental Romance (1440–1550): Redefining a Genre*, ed. Joseph J. Gwara and idem (London: Tamesis, 1997), 3–20; and Marina Scordilis Brownlee, "Medusa's Gaze and the Canonicity of Discourse: Segura's *Proceso*," in *Studies on the Spanish Sentimental Romance (1440–1550)*, ed. Gwara and Gerli, 21–36.

[179] Gwara argues that this text was written by Flores: see Joseph J. Gwara, "Another Work by Juan de Flores: *La coronación de la señora Gracisla*," in *Studies on the Spanish Sentimental Romance (1440–1550)*, ed. idem, 75–110.

[180] Menéndez y Pelayo, *Orígenes de la novela*, 2: 3–4.

two main sources: *Amadís de Gaula* and *Fiammetta*.[181] His definition is apt as the *novela* is marked by its emphasis on sentiment instead of action, and it contains both chivalrous and erotic elements to varying degrees. Menéndez y Pelayo is also correct when he writes that the *novela* was influenced by the chivalrous romances and other literary forms, such as Italian novellas. However, despite the perceptiveness of these few observations, as a definition for the genre they are inadequate. The problem with his definition is threefold. The first problematic aspect is related to his proposed sources of the genre. While *Amadís* and *Fiammetta* may have influenced some *novelas*, they are not the only sources of all or even of individual *novelas*. The second pertains to the lack of any defining formal, structural, or stylistic features; and the third is because he neglects to elucidate this "concepto de la vida muy diverso" to which he says the *novelas* respond.

Carmelo Samonà argues specifically against the purely thematic nature of Menéndez y Pelayo's definition and discusses the heterogeneous structure of the various works.[182] Marina Brownlee agrees with Samonà and furthers his attack on thematic definitions of the genre by focusing on the various linguistic ideologies and discursive environments of the texts which, in her opinion, supersede subject matter in the context of generic definitions.[183] Despite the difficulties surrounding Menéndez y Pelayo's definition, it represents a significant step in the evolution of the modern critical reception of the *novela*. Prior to his work, the *novela* was conceived of as a sub-genre of the chivalrous romance—the black sheep of an illustrious family—and treated as a romance derivative, only slightly and poorly modified.[184] Following Menéndez y Pelayo's work the *novela* began to attract serious critical attention. Some scholars continue to explore possible Italian origins (including Boccaccio's *Fiammetta*);[185] while others look to French

---

[181] Menéndez y Pelayo, *Orígenes de la novela*, 2: 12.

[182] Carmelo Samonà, *Studi sul romanzo sentimentale e cortese nella letteratura spagnola del Quattrocento* (Rome: Carucci, 1960), 34.

[183] She also points to the false dichotomy of erotic and chivalric, positing that chivalrous romance is "more erotic, in fact, than *Fiammetta's* solipsistic, retrospective account of unrequited passion," and that romances are replete with intimate encounters and acts of chivalry motivated by love: see Brownlee, *The Severed Word*, 3.

[184] For example, Gayangos includes some of the *novelas* in his list of chivalrous romances while noticing that they have certain unique features. In his opinion, the major difference between the romances and the *novelas* is that the latter are more marital as opposed to martial as the result of their predominantly female target audience: see Pascual de Gayangos, "Discurso preliminar y Catálogo de los libros de caballerías," in *Libros de caballerías*. Biblioteca de Autores Españoles, 40 (Madrid: Rivadeneyra, 1857), lvi. For Amador de los Ríos and Sanvisenti the *novela* is romance with added allegory, due to Dante's influence: see José Amador de los Ríos, *Historia crítica de la literatura española* (Madrid: José Fernández Cancela, 1865) 6: 347; Bernardo Sanvisenti, *I primeri influssi di Dante, del Petrarca e del Boccaccio sulla letteratura spagnola* (Milan: Hoepli, 1902).

[185] See C. B. Bourland, "Boccaccio and the *Decameron* in Castilian and Catalan Literature," *Revue Hispanique* 12 (1905): 1–232; Arturo Farinelli, *Italia e Spagna*. 2 vols.

influences;[186] to native *cancionero* lyrics;[187] or to the Ovidian tradition.[188] Eschewing source studies, other critics select a formal, stylistic, or thematic feature as essential and definitive, and use it to define and explore the *novelas*. Some of the most common are epistolarity,[189] autobiographical qualities,[190] rhetoric,[191] subjectivity,[192] or narrative and plot motifs.[193] Others look to political and cultural

(Turin: Fratelli Bocca, 1929); Samonà, *Studi sul romanzo*; Antonio Linage Conde, "Los caminos de la imaginación medieval: de la *Fiammetta* à la novela sentimental castellana," *Filología Moderna* 15 (1975): 541–61; Antonio Prieto, *Morfología de la novela (Ensayos de lingüística y crítica literaria)* (Barcelona: Planeta, 1975); Pedro Bohías Balaguer, "La novela caballeresca, sentimental y de aventuras," *Historia general de las literaturas hispánicas*, ed. Guillermo Díaz-Plaja, vol. 2. (Barcelona: Barna, 1951), 189–236.

[186] See Frederick Bliss Luquiers, "The *Roman de la Rose* and Medieval Castilian Literature," *Romanische Forschungen* 20 (1907): 284–324; Chandler R. Post, *Medieval Spanish Allegory*, Harvard Studies in Comparative Literature 4 (Cambridge, MA.: Harvard UniversityPress, 1915; repr. Westport: Greenwood Press, 1974).

[187] Prieto, *Morfología de la novela*; Cvitanovic, *La novela sentimental*; A. D. Deyermond, *A Literary History of Spain: The Middle Ages* (London: Ernest Benn, 1971); Waley, "Love and Honour."

[188] Olga T. Impey, "Ovid, Alfonso X, and Juan Rodríguez del Padrón: Two Castilian Translations of the *Heroides* and the Beginnings of Spanish Sentimental Prose," *Bulletin of Hispanic Studies* 57 (1980): 283–97; Rudolph Schevill, *Ovid and the Renaissance in Spain*. University of California Publications in Modern Philology 4 (Berkeley: University of California Press, 1913; repr. Hildsheim: Olms, 1971); Antonio Alatorre, *Las 'Heroidas' de Ovidio y su huella en las letras españolas* (Mexico City: Universidad Nacional Autónoma de México, 1950); Juan de Segura, *Proceso de cartas de amores: A Critical and Annotated Edition of the First Epistolary Novel (1548) together with an English Translation*, ed. and trans. Edwin B. Place (Evanston: Northwestern University Press, 1950, repr. New York: AMS, 1970); Pamela Waley, ed., Juan de Flores, *Grimalte y Gradissa* (London: Tamesis, 1971), xxviii; Brownlee, *The Severed Word*.

[189] Charles E. Kany, *The Beginnings of the Epistolary Novel in France, Italy and Spain*, University of California Publications in Modern Philology 21 (Berkeley: University of California Press, 1937); Françoise Vigier, "Fiction epistolaire et *novela sentimental* en Espagne aux XVe et XVIe siècles," *Mélanges de la Casa de Velázquez* 20 (1984): 229–59, here 229, 230.

[190] Agustín Milares Carlo, *Literatura española hasta fines del siglo XV* (Mexico City: Robredo, 1950); Varela also looks at autobiography, but for him it is only one of many important generic traits: see José Luis Varela, "Revisión de la novela sentimental," *Revista de Filología Española* 48 (1965): 351–82.

[191] Edward Dudley, "The Inquisition of Love: *Tractado* as a Fictional Genre," *Mediaevalia* 55 (1979): 233–43; Anna Krause, "El 'tractado' novelístico de Diego de San Pedro," *Bulletin Hispanique* 54 (1952): 245–75; Samonà, *Studi sul romanzo*; Gómez discusses rhetoric as well as other features: see Jesus Gómez, "Los libros sentimentales de los siglos XV y XVI: sobre la cuestión del género," *Epos* 6 (1990): 521–32, here 526.

[192] On subjectivity see Gómez, "Los libros sentimentales," 526

[193] Régula Rohland de Langbehn, "Argumentación y poesía: función de las partes integradas en el relato de la novela sentimental española de los siglos XV y XVI," in

factors, such as women's social and literary position or the rise of new bourgeois values to explain the popularity and value systems of the *novelas*.[194] These approaches all increase our understanding of the *novelas* and ought not to be viewed as mutually exclusive. Just as we cannot expect all the *novelas* to share an entire range of generic attributes, it is equally disadvantageous to privilege one attribute over all of the others. The use of epistles and other rhetorical set pieces, the elaborate style of many of the *novelas*, their quasi-autobiographical nature, the use of

---

Actas del IX Congreso de la Asociación Internaciónal de Hispanistas, ed. Sebastián Neumeister (Frankfurt: Vervuert Verlag, 1989), 575–81; idem, "Fábula trágica y nivel e estilo elevado en la novela sentimental española de los siglos XV y XVI," in *Literatura Hispánica Reyes Católicos y Descubrimento. Acta del Congreso Internacional de la literatura hispánica en la época de los reyes Católicos y el Descubrimento*, ed. Manuel Criado del Val (Barcelona: PPU, 1989), 230–36.

[194] For studies that draw direct connections between the *novelas* and specific political events, see Francisco Márquez Villanueva, "*Cárcel de amor*, novela politica," *Revista de Occidente*, 2nd ser. 14 (1966): 185–200; idem, "Historia cultural e historia literaria: el case de *Cárcel de amor*," in *The Analysis of Hispanic Texts: Current Trends in Methodology*, ed. Lisa Davis and Isabel Taran (New York: Bilingual Press, 1976), 144–57; Santiago Tejerina-Canal, "Unidad en *Cárcel de Amor:* el motivo de la tiranía," *Kentucky Romance Quarterly* 31 (1984): 51–59; Régula Rohland de Langbehn, "El problema de los conversos y la novela sentimental," in *The Age of the Catholic Monarchs 1474–1516: Literary Studies in Memory of Keith Whinnom*, ed. Alan Deyermond and Ian Macpherson (Liverpool: Liverpool University Press, 1989), 134–43; Julio Carlo Baroja, *Vidas mágicas e Inquisition* (Madrid: Taurus, 1967), 1: 284. On the woman debate see Joseph F. Chorpenning, "Rhetoric and Feminism in the *Cárcel de Amor*," *Bulletin of Hispanic Studies* 54 (1977): 1–8; Gascón Vera, "La ambegüedad en el concepto del amor," 119–55; E. Michael Gerli, "La 'religión' de amor' y el antifeminismo en las letras castellanas del siglo XV," *Hispanic Review* 49 (1981): 65–86; Jean Gilkison, "Language and Gender in Diego de San Pedro's *Cárcel de Amor*," *Journal of Hispanic Research* 3 (1994–5): 113–24; Patricia E. Grieve, *Desire and Death in the Spanish Sentimental Romance (1440–1550)* (Newark: Juan de Cuesta, 1987); Haywood, "Female Voices," 17–35; Louise M. Haywood, "Gradissa: A Fictional Female Reader in/of a Male Author's Text," *Medium Aevum* 64 (1995): 85–99; Elizabeth T. Howe, "A Woman Ensnared: Laureola as Victim in the *Cárcel de amor*," *Revista de Estudios Hispánicos* (USA) 21 (1987): 13–27; Indini, "Nicolás Núñez," 489–504; María Eugenia Lacarra, "Notes on a Feminist Analysis of Medieval Spanish Literature and History," *La Corónica* 17 (1988–9): 14–22; Lacarra, "Representaciones femininas," 159–75; Jacob Ornstein, "La misogonia y el profeminismo," 219–32; Parrilla, "'Acresentar lo que de suyo,'" 241–56; Van Beysterveldt, "La nueva teoría," 70–83 and "El amor caballeresco," 1–13. And on bourgeois values, see Julio Rodríguez-Puértolas, "Sentimentalismo 'burgués' y amor cortés: la novela del siglo XV," in *Essays in Narrative Fiction in the Iberian Peninsula in Honour of Frank Pierce* (Oxford: Dolphin, 1982), 121–39; J. H. H. Lawrance, "On Fifteenth-Century Vernacular Humanism," in *Medieval and Renaissance Studies in Honour of Robert Brian Tate*, ed. Ian Michael and Richard A. Cardwell (Oxford: Dolphin, 1986), 63–79; Wardropper, "El mundo sentimental," 168–69.

allegory and debate, and the tendency towards narrative innovation and experimentation evidenced in the *novelas* are important generic features, even though they do not all apply to absolutely every text that may be included under the rubric *novela*. Moreover, while Italian erotic literature and chivalrous romances are the sources for some of the *novelas*—for instance, who can argue that Juan de Flores's *Grimalte y Gradissa* was not inspired by *Fiammetta*, or that duels, jousts, and challenges were not first seen in romances?—these are not the only influences, not do they influence all the *novelas*. The *novelas* contain elements from various genres, especially chivalric romance, lyric poetry, Ovidian verse, and Italian erotic literature; however, the degrees of influence are hard to determine, are rarely agreed upon, and differ for each work.

The most comprehensive definition of the *novela* is provided by César Hernández-Alonso, who writes:

> Entiéndese por *novela sentimental* un tipo de narración que surge en la España del siglo XV, que combina y conjunta la poesía de cancionero con narraciones caballerescas que toma como eje temático el amor cortés en sus diversa variantes, con la correspondiente idealización de la mujer, y que analiza un proceso amoroso generalmente frustrado.[195]

> [The *novela sentimental* is a type of narrative that peaks in fifteenth-century Spain, which combines and conjoins *cancionero* poetry with chivalrous tales, which takes as its theme courtly love in its diverse guises with the corresponding idealisation of women, and which analyses a love story which is generally frustrated.]

He further explains that it is not a realistic genre, but inclines towards allegory and the imaginative, and tends to avoid explicit description. The stories are generally timeless. The *novelas* may be set in exotic or foreign locations, or the author may allude to a known city through veiled illusions, but the setting does not affect the story nor is it described in great detail.[196] Diverse modes of rhetorical expression are combined, such as prose, verse, discursive monologues, dialogue, letters, laments, challenges, and rapid narration. These texts exhibit a concern with rhetoric and style, the latter being generally artificial with Latinate syntax.[197] They often take an autobiographical form although the content is not necessarily autobiographical. The tone is querulous, whining, plaintive, and sentimental, due to the hero's un-reciprocated love which drives the hero to desperation, grief, or even death.[198]

---

[195] César Hernández Alonzo, *Novela Sentimental Española* (Barcelona: Plaza & Janés, 1987), 11.

[196] Hernández Alonzo, *Novela Sentimental*, 13

[197] Hernández Alonzo, *Novela Sentimental*, 13

[198] Hernández Alonzo, *Novela Sentimental*, 12.

The majority of scholarship on the *novela* still operates in the shadow of Menéndez y Pelayo and defines the genre through comparisons to the romance.[199] Such evaluations are problematic as they relegate the *novela* to a secondary position and they operate according to the assumption that the romance is a clearly defined and definable genre. They are useful nonetheless, as they are able to gesture towards some of the dominant features of the *novela*. On the most basic level, there is scant action in the *novelas* while the romances depend on a steady proliferation of events. The protagonists in the *novelas* write letters and poems and issue long laments. While they may challenge their rivals, combat is rare, and when it does occur, it is dealt with summarily, as in *Cárcel, Arnalte y Lucenda*, and *Grisel y Mirabella*. The heroes of the *novelas* must face a different type of challenge from that of the knights of chivalrous romance. While the heroes in both genres are trying to win the love of their ladies, in the sentimental romance the amorous conquest is rhetorical in nature and its success or failure is dependant on the heroes' verbal dexterity and eloquence.[200] In the *novelas*, the errant knight becomes a talking knight, prefiguring the Renaissance courtier.[201]

The chivalric romance is not the only genre that affected the development of the *novela*. All the sources mentioned above exerted influences of varying degrees, not only on the many individual authors of the *novelas*, but even on different aspects of the same work. This is especially notable in the depiction of love in the *novelas* which is based on diverse traditions, such as Ovid's verse, Boccaccio's novellas, chivalric romance, and *cancionero* poetry.[202] In various *novelas*, all or some of these types of love are at play. This is most obvious in a comparison of the two pairs of lovers in each of *Grimalte y Gradissa* and in *El Siervo libre de Amor*. Different modes of expression also affect the *novelas*. Ovid's formal influence on the *novelas* stems from his *Heroides*: it showed the Castilian writers how

---

[199] See Enrique Moreno Báez, ed., Diego de San Pedro, *Cárcel de amor* (Madrid: Cátedra, 1989); A. D. Deyermond, "The Lost Genre of Medieval Spanish Literature," *Hispanic Review* 43 (1975): 231–59; Bohías Balaguer, "La novela caballeresca," 201; Durán, *Estructura y técnicas*, 178; Harvey L. Sharrer, "La fusión de las novelas artúrica y sentimental a fines de la Edad Media," *El Crotalón* 1 (1984): 147–57; Emily Spinelly, "Chivalry and its Terminology in the Spanish Sentimental Romance," *La Corónica* 12 (1984): 241–53, here 242.

[200] Gómez, "Los libros sentimentales," 526.

[201] Gómez, "Los libros sentimentales," 527.

[202] On these traditions, see Schevill, *Ovid and the Renaissance*; Ivy A. Corfis, *Diego de San Pedro's* Tractado de amores de Arnalte y Lucenda: *A Critical Edition* (London: Tamesis, 1985); Bohías Balaguer, "La novela caballeresca"; Van Beysterveldt, "El amor caballeresco," 407–25; idem, "La nueva teoría del amor en las novelas de Diego de San Pedro," *Cuadernos Hispanoamericanos* 349 (1979): 70–83; Alexander A. Parker, *The Philosophy of Love in Spanish Literature, 1480–1680* (Edinburgh: Edinburgh University Press, 1985), 11–40; René Nelli, *L'Érotique des Troubadours* (Toulouse: E. Privat, 1963).

the epistle could be used to narrate an emotional and subjective narrative told by either male or female speakers. His *Ars Amatoria* described the art of letter writing and linked it to the art of seduction. Epistolary and other rhetorical techniques were also learned from classical and medieval rhetorical manuals. The lyrics and the romances affect the presentation of love, but they also influence the tone of the *novelas*. The long expressive speeches and letters articulated and issued by the lovers in the *novelas* are indebted to lyric utterances. The narrative style which involves glossing over events in a short amount of space, typical of the *novelas,* can be seen in the "now turn we . . ." and "now leave we . . ." formulae of the romances (although the romances are, of course, also notorious for their long digressions).

When faced with such a large body of generic scholarship, open-mindedness is as important as discretion: each critical attempt can tell us something new about the *novelas* or about an individual text, such as *Cárcel*. Even on the basic level of plot, noting similarities between *novelas* can indicate where their authors deviate from or respect the norms, as Régula Rohland de Langbehn's structuralist analysis demonstrates. Rohland de Langbehn isolates a basic story-line in the *novelas* and subdivides it into eight stages which correspond to the dénouements of almost all the *novelas*.[203] The initial step is that the lover, usually a noble, loves a woman who rebuffs him.[204] Communication is then established between the lover and his beloved when he confesses his love to her, and in some works his emotional disclosure occurs through the assistance of a go-between.[205] After initial contact is established, the lover continues to court his lady who is persistent in her rejection.[206] She may eventually have mercy on him, but the movement towards a union will be interrupted in one of two ways. First, either the lover ceases to observe the behavioural norms dictated by the social and amorous code of conduct, and his lady, offended and frightened, returns to her original rebukes;[207] or, second, the suspicions of others are aroused and her family or other individuals intervene to separate them.[208] Following the separation there are three possible outcomes: the separation may be final with no hope of reunion;[209] one of the lovers may die;[210] or the lady will reject her lover completely.[211] Any one of these

---

[203] Rohland de Langbehn, "Fábula trágica," 230.

[204] In some texts, such as *Sátira de felice e infelice vida, Veneris tribunal,* and *Repetición de amores* this is the extent of the dénouement.

[205] For instance, Belisa in *Arnalte y Lucenda,* Auctor in *Cárcel,* Grimalte in *Grimalte y Gradissa,* and Actalasia in *Queja y aviso contra Amor.*

[206] This does not occur in *Grimalte y Gradissa* and *Cuestión de amor.*

[207] See *El Siervo libre de Amor, Arnalte y Lucenda, Tratado llamado Notable de amor.*

[208] See *Proceso de cartas de amores, Cárcel, Grisel y Mirabella.*

[209] See *Triste deleitación, Proceso de cartas de amores, Penetencia de Anor.*

[210] Such as Liessa in *El Siervo libre de Amor* and Grisel in *Grisel y Mirabella.*

[211] Laureola in *Cárcel* is one such example.

two outcomes, or the consequences of step three (where the lady refuses to have mercy on her lover), will cause the death of the (other) lover.[212] And finally, the death of one of the lovers may cause the other to repent.[213] As this schema makes evident, there are always obstacles to the amorous adventure, and the end of the *novela* is invariably tragic.

b) Counsel Literature

The consequences of accepting bad counsel are explored in *Castell* as Laureola is unjustly imprisoned because her father, King Guallo, heeds the malicious advice of his evil advisors. Despite the evidence of Laureola's innocence provided by the judicial duel, Guallo stubbornly asserts his daughter's guilt, even though everyone at his court, with the exception of the evil counsellors, tries to convince him otherwise. His subjects are faced with a grave problem: they must devise a way to inform their tyrannical ruler that he is behaving unjustly and steer him back to virtue. This theme is not new to *Castell*, and it is precisely its lack of originality that is of interest. Like so many of its contemporary and antecedent texts, *Castell* engages with issues of political leadership: how to give and recognise good counsel; what is tyranny; how a leader can take responsibility for errors in judgement and still preserve his honour. These political themes place Berners's translation within a contemporary tradition of counsel literature. *Castell* deals specifically with ideas of tyranny and counsel which were heavily debated and discussed during the 1520s, and indeed throughout most of the Middle Ages and the sixteenth century. In this section, *Castell* will be read alongside texts such as Thomas Elyot's *Boke of the Governor, Pasquil the Plain,* and *Of the Knowledge which Maketh a Wise Man*, Thomas Starkey's *A Dialogue Between Pole and Lupset,* Thomas More's *Utopia,* as well as earlier romances, including *Havelok, Athelston,* and *Seven Sages of Rome.* In these texts, ideas of good leadership are advanced: counsel is advocated, tyranny is condemned, and the ruler is encouraged to place the benefit of the commonweal above personal interest.

That counsel was an important subject among the early Tudors is incontestable. According to T. F. Mayer, debate over the function of counsellors "became one of the principal forms of sixteenth-century resistance."[214] A predominant theme in early Tudor literature is counsel: the merits of taking counsel; the difficulty of discerning good from bad counsel; the consequences of taking bad

---

[212] For example, Andalier in *El Siervo libre de Amor,* Fiometa in *Grimalte y Gradissa,* Leriano in *Cárcel,* Mirabella in *Grisel y Mirabella,* Flamino in *Cuestión de amor,* Cristerno in *Tratado llamado Notable de amor,* and Lucíndana in *Queja y aviso contra Amor.*

[213] For instance, Laureola in Núñez's *Cárcel* and Pánfilo in *Grimalte y Gradissa.*

[214] Thomas F. Mayer, "Nursery of Resistance: Reginald Pole and his Friends," in *Political Thought and the Tudor Commonwealth: Deep Structure, Discourse and Disguise,* ed. Paul A. Fideler and T. F. Mayer (London and New York: Routledge, 1992), 50–74, here 53.

counsel; and a trope which I have named the shield of counsel. In this trope, the advisor uses the forum of counsel to veil criticism of the monarch and other advisors, thus advancing potentially controversial or dangerous issues within a safe framework. The shield of counsel is also used by the king, who blames any poor decisions he has made on the advice of his counsellors. Tudor counsel literature is also concerned with the counsellor's moral obligation to give advice, which differentiates early Tudor from medieval discussions of counsel. With the early modern re-discovery of the idea of civic duty, inherited from classical texts such as Plato's *Republic* and *Epistles* and Cicero's *On Duties*, the portrayal of counsel was altered as the scope widened to include not only the king's duty to take advice, but also the citizen's duty to give advice. Medieval texts, especially romances and political treatises, concentrate on the former: they are concerned with the king's responsibilities and the consequences of his virtuous or vicious actions. However, the moral dilemma of the counsellor to give or not to give advice, prevalent in later texts, is absent. As I will demonstrate, *Castell* stands at the gateway of these two traditions, sharing concerns with both medieval and Tudor texts of counsel.

In *Policraticus* by John of Salisbury and in John Fortescue's *On the Governance of England*, for instance, the emphasis is on the king's duty to take advice, not on the counsellor's responsibility to advise, and the king is characterised as good or evil depending on whether or not he listens. *Policraticus* advances an image of ideal kingship similar to that of *Castell*.[215] Salisbury (like the early Tudor authors noted above) contrasts the ideal prince with the tyrant whose state of pride and wilfulness is likened to the illness of leprosy, which is inflamed by flatterers and dishonest people.[216] These flatterers are especially harmful to the prince as, if heeded, their words will dull his senses and impede his reason, thus transforming him into a tyrant, as occurs to Guallo in *Castell*.[217] The ideal prince ignores

---

[215] John of Salisbury, *Policraticus. Of the Frivolities of Courtiers and the Footprints of Philosophers*, ed. and trans. Cary J. Nederman (Cambridge: Cambridge University Press, 1990).

[216] Salisbury, *Policraticus* 3.3, 8.17.

[217] Salisbury, *Policraticus* 3.4. In contrast to tyrants, princes are preoccupied with the welfare of their people (4.1), they protect the poor and all who cannot fend for themselves (4.3, 5.7). They are pious and God-fearing as they recognise that all wisdom derives from God (4.7). The importance of tempering justice with mercy, a quality that King Guallo must learn, is also stressed (4.8). These ideas are echoed in the Latin poem, *The Battle of Lewes*, which presents the ideal king as God-fearing, just, merciful, compassionate, and one who seeks and heeds counsel: see T. Wright, ed., *The Political Songs of England* (London: Camden Society, 1839), 70–120. The positive depictions of Edward I in the *Chronicle of Matthew of Westminster* and the *Chronicle of Bury St Edmund* also use similar terms. Cf. David Staines, "*Havelok the Dane*: A Thirteenth-Century Handbook for Princes," *Speculum* 51 (1976): 601–23.

the flatterers and follows wise men: "For it is impossible that he should dispose rulership advantageously who does not act on the counsel of wise men."[218] The importance of counsel to good governance is similarly articulated by Fortescue. He describes the dangers of heeding counsellors who act in self-interest, outlines the duplicitous and dishonest nature of evil counsellors, and gestures towards the difficulty of having discreet counsellors. He firmly espouses the benefits of counsel and even offers his own model of Council to safeguard against corruption.[219] Fortescue's high estimation of counsel and Council is based on Roman, Athenian, and English historical precedent.[220] In his estimation, Rome and Athens prospered when ruled by Council, and failed when they were not. Likewise, in England, those kings ruled by wise advisors were "the mightieste kinges of the worlde," but those ruled by "private counsellours" disgraced the country.[221] "Be wich ensample," Fortescue concludes, "yff the kyng haue such a counsell as is before specified, his lande shall not only be ryche and welthy, as were [th]e Romans, but also [h]is hyghnes shalbe myghty, and off poiar to subdue his ennemyes, and all o[th]er that he shall liste to reygne uppon."[222] Fortescue is highly dubious of private counsellors and he puts his faith in public forums, such as Council, since they are answerable to the people, and less prone to secretive, duplicitous scheming. This same confidence in public assemblies is articulated in medieval romances such as *Althelston* and *Havelok*, to be discussed below. Similarly, in *Castell*, Lereano and Persio's duel, and the public addresses to the king by Auctor, the queen, and the cardinal, are preferred (by everyone except the king himself) over the secret, private advice given to the king by Persio and his accomplices. Salisbury and Fortescue look to the king and examine the consequences of his taking or refusing advice. There is no reference made to the problems or responsibilities of the counsellor in advising his ruler.

Medieval romances address the theme of counsel in a similar way. Geraldine Barnes situates medieval romance within a continuing thematic tradition of advice literature, observing that

> romance makes it [counsel] the basis of a code of chivalry in which wise counsel regulates prowess, channels it to constructive ends, and constitutes the medium for devising successful strategy. The principle of policy- and

---

[218] Salisbury, *Policraticus* 5.6.

[219] John Fortescue, *The Governance of England: Otherwise Called the Difference between an Absolute and a Limited Monarchy*, ed. Charles Plummer (Oxford: Clarendon Press, 1885), 145–46, 347–48. On specific links between Fortescue and humanist counsel literature, see John Guy, "The Henrican Age," in *The Varieties of British Political Thought, 1500–1800*, ed. J. G. A. Pocock (Cambridge: Cambridge University Press, 1993), 13–46.

[220] Fortescue, *The Governance of England*, 348.

[221] Fortescue, *The Governance of England*, 348.

[222] Fortescue, *The Governance of England*, 150–1.

decision-making by consultation, are officially, if not always willingly, espoused by thirteenth- and fourteenth-century English monarchs, is integral to the ethos of Middle English romance, where to 'work by counsel' extends beyond a proverbial commonplace and the 'problem of counsel', a fully articulated issue in the literature of the fifteenth- and sixteenth-century political commentary, is an underlying discourse.[223]

Counsel is used in romance to measure the abilities of both kings and knights and to judge their worth. The king who gives and receives good counsel is esteemed and his opposite is condemned as a tyrant. The ability to accept good counsel is a sign of wisdom, and asking for, and the ability to differentiate between good and bad, advice is the hallmark of a successful hero. The tyrannical king emerges as a stock character of the genre whose presence is usually signalled by his irrationality, his complicity with evil advisors, and his refusal to take good advice, like King Guallo in *Castell*. These ideas are explored in romances such as *Havelok the Dane*, *Seven Sages of Rome*, and *Athelston*.[224]

In *Havelok*, Athelwold and Birkabeyn are ideal kings who, despite their virtue, both fall prey to evil counsellors and leave their respective realms in the hands of a villain.[225] The romance concludes with Havelok's correction of Athelwold's and Birkabeyn's errors as he restores social harmony and rightful rule: he

---

[223] Geraldine Barnes, *Counsel and Strategy in Middle English Romance* (Cambridge: Brewer, 1993), 18–19.

[224] The link between counsel and virtue also is vividly illustrated in *Gamelyn* and *Beves of Hamptoun*. In these romances, the person who cannot take good advice is perceived as immature, impetuous, and incapable of ruling himself, let alone others. *Gamelyn* stresses the need to take counsel: the eponymous character is subjected to continued harsh treatment from his brother, and only when he requests counsel from Adam does his situation begin to change. Adam's advice of prudence, requesting assistance, and not acting violently mark him out as a good advisor, and a worthy match for the hero who has approached him. The fact that Gamelyn requests advice shows him to be on his way to success. Similarly, Beves's situation does not ameliorate until he begins to ask for and accept advice. Boniface advises Beves three times and each time his words temper Beves's behaviour, preventing him from acting rashly, as is the usual function of counsel. In each of these three instances Beves's fortune improves. He also benefits from Saber Florentin's advice, and this instance marks a significant step in Beves's development: it is the first time that he requests advice, representing a definitive move towards maturity and away from rash behaviour. See Walter W. Skeat, ed., *The Tale of Gamelyn*, 2nd ed. (Oxford: Clarendon Press, 1893); Eugen Kölbing, ed., *The Romance of Sir Beues of Hamtoun*, EETS ES 46, 48, 65 (London: Trübner, 1885–1894).

[225] See the description of Althelwold as just, clement, pious, a good military leader, fearless, strong, and open to counsel and the similar picture of Birkabeyn in Walter W. Skeat, ed., *The Lay of Havelok the Dane*, rev. Kenneth Sisam, 2nd edn. (Oxford: Clarendon Press, 1915), li. 340–357.

punishes the traitors, pacifies his enemies, rewards his loyal subjects, and consults his subjects on policy.[226] Havelok, Athelwold, and Birkabeyn are opposed by the treacherous usurpers, Godard and Goderich. Goderich rules without counsel, relying on threats, fear, and an oppressive bureaucracy.[227] They both govern autocratically, demanding loyalty without offering their subjects anything in return, unlike Havelok who offers his subjects a participatory role in government.[228] Not only is Havelok an ideal ruler, but he is also blessed with ideal subjects who recognise their civic responsibility through their acceptance of partial blame for allowing Birkabeyn to accept bad advice and relinquish the rule of his kingdom to an evil advisor.[229] "This consultation, the mark of constitutional monarchy, is emphasised by the writer, and is one of the most striking additions to the Havelok story."[230] It also sets *Havelok* apart from contemporary texts, foreshadowing the importance ascribed to the citizen's duty to his country in later Tudor texts, including *Castell*, as will be seen below.[231] The lack of blame ascribed to the good kings for their misguided actions alludes to the trope of the shield of counsel: the monarch's misdemeanours are excused because they are attributed to his being manipulated by evil counsellors rather than being of his own invention.

Like *Havelok*, *Athelston* has many themes and features in common with *Castell*. *Athelston* and *Castell* share the motifs of the tyrannical ruler; the jealous counsellor; the unjust imprisonment of the innocent; an unsuccessful, virtuous, intercessory queen; a high-ranking clergyman who also fails to persuade the ruler; the punishment of the traitors; an unpunished king; treasonous advice given in private; the request for just, public action; and the opposition of treason and secrecy to public justice. Moreover, King Athelston, like Guallo, has a misplaced sense of justice. The former desires to keep the traitor's name secret because he

---

[226] See Skeat, *The Lay of Havelok*, li. 2809–2841, li. 2858–2883, li. 2897–2927, li. 2808–2817.

[227] Skeat, *The Lay of Havelok*, li. 266–279, 2564–2565.

[228] Skeat, *The Lay of Havelok*, li. 249–262, 437–442.

[229] Skeat, *The Lay of Havelok*, li. 2797–2807.

[230] Judith Weiss, "Structure and Characterisation in *Havelok the Dane*," *Speculum* 44 (1969): 247–57, here 250. David Staines, Geraldine Barnes, and Sheila Delaney all argue that *Havelok* responds to the contemporary political situation and is part of the growing concern in the 1200s regarding the ideals of kingship, and the importance of the participation of the people in governmental affairs: see Staines, "*Havelok the Dane*," 602–23; Barnes, *Counsel and Strategy*, 41–46; Sheila Delaney, *Medieval Literary Politics: Shapes of Ideology* (Manchester and New York: Manchester University Press, 1990), 61–72.

[231] This image of theocratic, political, and contractual rule is paralleled in Henry of Bracton's *De Legibus et Consuetudinibus Angliae* in which the ideal ruler closely resembles Havelok, Athelwold, and Birkabeyn. This highly influential text presents the king as being both above and below the law and hence obliged to govern justly. Cf. Delaney, *Medieval Literary Politics*, 62.

feels beholden to the oath he made to the evil man. His stubborn belief in the justness of his actions is reminiscent of Guallo's similar insistence upon Laureola's guilt and his need to punish her. Guallo and Athelston are surrounded by good advisors—their respective queens and the cardinal (*Castell*) and the archbishop (*Athelston*)—as well as bad advisors, but they fail to distinguish between the two. Also both romances allude to the fact that the only way to guarantee justice is through public arenas, be they public trails or judicial duels, and both romances end with the flawed rulers still on the throne. Like *Castell*, *Athelston* "holds out the possibility of rehabilitation for rightful monarchs, whose misplaced trust in bad counsel has steered them in the direction of despotism," again showing how the prince can avoid recrimination by blaming his corruption on having received bad counsel. [232]

The Emperor in *Seven Sages of Rome* is also ultimately forgiven for his evil behaviour. [233] In *Seven Sages*, Florentine, like Laureola, falls victim to his father's anger, but in *Seven Sages* it is his stepmother who poisons his father against him. Like Persio, the stepmother's jealousy inspires her to use counsel to treacherous ends. She approaches the Emperor and accuses Florentine of raping her, when really she had approached, and was rebuffed by, him. Emperor Diocletian and Guallo both take rash, harsh measures against their own kin, having them imprisoned without due deliberation. Again like Guallo, Diocletian is immediately admonished by his good advisors: his barons "blamed hi*m* he dede [*th*]at dede / wi[*th*]outen counseil *and* rede," and they implore him to wait until they have deliberated, arrived at a solution, and counselled him before he acts. [234] He is also, like Guallo, reproved for wanting to put his offspring to death without his subjects' consent, and he is warned that he will incur his subjects' hatred should he do so. These events and their resolution frame a battle of wits, in which the sages and the empress fight for the king's favour through a story-telling contest. Just as counsel permeates the frame, it is perpetuated in the debate as their tales revolve around the ideas of counsel and good leadership. [235] From beginning to end, the story is concerned with power and with the reliability of counsellors: "The principal issue in *The Seven Sages* is the loss of royal authority and miscarriage of justice, caused by malign counsel and treachery and rectified by wholesome counsel

---

[232] Barnes, *Counsel and Strategy*, 59.

[233] His actions are condemned in the F version of the story by his son, Florentine, who, reprovingly, says: "Wi*th*owt councell slee me [*th*]ou wylt, /Agenste ryght, wi*th*owten gylte": Karl Brunner, ed., *The Seven Sages of Rome (Southern Version)*, EETS 191 (London: Oxford University Press, 1933), ll. 3723–3724. This accusation easily could have been uttered by Laureola, or indeed, by numerous other victims of tyrannical rulers.

[234] Brunner, *The Seven Sages*, li. 499–500, 504.

[235] The theme of counsel is also highlighted by the events which lead up to the Empress's betrayal, such as the processes of advising Diocletian to educate Florentine away from home and urging him to remarry.

and strategy."[236] The rehabilitative nature of counsel is stressed in this and many other romances. They advance the belief that if the ruler heeds the right advice he will be freed of tyranny and become (again) or remain a good ruler.

These ideas are found not only in romance: many texts from a wide range of literary genres articulate similar concerns regarding counsel. For instance, in Chaucer's *Tale of Melibee,* Prudence forcefully stresses the importance of counsel to good government, recognising the dangers of following bad advisors. She urges him to "Taak no conseil of a fool," and reminds him of the maxim: "Salomon seith, 'Werk alle thy thynges by conseil, and thou shalt neuer repente.'"[237] She further admonishes Melibee for allowing his advisors to become aware of his desired course of action, because this encourages them to flatter him by concurring with his opinion rather than to provide him with impartial advice.[238] Likewise, texts in the *Secretum Secretorum* tradition stress the need to take advice and the dangers of taking the wrong advice, and they explore how to chose the right counsellors and elicit the best advice from them.[239] A point that is repeatedly stressed in texts of this tradition is the importance of not trusting an advisor who has his own personal interests at heart. *Secretum* works are also concerned with tempering the king's natural desires and emotions through advice, corresponding to the premise advanced in *Castell* (as we will see below) that counsel inhibits the ruler's irrational impulses. In her examination of the *Secretum* tradition Judith Ferster discusses the paradox inherent in advice to princes literature, alluded to above, whereby the ruler must surrender himself to his counsellors in order to retain his power: in order to rule well, the ruler must be ruled. This paradox, which will be discussed further below, forms part of the shield of counsel trope, and was addressed continually by political theorists through and beyond the sixteenth century.[240]

---

[236] Barnes, *Counsel and Strategy*, 118.

[237] Geoffrey Chaucer, " The Canterbury Tales," in *The Riverside Chaucer*, ed. Larry Dean Benson, et al., 3rd ed. (Boston: Houghton Mifflin, 1987), li. VII 207, 1002–1003.

[238] Chaucer, "The Canterbury Tales," li. VII 1450–1452.

[239] At the root of the tradition is the ninth-century Arabic *Kitab sirr al-asrar* which was translated numerous times into Latin and English during the Middle Ages. On the Arabic text, see Robert Steele and A.S. Fulton, *Secretum Sectretorum*, Opera hactenus inedita Rogeri Baconi (Oxford: Clarendon Press, 1920), 5: iii–lxiv, for a translation of the Arabic text, see 176–266, and for an Anglo-Norman version, see 287–313. For some Middle English translations see Robert Steele, ed., *Three Prose Versions of the Secretum Secretorum*, EETS ES 74 (London: Trübner, 1898). On this tradition see also Judith Ferster, *Fictions of Advice: The Literature and Politics of Counsel in Late Medieval England* (Philadelphia: University of Pennsylvania Press, 1996), 39–41.

[240] For instance, many of the same arguments are advanced by Francis Bacon, in Sir Francis Bacon, "Of Counsel," in *The Essayes or Counsels, Civill and Morall*, ed. Michael Kiernan, The Oxford Francis Bacon, 15 (Oxford: Oxford University Press, 2000), 63–68.

As demonstrated by these examples, medieval romances aim to show that a king without good counsel is a tyrant. In later works, to be seen below, the tyrannical king exists as a catalyst for a discussion of the counsellor's role, as the classical notion of civic duty, mentioned earlier, accrues in importance and contentiousness. *Castell* stands at the gateway of these two traditions, or methods, of treating counsel, as it encompasses both approaches and ideologies. It draws on the evil king prototype, but equally engages with the theme of counsel from an early modern perspective, questioning the counsellors' functions, their degree of moral responsibility to offer advice, and the methods they should to adopt in order to influence the king. This concern with the counsellor's obligations, central to Tudor political treatises and dialogues, manifests itself in discussions of political responsibility and virtue, which are themselves inseparable. At the basis of this junction is the idea of civic duty, derived from Plato and Cicero, and taken up with enthusiasm by More, Erasmus, Starkey, and many of their contemporaries. Harking back to Plato, Cicero posits:

> as Plato has admirably expressed it, we are not born for ourselves alone, but our country claims a share of our being, and our friends a share . . . and as men, too, are born for the sake of men, that they may be able mutually to help one another; in this direction we ought to follow nature as our guide, to contribute to the general good by an interchange of acts of kindness. By giving and receiving, and thus by our skill, our industry, and our talents to cement human society more closely together, man to man.[241]

Closely related to civic duty is the Platonic tenet, important to Tudor writers, which holds that social harmony depends on the ruler's philosophical nature, namely his degree of understanding and appreciation of ethics and morality.[242] Plato affirms that if the king is not a philosopher then philosophers must surround the king:

> Unless, I said, philosophers bear kingly rule in cities, or those who are now called kings and princes become genuine and adequate philosophers, and political power and philosophy are brought together, and unless the numerous natures who at present pursue either politics and philosophy, the one to

---

[241] Marcus Tullius Cicero, *On Duties*, ed. and trans. M. T. Griffin and E. M. Aitkins (Cambridge: Cambridge University Press, 1991), I 22.

[242] On the importance of the image of the philosopher-king in the early Tudor period see Greg Walker, *Persuasive Fictions: Faction, Faith and Political Culture in the Reign of Henry VIII* (Aldershot: Scolar Press, 1996); idem, *Plays of Persuasion: Drama and Politics at the Court of Henry VIII* (Cambridge: Cambridge University Press, 1991); J. Christopher Warner, *Henry VIII's Divorce: Literature and the Politics of the Printing Press* (Woodbridge: Boydell Press, 1998).

the exclusion of the other, are forcibly debarred from this behaviour, there will be no respite from evil . . . for cities, nor, I fancy, for humanity . . .[243]

A just realm depends on the ruler's moral and spiritual state. If the ruler is not a paragon of virtue, he will act without justice, and will be susceptible to vicious advisors who will create evil laws, leading to civic unrest, disobedience, and general immorality. Hence, if the king is not a philosopher then philosophers must surround and advise him so that he acts honourably: social harmony and the morality of the entire realm are at stake.

The importance of the advisor forms the vital core of most early Tudor texts of counsel. These texts present the advisor as crucial to the well being of the state, echoing Erasmus's contention, "A country owes everything to a good prince; but it owes the prince himself to the one whose right counsel has made him what he is."[244] For example, in trying to convince Raphael to enter into the king's service in Book 1 of *Utopia*, the More persona makes a claim analogous to Erasmus's. He tells Raphael that the highest aim of man is to contribute to public affairs through counsel, declaring: "I do not see any other way in which you can be so useful to . . . the general public . . . your advice to a prince would be of the greatest advantage to mankind. No part of a good man's duty—and that means yours—is more important than this."[245] Similar arguments are advanced in Starkey's *Dialogue*. The entirety of the dialogue is devoted to Lupset persuading Pole to become a counsellor, and throughout the text performing public service as an advisor is stressed as the highest possible good. Elyot also makes the point repeatedly. His *Boke of The Governor* is a veritable monument to the importance of the counsellor. Elyot posits that "The end of all doctrine and study is good counsel . . . wherein virtue may be found," and it is also the goal of his educational project in *Governor*.[246] The manual concludes with a discussion of consultation and counsel, wherein Elyot stresses the import of counsel and counsellors for the maintenance of the commonweal.

The large degree of social, political, and moral weight ascribed to the counsellor in these texts is directly related to the counsellor's role in maintaining peace and justice: the counsellor is obliged to teach the prince how to be just and

---

[243] Plato, *The Republic*, trans. A. D. Lindsay (London: Everyman's Library, 1906; repr. London: David Campbell, 1992), V 473c–d. Cf. Plato, "Epistle VII. Plato to the relatives and friends of Dion. Welfare," in *The Platonic Epistles*, trans. J. Harvard (Cambridge: Cambridge University Press, 1932), 326 a–b.

[244] Desiderius Erasmus, *The Education of a Christian Prince*, ed. and trans. Lisa Jardine (Cambridge: Cambridge University Press, 1997), 6.

[245] Thomas More, *Utopia*, ed. and trans. George M. Logan and Robert M. Adams (Cambridge: Cambridge University Press, 1989), 13–14, 28, 36.

[246] Sir Thomas Elyot, *The Book named The Governor*, ed. S. E. Lehmberg (London: Dent, 1962), 238.

to show him how domestic and foreign harmony can be attained. In *Castell*, the cardinal is responsible for peace and justice as he works to free Laureola. The pacifist policies of the humanists are well known, and their desire for peace is made manifest in discussions of advice as they use the advisory forum to teach the prince the value of peace, and to steer him towards that goal. As writers of advice literature they present themselves, similarly to the cardinal, as spokesmen of peace and justice, and they use their texts to persuade princes and other actual or potential advisors to act likewise. For instance, Erasmus devotes a large section of *Education* to "the arts of peace," and he adopts the role of advisor and peacemaker, declaring "our first and foremost concern must be for training the prince in the skills relevant to wise administration in time of peace, because with them he must strive to his utmost for this end: that the devices of war may never be needed."[247] Likewise, in *Governor*, Elyot presents himself as a just advisor and simultaneously teaches future leaders and advisors the importance of justice. He posits, "The most excellent and incomparable virtue called justice is so necessary and expedient for the governor of a public weal that without it none other virtue may be commendable, nor any manner of doctrine profitable."[248] Raphael's experience at Morton's home, narrated in *Utopia*, gives a practical demonstration of how the advisor can and ought to ensure justice, despite the fact that Raphael concludes the opposite. The other topic More and Raphael discuss with regards to counsel is peace, and whether or not the counsellor could act as an effective peacemaker.

These writers value the advisor by linking him to the sage philosopher and opposing him to the tyrant and the flatterer. This dichotomy of vice and virtue is manifested specifically through the common practice of defining the prince in opposition to the tyrant, the counsellor in opposition to the flatterer, and the tyrant or errant prince in opposition to the good counsellor. In *Castell*, the impression of the cardinal's goodness is reinforced through his opposition to both the king and Persio. Erasmus strongly contrasts princes and tyrants, writing: "Only those who dedicate themselves to the state . . . deserve the title 'prince.' For if someone rules to suit himself . . . in practice he is certainly a tyrant, not a prince. Just as there is no more honourable title than 'prince,' so there is no term more detested and cursed on every score than 'tyrant'."[249] To best instruct the prince, Erasmus suggests presenting the prince with examples which sharply contrast princes and tyrants. He also devotes many pages to the danger of flatterers, like Persio in *Castell*, and even prefaced the first edition of *Education* with his translation of Plutarch's essay "How to distinguish a friend from a flatterer." These issues are given life in Book 1 of *Utopia* and in Elyot's dialogues. In their discussion

---

[247] Erasmus, *The Education of a Christian*, 65.
[248] Elyot, *The Book named The Governor*, 159.
[249] Erasmus, *The Education of a Christian*, 25.

of the merits and disadvantages of being an advisor, Raphael and More polarise flatterers and good advisors. For Raphael, the ubiquity of flatterers forms part of the reason why he will not enter into public service. Regarding the events in Morton's household, he concludes, "In fact they went so far in their flattery that they indulged and almost took seriously ideas that he only tolerated as the jesting of a fool. From this episode you can see how little courtiers would value my advice."[250] Elyot's *Pasquil the Plain* is an obvious example of the opposition between flatterers and good counsellors, as it narrates a debate between Pasquil, the good advisor; Gnatho, the flatterer; and Harpocrates, the hypocrite. The tension between prince and advisor, as exemplified through the contrast of the king and cardinal in *Castell*, is explored in Elyot's second dialogue, *Of the Knowledge*, which narrates Plato's experience in the court of the tyrannical Dionysius of Syracuse. This opposition is, in fact, inherent in the mirror for princes genre as the advisor presents himself as wise and able, and the prince in need of his instruction.

The philosophical nature of the advisor is also taken up in *Castell* as the cardinal is presented as the paragon of justice, virtue, and wisdom. But not only do Berners and his peers borrow the terms of the dichotomy from Plato and Cicero, they also engage frequently in the moral debate regarding the citizen's duty to advise his king. In *Utopia*, Peter Giles, More, and Raphael debate whether or not Raphael should enter into the king's service as a counsellor. While Raphael asserts that he has no place in politics, More argues that as a wise man he has a civic and moral responsibility to advise his prince.[251] More cites the popular Platonic argument in his defence, positing "No wonder we are so far from happiness when philosophers do not condescend even to assist kings with their counsels."[252] According to More, this type of philosopher must do all he can to ensure the well-being of the realm. Like Erasmus, Plato, and Berners, More associates counsel with philosophy, reason, virtue, and civic harmony, suggesting that if the king is lacking in counsel he will rule irrationally, viciously, and according to his passions.

Similarly, in Thomas Starkey's *A Dialogue between Pole and Lupset,* the importance of counsel and the individual's duty to his country is stressed. Lupset contends that "al men are borne & of nature brought forth, to commyn such gyftys as be to them gyven, ychone to the profit of other, in perfayt cyvylyte, & not to lyve to theyr owne plesure & [profyt], wyth [out] regard of the wele of theyr cuntrey, forgettyng al justyce and equyte."[253] He pits pleasure and personal gain against justice and equity, and the latter are linked to civility and to a prosperous realm. To live for personal gain is to propel the realm downwards and to

---

[250] More, *Utopia*, 28.

[251] More, *Utopia*, 28.

[252] More, *Utopia*, 28.

[253] Thomas Starkey, *A Dialogue Between Pole and Lupset*, ed. T. F. Mayer, Camden Fourth Series, 37 (London: Royal Historical Society, 1989), 1.

negate one's fundamental and natural obligation to one's fellows. Thus, as More and Erasmus also claim, it is not a matter of personal choice—the philosopher is morally obliged to share his knowledge, which entails advising the king despite the consequences. These texts place a large onus on the individual's devotion to the realm. Moral and personal integrity depends upon patriotic and social dedication, and no one can be called virtuous without subscribing to this principle: social responsibility is part of virtue.

These ideas are advanced in *Castell*, but rather than present them as a philosophical or political debate, we are shown the damage that can be done if the ruler is not properly advised. Issues debated by the fictional characters created by More, Elyot, and Starkey are made concrete in *Castell* as potential advisors must decide whether or not to intervene to save Lereano and Laureola from unwarranted death and dishonour. But while *Castell* articulates these contemporary political concerns, it does not distance itself from the medieval romance tradition. It exploits its romance heritage utilising romance tropes of counsel and character prototypes, like the tyrannical king and the shield of counsel seen earlier, to explore the theme in a specifically Tudor context. Furthermore, in *Castell*, the term "counsel" is imbued with many layers of signification: as the term is reiterated its lexical and semantic frames of reference widen, layers of meaning accrue, and the term "counsel" comes to connote and denote much more than the act of giving advice. The term is broadened to encompass rationality, virtue, and their concomitant attributes, while lacking in counsel is linked to irrationality, sin, and madness.

At the start of *Castell*, Lereano is held captive by Amours, the god of love. The events leading to his imprisonment are clearly described in order to present Amours according to the ideal of the just prince. Lereano explains that although Amours has indeed imprisoned him, his prison is composed of his own mental faculties—Will, Memory, Reason, and Understanding—who were all asked by Amours if Lereano should be captured, and all of whom consented. The process of consultation is clearly defined. It is explained that Amours decides to capture Lereano only after due deliberation and advice, and it is only because the advice he receives is unanimous that Amours imprisons Lereano. In the model of the ideal judge, or of the humanist king, Amours takes counsel, deliberates, and does not privilege the advice of any one person, nor does he act on his own whims. A comparison with the other ruler and judge in *Castell*, King Guallo, furthers the impression of Amours's virtue. Like the tyrant, described above, King Guallo acts on the testimony of false witnesses, ignores good counsel, and shuns due process by refusing to recognise the outcome of the duel. Amours's presentation as the humanist king emphasises King Guallo's depravity since if even Love, who is traditionally opposed to reason, can act rationally and affably, then there is no excuse for the king's inability to do so.

When the text moves away from the allegorical realm, the prototype of the good judge established in the allegorical opening in the character of Amours is replaced by God who is the ideal judge in the real world. The characters in *Castell* realise that justice will not be done by God's earthly representative, the king, and so they turn to God for true justice. Laureola makes "Hym judge of my mynde, to whome the trouthe of all thynges is manyfest & knowen," and encourages her father to do likewise by reminding him of God's justice and mercy (Chap. XVII; E2r). She writes to Guallo: "For syn God is juste he shall clere my trouth" (Chap. XXXV; H7v). Auctor consoles Lereano by referring to God's justice and mercy, explaining, "syn hevyn dysposith that is wrought upon the erthe, it can be none other wyse but that God wyll receyve *the* wepynges of innocentes and thy juste petycions" (Chap. XXIV; F8r). In admonishing the king and reminding him of God's true judgement, the cardinal clearly opposes God's good judgement with the king's error in judgement. This dichotomy is articulated as the cardinal asks the king, "And, Syr, why gyve you more fayth to theyr informacion, rather then to *the* judgemente of God, the which was clerely sene in the batayll bytwene Persio & Lereano?" (Chap. XXX; G7v). Auctor, Laureola, and the cardinal all refer to God as the true judge, who rewards and punishes equitably: as an arbiter of justice His probity is unfailing. God in the literal realm, like Amours in the allegorical realm, represents good judgement.

Amours, however, has one flaw: he "never perdonyth" (Chap. II; B5r). This attribute serves to align him with Guallo as they are both unwilling to alter their decisions and free their prisoners. Amours will not release Lereano; King Guallo will not release Laureola. Amours's lack of mercy also differentiates Amours from God, especially as throughout *Castell* God is presented and appealed to according to the twinned characteristics of justice and mercy. Despite this difference, Amours and God both rule justly. As such, they are antithetical to the king who, like the dreaded tyrant seen earlier, is incapable of sustaining justice. In *Castell*, a hierarchy of kingship is established with God, who in His omniscience knows what is right, at its head. Next comes Amours. He also knows what is right, but his knowledge is not innate; it derives from counsel and deliberation. At the bottom of the chain is King Guallo, who is ignorant and incapable of acting justly and rationally, and who does not compensate for his shortcomings, as does Amours, through deliberation and (good) counsel. The king is, in fact, "lacking in counsel," a polyvalent phrase repeated with frequency in *Castell*.

The state of being without counsel is described in detail by Auctor in Chap. XII, following his meeting with Laureola. He depicts himself as bewildered, fearful, unable to understand Laureola or the situation, and lacking in hope, guidance, and reason. He sums up this condition of bewilderment, despair, terror, and irrationality by comparing himself to "a man without counsayll" (D4r). In this instance the term "counsel" comes to denote an altered and profoundly disturbed state of mind. In Auctor's discourse, counsel is associated with reason as its opposing state of lacking in counsel is linked to irrational passion. Lereano suffers from a similar condition of lacking in counsel, also inspired by Laureola. Lereano's love drives him to a state of confusion, despair, and disordered understanding: as he explains to Laureola, he is blinded by her and his understanding and reason cannot function (Chap. XV; D8r). When Auctor takes on the responsibility of nursing Lereano back to health, he makes the link between Lereano's pain and his need for counsel. Auctor explains how he "went to Lereano, thynkyng to gyve hym some counsayll and . . . to remedy parte of his evell" (Chap. XII; D4r). In this instance the process of giving counsel is equated with raising Lereano's spirits and relieving him of some of his pain, thus implying that passion and irrationality can be alleviated through good counsel. This connection is further articulated in Lereano's and Auctor's reactions to the king's refusal to recognise Lereano's and Laureola's innocence. When Lereano hears that the king is ignoring the result of the duel, Lereano, "with great fury and passion desperate . . . was therwith nere oute of his wytte [and] . . . in a great perplexite" (Chap. XXIII; F5v). Observing Lereano's state, Auctor resolves, "And when I saw hym stande in suche a dysmayde trance, I thought then to serve hym with my counsayll, to th'entent he shuld not do that thyng in haste wherby to repent hym after" (Chap. XXXIII; F5v). In this situation, Lereano is angry and confused, but fortunately he is prevented from reacting hastily by Auctor's counsel, which steers Lereano towards sage and virtuous behaviour. Auctor's counsel to Lereano further elucidates the association of counsel and reason and the dichotomy between passion and counsel: he instructs Lereano to act with "sage pacience" and to "folow my symple counsayll" even though his "understandyng be occupyed *with* passion" (Chap. XXIV; F6r). Auctor advocates counsel, because when passion is involved, understanding is crippled and counsel is the best remedy. He pronounces, "demuer delyberacion shulde be determynyde or yt were executyd all wayes in a thyng doughtfull the most surest way wolde be taken" (Chap. XXIV; F6v). Counsel and deliberation are stressed as being essential, since anger, jealousy, and other strong emotional responses cloud the understanding, rendering reasonable actions impossible. The opposition between passion and counsel has as its corollary the link of counsel and reason: a lack of reason is synonymous to a lack of counsel, and reason can be restored through counsel.

Auctor provides Lereano with an endless stream of counsel, which ensures that Lereano remains rational and in control. In contrast, Persio does not have an advisor, and his false accusation of Laureola and Lereano consequently derives directly from his lack of counsel. Persio is confused, his mind is "disordered," and because he is "*with*out deliberacy*on* or co*un*sayll" he acts according to his "gelous suspecte" (Chap. XVIII; E5r). Persio is shown to be evil because he acts without advice, and the lack of counsel is specifically linked to the presence of passion. By clearly stating that this evil action was taken without deliberation and counsel, the jealous passion is opposed to counsel and deliberation.

Counsel is the best remedy for disordered emotions and, in *Castell*, a lack of counsel is associated with pain and affliction as well as with passion. Lereano reinforces this association when he tells Laureola, "And I ame so accustumyd to lyve in hevynes that I ame fayne to take counsaill for your cause. But in the payne *that* I fele now I take no counsayl, nor I have no rest, nor my harte can not be quyt for the payne that ye suffre" (Chap. XXVI; G1r). This point is again reiterated when Lereano despairs upon receiving Laureola's final letter: "when he hadde redde it, he sayd he wolde nother take strength nor receyve any counsayll, syn it was so good reason that he shulde dye" (Chap. XLII; K5r). The absence of counsel here is linked to anguish as well as to death. Since counsel is the only thing that can save Lereano, by refusing counsel he resigns himself to death.

While Persio acts out of passion because he lacks counsel, the king acts irrationally because he listens to the wrong type of counsel. Like the tyrant of counsel literature, he is easily misled by evil advisors. Following Persio's accusation of Lereano and Laureola, the king undergoes a long process of deliberation: he ponders, he "studyed long or he was determynyd to aunswere . . . he had slept on *the* mater" (Chap. XVIII; E5v). But while he ruminates prior to acting, he still neglects to take counsel. As a result, he deems Persio to be honest and heeds the accusation of this evil counsellor: "he bileved Persius' sayeng to be true. Consyderyng his vertue and auctoryte, he wolde shew nothyng, but of troug[*th*]" (Chap. XVIII; E5v). The king is not as impetuous and impatient as Persio; but while he tries to refrain from acting recklessly through the process of deliberation, he still cannot choose the proper course of action because he takes advice from the wrong person, namely Persio. His actions are misguided since he fails to heed his good advisors. The king repeats this mistake during Lereano and Persio's judicial duel, when he listens to Persio's friends and interrupts the fight prior to its conclusion even though Lereano clearly has the advantage. This prevents justice from being done. Moreover, following the duel, when Lereano petitions the king to exonerate him and Laureola, the king "aunswered that he wold take counsayll what was best to do, and sayde that in suche a case delybercion wold be taken or any sentence shuld be gyvyn" (Chap. XXIII; F4r). Unfortunately the king, for the third time, listens to the wrong people, this time to Persio's paid accomplices. The king examines them carefully, but fails to perceive their craftiness. Therefore, "by reasone of theyr informac*ion*, *the* kyng reputyd Persyo for trew servant and belevyd that it was more by reasone of his fortune, rather then by his untr[e]w[e] quarell, that he lost the batayll" (Chap. XXIII; F5r). The harm that can be caused by listening to bad counsel, warned against in the advice literature discussed above, is clearly demonstrated through the king's actions. The error is repeated three times in order to articulate the point: just as good counsel leads to rational action, bad counsel leads to passionate reactions, which prevent justice from being served and which disrupt civic harmony.

The association of bad counsel or a lack of counsel and passion is furthered through the different characters' reactions to the king as they unanimously ascribe his unjust actions to his irrationality and his refusal to take good counsel. Lereano realises that the king's lack of reason must be remedied in order for justice to be done. Accordingly, Lereano and Auctor try to steer the king back to reason through the good advice which is presented to the king by Auctor, the cardinal, the queen, and Laureola. Laureola agrees with Lereano's prognosis regarding her father's condition, and in writing to Guallo she polarises "the furour of [his] ire" and "the trouth" (Chap. XXXV; H5v). She further opposes his "furour" to "good counsaill and naturall prudence," and reminds him of God's justice, providing him with the perfect example on which he should model his behaviour, and reminding him that he is ultimately accountable for all of his actions (Chap. XXXV; H7r). Because she recognises that counsel will restore his reason, she does not beg for mercy, as her mother does, but rather offers him advice in the style of *speculum principis*. Not only does her political discourse allude to such an understanding of the curative force of counsel, but she also makes the point explicit when she writes: "or ye determyne take good advyse, for as sure as God is true I never dyd thyng to deserve to suffre any payne" (Chap. XXXV; H6r).

The cardinal's approach is similar to Laureola's. He counsels the king in the advice to princes tradition in order to obtain Laureola's liberty. In fact, his lengthy speech on counsel can be read as a mini-*speculum principis*. He provides the king with six reasons why counsel ought to be heeded, followed by general remarks on the value of counsel in all situations, and he concludes by addressing the value of counsel in this specific instance. In his oration, he has recourse to the dichotomy of counsel and passion, positing that counsel is necessary, "for the harte of hym that the mater tochyth can not be with oute some ire, covetesnes, affection, or desire, or some other lyke condicion, so that he shall not determyne the cause as he ought to do" (Chap. XXX; G5r–G5v). As Lereano, Laureola, and Auctor allege, emotions block reason and the only available remedy is counsel. Recalling Lereano's blindness due to his passion for Laureola, the cardinal further cautions the king, "Certaynely, Syr, it is but a blynde counsayll, a man to counsayll hym selfe knowynge hym selfe in any furour or passion" (Chap. XXX; G5v). Like Laureola and the authors of the counsel literature seen above, the cardinal associates "furour or passion" with a lack of counsel (Chap. XXX; G5v). Wise rulers ought to think of all the consequences of their actions and follow reason, "And if they fynde them selfe troublyde with any passion, tyll they be cleryd therfro they shulde gyve no sentence. And yf they debate and delaye ther deades, then they do well. For in all suche weighty maters hast is daungerouse and tariynge is suretie" (Chap. XXX; G6r). Echoing Laureola's, Lereano's, and Auctor's statements, the cardinal contends that arguing and deliberating matters allows the truth to be perceived with greater ease. The good prince must also exert caution in choosing his counsellors "and not to determyne upon a lyght credence," as the king does by heeding Persio's accusations (Chap. XXX; G6v). No decision should be made, nor any advice taken, unless the prince is convinced of the advisor's honesty. The cardinal makes the opposition between wisdom (and counsel) and fury clear, just as Auctor, Laureola, and Lereano did before him. Similarly to Laureola and Auctor, the cardinal invokes God as the ultimate judge by referring to the duel between Persio and Lereano. The duel revealed God's judgement, and by mentioning the fight and the king's poor assessment of it, the cardinal reminds the king that he is acting against God as well as contrary to reason and counsel. Throughout his speech, the virtues of honesty, temperance, pity, reason, and justice are linked to form a moral core and this conceptual nexus is associated with counsel; the opposing vices of haste, fury, irrationality, and dishonesty are attached to the king and to his act of taking bad advice.

The king's reply to the cardinal does little to reassure his subjects. He agrees with the general remarks uttered by the cardinal, but he contends that he is "more bound to punyshe then to perdone" and so will not heed the cardinal's advice (Chap. XXXI; G7v–G8r). While he is aware "that great prynces ought to receyve conusayll," he says that his "harte is chargyd with passione" and so it is "locked fro herynge of any counsayle" (Chap. XXXI; G8r). He knows that his thinking is clouded and that he ought to follow the advice of his counsellors, but he will not do so, because he is too angry. His statements reinforce the link between counsel and reason and the polarity of counsel and passion. The king continues by providing many arguments regarding why the guilty must be punished, but as they are founded on a fundamental untruth — Laureola's guilt — his reasoning is ineffective and unpersuasive, and it demonstrates a lack of common sense and reason.

While such a king is deserving of condemnation, the trope of the shield of counsel is employed to deflect blame from the king. As the cardinal asserts, "yf by another manne's counsayll the besynes fayleth and takyth none effecte, yet he that demaundeth the counsayll is oute of blame & charge and they that gave the counsayll muste bere the charge & faulte" (Chap. XXXI; G5v). This is precisely what happens in *Castell*, as the evil advisors are held responsible and it is made plain that there was no way the king could have recognised their deceit. Auctor explains that the king:

> examynyd eche of them a parte by subtyle and sharpe perswasions to se yf they any thyng swarvyd in ther sayenges. But they were such persons that if a man shulde have wastyde all his lyfe in falsenes, coulde not be lyke them. They were so sure of theyr wordes, the more they were examynyde the surelyer they fortefyed theyr false lyes, so that therby the kyng gave to theyr false sayenges fayth and beleve. (Chap. XXIII; F5r)

This passage indicates that the king behaved impeccably in his cross-examination of the evil counsellors, but that no matter how good his investigation was, there was no way that he could have discovered their deceit. As such, the king can emerge from his blunder of heeding the wrong advice unscathed. His advisors are to blame, and by rectifying the situation and freeing Laureola, the king is shown to return to his senses.

Blame does not always exclusively rest on the shoulders of the bad advisors; when the king errs, all of his advisors are in danger of recrimination. The risks involved in the advisory process occupy a central role in the Tudor discourse of counsel: as I discussed above, the debate over the extent of the wise citizen's duty to advise his prince was ubiquitous. I also observed that these concerns formed the main site of difference between medieval and Tudor counsel literature. In a manner analogous to contemporary counsel texts, *Castell* employs the medieval prototypes of the just prince and the tyrant to articulate the importance of counsel to good government; and *Castell* is simultaneously interested in the counsellor's obligations to advise his prince and in the inherent dangers in the advisory process. While the king shares attributes with his medieval predecessors, the advisors in *Castell* differ from the romance-counsellor prototype. Unlike in medieval romance, where the counsellors' duty to advise does not figure, the counsellors in *Castell* demonstrate an awareness of their responsibility, and articulate that duty in terms of the same polarities seen in the humanist political texts. For instance, when addressing the king, the cardinal says: "Therfore, Syr, blame us not, though in the fercenes of your ire we be come to trouble you, for we hadde rather that ye shulde in your ire reprehende us for our comynge to you, then that after ye shulde repent you and condempe us bycause we gave you no counsayll" (Chap. XXX; G6r). Laureola implores her father to accept the advice of his counsellors, writing: "Howbeit, I requyre you, or ye determyne take good advyse ... if ye thynke the opinyon of your furour better than good counsaill and naturall prudence, then unhappy is that daughter . . ." (Chap. XXXV; H7r). The cardinal and Laureola demonstrate an awareness of the advisor's responsibility to counsel the king and thus lead him to virtue. The cardinal states his duty clearly and vocalises the risks involved—by offering advice he may be reprimanded, but his duty outweighs the potentially negative consequences. The counsellors' responsibility is also implied in their language, as they oppose counsel and reason to passion. Laureola expresses the dichotomy of anger and good counsel and prudence, and suggests that good advice will prevent him from dishonour. Likewise the cardinal contrasts the fierceness of the king's ire with counsel, because counsel will lead the king from passion to reason and ensure his virtuous action.

The themes of counsel addressed by *Castell* situate the text within the tradition of counsel literature—both the literature of medieval romance and Tudor dialogues and instructional manuals—allowing it to be read as such by its audience. *Castell*'s affinities to the counsel literature tradition may explain why the text may have appealed to Berners as matter suitable for translation and why he thought that his contemporaries would enjoy it. *Castell* shares themes and concerns with antecedent and contemporary literature. Its negotiation of early Tudor and medieval ideologies of counsel situates it specifically within an English, humanist context enabling it to address the concerns of Berners and his contemporaries. Such a thematic and ideological combination situates *Castell* within a larger, atemporal tradition of counsel literature, and simultaneously positions it at a specific moment in time as it responds to the predominant concerns of the literary traditions of counsel at its point of translation.

5. The Texts

The three early printed editions of *Castell* (1548?, 1552?, and c. 1555) are virtually identical, with the exception of some changes which are preserved in the second and third editions of the romance. There are three main types of alterations made to the text: the addition of poems, including the verse prologue; the addition of marginal notes; and the excision of references to the Virgin Mary. It is likely that Andrew Spigurnell, an unknown Tudor writer, is responsible for these revisions. It is not possible to ascertain the extent of Spigurnell's agency in the latter two types of revision, but it is certain that the poems are his. The verse prologue names him as its author, "Androwe Spigurnell to the reader in maner of a prologue," and it implies his responsibility for further alterations to the text, reading (Prol.; A1v):[254]

> I have taken upon me presumptuosly
> Newly to penne the matter though unable
> Yet have I done it and also rudely
> Have added somwhat unconnyngly . . . (Prol.; A2r)

Moreover, given the similarities in style and language, it is likely that the three additional poems—in Chaps. XVIII and XXXVIII—were also penned by him.

This prologue is written in nine rhyme royal stanzas. In a manner analogous to Núñez's prologue, this prologue imparts its author's interpretation of *Castell*, and given that Spigurnell read the addition, it is not surprising that Spigurnell's analysis is quite similar to Núñez's. He engages critically with the book, and deems it

> a present moche unworthie
> To be presented to a Lady or a Quene,
> That declare them selfe in every case
> To have pytie mercy and grace. (Chap. Prol.; A1v–A2r)

This assessment of *Castell*'s unsuitability for a gentle female audience is directly related to Spigurnell's reading of Laureola as cruel and heartless. While he admires her concern for her honour, he concludes that she erred in refusing Lereano: "For though honour before lyfe is to be preferred / Yet another's lyfe is to be regarded" (Prol.; A2r). Picking up on key terms used in *Castell*, he argues that it is woman's *natural* state to be *piteous* and *merciful*, and thus posits that Laureola damages her honour through her lack of pity.

---

[254] Signature numbers for Spigurnell's additions refer to the second edition of *Castell*, printed by Wyer in 1552?.

So that it appereth in the conclusyon
A Lady pyteles and endewed with cruelte
Is to her honour reproche and obloquie. (Prol.; A2r)

Spigurnell has clearly engaged with the text and considered its meaning. In his prologue he alludes to some central issues raised by *Castell*: honour and love; pity and cruelty; and woman's natural condition. However, his interpretation, owing to his reading of Berners's amalgamated text, is diametrically opposed to the message of San Pedro's *Cárcel*, which argues that woman's honour takes precedence over man's love and life. While San Pedro's text advances woman as supremely powerful and presents her honour and concerns as superior to man's, Spigurnell, following Núñez, uses the paratext to reverse this message. He thus cannot see how *Castell* could be presented as a laudatory gift to a lady such as Elizabeth Carew; rather, he presents the book as a warning to all women to take heed and not value themselves and their honour too highly, lest disaster ensue. He writes:

But to the intent that women in generall
By theyr disdayne and lacke of pytie
Shal note, what inconvenyence mai come and fal
To lovers that be tormented crewly
Therfore I have taken thus upon me
This booke to peruse and reade with payne
In wyll to have it prynted agayne. (Chap. Prol.; A2r)

Laureola loved Lereano, but because of her "disdayne and lacke of pytie," Lereano died. This alteration is striking in light of the fact that *Castell* is the first secular English translation made for a woman that does not claim to be didactic, and that was "made purely on the grounds that young women would find it entertaining."[255]

Spigurnell's subsequent three poems are sung by Lereano at moments of particular emotional intensity. The first poem, in Chap. XVIII, occurs when Lereano reaches a point of despair because he thinks that he has received Laureola's ultimate rejection (E1v–E2r). The poem has an inconsistent rhyme scheme: the first stanza is in rhyme royal; the second is almost rhyme royal, except that it has only six lines; and the third stanza is composed of three rhyming couplets. The last two lines of the first stanza form the refrain, "My care sorowe and my burest / And welcom her sonde that I love best," but the second stanza only uses

---

[255] Alexandra Barratt, "Carried Forward: Translations for Women to 1550," Australian and New Zealand Association for Medieval and Early Modern Studies Fifth Biennial Conference, Auckland, New Zealand, 2–5 February 2005, unpublished conference paper.

the first of the two lines for the refrain and the third uses both, while varying
the first line to "Agaynst care sorowe and all burest." This repetition and modification of the refrain resembles the ballade technique of incremental repetition.
The first and third stanzas repeat the term "welcome" followed by a term of relief or happiness (solace, comfort, joy, mirth, hope). The second repeats "blessed
be" followed by terms related to epistolary composition (the hand that wrote, the
pen, paper, messenger). The poem proceeds by anaphora, and the accumulation
of clauses creates the effect of increasing happiness and solace from the pains of
love. Two distinct, but related, language clusters are formed—one of positive
amorous emotions and the other of epistolarity. This poem makes the specific
link between the relief from the pains of love and the receipt of a letter, reflecting
the importance of letters in *Castell*.

After finishing his first song, Lereano "concludyd and determyned to go
to the courte, but fyrste" he sings again (Chap. XVIII; E2r–E2v). This second
composition is composed of four stanzas of eight lines organised according to the
rhyme scheme aaabcccb. The rhymes are repetitive and unoriginal: for instance
in the first stanza the term "payne" is repeated in the rhyme position; and in the
third stanza "alone" rhymes with "all one." The poem lacks a refrain, but the line
"In this lyfe mortall" is repeated in two of the four stanzas. This poem contrasts
with the first poem in terms of both poetic sophistication and tone. Whereas the
first poem is hopeful, this poem employs imagery of death and despair to present the lover as hopeless, and it advances death as Lereano's only possible form
of relief.

The third "dytie" is sung by Lereano to increase his sorrow and hopefully
"therby to abbrydge his myserable and most payneful lyfe" (Chap. XXXVIII;
I6v). It occurs in Chap. XXXVIII after Laureola rejects Lereano (yet again),
even though he has freed her from her imprisonment and placed her in the safe-
keeping of her uncle (I6v–I7r). This poem resembles the first poem formally and
the second tonally. It is in three monk's tale stanzas (rhyme scheme of ababbcbc),
and employs a refrain which varies on "Up for to ryse and throwe me downe
agayne." The first stanza is an invocation to Fortune, lamenting her fickleness.
The same technique of anaphora is used as in the first poem: lines begin with
"O fortune . . ." This accumulation of clauses gives the impression of increasing
despair, accurately reflecting Lereano's emotions. The second stanza proceeds by
opposition, repeating the contrasting terms "farewell" and "welcome" followed
by positive and negative terms, respectively. This creates two contrasting nex-
uses of vocabulary as the negative is welcomed and the positive is eschewed. The
repetitive nature of these stanzas, particularly through the use of the term "welcome," recalls and opposes the first poem. Feelings of hope evidenced in the first
poem are replaced by despair, especially as articulated in the final stanza, which
expresses a longing for death. This despair echoes the second poem, as it presents
an equally despondent message.

Unlike the prologue, these three poems do not detract from, or interfere with, the story or any of the characterisations. By reflecting Lereano's feelings, as he alternately hopes for, and despairs of, Laureola's love, they reflect the narrative progression. The poems also present him as increasingly sincere: they are sung by him in private moments of reflection, and so we see that even without his usual audience of either Laureola or Auctor, his feelings are constant. This prevents us from sharing Laureola's doubts regarding his *troth*. While not exceptional poems, they are good enough not to disrupt our impression of Lereano as an eloquent speaker and writer, as demonstrated through his letters and orations, and they further demonstrate his ability to express his emotions accurately. The juxtaposition of the first two poems is particularly effective since it reflects Lereano's predominant state of confusion throughout *Castell*, as he is trapped between hope and despair.

The majority of the marginal notes in the second and third editions of *Castell* highlight plot elements, descriptive passages, or changes in speaker. The most interesting notations are those related to the arts of rhetoric, specifically to letter writing. For instance, in the letters of challenge and response exchanged by Persio and Lereano there are marginal glosses which indicate the rhetorical divisions of their epistles. The notes to the challenge letter indicate the "Introduction o the satyde mater," the "Declaracion of the said mater," "The accusement," "The appele," and the "Conclusyon" (Chap. XIX; E4r–E5r). And, in Lereano's response, the glosses direct our attention to "The proheme of the letter," "The argument," "The defence of treason," "The answere," and "The devyse of the armure" (Chap. XX; E5r–E6r). These glosses indicate the different rhetorical parts to the letters in the same manner adopted in instructional treatises, such as Erasmus's *De conscribendis epistolis*. There were numerous Castilian manuals available in the fifteenth century describing the procedures involved in issuing, and responding to, a challenge, the most notable being the texts written by Alfonso de Cartagena and Diego de Valera.[256] The letters in *Castell* follow the guidelines provided by these models, as demonstrated by Corfis.[257] Corfis and Whinnom also both compare Persio's missive to a historical challenge letter written by Diego López de Haro, demonstrating their verbal and structural similarities.[258] These marginal notations to the letters of challenge and reply suggest that the letters may have been intended to function didactically, to instruct readers how to compose model

---

[256] Whinnom, *Obras Completas, II*, 84.

[257] Ivy A. Corfis, "The *Dispositio* of Diego de San Pedro's *Cárcel de Amor*," *Ibero-Romania* 21 (1985): 32–47, here 39.

[258] Corfis, "The *Dispositio*," 39ff.; Whinnom, *Obras Completas, II*, 56, 84–86; Cf. Erasmo Buceta, "Cartel de desafío enviado por D. Diego Lopez de Haro al Adelantado de Murcia, Pedro Fajardo, 1480," *Revue Hispanique* 81 (1933): 456–74.

epistles. While Persio's letter and Lereano's reply have strong Iberian precedents and were written according to both Spanish court etiquette and the dictaminal arts, they were so well understood in England more than fifty years after their composition that Spigurnell was able to identify all of their parts in the marginal notations. His glosses show that he could easily recognise these epistolary divisions, that he was interested enough to do so, and that he thought his annotations would appeal to his readers' interest in rhetoric and epistolary composition. As Corfis observes, "An unexpected confirmation of the importance which sixteenth-century readers attached to the rhetorical nature of the letters and speeches in books such as *The Castell of Love* comes from Spigurnell's marginal notes."[259] Spigurnell's concern with epistolarity is reinforced by the poem that he adds to Chap. XVIII, discussed above, in which he employs the language of epistolarity. And further drawing attention to the epistolary exchange, in Chap. IX there is a gloss which reads, "Note the wrytyng of leters" (C4r). Moreover, he adds "To the good and vertuous Lady, the Lady Carewe, gretynge" to the start of the prologue, providing it with a salutation (Prol.; A2v).

Spigurnell's interest in epistolarity in conjunction with the exemplary nature of all the letters in *Castell* and with the centrality of the letters in terms of structure and theme further suggests that the letters may have been intended as didactic models. Not only could fictional letters be used as models for emulation by sixteenth-century composers, but they could also be lifted out of their fictional contexts and pilfered by unoriginal letter-writers. For instance, Barbara Weissberger cites an instance of *Cárcel* being used in this way. She explains how, in an historically documented courtship, one of Lereano's letters was copied and sent by an early sixteenth-century lover to his lady. The lady recognised the letter's source and refused to accept it, stating "Esta carta no viene a mi, sino a Laureola" (Sp, This letter is not for me, but for Laureola).[260] This is reinforced by the similar use of glossed, exemplary epistles in other contemporary texts. For instance, Claudius Hollyband's translation of *Arnalte and Lucenda*, Young's translation of *Fiammetta*, and Thomas Underdowne's translation of Heliodorus's *Aethopian History* of 1569? all have glosses indicating speeches, descriptions, orations, letters, and complaints. The marginal notations suggest that these fictional works were used didactically—that their letters, and other rhetorical units, were meant to be studied, copied, or imitated by aspiring letter writers. This method of using fiction for practical purposes is also supported by the borrowing of fictional letters by writers of instructional manuals. For instance, in the English letter-writing manual by William

---

[259] Corfis, "The *Dispositio*," 40.

[260] The instance occurs in Melchor de Santa Cruz's *Floresta española*, which dates from the mid-sixteenth century: see Barbara Weissberger, "Resisting Readers and Writers in the Sentimental Romances and the Problem of Female Literacy," in *Studies on the Spanish Sentimental Romance 1440–1550*, ed. Gwara and Gerli, 173–90, here 176–77.

Fulwood, *The Enimie of Idleness*, letters are borrowed from fictional compositions: in all the editions of Fulwood's manual, the first amatory letter is derived from *De duobus amantibus*; and in the third edition, three of the model amatory letters are copied from *Amadís de Gaula*. The most extensive culling of letters from *Amadís* was in *The moste excellent and pleasaunt booke, entituled: The treasurie of Amadis of Fraunce*, Thomas Paynell's translation of the letters and other rhetorical pieces from the Spanish chivalric romance. His text was composed entirely of extracts from the romance and had the express purpose of epistolary instruction. Moreover, in the first edition of Angel Day's *The English Secretorie* from 1586, rather than present a series of model love letters, as he does in the revised edition of 1599, a story is recounted using epistles and short narrative links. Such texts bear witness to a high degree of slippage between the fictional and didactic modes, suggesting that fictional letters could be, and indeed were, used for instructional purposes.[261]

In Lereano's defence of women he presents the Virgin Mary as an example of supreme virtue and proclaims her importance in salvation. In the second and third editions, however, Christ is praised instead of the Virgin, and Mary's role is limited to having borne Christ. The first edition reads:

> For where can ther be a greatter synne then to put out of knowledge, and to forgette the welth that is to come to us by reasone of the Vyrgyn Mary and dayly cometh. She delyvered us fro payne, and causeth us to meryte the glory of heven. She saveth us, she susteyneth us, she defendeth us, she gydeth us, she gyveth us lyght of grace. Then seynge she was a woman, then all other for her sake ought to be crowned with lawde and prayse. (Chap. XLIII; K8r)

The second and third editions preserve the first and last sentences in their entirety, including the naming of Mary in the initial sentence; the alterations, however, begin at the start of the second line. The passage from the revised editions reads:

> For where can ther be a greatter synne then to put out of knowledge, and to forgette the welth that is to come to us by reasone of the Vyrgyn Mary and dayly cometh. *Her sede* delyvered us fro payne, and causeth us to meryte the glory of heven. *Her sede* saveth us, *[ ]* susteyneth us, *[ ]* defendeth us, *[ ]* gydeth us, *[ ]* gyveth us lyght of grace. Then seynge she was a woman, then all other for her sake ought to be crowned with lawde and prayse. [emphasis added] (K6v)

The changes are slight, but through the two substitutions of "Her sede" for "She" the focus is changed from the Virgin to Christ. Likewise through the four omissions of the pronoun "she," "her sede" becomes the subject of the sentence, so that

---

[261] For more information see Boro, "A Critical Edition," Chap. 4.

Christ's actions are commended rather than Mary's. In the revised edition, the final line seems like an afterthought, as the Virgin is praised only because of her Son's actions. Her role is limited to giving birth to Him and she ceases to have any larger spiritual role. This alteration is, of course, in keeping with the religious changes of the sixteenth century, and corresponds to similar alterations in other romances.[262] It is also not incongruous with Wyer's corpus as he is known to be a Protestant printer. It is possible that the changes were made by Wyer, or at his request by someone in his print-shop. Spigurnell's religious beliefs are unknown and so cannot aid in attributing the changes to him.

---

[262] For instance, in the copy of *Bevis of Hamptoun* at Bod. (*STC* 1988), a reader has erased two occurrences of "Pope" and in later prints the term is emended to "bishop." Likewise "masques" replaces "Masses" in the copy of Sir Degarre in the Percy Folio MS. See Andrew King, The Faerie Queene *and Middle English Romance: The Matter of Just Memory* (Oxford: Clarendon Press, 2000), 34. King further observes that many romances retained these Catholic references.

Editorial Policy

This edition takes as its base text the first edition of *Castell*, which was printed by John Turke in 1548 (*STC* 21739.5). This print has been collated with the subsequent two prints of the romance: the second edition was issued by Robert Wyer for Richard Kele in 1552?; and John Kynge published the third in c. 1555 (*STC* 21740 and 21742, respectively). Turke's edition is extant in one complete copy, B.L. C.57.aa.36 and a fragment is preserved at the Bod., shelfmark Douce Fragm. f 51 (11). This fragment is of folios K2r–K7v of Turke's edition, Chaps. XXXIX–XLIII of this edition; its exact start and end are indicated in the notes to this edition. I have worked directly with Turke's edition, making my transcription of the text of *Castell* from B.L. C.57.aa.36, and I have likewise examined Bod. Douce Fragm. f51 (11), finding its readings to be identical to the complete copy. My transcription of Turke's edition has been collated with the two later editions. There are two copies of the second edition, B.L. G10332 and Huntington Library 69228, and I have used the B.L. copy for my collation. The third edition exists in a unique copy, housed at the Huntington Library, shelfmark 27912. My collation of the third edition is based on the STC microfilm (reel 469:9) and the electronic facsimile provided by Early English Books On-line (EEBO, http://wwwlib.umi.com/eebo/). In addition to the B.L. copies, I have also had recourse to the STC microfilms and the EEBO facsimiles for the first and second editions: these are STC reel numbers 1670:9 and 146:3, respectively.

In this edition, textual variants are given at the foot of the page, using the sigla 2 and 3 to refer to the second and third editions, respectively. Typographical errors, such as turned letters, have been corrected, and all emendations are enclosed within square brackets. I have included Andrew Spigurnell's additions to the second and third editions, and these are clearly demarcated from the first edition through the use of italics and square brackets. The chapter divisions and chapter titles from Turke's print are preserved; the numbering of the chapters is editorial. Spelling follows that of the base text, except the use of i/j and u/v which have been regularised in order to conform to modern practice. Abbreviations have been expanded and are italicised, and punctuation and capitalisation have been modernised. Word division is editorial. The page signatures of Turke's print are given in the text in square brackets. Words and expressions which are included in the glossary are marked with the symbol °, and superscript roman numerals refer to the critical and linguistic notes to *Castell*, which can be found at the end of the edition. These notes focus on *Castell*'s relationship to its Spanish and French sources, as well as provide explanations of difficult passages, and explications of historical and literary allusions.

This editorial policy has enabled me to present the most authoritative text, the text closest to what Berners actually wrote, while simultaneously valuing and considering the subsequent layers of authorship manifested in the textual variations of the second and third editions, whether they are created by the compositors, printers, or later writers. Whereas Spigurnell's verse insertions and the textual footnotes look forwards from Berners and the base text to subsequent moments of textual activity, the linguistic endnotes look backwards to *Castell*'s Spanish and French roots, pointing to variations and consistencies in Berners's translation, and illuminating the layers of authorial intervention and creativity which precede his translation. By bearing witness to the lengthy process of transformation and rewriting that lead up to and followed the creation, transcription, publication, and dissemination of *Castell*, I aim to present *Castell* as an evolving, developing text. This introduction, which surveys the authorial and generic diversity of *Castell*, shares this aim. The introduction and edition thus complement each other in ways other than those usually defined by the traditional relationship of edited text and study. They work together to reveal the complex and heterogeneous nature of the textual and literary history of *Castell*.

Bibliographical Descriptions

John Turke, 1548. Complete copy: B.L. C.57.aa.36. Fragment: Bod. Douce
Fragm. f 51 [11]. *STC* 21739.5.

TITLE PAGE: [within a frame of four separate pieces, 76 × 120 mm: top piece, 57 ×
12 mm, a foliate pattern with an animal in the centre; bottom piece, 56 × 12 mm,
a floral and foliate motif; left-hand piece 9 × 119 mm, a bird, grapes, leaves, and
vines; right-hand piece, 9 × 120 mm, foliate design] The castell of | loue, trans-
lated out of Spa= | nishe in to Englyshe, by Iohan | Bowrchier knyght, lorde Ber=
| nis, at the instaunce of the lady | Elizabeth Carew, late wyfe to | syr Nicholas
Carew knyght. | The whiche boke treateth | of the loue betwene | Leriano and |
Laureola | doughter to the kynge of | Masedonia. | ¶ Cum priuilegio ad imprt=
| mendum solum.

COLLATION: 8°. A⁴, B–O⁸, [$5 (–A1, A3, A4, D2; E4 misigned C4) signed].
216 unpaginated pages.

CONTENTS: Title page (A1r); Prologue (A2r–A3r); Text (A3v–O8r); Colophon
(O8r): ¶Prynted at London in Pauls | churcheyarde, by Iohan | Turke, at the
sygne | of the byble.

TYPE: Three sizes of black letter type are used. The bulk of the text is written in
a font of 94mm to 20 lines. A slightly larger font is used for the first line of the
title page. The third, still-larger font is used for the initial capital letters at the
beginnings of chapters. These initial letters are about two lines deep, and occupy a space of two to three lines. All chapters, with only three exceptions, are
introduced by this sort of capital letter: the initial T on D2r is in a Roman font;
and the prologue and first chapter are adorned by large decorated initial letters.
A decorated letter F, six lines deep, starts the prologue on A2r. The white letter is set against a black background ornamented with a hare and a crude foliate
motif. On A3r, a large, decorated letter A appears. The letter, seven lines deep, is
black and positioned against a black background with a foliate and floral motif,
replete with strawberries.

DECORATION: Decoration is minimal. In addition to the two large initial letters,
a paragraph symbol is used to mark chapter titles. The top section of the border
is reused on the final leaf of the narrative (O8v) in an upside down position.

Copy-specific information:

a) B.L. C.57.aa.36.

BINDING: The nineteenth-century binding, produced by Riviere and Son, is of dark green morocco. The fore-edges are gilt, and an ornamental gilt design and a double blind rule adorns the front and rear covers. In the centre of the front cover, in gilt letters, is the inscription: (DIEGO DE SAN PEDRO) | CAS-TELL OF LOVE | TRANSLATED BY JOHAN BOWRCHIER. The title, CASTELL | OF | LOVE, appears in gilt lettering on the spine, surrounded by additional gilt decoration. Three leaves are added by the binder at the front and the back of the volume, increasing the total number of pages to 228.

SIZE: The copy measures 90 × 135 mm and the leaves are of the dimensions 83 × 133mm. The maximum printed space, with catchwords and signature mark-ings, is 73 × 120 mm; without the catchwords and signatures, the average printed space is 73 × 115 mm. Each page contains 24 lines of type. Catchwords and sig-nature markings, when they appear, are positioned on the 25th line.

PROVENANCE: The rear pastedown bears the pencil inscription: "Perfect / (one or two letters restored in / outer margin of Hi) / B. Quartich / F. S. Fergusson." Ferguson only began to work with Quartich in 1897, and so his name on the rear pastedown suggests that Quartich acquired the book after that date. Inciden-tally, it does appear as though the final letters of lines 18–20 on H1r have been restored with black ink. The stamp of the British Museum, on O8v, bears the date of acquisition 11 July 1911.

WATERMARKS: No watermarks are distinguishable.

b) Bod. Douce Fragm. f 51 [11].

The four-leaf fragment of this first edition represents signatures K2, K3, K6, and K7 of Turke's edition. The central leaf of the gathering is lacking and all four pages are seriously damaged. Only about 1/6 of the top left hand corner of K2 remains. K3 is lacking the right third of the page and the lower margin is also ab-sent. K6 has been repaired, but the bottom is torn and a portion of the text from right lower portion of the page is missing. The fourth page, K7, has also been repaired; the left lower portion of the page is lacking and the top of the page is torn. The poor condition of this page coupled with the quality of the hand ren-ders the marginalia at the top of K7v illegible.

MARGINALIA: K3v and K6r contain manuscript notations in the top and central margins, which can be read once the book is rotated 180 degrees. The central marginalia reads: "Thow / shalte/ not/ underst/ande / Yow /shall/ under/stande/ Yow shall." In the same late sixteenth-century hand, at the top of the page, is the inscription: "Mr Tutte at the signe of the kyng." The writing extends through the middle fold of the page, indicating that the notes were made after the fragment was separated from the book. The absence of the middle leaf of the gathering further confirms that the central marginalia could only have been written once the central leaf had been lost.

VARIANTS: There are no press variants between this fragment and the complete edition.

WATERMARKS: No watermarks are distinguishable.

Robert Wyer for Richard Kele, 1552?. Complete copies: Huntington Library 69228 and B.L. G10332. *STC* 21740.

TITLE PAGE: ¶ The Castell of | loue, translated out of Spanyshe into | Englysshe, by Iohn Bowrchier | knyght, lorde Bernes, at the in= | staunce of the Lady Elyzabeth | Carewe, late wyfe to Syr | Nicholas Carewe | knyght. The whiche boke | treateth of the loue betwene Leriano and | Laureola | doughter to the kynge of | Masedonia.

A woodcut, 47 × 66mm, follows (Luborsky 7272/8).[1] Framed by a slim double border, the woodcut depicts Lereano and the crowned King on the left hand side and the Queen and Laureola on the right. The woodcut is almost equally divided in two by the horizon line that is suggested by small hills in the middle of the image. Some grass and a flower are positioned on the middle bottom section of the woodcut. The four characters are gathered in a field and are gazing upwards toward the middle of the woodcut at a heavily draped, female figure, who is surrounded by a cloud; their arms are extended outwards in the direction of the apparition. Lereano is wearing a hat and a fur-lined, calf-length mantle; he is holding the King's robes above the ground. The women wear long dresses and their heads appear to be covered. Proportions are exaggerated: the women's faces are larger than those of the men, and they are taller.

COLLATION: 8°. A–O^8, [$5 (–D5, A4 missigned A3, A5 missigned A4, C5 missigned C4) signed]. The edition consists of 224 un-paginated pages.

CONTENTS: Title page (A1r); Andrewe Spigurnell's Prologue (A1v–A2v); Berners's Prologue (A2v–A3v); Text (A4r–O8r); Colophon (O8r): ¶ Thus endeth this | Castell of loue. | ¶ Imprynted by | me Robert wyer, | for Richarde | Kele.

---

[1] Ruth Samson Luborsky and Elizabeth Morley Ingram, *A Guide to English Illustrated Books, 1536–1603* (Tempe, AZ: Medieval and Renaissance Texts and Studies, 1998).

TYPE: Four different size fonts of black letter type are used: a medium sized black letter, of 94mm to 20 lines, is used for the majority of the text; the largest font is used for the first line of the title page, most of the initial chapter letters, and the colophon; a slightly smaller black letter font than the average size is used for the first line of the chapter title on L1r; and the smallest font is used for Andrew Spigurnell's prefatory poems (A1v–A2v) and for the marginal glosses throughout the volume. Two sizes of Roman font are also used. The larger of the two is used for some initial capital letters, such as the letter B on A1v, the S on A8v, and the Os on each of M4r and O2r. Smaller Roman characters are used for two letter Os on I6v and I7r, and for a letter V on L8r.

DECORATION: The edition contains three decorated initial letters. The most ornate is the letter T on signature A2v, which begins the dedication to Elizabeth Carewe. It is five lines deep and the letter is surrounded by a floral and foliate motif. The initial letter A, at the start of the narrative on signature A3r, is six lines deep. The white letter sits against a black background with foliate ornamentation. The simple decorated W on signature O4r is three lines deep; the letter is set against a black background with no embellishment. Chapter titles and beginnings of verse stanzas are marked with the paragraph symbol and several pointing fingers also adorn the margins.

Five woodcuts are contained in the volume, including the title page woodcut, already described. The woodcut on L1r, 74 × 59 mm, depicts Lereano's deathbed scene (Luborsky 7272/43). A canopied bed, on the left, occupies two thirds of the woodcut, and an arched and decorated doorway occupies the extreme right third. Lereano is in the bed, with his neck and shoulders exposed. Teseo stands to the right of the bed, close to the middle of the woodcut. He is bearing a deep dish and is richly dressed in an ample-sleeved robe, fur-lined collar, wide-brimmed hat, and a medal hangs on a chain around his neck. Three women stand in the doorway as onlookers. The first woman has long hair and wears a dress with fluted sleeves and a simple neckline, and a long tasselled rope serves as her belt. Of the second woman, just her visage is shown. The third woman is only roughly sketched in the background.

The woodcut on O4r, 65 × 49 mm, needs to be rotated 90 degrees counterclockwise to be correctly viewed. It corresponds to Hodnett 901.[2] It depicts Auctor in bed, lying on his right side, wearing a nightcap and gown. He leans back on the pillows and his head is propped up with his right hand. His left harm hangs by his side. An ornately embroidered bedspread with flowers covers his body from the knees down, and a draped bed-skirt hangs from the bed. To his right is an open doorway and a wall, over which fabric is draped.

---

[2] Edward Hodnett, *English Woodcuts, 1480–1535* (Oxford: Oxford University Press, 1973).

Laureola is depicted writing in the woodcut on O6v, 58 × 55mm, which is a version of Wyer's device. A turreted castle occupies the top right section of the woodcut, and a diamond-pattern borders the left hand side. Beyond the castle's moat, to Laureola's right, is a turret with a crenellated parapet, which is joined to a portico path leading up to the castle. Laureola is seated at the edge of the moat, with a pen in her right hand, writing on a blank scroll that curls over the inside of her right knee. She holds a corner of the scroll in her left hand. She is wearing a hooded cloak over a long dress with ruffled sleeves. The dress has many folds, which are draped around her knees, extending outwards behind and around her. The material forming her sleeves is equally abundant. Her head is uncovered, revealing her shoulder-length curly hair.

A similar image of Laureola forms the centre of Wyer's device on O8v (the image measures 61 × 73 mm; the bottom piece of the device, Wyer's name, measures 60 × 12 mm; and the whole woodcut is 61 × 85 mm). In this instance, rather than a scroll, an eagle with its wings raised is seated on her right wrist. It bears a vial in a sling in its beak. The background is slightly altered, so that the female figure is seated on an island. On the left hand side of the woodcut, above the eagle, is an indistinguishable mass, possibly intended to represent a tree or clouds. Extending about two-thirds across the top right hand side of the woodcut is the castle, a cityscape, and rounded hills. Robert Wyer's name is printed below the image.

Copy-specific information:

a) Huntington Library 69228.

BINDING: The copy has a single blank leaf added by the binder at both the front and back of the volume, resulting in a book of 228 pages. The binding, which dates from the late sixteenth century, is of dark brown calf-leather decorated with a triple blind rule. Stubs of silk green ties are visible. A medium-brown leather tab on the spine bears the following worn, gilt, capital lettering: "CASTE[L] / OF LO[VE] /LON[D]/ PRWYER . . ." On the top fore-edge "Carcell Damor" is written in a brown italic script; the bottom fore-edge has the very faded, italic inscription, also in brown ink: "Castell of Love."

SIZE: The copy measures 103 x153 mm. The size of the leaves is 92 × 144 mm. The maximum printed space on pages with catchwords and marginal glosses is 81 × 115mm; on pages without catchwords and marginal glosses, the type fills 66 × 111mm of the page. An average page has 24 lines of black letter type; the catchwords and page signatures are on line 25.

PROVENANCE: The copy bears the bookplate of Horace (Horatio) Walpole (1717–79) on the front pastedown. After passing from Walpole's ownership, it formed part of the library at Britwell Court, and it was bought by the Huntington, as lot 685, at the Britwell sale at Sotheby's on 4 April 1924, for £200.

WATERMARKS: (1) closed hand holding the stem of a flower with four petals, 25 × 70mm; (2) pot, with conical lid, rounded body, and narrow stem attached to a rounded base, bearing the initials R.M., 23 × 52 mm.

b) B.L. G10332.

BINDING: Four blanks leaves have been added by the binder (two at the front and two at the rear), forming a book of 232 pages. The outermost added leaves are of a red marbled paper, which is also used for the front and rear pastedowns. The binding is of dark green morocco, with a triple blind rule on the front and rear covers. Both covers bear the gilt insignia and name of The Right Honourable Thomas Grenville. The spine is decorated with a gilt floral motif and boasts the lettering "CASTELL / OF / LOVE/ LD. BERNERS." The fore-edges are gilt.

SIZE: The volume measures 95 × 134mm, and the leaves measure 92 × 129 mm.

WATERMARKS: (1) closed hand holding the stem of a flower with four petals, 25 × 70mm; (2) pot, with conical lid, rounded body, and narrow stem attached to a rounded base, bearing the initials R.M., 23 × 52 mm.

PROVENANCE: Grenville is the only known owner.

VARIANTS: There are no press variants between the two copies.
John Kynge, c. 1555. Complete copy: Huntington Library 27912. *STC* 21742.
TITLE PAGE: [within a frame, 66 × 112 mm, the left hand side of the border is adorned with a floral motif; a swan and three baby swans decorate the bottom of the page; the right hand side of the page is trimmed with a floral and foliate motif; and five heads embellish the top edge of the page] ¶ The Castel | of loue, translated oute of | Spanysshe into Englyssh, | by Iohn Bowrchier kny= | ght, lorde Bernes, at the in | staunce of the Lady Eliza= | beth Carewe, late wyfe to | syr Nicholas Carewe kni= | ght, The which booke trea | teth of the loue betwene | Leriano and Laureo | la doughter to the | kynge of Ma= | cedonia.

Following the text are three dots forming a triangle, contained within parentheses.

COLLATION: 8°. A–Q⁸, R⁴, [$5 (–B4, C4, D4, E4, G3, G5, H5, I4, I5, K5, L4, L5, M5, N5, O5, P5, Q5, R2, and R4) signed]. The edition is composed of 264 unpaginated pages.

Contents: Title page (A1r); Andrewe Spigurnell's Prologue (A1v–A2r); Berners's Prologue (A2v–A3v); Text (A4r–R4v); Colophon (R4v): ¶ Thus endeth this Castell |of loue. | ¶ Imprinted at London, in | Crede lane by Iohn | Kynge.

Type: Four sizes of black letter type are used. The main body of the text is of 94mm in 20 lines; a smaller type is used for Spigurnell's prefatory verses and the marginal notations; a slightly larger type than that used for the bulk of the text is used for the heading of Spigurnell's prologue; and a larger type is used for the first line of the title and for the introductory initial letter Ws throughout the text. With the exception of the initial letter Ws, all other initial letters are in Roman type.

Decoration: Two decorated initial letters adorn the volume: a letter T begins the dedication to Elizabeth Carewe (A2v), and a letter A marks the start of the narrative. Both letters, which are five lines deep, are white on a black background decorated with a foliate pattern. The chapter headings of these two sections are marked by pointing fingers, and all other chapter headings are preceded by the paragraph symbol, which is also used to signal the beginning of verse stanzas.

Binding: Three blank leaves were added to the front and back of the volume by the binder, resulting in a total of 276 pages. The binding is early eighteenth- or possibly late seventeenth-century. It is dark tan calf with a gilt dotted rule around the edge of the front and rear boards. Gilt flowers and other ornamentation decorate the spine. A red leather tab on the spine reads "CASTEL/ OF / LOVE" in gilt lettering. The front and rear pastedowns are blue marbled paper.

Size: The volume is 95 × 135 mm, and the pages measure 90 × 130 mm. The type occupies 59 × 112 mm on most pages, and with the catchwords and the marginal glosses the space increases to a maximum of 75 × 116 mm. An average page contains 24 lines, with the catchword or page signature occupying the 25th.

Provenance: The earliest known owner of the book was George Mason (1735–1806), revealed through the inscription: "Bought at Mason's sale 25th April 1779 - £ 0.19." Under this notation is the stamp of the "Biblioteca Heberiana," revealing the subsequent owner: George Heber (1774–1833). From the Heber collection the book was acquired by Britwell Court Library. It was sold at the Britwell sale at Sotheby's on 15 June 1920, as Lot 270, for £138, and bought by the Huntington in January 1922.

Watermarks: No watermarks are distinguishable.

Marginalia: The title page bears the inscriptions "H ?" and "MS," and the date "23.10.1760," all in an eighteenth-century hand.

Notes: Policy and Practice

The notes draw attention to significant instances where Berners diverges from either or both of his sources, including omissions, additions, and alterations. By significant, I mean changes which demonstrate his dependence on one source rather than the other, or changes which alter the sense of his originals. The notes also provide clarification of some passages of *Castell* that may be difficult to understand; they indicate specific words with which Berners has repeated difficulty; and they point to larger trends in his translation style and methodology, which are further discussed in section 3 of the introduction. References to historical and literary characters are explicated. Proverbs are identified according to their reference numbers in Morris Tilley's and Bartlett Jere Whiting's dictionaries of proverbs.[1] Finally, where a specific passage represents a point of scholarly debate or attention, I cite the main, relevant critical sources. Several of my notes are based on Carmen Parrilla's notes to her 1995 edition of *Cárcel*; these notes are cited according to her referencing system: for instance, Parrilla 1995 3:12, refers to note number 12 to page 3 of *Cárcel*.

---

[1] Morris Palmer Tilley, *A Dictionary of the Proverbs in England in the Sixteenth and Seventeenth Centuries. A Collection of the Proverbs Found in English Literature and the Dictionaries of the Period* (Ann Arbor: University of Michigan Press, 1950); Bartlett Jere Whiting, *Proverbs, Sentences, and Proverbial Phrases; from English Writings Mainly Before 1500* (Cambridge: Harvard UP, 1968).

Castell of Love

Title Page

The Castell° of Love, translated out of Spanishe in to Englyshe by Johan Bowrchier Knyght, Lorde Bernis, at the instaunce° of the Lady Elizabeth Carew, late
wyfe to Syr Nicholas Carew, Knyght.[i] The whiche boke treateth of the love betwene Leriano and Laureola, doughter to the Kynge of Masedonia.[ii]
    Cum priuilegio ad imprtmendum solum.[1] [A1r]

The Prologe[1]

For[2] the affeccyant°, desyre, and obligacyon that I ame bownde in towardes your[3]
ryghte vertuous and good Lady, as well for the goodnes that it hath pleased you
to shewe me, as for the nyrenesse° of consanguinite, hathe pleased[4] me to accomplyshe your desyre as[5] in translatynge this present boke.[i] And though my so
doynge can not be correspondente any thynge to recompence your goodnes, yet
not beynge ignorante of your [6] wyll and desyre, the whiche in this cause I take
for the hole effecte. Thynkynge thereby to do you some smale rememoracyon°,
and also bycause the matter is very pleasante for yonge ladyes and gentle wom-
en, therfore I have enterprysed° to translate[7] the same out of[8] Spanyshe in to[9]

---

[1] Cum priuilegio ad imprtmendum solum] 2 3 Omitted.

---

[1] The Prologe] 2 3 *To the good and vertuous Lady the Lady Carewe gretynge*
[2] For] 2 3 Omitted.
[3] your] 2 3 *you*
[4] pleased] 2 3 *encoraged*
[5] as] 2 3 Omitted.
[6]] 2 *good*
[7] translate] 2 3 *reduce*
[8] out of] 2 3 *from*
[9]] 2 3 *the*

Englyshe ¹⁰, [A2r] not adorned° with so fresshe° eloquence that it shulde meryte to be presented to your goodnese.ⁱⁱ For or° I fyrste entred in to this rude° laboure I was brought into greate doubtfulnesse and founde my selfe in dyvers ymagyn-acyons°.ⁱⁱⁱ For seynge° the quycke° intellygence of your spyryt, I feared, and agayne the remembraunce° of your vertue and prudence gave me audacyte.ⁱᵛ In the one I found feare, and in the other suertie° and hardynesse°.ᵛ Fynally I dyd chose the moste unvaylable° for myne owne shame, and most utilitie° in any reprehencion or rebuke. For the moche boldenesse in that I have not taken suche respyte° as I oughte to have done. Yet in consyderacyon of your gentlenesse°, myne affeccy*on* is alwayes in truste° to skape° blameles.ᵛⁱ I have taken this entrepryce on me more b[y]¹¹ desyre to have blame thereby then to atteyne° by my prayse or laude. Wher-fore, ryghte vertuous Lady, maye [A2v] it please you of your goodnes to accept this lytle presente treatyse and to receyve this my good wyll or° ye condempne° the faulte.ᵛⁱⁱ And also to have the¹² more affeccyon to the presenter then to the valewer°¹³ of the thynge presented, requyrynge° you to holde and repute° me al-wayes as one of the nomber of them that alwayes shal be redy to do you pleasure. And for the surplus, I desyre the Creatour of the Fyrst Cause long to indure and to encrease your happy° prosperite. Amen. The ende of the prologe. [A3r]

[Prologue to the 2ⁿᵈ & 3ʳᵈ Editionsᵛⁱⁱⁱ

Androwe Spigurnell to the reader in maner of a prologue:

Beholde you readers of this boke present
Which the Lord Barnes¹⁴ out of the Spanyshe
Hath translated to a good intent
And reduced the same into our Englyshe.
And thankes to have the same dyd he fynyshe
Wherin it appereth moche paynes he dyd take
At the instaunt° request, and for a¹⁵ Ladye's sake.

Betwene two persone¹⁶ it doth procede
The one ¹⁷ a lovre named Leriano
Sone and heyre° he was in dede
Unto the noble Duke of Guerro

---

¹⁰] 2 3 *tonge*
¹¹ by] 1 *be*
¹² the] 2 3 Omitted.
¹³ valewer] 2 3 *valew*
¹⁴ Barnes] 3 *Barner*
¹⁵ a] 3 Omitted.
¹⁶ persone] 3 *persons*
¹⁷] 3 *of*

The other was doughter to Kynge Gallo
Who was kynge of Macedonia
And named she was Laureola.

I havyng case° to syt and muse
By my selfe all alone[18]
I toke a boke as I do use
For to rede and loke upon
Upon this I chaunced and then anon
The boke's name rede, I was[19] *therwithall*
Incoraged to procede and rede it all.

The booke ones° redde & the matter sene
I thought it a present moche unworthie
To be presented to a Lady or a Quene
Seynge° it is to a Ladye's insance°[20]
Specially notyng a Ladye's crueltie
That declare them selfe in every case°
To have pytie mercy and grace.

For though she dyd her moost endevoure
Alwayes regardynge howe she myght save
Her estate nobilite and honoure
Yet reason would pytie she shold have
And not her lover's lyfe deprave
For though honour before lyfe is to be preferred
Yet another's lyfe is to be regarded.

For seyng° that nature hath formed naturally
Women to be mercyfull of naturall dispocisyon
It must therfore double in women of sabilite°
For it is to them theyr propre condicion
So that it appereth in the conclusyon
A Lady pyteles and endewed° with cruelte
Is to her honour reproche and obloquie°.

But to the intent that women in generall
By theyr disdayne and lacke of pytie
Shal note what inconvenyence°[21] *mai come and*[22] *fal*

---

[18] alone] 3 *as one*
[19] was] 3 Omitted.
[20] insance] 3 *infance*
[21] inconuenyence] 3 *it conuenience*
[22] and] 3 *a*

To lovers that be tormented crewly
Therfore I have taken thus upon me
This booke to peruse and reade with payne
In wyll to have it prynted agayne.

And bycause to the reader it shold be more delectable
I have taken upon me presumptuously
Newly to penne the matter though unable
Yet have I done it and also rudely°
Have added somwhat unconnyngly
The rudenes° therof I do submyt
Unto the readers to amende it.

Desyrynge them with herty submyssyon
To regarde my mynde and°²³ intent
And not to ponder my presumpcyon²⁴
But esteme the meanyng and what intent²⁵
And of my good wyll to gyve theyr judgement
Unto my rudenes° the blame aplyenge°
Which in this doynge and chyefe ofending.]

I: The Auctorⁱ

After *the* warres done and finyshyd in my countrey, beynge in my poore mansion°, in a mornyng whan the sonne illuminyd the earthe, in a shadowyde darke valey, in the mountayne called Serua de Maren*us*°, in the cou*n*trey of Masedonia, as I walkyd in a strayte way shadowyd *with* fayer trees sodenly I mette with a knight fyers and furious, whose presence was ferfull to regarde°. ¹ ⁱⁱCoveryde all in here° lyke a savage creature, in his lyfte° hande he bare a bryght schilde° of stele, & in his ryght hand a shynynge ymage entaillid° in a clere stone, of such plesure & bewtie, that *the* clerenes° troublyd the syghte of myne eyen°, out of the whiche there issuyde dyvers rayes of fier enbransing°² & enflaming *the* body of a man.³ ⁱⁱⁱ The which the sayd knight forceably [A3v] ledde behynd hym, who with dolorous

---

²³ and] 3 *an*
²⁴ And not to ponder, my presumpcyon] 3 Omitted.
²⁵ But esteme the meanyng, and what intent] 3 Omitted.

---

¹] 2, 3 Marginal note *Note*
² enbransing] 2 *enbrasyng* 3 *enbrasing*
³] Marginal note 2 *The discriptio*n *of desyre* 3 *The discriptio*n *of desire*

playntes° and sorowfull passions° sayde:[iv] [4] "By reason of my hope, I suffre all this."[v] And when he aprochyd, and that I was nere hym, he sayd with mortall anguysh: "Frende, for the love of God I pray the folow me and ayde me in this my great beisynes°." And I as then had more cause of feare then reason to aunswere, but I set myne eyen°[5] on this strange vision, judgyng in my hart dyverce consideracions. As to leve my way, me thought it symplenes°, and to accomplysh the desire of the pacient°, I thought it dangerous.[vi] To folow hym was perell, and to leve hym in that turbacion° was pite°, so that I wiste° not whiche was beste to chose.[vii] How be it, after that feare had left myne alteracion°[6] in some ease and that my spirites° began to respyre°, then I consyderyd well that I was more bounde to the vertue then to the lyfe.[viii] And then determynyde° for the dought that I was in, to folow *the* way of hym who desyred myne [A4r] ayede. And I hastyde° me to go after in suche sorte that shortely I overtoke them.[ix] So we went all .iii. a long space°, with no lesse anoyance then to be solytary alone fro° pleasur or company. And though the desyre of the dolorous was cause of my folowynge, yet to speke to hym that ledde the pacient I faylyde audacyte, and to desire° hym, me thought nothynge avayleable° nor I hadde not deservyd it. Though in this case° I fayled counsayll, yet after I had revolvyde° my thoughtes in the remembrance°[7] of many thynges, I thought it beste to put to hym some maner of purpose to th'entent that accordyng to his aunswere I shuld determyne° further.[x] And with this delyberacion I requyrede° hym in the moste curtes° wyse° that to me was possible, to shew° me what he was. Who aunswered me, & sayd: "Frende, certaynly accordyng to my naturall condycion I oughte to gyve the none° aunswere bycause myne offyce is rather to assure° evyll° then to [A4v] aunswere well. How be it in that I have bene alwayes norished° among men of good nourture°, I shall use to the of the gentylnes° that I have lernyd and not of the fercenes of my nature[8].[xi] Thou shalt understand, sence thou wylt know it, that I ame principall officer in the house of the God of Love and I ame namyd by my ryght name, Desire.[xii] [9] And with the force of this chylde°[10] I resyst & defende all[11] hoopes°. And with the beautie of this image I cause *the* affections wherwith I broyle and enflame the lyves, as thou maist se by this prisoner whom I lede in to the prisone of love, who all onely by dethe hopeth his delyverance."[xiii] Whan this tormentour hadde shewed° me all

[4]] Marginal note 2 *The lamentacion of Leriano* 3 *The lamentacion of Leriano*

[5] I set myne eyen on] 2 *myne eyen beyng fixed on* 3 *mine eyen being fired of*

[6] left myne alteracion] 3 *lefte alteration*

[7] thoughtes in the remembrance] 2 *thought in remembraunce* 3 *thoughtis in remembraunce*

[8] of my nature] 2 3 *of nature*

[9]] Marginal note 2 *The exposicion of desyre the chefe offycer in the castel of loue with his armour* 3 *The exposicion of desyre the chief officer in the castell of loue with his armour*

[10] chylde] 2 3 *shilde*

[11] all] 2 Omitted.

these thynges, we mountyd up a sharpe° & an hygh mountayne, that further to
travaylle° my force fayled. ˣⁱᵛ And with greate payne we aryvyd to the heyght. In
receyvynge this aunswer¹², then I studyed° how to thanke hym of the grace that
he hadde shewed me. And [B1r] ther *with* sodenly he vanyshed fro° my presence.
This was in the begynnynge of the night wherfore I coulde not kepe my waye,
nor knowe whether I shulde drawe° for the darkenes of the nighte & the small
knowledge that I had of the cou*n*trey. Howbeit, I thought it best not to returne
nor to departe fro° the p[la]ce¹³ that I was in. Then I began to course° myne ad-
venture°, abandonyng my selfe fro° all hope, abiding there my p*er*dicio*n*. Thus in
the myddes° of my tribulacyon I never repentyd of that I had done, for I estemyd
better to lese° my lyfe accomplyshynge vertue than to save it doing the contrary.
Thus I was all *the* nyght in hevynes° and travelous° contemplacion. And when the
light of the day discoveryd° *the* wayes°, I sawe before me, on the most highest
place of *the* mountayne, a tower so hygh that me semyd it atteynyd to the hevyn.
Hit°¹⁴ was made by suche artifice¹⁵ that of the strangnes therof I began to mer-
vayll° & I joyned [B1v] my selfe to the foote therof. The tyme offeryd me more
to feare then to regard° or note it, beholding the strange overage° & newelte° of
the edefice.ˣᵛ The fundacio*n* wheron it was foundyd was of a stone clere and
stronge of nature, wherupo*n* was reysed .iiii. great pillers of violet marble, so
fayre and so hygh beyonde the comon forme that it was mervayll° how they were
systeynyd. ˣᵛⁱ ¹⁶ Above the whiche was fabricate° a tower .iii. square°¹⁷, the most¹⁸
strongest that could be devised. On every square° therof, on *the* height, there
stode an humayn image made of metall payntyd *with* theyr owne colours, one
tawny°, a nother blacke, & the thirde gray, eche of them holding a chayne in
theyr handes, made of great force°.ˣᵛⁱⁱ And on the heyght of the tower ther was a
pynacle full of great clerenes° & light comyng fro° a raye of light issuyng out of
the tower.ˣᵛⁱⁱⁱ I harde .ii. watches° who never seaced°, but still° wakyd. Of these
thynges greatly I mer[v]ayled° [B2r] & could not tell what to thynke or to¹⁹ say.
ˣⁱˣ Thus beyng in great dought and confusion, I sawe joynynge to the marbell a
stayre mountyng to the gate of the tower, wherof the entre° was so darke that to
mount up semyd impossible.ˣˣ How be it, I deliberyd°²⁰ wyllynge rather to go to
my perdicyon in mountyng then to save my self with tarieng. Thus, takyng harte,

---

¹² aunswer] 2 *an were*
¹³ place] 1 *palce*
¹⁴ Hit] 2 3 *It*
¹⁵ artifice] 3 *artificer*
¹⁶] 2 Marginal note *The discription of the Castell of loue outwartle* 3 *The discription of
the Castell of loue outwartly*
¹⁷ square] 3 *sware*
¹⁸ most] 2 3 Omitted.
¹⁹ to] 2 3 Omitted.
²⁰ deliberyd] 2 *delyveryd* 3 *delivered*

I began to mou*n*te. And when I was up .iii. steppes, I found a dore of iron, the which satisfied[21] me rather to tast°[22] *with* my handes then to attayne° therto by syghte by reason of *the* darknes that I was in.[xxi] And when I came to the gate, I founde ther a porter, of whome I demaundyd° licens to entre. He aunswered, how he was content so that fyrst I shuld leve behynde me myne armure. I grauntyd hym to leve suche as I bare customably upon me.[xxii] Then he sayd: "My ffrend, it aperith well that of the usage & custome of this house° thou knowest but lytle. The [B2v] armoure that I demaunde°, and those that it behoveth° the to leve are suche as the harte is wonte to be defendyd withall° fro° hevynes° & sorowe as are, hope, rest, & contentacion°.[xxiii] For to have those condicions, ther may none° joy of the demaunde° that thou desyrest°." [23] And when I knew his entension, with-oute any further advyse° I aunswered & assuryd hym that I was come thyther° with out any of those armours. The*n* he grau*n*tyd the openyng of the gate. & so with greate travaill° and sore° trouble I aryvyd to the height of the tower where I found a nother porter wh[o][24] demaundyd° of me as *the* other dyd. And when I had made hym lyke aunswere he gave me place° to entre.[25] Then I went all the length of the tower and enteryd in to a halle, where in *the* myddes° therof stode a chayre brennynge° full of fyre, in the whiche satte he who made to me the re-quest, and causer of my perdicion. And myne eyen were so chargyd° *with* regard-ing° [B3r] of this overage° & my tonge° was so oppressed° that I could demaund° no questio*n* of all these mervails°. And as I regardyd° them, I sawe the .iii. chaynes that the images held on the height on *the* tower were fast° tyed about this poore captyve prysoner, who alwayes brent° and never consumyd°.[xxiv] Then I saw two sorowful women, theyr faces ful of wepynges and dolours. They ordeyned° to sette on his hed°, with greate crueltie, a crowne full of sharpe poyntes of steale, without pyte, persyng° his hed° to the brayne.[xxv] Also ther was a blacke morion°, vestured° in yelowe, who came often tymes *with* a great fawchon° to strike hym. And ever I saw how the pacient° receyved the strokes with a shelde, subtilly° is-suyng out of his hedde°, the which covered hym to the feete.[xxvi] I saw other .iii. servau*n*tes ryght diligent, who brought hym meate on a blacke cloth and with great fury gave him mete of bitter taste.[xxvii] And on the one syde of the table I sawe [B3v] an olde man syt in a chaire lenynge° his hedde° in one of his handes, lyke a man solitary in thought & pensyfenes. All these thynges I could scant se for the darkenes of the towre, but by reason of a clere shynynge lyght that issuyd out of the prisoner's harte, which gave clere lyghte over all. And when this

---

[21] satisfied] 3 *satisfird*

[22] tast] 2 3 *cast*

[23]] Marginal note 2 *The armoure against love* 3 *The armoure agaynst love*

[24] who] 1 *whe*

[25]] Marginal note 2 *The discripcion of the Castell inwardely* 3 *The discripcio*n *of the Castel inwardely*

prisoner saw me so astonyd° to se²⁶ thinges of²⁷ suche mystery, and that he saw
tyme to pay me *with* his wordes, though he were not in my det. Yet²⁸ to gyve me
some rest & solacious° comforte with his discrete° reasons medlyd° with piteous°
wepynges, he began to say in this maner.ˣˣᵛⁱⁱⁱ

II: The prisoner¹

Some parte of my harte I shall discover° as I oughte to do for the sorowe that I
have of the accordyng to thy² deserte°. How be it, thou seist° well that in my trybulacion I have no powre to feale any other man's evil, myne owne is so great. I
pray the take³ for satisfaction not that I do, but that I [B4r] desire. Of thy comyng
hyther I ame the cause. I ame⁴ he whome thou sawest led as a prisoner. Bycause of
the tribulacion that thou arte in thou knowest me not. Torne agayne to thy spir-
ites° and take rest and quyet judgement to th'entent thou mayst be ententyve° to
that I wyll say.ⁱ Thy comyng was to remedy° me, my wordes shall be to advertyse°
thee. Who I ame, I shall shew° the. And of the mysteryes that thou hast seene, I
shall infourme the. The cause of my prison, I wold° thou knewdest, and I requyre°
the to delyver me if it be in thy puissaunce°.ⁱⁱ Knowe for certayne I ame Lereano,
sonne to the⁵ Duke Guerro, whome God perdon, & of the Duches Colerea.ⁱⁱⁱ My
byrthe was in this realme, where thou arte⁶ present, named Macedonia. My fortune ordeynyd°⁷ that I became amorous of Laureola, doughter to Kynge Guallo
who at this present tyme reygneth, whom I shuld rather have fledde fro° then to
have fallen in to the trace° of love, and [B4v] specially in so hygh a place.ⁱᵛ But
as the fyrst movynge°⁸ maye not excuse me, in stede of forsakynge therof by reason I have confermyd it by good wyl.ᵛ Also Love hath vanquyshed me & brought
me in to this howse°, namyd the Castell° of Love, who never perdonyth. For he,
seing° displayed the vailes° of my desyre, hathe broughte me in to *the* state that
thou seist° me in. And to the entent thou shuldest the better note and marke the

---

²⁶ to se] 3 Omitted.
²⁷ of] 2 3 Omitted.
²⁸ yet] 3 *ye*

---

¹] 2 3 *Laureola*
² accordyng to thy] 2 3 Omitted.
³ take] 3 *rake*
⁴ the cause, I ame] 3 Omitted.
⁵ the] 2 3 Omitted.
⁶ arte] 2 *act*
⁷ ordeynyd] 3 *orderueth*
⁸ mouynge] 2 3 *monyng*

fundacion of this and of al that thou hast sene,⁹ thou shalt know that the stone
wheron the pryson is foundyd is my fayth, who determineth° utterly to suffre the
dolour of this payne for the welth° of his evill°.ᵛⁱ The great pyllers that are assys-
ted° to this stone ar[e]¹⁰ my understandynge, my reason, my memory, & my wyll,
whom Amours commaundyd to apere before his presence or° he wolde° gyve any
sentence apon me.ᵛⁱⁱ And the better to execute on me his true justyce, demaun-
dyd° of eche of them yf they consentyd that I [B5r] shuld be taken prisoner, bicause if any of them wolde° not have consentyd, he wolde° have asoyled° me fro°
payne and blame. To the whiche demaunde° all .iiii. aunswerd in this maner.
First Understandynge said: "I consent to the evill° of the payne for the welth° of
the cause, wherfore my wyll is that he be taken." Then sayd Reason: "& I consent not allonely° that he be in prison, but I ordeyne° that he there abyde and dye.
For it were better for hym the happy° deth, then to lyve in dispayre, considering
for whom he shal suffre it."ᵛⁱⁱⁱ Then sayd Memory: "Syn° that Understanding &
Reason connsentyth that without deth he can not be delivered, I then promyse he
shall never forget it, but alwayes have it in his remembraunce°." Then sayd Wyll:
"Seyng° it is thus I will then be the key of his prisone, and determyne° always
to be persecuter of Wyll and Desyre."ⁱˣ This seing° the God of Love, who ought
to have savid me, condemned me & gave this cruell sentence agaynst [B5v] me.
As for *the* .iii. images standing on *the* walles of *the* towre, eche of them of a con-
trary° colour as tawny°, blacke, & gray,¹¹ the one is hevynes°, the other anguish,
and the thirde travaill°.¹² ˣ The cheynes° in theyr handes are their strengthes,
wherwith they holde faste° tyed the harte in such wyse° that it can recover none°
ease nor rest.¹³ ˣⁱ The great clerenes° & shynyng that the egle° hath in his bek°
& wynges, as¹⁴ thou hast sene in the hyghest parte of the towre, whiche is myne
inwardes° thoughtes, whiche hath so great clerenes° in it selfe that it suffiseth to
enlumyne° *the* darknes of this clowdy° prison. ˣⁱⁱ And the force therof is so great
that the strength of the thick walles can not let it, but that it wyll attaigne° to
the egle° in suche wyse° *that* they wyll go together in company, bycause they are
the thinges that mountyth and ascendyth hyghest.ˣⁱⁱⁱ For the which cause my
pryson is in the hyghest place of the lande. The .ii. watches° that thou herest so
dilygently watchyng° [B6r] be Mishap° & Hate.¹⁵ They be of that dev[ys]e¹⁶ *that*

---

⁹] Marginal note 2 *The exposicion or declaracion of the castell & of love The maner of a*
lover 3 *The exposicion or declaration of the castel & of love The maner of a lover*

¹⁰ are] 1 *ary*

¹¹] Marginal note 2 *The .iii. ymages* 3 *The thre ymages*

¹²] Marginal note 2 3 *The cheynes*

¹³] Marginal note 2 *The greate shynyuge* 3 *The greate shynynge*

¹⁴ as] 2 *whiche* 3 *whych*

¹⁵] Marginal note 2 *The ii watches* 3 *The two watches*

¹⁶ devyse] 1 *deuile*

no hope nor remedy° shuld entre into me.[xiv] *The* darke stayres to mount on is An-guysh, wheron I mountyd as thou seyst°.[17] The fyrst porter[18] was Desyre, who to all hevynes° openyth the gate.[19] Therfore he sayd to the *that* thou shuldest leve al thyne[20] armure of pleasoure. The other porter was Torment, who brought me hyther, who is of the same condicyon.[xv] [21] The chayre of fier wherin thou seist° me syt is my Juste Affection, whose flames alwayes brynneth° in myne entray-les.[22] [xvi] The .ii. women *that* gave me the crown of martyrdom are called Payne & Passyon°, who satisfyeth my fayth with this present reward.[23] The olde man *that* thou seyst° syt in so great study representeth Great Thought & Pensyfenes *with* Grevous° Care and Solicitude.[xvii] [24] The which (joyned with *the* other evyls°) manisheth°[25] my poore lyfe.[xviii] [26] The blacke more° vesturyd° in yelowe, who traveyleth° to take awaye my lyfe, is named Dispayre.[27] & the sheld that issueth [B6v] out of my hed°, defending me fro° his strokes, is my Wytte°, who (seynge° *that* Dispayre wold° slee me) commandeth me to defende my lyfe. Consyderyng the deserte° of Laureola, he commaundeth me to desyre a[28] long life *with* suffer-ance, rather then with deth to make an ende.[xix] [29] The black boord° for me to eate on is Ferme° Stedfastnesse wheron I eate,[30] thynke & slepe. Theron are the hevy° meates of myne conteplations.[31] The .iii. diligent servaunts[32] *that* serveth me are named Evyl°, Payne and Dolour.[33] One bereth the meat of doubtfulnesse, wherof I eate.[xx] Another bereth dispayre, wherin *the* meat is brought. & another bereth *the* cup of tribulation, wherin I drink, drawing water fro° *the* hart to the eyen° & fro° *the* eien° to the mouth.[xxi] Now judge thy self if I be wel served. If I have nede of remedy° *thou* seyst°. [34] I requyre° the, syn° *thou* arte here aryved that thou wilt

---

[17]] Marginal note 2 3 *The stayres*

[18] porter] 3 *port*

[19]] Marginal note 2 *The fyrst porter* 3 *The first porter*

[20] thyne] 2 3 *thy*

[21]] Marginal note 2 *The .ii. porter* 3 *The seconb porter*

[22]] Marginal note 2 3 *The chayre*

[23]] Marginal note 2 *The .ii. women* 3 *The two women*

[24]] Marginal note 2 3 *The olde man*

[25] manisheth] 3 *menasseth*

[26]] Marginal note 2 *The blake more* 3 *The blacke more*

[27]] Marginal note 2 *the shelde* 3 *The sheld*

[28] a] 2 3 Omitted.

[29]] Marginal note 2 3 *Laureola the cause faled love*

[30]] Marginal note 2 *The blake borde* 3 *The blacke borde*

[31]] Marginal note 2 3 *The meates*

[32] servaunts] 1 *seruates* 2 *servaunt*

[33]] Marginal note 2 *The .iii. servauntes* 3 *The thre servauntes*

[34]] Marginal note 2 *The prisoner requyre* 3 *The prysoner requyre*

serc[h]e³⁵ fo[r]³⁶ me some remedy° & sorow° myne evyll°. I desyre of the none° other good, but that Laurelola may be advertysed° & knowe [B7r] by the ³⁷ state how thou seyst° me. And peradventure° thou wylt excuse the bycause thou seyst° me fayle power to make the a recompence.ˣˣⁱⁱ I requyre° the, let it not be undone for that cause. For more vertue it is to remedy° them that be in tribulation, then to susteyne them that be in prosperite.ˣˣⁱⁱⁱ Let thy workes be suche that thou repente not thy selfe for lacke of doynge it when thou myghteste have done it.

III: The aunswer of the auctor to [Lereano]¹

Thy wordes shewe well that love hath taken and occupieth thy lybertie but not thy vertue, the whiche I prove° by that I se in the to be more redyer to dye then to speke. ⁱ How be it, thou hast forcyd thy wyll to prove° the werynes° of my² lyfe, judgynge what for travels° passyd & for my solycitude present that I have but small hope to lyve.ⁱⁱ & without doubt, so it is, for thou causest my perdicion, desyrynge doughtes° [B7v] remedy°. And yet thou doest remedy° the same as a perfight° judge. ⁱⁱⁱ And surely I have hadde no lesse pleasour to heare the, then I have had sorowe to se the. For by thy persone is well sene thy payne, & by thy reasons knowen is thy bountie° in gyuvnge socour and ayde to the ned[y]³, lyke as thou hast done now to me.ⁱᵛ For I, consyderynge the strange mysteries° of this thy pryson, I doubted of my salvacyon, belevynge all had ben but illusions done by arte diabolycke° rather then by any condycyon amorous. For this thou hast shewed° me, I thanke the. And nowe I knowe what thou arte, I thynke well en-ployed°⁴ the travayll° that I have enduryd for thy sake.ᵛ The knowledge of the moralite° of these figures hath ryght well pleased me, for though I well regardyd° them yet for lacke of knowlegde my harte was in captyvyte and prisone, and now I ame out of doubt & feare.ᵛⁱ And where as thou hast commaundyd me that I shuld gyve [B8r] knowledge to Laureola in what case° I have sene *you*, the which to do I fynd gret perel for a man of a strange° nacion. What maner & forme shuld he fynde to execute such a message? I have not alonely° this doubt but dyverce other. The rudenes° & dulnes° of my wytte°, the dyfference of oure speche & tonge°,

---

³⁵ serche] 1 *serce*
³⁶ for] 1 *foe*
³⁷] 2 3 *the*

---

¹ Lereano] 1 *Laureola* 2 3 *Leriano*
² my] 3 Omitted.
³ nedy] 1 *nedr*
⁴ enployed] 3 *enploi*

the noblenes of Laureola, and the gravite of this besynes°.^vii So that in this case° I fynde but small remedy°, but alonely° my good will whiche vanquyssith°5 all other inconvenientes°6 and daungers.^viii For to thy service I offre my selfe as moche as though I hadde bene thyne owne servant all the dayes of my lyffe.^ix And I promyse the *that* with good hart I shal acco*m*plish to my power al thy co*m*mandeme*n*ts. ^x I pray to God I may be as happy° as I ame desyrous° to serve the, so that thy deliverance may bere witnes of my true dilygence.^xi So great affeccion I bere to the & so moche I ame bound to love thy noblenes, that if I myght remedy° [B8v] thy trybulacions I shuld repute° my selfe well rewardyd for all my travyls°.^xii So that in the meane tyme thou wylt bere al maner of assautes° pacyently, in trustyng upon me that when I returne and bryng *thee* any remedy *that* thou mayste take suche corage in thy lyfe that thou mayst feale the sparkels° therof.^xiii

IV: The Auctor

When I had endyd myne aunsewre to Lereano, then I depa*r*tyd fro° hym and lernyd the waye to the cytte of Suria, where as lay° *the* Kyng of Mazedonia¹, ² which was halfe a ³ journey fro° *the* prisone fro°4 whence I depa*r*tyd.^i 5 Thus I came to the courte & 6 wente to *the* palays to treat° and7 to se *the* maner of the people of that courte, and to regarde° the forme and situacion of the palayce, and how I myght resorte°, goo, come, or abyde to entre in to the enterprice that I had in hand.^ii And this I dyd dyvers dayes, to lerne and to se what way shulde be best & moste covenable° to my purpose. & [C1r] the more I studyed, the lesse disposytion8 I found to attayne to that I desyryd.9 & when I had serched al maner of wayes, I thought most avayleable° to my purpose to acquaynte my selfe *with* the yong courters and with the principall of *the* courte°, for generally among them is found good maner and curtesye. And thus I drew so longe to theyr company,

---

⁵ vanquyssith] 3 *vanissheth*
⁶ inconuenientes] 3 *inconveniences*

---

¹ Mazedonia] 2 3 *Stone*
²] 2 3 *the*
³] 2 3 *dayes*
⁴ fro] 2 3 *that*
⁵] 2 3 *And*
⁶] 2 3 *then*
⁷ and] 2 3 Omitted.
⁸ disposytion] 2 3 *comforte*
⁹] Marginal note 2 3 *I meane to enter in the lyke purpose*

with in a breve tyme I was estemydde among them as though[10] I had bene one
of theyr propre nacion. [iii] And at last I fell in aquayntance among the ladyes, and
lytle and lytle° I fell in acquayntance with the Ladye Laureola.[iv] And dyverce
tymes I recountyd to her of the mervayls° of Spayne and of other places where as
I had bene, the whiche she gretly delyghtyd to here.[v] Then I, seyng° my selfe in
maner with her as a servant, I thoght then I myght shewe° her that thyng that I
desyryd[11].[vi] And on a day, as I saw her aparte fro° other ladyes, I knelyd downe
and sayd as folowith. [C1v]

V: The Auctor to Laureola [1]

It is lesse goodnes to perdone the great & puyssante°[2] persones when they have
d[es]rvyd[3] trespace, then to be revengyd upon the symple° & small° personages°
when they have done injury.[i] For *the* one wyll make amendes by reason of theyr
honour, and the other are[4] perdonyd by vertue.[ii] The whiche is due to be usyd
amonge greate personages°, and most specyally to noble ladyes & gentle women
having noble hartes. According to theyr birth they ought naturally to have pyte
in theyr condicions.[5] [iii] Lady, I say thys for peradventure° in shewyng° to you
myne entent I shal be reputyd° to bolde, not havyng respecte to your great mag-
nyficens. [iv] In the begynnyng, or° I was determyned° to speake to you, I was in
great doubt, but at the ende I thoughte it for the best that yf ye entreate me in-
humaynly to suffre *the* payn for my speakyng rather then to endure in dolour for
beynge styll.[v] [6] Lady, ye shal [C2r] knowe that rydynge on a daye amonge sharpe°
mountayns I sawe, by the commandement of Amours, how Lereano, sonne to
Duke Guerro, was taken & led to prison as a prisoner, who prayed me to ayde
hym in his trouble and besynes°. By whose occasion I lefte the waye of my reste
and toke the daungerous way of his travayle°.[vi] And after that I hadde longe gone
with hym, I sawe howe he was put in to a swete prisone as toward his wyll, but it
was ryght bytter as to his lyfe. For there he susteyneth all the evyls° and paynes of

---

[10] though] 3 *thought*
[11] desyryd] 3 *desyre*

---

[1]] 2 3 *beloved*
[2] puyssante] 2 3 *noble*
[3] desrvyd] 2 *commytted any* 3 *committed any*
[4] are] 2 3 *may be*
[5]] 2 3 Marginal note *Noble women must have pyte*
[6]] 2 3 Marginal note *The doynge of the message*

the world. [7] [vii] Dolour turmenteth hym, passyon° foloweth hym, dispaire destroieth him, deth manasheth° hym, payne executeth hym, thoughtes waketh hym,
desyre troubleth hym, hevynes° condemneth hym, his fayth wyll not save hym. [viii]
& I knewe by hym that all this ye are the cause. And I judge, by that I sawe hym,
his dolour (whiche he kepethe secrete in his mynde) to be more greater then he
hath discovered° [C2v] to me by wepinges. [ix] But by reason of the syghte *that* I se
of your presence, I fynde that his torment is not without a juste cause. [x] And *with*
sore° syghes issuynge fro° his harte, he desyred°[8] me to gyve you knowledge of
his evyl°. [xi] His request was with payne & dolour, & my obedience of pure compassyon of his payne & torment. Though I judge you cruel, yet by *the* frequenta-
tion° of your gentlnes° I se & thinke ye be piteous, & not without reason. [xii] For by
reason of your excellent fayrenes & dignite he beleveth the one, & by your noble
condicion hopeth on *the* other. [xiii] & his payne wherof ye be causer, yf ye wyll rem-
edy° *with* pitie accordyng to his deservinge, ye shal be then praised above al other
women *that* ever were. [xiv] [9] Remembre nowe & behold whether it is better to be
praysed for gyvynge remedy°, or els to be blamyd for sleyng of hym. [xv] Consyder
how moch ye be bound to hym, *that* for al his passion° & adversite yet he doth
serve you. [xvi] & if ye remedy° hym, then he is *the* occasion to cause you to do [C3r]
as moch as God maye do. [xvii] For it is of[10] no lesse esteme the redemer then is *the*
creator. For in takynge fro°[11] hym the deth, ye shall do as moche as God to gyve
hym lyfe. I knowe not what excuse ye can make not to remedy° hym without ye
beleve that sleynge is a vertue. I desyre° of you none° other good but to be sory
for his [12] evyll° and payne. [xviii] This desyre shall be to you nothynge grevable, for
he had rather [13] endure in hym selfe styll payne and adversite then to cause you
to feale any payne & displeasour. [xix] This, my bolde speakynge, condemneth me,
but the dolour of hym that hathe sente me assoyleth° me agayne. His payne is
so great that none°[14] evyll° can come to me to be equall to his payne. [xx] I requyre°
your gentlenes°, let your aunswer be comfortable°[15] to your vertue and not to the
fercenes that ye shew by your regardes°. And in your so doynge, ye shal be praysed, and I[16] reputyd° a good messenger, and the paynefull° prisoner Lereano delyvered [C3v] quyte° fro° all payne. [xxi]

---

[7]] Marginal note 2 *The dyversyte of the prison betwene lyfe and wyll* 3 *The dyrersyte of*
the prison betwene life and wyll

[8] desyred] 3 *desireth*

[9]] Marginal note 2 *The recorde of pytie* 3 *The recorde of pytye*

[10] it is of] 2 3 Omitted.

[11] fro] 3 *for*

[12]] 2 3 *great*

[13]] 2 3 *for to*

[14] none] 3 *no*

[15] comfortable] 2 3 *conformable*

[16] I] 2 3 Omitted.

VI: The aunswer of Laureola to the auctour

Lykewyse as thy reasons be temerous° and fearefull to declare, semblably they are great and grevous to perdone. Yf thou were of Macedonia [1] as thou arte of Spaygne, thy reasons and thy lyfe shuld fynishe together. But thou beynge a straunger shalte not receyve the payne° that thou deservyste. And as for the pytie that thou thynkest to be in me, I wolde° thou knewest that in suche lyke cases° doubtefull justice & crueltie is[2] as ryve° and dewe° as is[3] clemence or[4] pitie, the whiche, yf I shulde execute upon the, shulde be cause of .ii. welthes°.[i] The one, therby al other shuld take ensample° of feare. And the other, all noble women shulde be estemed and reputed° accordynge to theyr demerites°. How be it, if thy fole hardynes° requyre punycion°, yet my[5] mekenes and benignite consenteth to perdone the, though [C4r] it be agaynst the ryght waye of justice.[ii] For not alonely° for thy[6] fole hardynesse° thou oughteste to dye, but also for the offence that thou hast done agaynst my bountie° and vertue, *the* which thou haste sette in the balance of doubt bycause this that thou haste sayde to me.[iii] Yf it came to knowledge of sundry persons, some wolde° beleve that thou foundeste me redy aparelled° to accomplyshe thy desyre, as in havyng pytie of the payne of Lereano.[iv] Thou oughtest to thynke that my dignyte shulde have put the in feare, rather than his[7] fole hardines° to have made the so bolde.[8] [v] Yf thou entend any further to procure his liberte, thou mayst well seke for his remedy° and fall° thy selfe in perell.[vi] Therfore I advyse the, seynge° thou arte a straunger, seke for thy naturall° sepulture, and not in Macedonia.[vii] And to comon° with the in such maters I offende my tonge°, therfore I wyll say no more. But I wy[l][9] thou know that this that I have sayde is suffycyent[10]. [C4v] And yf any hope be in the to speake any further in this case, thy lyfe shal be shorte, or if thou thynke to come to me with any mo° such ambassades°.[viii]

---

[1] Macedonia] 2 3 *Stone*

[2] iustice & crueltie is] 2 *judgement crneltie are* 3 *judgement cruelte are*

[3] is] 2 3 *are*

[4] or] 2 3 Omitted.

[5] my] 2 3 *thy*

[6] thy] 2 3 *my*

[7] his] 2 3 *thy*

[8]] Marginal note 2 3 *The cause of feare*

[9] wyl] 1 *wy* 3 *wyll*

[10] suffyeyent] 2 *suffycyent* 3 *sufficient*

VII: The Auctor

When Laureola had endyd her wordes I sawe well her reasons were short, but longe was her trouble & displeasour. So I departed fro° her & thought upon many thynges, the which grevously° tormented me. I remembred how farre I was out of Spayne & of my longe taryeng thence.[i] Also I callyd to my mynd *the* great dolour of Lereano, sore° mistru[s]tyng[e][1] his helthe. & I perceyved well I could not accomplysh that I was purposyd° to do, as to bryng Lereano to lyberte *without* great perel. Yet I determyned° to folow myne enterpryse duryng my lyfe, or els to brynge Lereano some hope of relefe.[ii] And *with* this purpose°, the next day I went to *the* palays to se what countenance Laureola made. And when she saw me, she entreated me as she [C5r] was accustomyd[2] to do before, without changynge of her porte° or chere°, whose sure demeanour brought me in greate suspecte°.[iii] I thought she dyd it to prove° yf I wolde° returne agayne to entre in to my fyrste reasons. I fearyd leste she hadde dissimuled° to cause me to take corage to have spoken agayne for Lereano, and then to have punysihed me for my folyshe enterprice.[iv] So I coulde not tell wherto° to truste.[v] Thus I passed that daye and dyverce other, and ever me thought by the apparence that I could se by her that I hadde more cause to be bolde then reason to feare. And in that byleve°, I wayted a tyme convinient & spake with her agayne, shewynge myselfe fearefull, though I was not so in dede.[vi] [3] For in such besynes° and with suche persons, it is behovable° to fynde some doubtfull turbation°, for in suche cases° to moche boldenes is reputyd° folye, for therby myghte be thought that the dignyte nor auctorite° of the persone [C5v] were not estemed.[vii] Therfore to save me fro° that errour, I spake to her with no great audacite, but in a fearefull maner. So I shewed° her all that I thought convenient for the remedy° of Lereano, but her aunswer was accordyng to the fyrst, savyng° she was not so force°[4] nor in such displeasour with me as she was before.[viii] [5] How be it, in her wordes she gave me knowledge that I shulde be styll and holde my peace°, but yet me thought her continance°[6] gave me lycence to speake.[ix] And thus, ever when I founde tyme & place I requyred° her to have pitie upon Lereano.[x] And so divers tymes I found her aunswers sharpe in wordes & meke in countenance.[xi] And when I had well advysed° al her demeanour, I hoped uppon some profytte seynge° in her dyvers thynges wherby an amorous harte myght be knowen.[xii] For ever when I saw her alone, she was pensyfe and

---

[1] mistrustyng] 1 *mistrutyng* 2 *mystrustynge*
[2] accustomyd] 2 3 *customed*
[3]] Marginal note 2 3 *Ferefulnes to appere is mete*
[4] force] 2 3 *ferce*
[5]] Marginal note 2 *Importance may get remedy*
[6] continance] 2 *comitinaunce* 3 *countenaunce*

full of study. And when she was amonge compa[n]y, she wolde° not be mery.[xiii] [7] She abhorred [C6r] company, and to be alone was her pleasour. Often tymes she wolde° fayne her selfe syke [t]o[8] eschewe other pleasurs, and if she were espyed she wolde° fayne some dolour or payne, and often tymes she wolde° gyve sore° sighes. [xiv] And if Lereano hadde bene named in her presence, she wolde sodeynly starte and leve her comynge°[9] and blushe redde as a rose & agayne pale. [xv] Her voyce wolde° change, and her mouth waxe° drye, and though she coveryd her thoughtes as moch as was possyble, yet her piteous passyon° surmounted her discrete° dissimulation.[xvi] I say pitefulnes, for without doubte, accordyng as she shewed after, she receyved these alterations more of pytie the*n* of love. Howbeit I thought otherwyse in her.[xvii] Seynge° the tokens that I sawe in her, I thought my selfe halfe spedde of° some good hope, and therwith I spedde me to Lereano.[xviii] And after that I hadde shewed° hym all *that* was passyd bytwene me and Laureola, then I counsayled [C6v] hym to wryte to her, offerynge my selfe to bere the lettre.[xix] And though he was as then more redyer to reme*m*bre what was best for hym to do, to write or not, at last he[10] toke ynke and paper and wrote suche reasons as foloweth.[xx]

VIII: The lettre fro° Lereano to Laureola

If I hadde as good reason to write to you as I have to love, then w*ith*out feare I durste° be bolde to do it.[i] But to thynke to wryte to you troubleth my wytte° so that I lese° myne understa*n*dynge.[ii] Therfore, or° I begynne I fynde my selfe at a greate confusyon. My beleve sayth I may do it boldly, and your hyghnes putteth me in feare & doubte.[iii] In the one I fynde hope, & in the other dispayre. At the ende I agreed to wryte, but myne unhap° is to begyn in *the* houre of sorow, for overlate° it is now to complayne me for I am now in *the* case°. If I have deservyd any grace or merite[1], ther is nygh no thynge lefte lyvynge in me [C7r] to fele it, savyng° alonely° my true fayth whiche can not dye, as for my harte is without strength, and my soule without power, and my wytte° without memory.[iv] How be it, yf it wold° please you to shewe me so moche mercy as to these my presente reasons to make some aunswer, the true fayth that I bere you shulde then suffice

---

[7]] Marginal note 2 3 *The outward tokens of a lover*

[8] to] 1 *so*

[9] comynge] 2 3 *commun̄yng*

[10] though he was as then more redyer to reme*m*bre what was best for hym to do, to write or not. At last he] 2 *he shewed hym selfe then more redye to wryte, then not to wryte* 3 *he shewed him selfe then more redye to write, then not to write*

---

[1] merite] 3 *mercy*

to restore agayne in me all the partes that are destroyed.[v] I repute° my selfe culpable to demaunde° of you any reward and never dyd you servyce. And though
ye take my servyce & payne in good gree°, yet ye paye[2] me alwayes with doubtfull thoughtes.[vi] Ye may say, how ame I so bolde to write to you?[vii] Yet have no
mervayl° therof, for your beautie causeth myne affection, and the affection myne
desyre, and desyre *the* payne, and the payne causeth the boldnes.[viii] And for this
that I have done, yf ye thynke I have deserved deth, commaund to gyve it me. For
it were better for me to dye for your cause then to lyve without the [C7v] hope
of your good wyll.[ix] And to say the trouth, without° ye gyve me the[3] deth I shall
gyve it my selfe to fynd therby the lybertie, the which lyvynge I have serchyd for.
This wolde° I do, and it were not that I shulde leve you defamyd as to be reno-
myd° a murtherer.[x] Unhappy° shulde be that remedye° to delyver[4] me out of payne
and to cause you to bere blame. Therfore, in eschewynge of all such inconvenien-
tes°, I requyre° you send me your lettre as a reward for all myne evyls° that I slee
not my selfe. For I can not lyve with that I suffre, & my deth shuld so toche your
honor that all the dayes of your lyfe ye shuld be defamyd.[xi] And yf it maye please
you to do me any relefe, tary not nor be not slowe, lest ye shall have no tyme to
repent you, nor no place to redeme me.[xii]

IX: The auctor

And where as Lereano, accordyng to the gravite of his passyons°, wold° further
have executed his wrytyng, but [C8r] then usyng prudent discrecion°, for all his
payne, wrote no larger°. For that he had wryten was sufficyent to cause Laureola
to knowe hys evyll° and payne.[i] For when letters be wryten at length, that is usyd°
when the writer thynketh that the reder hath as good wyll to rede[1] them as the
sender hath to write them, but Laureola[2] was quyte° delivered fro° that presump-
cion, wherfore he extendyd hys letter no larger°.[ii] The which, when it was endyd,
I receyvyd with greate hevines° to se the sore° wepyng that Ler[e]ano[3] made, the
which I felt more then I can expresse.[iii] [4] Then I went fro° hym and spedde me
to Laureola. & when I came ther as she was, I found a tyme propyse° to speke to
her, and or° I delyvered the letter, I said to her as foloweth.[iv]

---

[2] paye] 3 *payne*
[3] the] 3 Omitted.
[4] delyver] 3 *dely*

---

[1] rede] 3 *redeme*
[2] Laureola] 2 3 *Leriano*
[3] Lereano] 1 *Laureano* 2 3 *Leriano*
[4]] Marginal note 2 *Note the wrytyng of leters* 3 *Note the wrytyng of letters*

X: The auctor to Laureola

Ryght excellent Lady, fyrst or° I say any thynge to you, I require° you to receyve
the dolour & payne of me, your poor kative° for the dischargyng° [C8v] of myne
importunat suet,° for wher so ever ye shall fynde me, of custome I shal be ever
more redy¹ to serve you the*n* to be importunate°.ⁱ And surely Lereano end[u]reth
more payne for the trouble that ye receyve then for the passio*n*° that he suffreth.
Wherof he wold° excuse hym selfe, though² his wyll desire to suffre it, to the
e[n]tent that it shuld not trouble you. Yet his sowle desireth not to suffre, but
rather to be in reste. The one co*m*maundeth hym to be styll, and the other bydd-
eth hym put oute his voyce°. But trustyng in your vertue, his dolour is oppressyd°,
desyryng to put all h[i]s³ evyll° into your presence, belevyng on the one parte ye
shuld be dangerous°, & on the other parte that it shulde cause you to have com-
passyon.ⁱⁱ Beholde how many wayes he deservyth meryte. To forget his trouble he
desyreth the deth, and not withoute ye consent therto. And bycause it shuld not
be said that ye consent therto, he desyreth the life in that he received [D1r] his
payne to be happy°. And for lacke of his desyre he loseth⁴ his understandyng, and
to prayse your beawte he desyreth ayde of all the worlde.ⁱⁱⁱ Beholde how moche
ye are bounde to him, for he prayseth them that distroyeth him. He hath all his
remembrance° upon that thyng that is the occasyon of all his evyl°.ⁱᵛ And by ad-
venture° I shuld be so unhappy° that he shuld lese° his love by my intercession,
which he hath deservyd by reason of his faythfull harte.ᵛ Yet I had rather I were
dede. Wherfore, I requyre° you to receyve this letter fro° hym, and in the redyng
therof to shew hym some mercy for the payne that he hathe sufferyd. And yf ye
blame hym ye are more culpable then he, for that ye have sufferyd hym to endure
payne so long. Ye perceyve well the sorow that he is in by the wordes in his letter,
the which though his mouth spake them & his hand wrote them, yet his⁵ dolour
dydde ordeyne° and devise them.ᵛⁱ & as God sende [D1v] you parte of heven as ye
have deservyd in the erth, that ye will receyve this his letter & make hym a*n* aun-
swere.ᵛⁱⁱ And alonely° with this reward ye maye redeme hym and therby do away
his debilite, & mynysh° hys torment, and favor his sykenes, and brynge hym in to
that state that he wyll desyre no more welth° nor endure no more payne.ᵛⁱⁱⁱ And
if ye wyll not thus moch do for hym to whom ye are so moch bounde, not at my
request, I maye then well repute° you cruell.ⁱˣ But I hope so moche in your vertue,
that accordyng to y[ou]r⁶ olde custome ye can do no thyng but vertue.

---

¹ more redy] 2 *ever redyer* 3 *ever redier*
² through] 2 *though* 3 *thoughe*
³ his] 1 *hus*
⁴ loseth] 2 3 *leseth*
⁵ his] 2 3 Omitted.
⁶ your] 1 *yuor*

XI: Th'aunswere of [1] Laureola to the Auctor

The perseverance in thy pursewt° bryngeth me to so streyght° a case° that many
tymes my thought is[2] dought° what to do, other to banysh the owt of this lande,
or els to jeobarde° my fame° in gyvyng the place° & leysure to say what thou lyst°.
[i] Yet I ame agreyd [D2r] not so to do, nor to put the to that extremyte by reason
of the compassyon that I have of the.[ii] For though thyne ambassade° be evyll°,
yet thyne entensyon is good as to fynd remedy° for *the* sorowfull.[iii] And the other
way I wyll not take bycause of myne honor, for he can not be delyvered fro° payne
without I be defamed.[3] Yf I could remedy° his evyll° withoute daunger or blottyng of[4] myn honour I wold° do it with no lesse affeccyon then thou desyrest,
but thou knowest well how that women are bounde to preserve theyr good fame°
rather then theyr lyfe. At the lest they shuld esteme it more then theyr bounte°.[iv]
For though *the* lyfe of Lereano shuld fynysh by deth, yet judge thy self whether
I ought rather to be piteful to me[5] self or to his evyll°.[v] And if all women ought
thus[6] to do, then specially such as be of noble blod ought so to do, for al peple
soner regardeth a smal spot in noble persons then a great fawte° in low *person-
ages*°.[vi] Therfore, in thy wordes [D2v] conferme the to reason for thy demaund°
is unjust. *Thou* thynkest I ame pleased *with* thy comoni[n]g°[7], which is contrary.
Though thy demaund° trouble me, yet thy condycion pleaseth me, & I have pleasour to shew the myne escuse *with* just reasons to save me fro° charge, blame, &
sclaunder°.[vii] The letter that thou woldest° have me to receyve maye well be excusyd, for my defence is of no lesse power than the perceverance of his hope. But
syn°[8] thou haste brought it I ame pleasyd to receyve it, but hope not of any aunswere, travayll° no more to desyre it, nor at [9] lest speke no more therof, lesse[10] that
my dysplesure trowble *thee* not as moche[11] as thou now prayseste my pacyence &
sufferyng.[viii] I blame my selfe, [12] that in .ii. thynges, bycause I comon° so longe
with the.[ix] The one is bycause *the* qualyte & heate° of the cause hath brought me
in trouble. The other is bycause thou mayst thynke *that* I ame well pleasyd to
speke with the in this mater, and belevest how I shuld [D3r] agre to Lereano.

---

[1] of] 3 *to*
[2] is] 2 *dothe* 3 *doth*
[3]] Marginal note 2 *She tendreth her honour* 3 *She tendreth her honoure*
[4] of] 2 3 Omitted.
[5] me] 2 3 *my*
[6] thus] 3 *this*
[7] comoning] 1 *comonig* 2 *commyng* 3 *comynge*
[8] syn] 2 3 *syns*
[9]] 3 *the*
[10] lesse] 2 *leste* 3 *lest*
[11] asmoche] 2 *to moche* 3 *to muche*
[12]] 2 3 *and*

Though thou thynke so, I have no mervayll°, for wordes is the image of the harte. ˣ Go thy way, content the with thyne owne judgement, and cary with the good hope of that thou desyrest, and not to be condempnyd in thyne own thought. For yf thou returne agayn to make new request thou wylt repent it. I will advyse the, lette this be the last spekyng of that mater or eles *thou* mayste well know thou shall repent it, for sekyng remedy° for a nother shalt fayle remedy° for thy selfe.ˣⁱ

XII: The Auctor

The wordes of Laureola dyd bryng me in to great confusyon, for when I thought best to understand her then I knew lest° of her wyl. Whan I had most hope, then I was farthest out of *the* way. And when I thought my selfe most sure, then I was in most feare, for *the* dyversyte of her jesture & behavour blyndyd myne understandyng.ⁱ The receyvyng of the letter satisfyed me, but [D3v] the ende of her wordes put me in dyspayre so that I know not what way to folow nor how I shuld fynd any hope.ⁱⁱ And thus as a man without counsayll, I departyd fro° her & went to Lereano, thynkyng to gyve hym some counsayll and to seke *the* best meanes that I coulde devyse to remedy° parte of his evell°. And when I cam to hym I said as foloweth.

XIII: The Auctor to Lereano

For the expedicion° that I bryng ye may well knowe where woordes fayle dylygence can not prevayll.ⁱ Thou dyddyst recommaunde thy remedy° to me, but Fortune hath bene to me so contrary in that she wolde° not be to me so favourable as to satysfye me in anythyng that is passyd. But fortune is rather myne enemy. Though in this case° I hadde good excuse to ayde the, for t[h]ough¹ I was the messenger thyne was the besynes°.ⁱⁱ The mater that I have passyd with Laureola, I can not understand it nor can not shew° it bycause it is of so [D4r] newe and dyverce° condycyons.ⁱⁱⁱ A thousand tymes I thought to have bene at the poynte to have gyven the remedy°, and agayne as often to have gyven the thy sepulture. Al tokens of her wyl (wonne & vanquysshed), I saw in her contenance, and² all the folysh frowardenes° of women withoute love, I harde in her woordes.³ Judgyng upon her demeanour, I was joyfull, and heryng her wordes, I was sorowfull. ⁱᵛ Sometyme I thought she dyd prudently dyssimule, and agayne I thought she wantyd love. But fynally when I saw her so moveable & changable, I belevyd then

---

¹ though] 1 *tough* 2 *thoughe*
² and] 2 3 Omitted.
³ I harde in her woordes] 2 3 Omitted.

veryly that ther was no love in her. For if a persone be taken with love, the hart shall be constante. And where as love lacketh, ther is [4] mutabylyte.[v] On the other parte I thought she dyd it for fare° of the cruell harte of the king, her father. What shall I say? She hath receyved thy letter & manyshed°[5] me to the deth yf I speke any further in thy[6] cause.[vi] Beholde [D4v] now this grevous° case° ther semyth in one poynt .ii. dyfferences. Yf I shuld shew° the all that was passyd bytwene her & me I shulde want tyme to speke yt.[vii] I requyre° the, enforce° thy wytte° and aswage° thy passion°, for in folowyng thy payne thou hast more nede of [7] sepulture thenne of comforte.[viii] For withoute thou take some repose, thou shalt leve here thy boones in stede of thy true fayth, the whych thou oughtest not to do. For satysfyng of thy selfe, it were more convenyent for the to lyve rather then to dye for to be out of payne.[ix] This I say bycause I se the gloryfye° in thy payne, but in sufferyng payne thou mayst attaygne to the crowne of lawde & prayse in that it may be sayd *that* thou enforcest° thy selfe to suffre payne for the ladye's sake.[x] Suche as be stronge & vertuous in theyr grettyst mysfortune shew grettest harte°.[xi] Ther is no dyfference bytwene the good & evyll, *with*out the bountye° be tempt° and provyd°.[xii] Consider that *with* [D5r] longe lyfe a thyng maye be wonne. Have good hope in thy fayth. Thynke *that* the purpose° of Laureola may change, and thy ferme, stedfast love never. I wyll not say all that I thynke for thy consolacion, for I perceyve by thy wepynges & complaynt that ardent° deth hath lyghtened° his flames.[xiii] But what so ever thou thynkyst that I can do for the, co*m*maund it, for I have no lesse wyl to serve the then I have to remedy° thy helth.

XIV: Lereano to the auctor

The dysposycion that I ame in, *thou* seyst°. The privasyo*n*° of my understandyng, thou knowest. *The* turbasyon° of my tong° thou mayst well note & merke. Therfore, have no mervaylle°, though myne aunswere be more with wepyng then with ornate wordes bycause *that* Laureola putteth fro° her harte the swete appetyght° of my wylle.[i] The thynges that be past bytwen *thou* and her, for all that, thou arte at thy liberte yet [D5v] thy judgement can not understande her meanyng.[ii] How shuld I the*n* knowe them for I ame so passyonyd° than I can not lyve but alonely°[1]

---

[4]] 3 *no*
[5] manyshed] 2 *monyshed* 3 *monisshed*
[6] thy] 2 3 *the*
[7]] 2 3 *a*

---

[1] alonely] 3 *onely*

to prayse her beautie?² & to repute° my last ende happy°, I wolde° these shulde be *the* last wordes of my lyfe bycause they be to prayse her. What gretter welth° can I have then *that*? If I were so happy° to be rewardyd therwith, as I deserve by reason of the payne that I suffre, who then shuld be lyke me?ⁱⁱⁱ Better it were for me to dye syn°³ I have servyd her, the*n* to lyve causyng her to have any trouble or dyspleasour.ⁱᵛ The thyng that most shall greve me is when I dye that the eyen° shall peryshe that hath seen her, and the harte that remembreth her. The which, consyderyng what she is, al my wyttes° are past the ordre of reason.ᵛ I say thus bycause thou seyst° that in the warkes of my harte, in steade of faynte love, my stedfast love encreaseth if in my captyve harte the⁴ consolacio*n*s could take any frute. This that thou [D6r] hast done to me suffyseth to enforce° me. But, as the heryng of them that be in hevynes° and lockyd in passyo*n* in to whose sowle can entre no wordes of comforte. And where thou saest° I shuld suffre none° evyll°, gyve me the strength therto and I shall put to my good wyll. As for thynges of honor that thou shewest° me, I know them by reason, and I deny them agayne by the same reasone. I say I know them for a man fre in liberte shuld use honor, and agayn I⁵ denye it as consernyng to my selfe. Yet I seke° in my grevous° payne to chose an honorable death. ᵛⁱ The travayll° that thou hast receyvyd for my sake, and *the* desyre that I se thou hast to delyver me fro° payne, byndeth me to offre for the my lyfe as often as it were nedefull.ᵛⁱⁱ But syn°⁶ ther is but smal lyfe left in me, take for satysfaction my desyre and not my power. Yet I requyre° the (syn°⁷ this shall be the fynall good dede that thou canst do for me, & the last that I shal receyve) [D6v] as to bere fro° me another letter to Laureola with suche newes as she shall be gladde of, and wherby she shall know how I dyspose° me to passe out of this transytory lyfe, and no more to trouble her.ᵛⁱⁱⁱ & to the entent that with good wyll thou shuldest bere it to her, I wyll begynne it in thy presence. Wherof the mater shal be as folowith.

---

²] Marginal note 2 *The difference betwene liberte & thraldo*m 3 *The dyfference betwene lybertie & thraldo*m

³ syn] 2 3 *syns*

⁴ they] 2 3 *the*

⁵ I] 3 Omitted.

⁶ syn] 2 3 *syns*

⁷ syn] 2 *syns* 3 *sins*

XV: The letter of Lereano [1] to Laureola [2]

Syn°[3] that the sepulture is the[4] rewarde of all myne evels°, I ame redy now to receyve it. Bel[e]ve[5] that deth shall not dysplease me, for he is of small wytte° that
abhorryth that thyng *that* gyveth libertie. But one thyng dyspleaseth me, that is
in[6] dyeng I shal lose al my hope ever to se you agayn, the whiche sore° greveth
me.[i] It may be sayd in so shorte a space as I have ben your servant, how shuld I
so sone lose my puyssance°? Ye ought not to mervail° therat, for *the* hope that ye
have brought [D7r] me in. And smalle comeforte with my greate passyon° suffyseth to put away & to destroy greater force then myne.[ii] Yet I can not beleve
that ye are cause therof without your workes do certifie the same.[iii] But alwayes I
have belevyd that your co*n*dycyon piteous shulde surmou*n*t your obstynate wyl.
But sin°[7] ye wyll that my life shal receve this domage°, *the* faute° therof is myne
owne mysfortune.[iv] [8] I am sore° abasshyd° that ye sorow not in your selfe, your
owne ingratitude. I have gyven you my liberte & intyerly° have gyve*n* you my
harte, nothyng retaynyng to my selfe. For all that, I can have no rewarde of love,
yet I desyre to serve you.[v] Who wold° thynke that ye shulde dystroy that thyng
that is your owne?[vi] Certaynly ye are your owne enemy withoute° ye fynde some
remedy° to save me.[vii] This ye o[u]ght to do, or els ye co*n*demne your selfe, for
my deth & perdycyon cannot profyght you.[viii] But I desyre° that ye wold° sorowe
for myne evyll°. Yet yf your [D7v] sorow shuld do you any payne then I desyre
it not.[ix] Syn°[9] that lyvyng I never dyd ye servyce, it were no ryght that dyeng I
shuld cause you to have trouble. They that loke agaynst the sonne, *the* more they
regard° it, the blynder they be. And so the more I remember your fayrenes, the
blynder is myne understandyng°.[x] This I say to th'entent that of this, my rude°
wrytyng, ye shuld have no mervayll°. For in the hard case° that I ame in, accordyng to my wyll, I am better dysposed to ende my lyfe then to make any reasones.
[xi] Yet I wolde° that thyng that ye ought to regarde° were so orderyd that ye shuld
not occupye your undersandyng° on a thyng so fayre° fro° your condycio[n]. Yf ye
consent that I shall dye bycause ye wold° have it publyshed°, ye have the power to
slee me.[xii] Then be ye evyll° cousayled, for without hope your beautie hath serty-
fyed me therof.[xiii] And if ye esteme my deth to be good bycause I ame not worthy

---

[1]] 2 3 *the lover*
[2]] 2 3 *beloved*
[3] Syn] 2 3 *Syns*
[4] the] 2 *the*n
[5] *beleve*] 1 *beloue*
[6] in] 2 3 Omitted.
[7] sin] 2 3 *syns*
[8]] 2 3 Marginal note *He accuseth her ingratitude*
[9] syn] 2 3 *syns*

to receyve [D8r] your grace, the whiche I have hopyd to wynne by reaso[n]e of my true fayth, the which[10] I lese for lacke of deservyng. And w*ith* this thought I thynk to suffre all my payne. And if it seme to you that the paynes that I endure for your sake can not be remedyed° withoute offence to your honor, thy[n]k that I wyll never desyre° *the* thyng that shuld torne you to blame.[xiv] What profyght shuld any thyng do to me that shuld be evyll° to you? Allonely° I desyre your aunswere for my fyrst & last reward. & to be brefe, I requyre° you, syn°[11] ye[12] make an ende of my lyfe, yet at [13] lest honor my deth. For in[14] the place where as the[15] desperate° sowles becometh, yf ther be any welth°, there I desyre to feale none°[16] other joy but *that* ye wyll honor my dede bones that I may joy a lytle with that great glory.

XVI: The auctor

The wordes and letter of Lereano finyshed, in stede of wordes myn [D8v] eyen° were satysfyed with greate wepyng.[i] & so witho[u]te power to speke, I departyd, thynkynge my judgement *that* it shuld be the last tyme that I had any hope to se hym agayn alyve. And as I was on my way I wrote a superscrypcion° upon the letter, to th'entent that Laureola shuld be in doubt fro° whence it came. And when I came in to her presence, I delyvered her the letter, who, belevyng that it had come frome some other persone, receyvyd it and began to rede it. And all the season° that she was redyng, I regardyd° styll° her vysage°. & when she hadde made an ende, I saw well she was sore° troubelyd as though she had sufferyd a great evyll°. [ii] Yet the regardyng° of her turbacyon° excusyd not my trouble. Then to assure° my selfe I demaundyd° of her other questyons no thyng concernyng to that purpose.[iii] [1] And to delyver her selfe fro° company, *the* whych in suche case is perelous lesse°[2] that the manyfest mutacions discover° [E1r] not the secrete thoughtes of the harte. Therfore she withdrew her selfe aparte and all that nyghte she was

---

[10] the which] 2 3 *and*
[11] syn] 2 3 *syns*
[12] ye] 2 3 *you*
[13]] 3 *the*
[14] in] 3 Omitted.
[15] the] 2 3 Omitted.
[16] none] 3 *no*

---

[1]] Marginal note 2 *A pretye meanes avoydig the Imynent dyspleasur* 3 *A pretye meanes avoyding the Imynent dyspleasur*
[2] lesse] 2 *lest* 3 *least*

without spekyng of any word to me as tuchyng that purpose.[iv] And the next day she sent for me & shewed° me many vertuous resons to dyscharge her selfe fro anythyng consentyng to release *the* payne of Lereano.[v] Howbeit, she sayd *that* she thought great inhumanite to lese° suche a man as Lereano for so small a pryce, as in wrytyng of a letter. "How be it in the redyng of his letter I take but smal plea-sour. Therefore here I have wrytten a letter, not *with* so[3] pleasant and swet wordes as be in his reasons. For who so ever here the wordes in this my letter, may well knowe *that* I have lytle studyed in the arte of eloquence."[vi] So for shamefastnes° sodenly her face was inflamyd, and as sodenly agayne pale. She was so sore° al-teryd and shorte wyndyd, that in maner she brethed for *the* deth. Her harte & voyce so sore° trymbled° that her dyscrecion° [E1v] could not enforce° her selfe to speke. Therfore, her aunswere was shorte. And also the place° requyred no lenger tyme.[vii] So she toke me the letter, and kyst her hand, and I receyvyd it. The ten-our wherof ensuyth.[viii]

XVII: The letter fro° Laureola [1] to Lereano [2]

The deth that thou lokest for, by reasone of thy payne I have rather deservyd it yf I shulde put my wyll to thyne.[i] But that is not so,[3] for this, my wryttyng°, is more to redeme thy lyfe then to satisfy thy desyre. What shulde it profytte me to ac-complysh it? For yf I were accusyd therof, I coulde have no wytnes to salve°[4] me, but alonely° my pure entensyon, which is so pryncypall a pertye[5]° that his wordes shulde not be taken nor [6] beleved.[ii] And with this feare, I have put to my hande to this paper, my harte & mynde beyng in hevyn makyng Hym judge of my mynde, to whome the trouthe of all thynges is [E2r] manyfest & knowen.[iii] [7] The cause why *that* I doubtyd to aunswere the was bycause withoute my condmnacion° thou canst not be assoyled°, as thou mayst well se.[iv] For though no creature know of this letter but thy selfe & the berer, yet I know not what judgement any of you may make upon me. Though it be but good, yet I ame spottyd° with *the* suspecte° therof. Therfore I desyre° the, when *thou* hast seen myne aunswere, remember the fame° & re[n]ome° of her that hath sent it.[v] Of this I hertely desyre° the, for often

---

³ so] 2 *a* 3 Omitted.

---

¹] 2 3 *beloved*
²] 2 3 *the lover*
³] Marginal note 2 3 *The cause of the letter*
⁴ salue] 2 3 *save*
⁵ pertye] 2 *partie* 3 *parte*
⁶] 2 *be*
⁷] Marginal note 2 *The pour of God* 3 *The power of God*

tymes suche fa[v]ors⁸ are publyshyd° for some hath more regard to the victory
then to the⁹ honour of them that shewith suche favour.ⁱ ¹⁰ And whether it were
better for me to be blamyd for crueltie, or to be spotted° or defamyd for beyng
to piteous, I reporte me to thy selfe.ⁱ & yet to gyve the some remedy°, I use now
the contrary. Thou hast that thou desyrest, and I that I feare.ᵛ I requyre° the
to turne & wynde°, and kepe secrete my letter in [E2v] thy remembrance°, for if
thou do beleve it then it nede not to be seen.ⁱˣ For that I have wryten, yf it were
sene it shuld be thought that I love the. And yf thou beleve the reasons that I
ha[v]e sayde to be spoken rather by dissymulacion then of trouth, then arte thou
begyled in that beleve°, for yt is clene contrary.ˣ For surely I say them rather with
a piteous entenscion then *with* any amorous entent. And to cause the to beleve
this, I wold° further extende my wordes yf I hadde leysour°. But to put the in to
none° other suspeccion, I make an ende of my letter. And to th'entent that my
warkes shulde receyve a just rewarde, thus wyll I endure my lyfe dayes.ˣⁱ

XVIII: The auctor

When I hadde receyved this letter of Laureola I departyd to go to Lereano.
Thynkyng then to have with me some company to ayde me in the glory of myne
ambassade° & to encorage therby Lereano, I callyd then to [E3r] me *the* grettest
enemyes *that* we had before, as Contentacion°, Hope, Rest, Pleysour, Myrth, and
Comforte.ⁱ I toke these with me for feare that *the* kepers of the prisone wolde°
resist & defende me the entre°, wherfore I thought to go in ordre of batayl°.¹ And
when I came to the heyght of an hygh hyll, I had a syghte of the pryson. Then
I dysplayed my baner all of grene so that our enemyes toke them to *the* flyght in
suche wyse° that he that fledde fastyst thought to be next° the jeoperdye°.ⁱⁱ And
when Lereano² harde this grete rumour°, not knowyng what it was, he came to a
wyndow of the towre and spake more with wekenes of spirite then with hope of
socour°. And when he saw me comyng in batayll *with* suche a goodly company,
then he knew what the mater ment.ⁱⁱⁱ & what for his feblenes & for his sodeyn
joye, loste his fealyng° and fell downe in a trance° in the howse° where he was.
And when I came to *the* steyres wheron I was wont to mount, Rest avauncyd

---

⁸ favors] 1 *fawors*
⁹ the] 2 3 Omitted.
¹⁰] Marginal note 2 *honour is to be preserved before pyte* 3 *Honour is to be preserved before pite*

---

¹] Marginal note 2 *The armour agaynst love* 3 *The armoure agaynst love*
² Lereano] 2 *Leriola*

[E3v] to marche on before, who gave clerenes° & chasyde away all the darkenes of the towre.[iv] [3] And when I came to hym & sawe hym in that mortall maner, I feared I came sone inough to wepe and to late to gyve hym remedy°.[v] Then with great dylygence, Hope stept to hym & cast a lytle water of comeforte° in his face. And therwith he returnyd agayne to hym selfe. And the better to strength hym, I delyvered hym Laureola's letter.[4] And all the season° that he redde it, all suche as I brought with me procured for his helth. Myrth gave joy to his harte, Rest comfortyd his spyrytes°, Hope brought hym in to good remembrance°, Contentacion cleryd his eyen°, Comeforte restoryd his helthe and strength, Pleasure quyckenyd° his understandyng°.[vi] [5] They treatyd hym in suche wyse° that when he hadde redde over the letter he was all hole°, as though he hadde never felte passyon°.[vii] And when he saw that my dylygence gave hym lyberte, he toke me often [E4r] tymes in his armes, offeryng hym selfe to be myne, and thought that but a small rewarde for the deservyng° of my servyce.[viii] His offers were to me in suche maner that I wyst° not how to aunswer hym as I ought to have done accordyng to his degre°.[ix] [6] And after that many thynges were passyd bytwene hym & me, he determy[n]ed° to go to the courte[7]. [x]

[He thynkynge somwhat to recreat° spirites & rejoyse his sorowfull herte, as well for gladnes of his comforte, as to advoyde dyvers fantasies that myghte happen to have commen to his doubtfull mynde, to be a base lute°, which on the one syde had this poysey° writen: "My death causeth[8] by absens." And on the other syde was[9] wryten: "Shal be redemyd with presens." & played this songe or balade folowynge:

Welcom solace, welcom comforte
Welcom joye, welcom myne ease
Welcom the socoure° that doth transporte
And brynge helth for my desease.
The thynge is welcom that doth apease
My care sorowe and my burest°,
And welcom her sonde° that I love best.

Blyssed be the hande that dyd wryte,
Blyssed be [10]pen that made the letter,

---

[3]] Marginal note 2 *Rest, in the vaward* 3 *Reste, in the vaward*

[4]] Marginal note 2 3 *hope & comfort*

[5]] Marginal note 2 *The dede of the sayd felde agaynste love* 3 *The dede of the sayd felo agayust love*

[6]] Marginal note 3 *Note*

[7] he determy[n]ed to go to the courte.] 2 3 Omitted.

[8] causeth] 3 *caseth*

[9] was] 3 Omitted.

[10]] 3 *the*

And blyssed be the memory that dyd indyght°,
And blyssed be the paper[11] *and the messenger,*
And blyssed be they that do transfer
My care sorowe, and my burest°.

Welcome myrth unto my harte,
Welcom hope that shall not departe,
Welcom pleasure unto my syghtes,
Welcom my comforte that dayly fyghtes
Agaynst care sorowe and all burest°,
And welcom her sonde°, that I love best.

And in the meane season° he concludyd and determyned° to go to the courte, but
fyrste. Etc.

O herte full of payne
The whiche to sustayne
Do me refrayne°
        In this lyfe mortall.
For death sertayne
Wyll helpe the agayne
And of all this payne
        Is medycyne pryncypall.

For thou mayst be suer°
It can not longe e[n]duer
Without some helpe and cure.
        Or when that plesaunt death
To the shall resorte
Unto thy comforte
And thy payne transporte
        In takynge awaye thy breth.

The lyfe that is yll
Death desyre wyll
It selfe for to spyll
        To put away his payne.
The lyfe that is deseased
With death wolde° be pleased
His sorowes[12] *to have peased°*
        Wherin[13] *he doth remayne.*

---

[11] paper] 3 *pay*
[12] sorowes] 3 *sorowe*
[13] wherin] 3 *when*

A herte with sorowe inwardly
Turmented contynually
And lyvynge for to dye
        In this lyfe mortall.
To hym selfe alone
Doth thynke sorowe care and mone[14]
To be to hym all one
        And unto death deruall°.]

And fyrst[15] we went to a towne of his, and taryed there a certayne season° to recover his strength and to newe aparell° hym agaynst°[16] he shuld go to the courte.
And when he saw his tyme, he set forth on his journey. And when his comyng
was knowen in the courte, many great lordes and yong courtyaers went to receyve
hym. But he toke more consolacion of his secrete glory then of all the open honour that was done to hym.[xi] Thus he was nobly accompanyd to the palace. And
his duetie done to the kyng, he kyst the hand of Laureola,[17] wherein was many
thynges to be notyd [E4v], and specyally to me who knew the mater bytwene
them.[xii] The one was overcome with [18] trybulacion, the other faylyd colour. He
wyst° not what to say, nor she to aunswere. [19] Suche force hathe the passyons of
love, alwayes it draweth the wyt° & dyscrecion° downe under his baner°, *the* which
I saw there by clere° experyence°. And though[20] that no man saw ther demanour
nor hadde no suspecte° bytwene them, yet Persio sonne to the Lorde of Gania
behelde them, and was as farre in love, as Lerea[no][21] was.[xiii] [22] And by reasone
that all gelous suspecte° disordereth° all thynges secrete, he regarded over° ther
wordes & contenaunces in so moch *that* he gave full credence to his own suspect°,
& gave not alonely° fayth to *that* he saw, *the* which was nothyng, but also belevyd
it surely in his imagynacion°.[xiv] & with *that* evyl° thought of jelosy, wi*th*out de-
liberacyo*n* or cou*n*sayll, he fy[n]dyng[23] the kyng in a secrete place sayd to hym
(affermyng *that* Laureola & Lereano lovyd to gether) [E5r] how that he hadde
seen them together dyverce nyghtes when the kynge was a bedde. Sayng how he
shewyd° this for the honour and servyce, that he bare to the kyng.[xv] [24] The kynge

---

[14] mone] 3 *more*
[15] and fyrst] 2 3 *Then*
[16] agaynst] 2 3 *agayne*
[17] Laureola] 2 *Laurealo*
[18]] 2 3 *very great*
[19]] Marginal note 2 3 *The metynge of the partyes*
[20] though] 2 3 *thought*
[21] Lereaon] 2 3 *Leriano*
[22]] Marginal note 2 3 *Persio*
[23] fydyng] 2 *fynding* 3 *fyndynge*
[24]] Marginal note 2 3 *The fayned accusement*

then beyng sore° troubelyd *with* those newes was in great doubte, and studyed long or° he was determynyd° to aunswere. And after he had slept on *the* mater, he bileved Persius' sayeng° to be true. Consyderyng his vertue and auctoryte, he wolde° shew° nothyng, but of trou[th]°25.xvi Then the kyng determynyd° what he wolde° doo. And therupo*n* he sent his doughter, Laureola, in to a towre in26 to a prysone.27xvii And then sent for Persio & commaundyd hym to accuse Lereano of treason accordyng to his lawes. Of the which co*n*mmau*n*deme*n*t he was sore° abashyde°, but the heate° of the busynes enforsyd° hym to grau*n*te it.xviii The*n* he acceptyd the Kynge's comma*n*dement, and sayde howe he thankyd God that he was offeryd suche a case° *that* his handes myght bere wytnes of his bounte° & [E5v] vertue.xix And bycause that in Macedonia28 suche deades were accustumed to be done by wrytyng & not in29 the kynge's presence by wordes, therfore Persio sent a wrytyng° to Lere[a]n[o]30 *with* suche reasons as ensue.xx 31

XIX: Persius' writtyng° to Lereanoi

Syn°1 that of good workes procedeth vertuous renome° and fame°, it is a iuste thynge that evylnes be chastysed to th'entent that vertue maye be maynteynyd.ii 2 And with great dylygence bounte° ought to be exaltyd, so that the enemyes therof, when ther wylfull operacions be to *the* co*n*trary, they ought to be co*n*straynyd to use bountie° for dread and feare of punyshement.iii I say this to the, Lereano, for the payne° that thou shalt receyve for the trespace that thou hast co*m*myttyd shal be a chastysement to the, and an ensample° for all other3 to feare.4 For if such thynges shuld be perdonyd and left unponyshed, vylany shuld then be no lesse favoryd in [E6r] them *that* do evyl, then noblenes in them *that* be good.iv Certainly evyl hath it profityd *thee* all the gentlenes° & honeste of thy lynage°, who gave the ensample° to folow bounte° and thou folowest the workes of treason.v Thy progenitours' bones wold° be redy to ryse agaynst the yf they knew how

---

25 trouth] 1 *trought*
26 in] 2 3 Omitted.
27] Marginal note 2 3 *Laureola to pryson*
28 Macedonia] 2 3 *Guallo*
29 in] 2 3 *by*
30 Lereano] 1 *Lereona* 2 3 *Leriano*
31] Marginal note 2 3 *The custome of the countree*

---

1 Syn] 2 3 *Syns*
2] Marginal note 2 *Introduction o the satyde mater* 3 *Introduction of the satyde mater*
3 all other] 3 *another*
4] Marginal note 2 *Declaracion of the said mater* 3 *Declaracion of the saide matter*

thou defoilyst° (with suche errour) theyr noble dedes.ᵛⁱ ⁵ Therfore now is the tyme
come that for thyne evyll deades, thou shalt receyve the ende of thy lyfe and de-
foyll° thy fame°. Cursyd be all suche as thou arte, that canst not chose an honourable lyfe.ᵛⁱⁱ And thou not regardynge thy servyce nor duetie to thy kyng!ᵛⁱⁱⁱ To be
so bolde, *with*oute shame, as to falle in love with Laureola, the kynge's doughter,
with whome, withoute shame, thou hast spoken dyverce tymes aloone after the
kynge's beyng a bedde, not folowyng the clere° lynage°.ⁱˣ ⁶ By which reasone I ap-
peale the as a traytour.ˣ And upo*n* that quarel° I thynk to sle the, or els to dryve
the oute of the [E6v] feld, or els to cause the ⁷ confesse with thy mouth my say-
eng° to be true, the which as long as the world endureth shal be an ensample° of
my trouth.ˣⁱ ⁸ And thus I leve, trustyng to prove thy falsenes, and to verify my
treuth. Chose thou the maner of our batayll & armur, and on the kynge's part I
shal make the assurance°.ˣⁱⁱ ⁹

XX: The aunswer of Lereano

More shal be my mysfortune then th[y]¹ malyce, withoute° the fault *that* thou
chargest me withall, of falsenes, shall gyve ² the payne by justice accordyng to thy
deserte°.³ ⁱ If thou were as discrete° as thou art evyll in escheweng of such perels,
first thou shuldest have knowen myne entension or° thou haddest gyven sentence upon my workes.ⁱⁱ But nowe I knowe by ⁴ that thou semyst better then thou
arte in dead°.ⁱⁱⁱ ⁵ I thoughte surely to have comoned° with the as with my frende,
havynge confidence in thy vertue, but nowe thou [E7r] shewyst thyne evyll
condicion.ⁱᵛ Lyke as here before thou shewydyst thy bountie° with frendly amyte°,
in lykewyse now *thou* discoverest° thy falshod, wherfor *thou* causest en[m]yte⁶
bytwene us, or I may say by reasone, enemy to thy selfe.ᵛ For by thyne owne wit-
nesse thou levyst the good memory of thy life with infamy, and shalte ende thy
life *with* shame. Why hast thou put thy serpentyne tonge upon Laureola, whose

---

⁵] Marginal note 2 *A similitude of his auncestours* 3 *A symylitude of hys auncestours*
⁶] Marginal note 2 3 *The accuseme*nt
⁷] 2 3 *to*
⁸] Marginal note 2 *The appele* 3 *The apele*
⁹] Marginal note 2 *Conclusyon* 3 *Conclusion*

---

¹ thy] 1 *the*
²] 2 3 *unto*
³] Marginal note 2 3 *The proheme of the letter*
⁴] 2 3 *the*
⁵] Marginal note 2 3 *The argument*
⁶ enmyte] 1 2 3 *enuyte*

alonely° bounte° suffiseth that if bounte° were loste throughoute all the worlde, it myght be recoveryd & founde in her?ⱽⁱ Thou mayntaynyst a c[le]re⁷° falsehodde, and I shall defend a just cause, and shall delyver & discharge° her fro° all fawtes°, and shall charge thyn honour *with* shame.ⱽⁱⁱ ⁸ I will not aunswere thyne unmesurable° wordes, for I repute° it a more honest way to vanquysh the with my handes, rather then to satisfye the *with* wordes.ⱽⁱⁱⁱ I desyre no thyng b[u]t alonely° to come to the case° to trye our debate°.ⁱˣ Thou accusyst me of treason, afferming [E7v] how I have ben dyverce tymes in the secrete chamber with Laureola after *the* kynge's beyng a bedde & at his rest. As well to the one as to the other, I saye *thou* falsely lyest, yet I denye not but that I have regardyd° her beawtie *with* an amorouse desyre.⁹ But though the force of love ordre the thoughtes, yet *the* vertue of trouth causyth clenlynes° of honeste°.ˣ I wold° be glad to have her favour, but for none°¹⁰ evyll thought. And moreover, I shall defende the quarel, and say¹¹ that I alone never enteryd in to her secrete chamber, nor never spake wordes of love to her, so that when the entension synnyth¹² not the judgement then shuld alwayes be hole withoute deformyte.ˣⁱ And syn°¹³ the determynacion° herof can not be withoute deth of one of us and not determynyd with our tonges°, therfore, lete us leve raylyng *with* our tonges° and abyde upon the day of our sentence, the which I truste in God shal be for my profyght, and honor to Laureola, and [E8r] shame and rebuke to the.ˣⁱⁱ Bycause thy dedes of malyce, and I to defende by reasone, the trough°¹⁴ shal be determyned° by justice. The armure that we shall chose shal be all ¹⁵ peces° acordynge to the custome of our countrey.ˣⁱⁱⁱ ¹⁶ Our horses bardyd°, with lyke speres and swordes, and with any other armure or wepyn that is usyd, with the whiche I truste to slee the, or to cause the to denye that ¹⁷ thou hast sayde, or els to chase the oute of the felde.

---

⁷ clere] 1 *celre* 3 *cleare*
⁸] Marginal note 2 3 *The defence of treason*
⁹] Marginal note 2 3 *The answere*
¹⁰ none] 2 3 *one*
¹¹ say] 3 *sayeth*
¹² synnyth] 2 *semyth* 3 *semeth*
¹³ syn] 2 *syns* 3 *synce*
¹⁴ trough] 2 3 *trouth*
¹⁵] 2 3 *of*
¹⁶] Marginal note 2 3 *The devyse of the armure*
¹⁷] 2 3 *that*

XXI: The auctor

Thus [1] evyll Fortune, envyous of the welth° & prosperite of Lereano, usyng againste hym her naturall chaungea[b]le[2] condycion, she[3] gave hym a torne whan she saw hym in his moste prosperite, whose mysfortune to behold was great passion°, and constreyned° the heres° to payne.[i] Thus levyng[4] to speke of this trouble,[ii] after Lereano had aunswered Persius' letter, the kynge, knowyng *the* covena[n]t of this batayll, assuryd° [E8v] the feld, assyngned° out the place where the batayll shuld be determyned°, & all thynges necessary was ordeyned that perteyned to suche deades, accordynge to the custome of Macedonia[5]. [iii] And on a day *the* kyng went to his stage and the knyghtes came in to the felde, eche of them accompanyd as they were favoured and as they hadde deserved.[iv] Savyng the equalnes of bothe pertyes'° honours, they were lyke brought in to the felde.[6] So they (after theyr reverence done to the kyng) ranne eche at other, so that by the force of theyr strookes they shewed the vertue of theyr hartes. And theyr speres broken at theyr fyrste encounter, then they dr[e]we[7] o[u]t[8] theyr swordes and fought so fercely that it was mervayll° to behold theyr deades and compassyon for that they sufferyd. [v] [9] And to be brefe in this history°, Lereano in gyvynge his hevy° strokes, at a stroke strake of Persyus' ryght hande so that it fell to the erth, sworde and all. [vi] When [F1r] Lereano saw how that Persyo had lost *the* best parte of his defence, sayde: "Persyo to th'entent that thy lyfe pay not his duetye for thy falseyes, reny[10]° that thou haste sayd."[vii] Then Persyo sayde: "Do as thou oughtest to do. Though myne arme fayle me to defende, yet my harte faylyth not to dye." Lereano, heryng *that* aunswere, preasyd° to hym and gave hym many sharpe & hevy° strokes.[viii] And when Persyus' frendes sawe hym in jeoperdy° of his lyfe, they requyryd° the kyng to caste downe his batone, assurynge° hym that Persyo shuld be brought forth to abyde suche jugement as it shuld please hym yf he were found culpable and gyltye.[ix] [11] To the which requeste the kyng condiscendyd°.[x] & so they were depertyd°, wher with Lereano was sore° agrevyd & not withoute good reasone, for he hadde great mervayll° why the kyng delte so with hym.[xi] Then they were conveyede oute of the feld with lyke seremonyes, how be it, they were not lyke

---

[1]] 2 3 *the*
[2] chaungeable] 1 chaungeale
[3] she] 2 3 Omitted.
[4] levyng] 1 *leuig*
[5] Macedonia] 2 3 *that countree*
[6]] Marginal note 2 *the daye of the battaill* 3 *the day of the battayl*
[7] drewe] 1 *drwe*
[8] out] 2 3 Omitted.
[9]] Marginal note 2 *The batayll* 3 *The batayle*
[10] reny] 3 *denye*
[11]] Marginal note 2 3 *The request of Persio's frendes*

in fame° & [F1v] honour.ˣⁱⁱ So they were brought to theyr lodgynges, and there taryed all nyght.ˣⁱⁱⁱ The next day in the mornyng, Lereano determynyd° to go to *the* palace¹² to desyre° the kyng in presence of all his courte to restore his honour & to do upon Persio ryghtwyse° justyce. ˣⁱᵛ But Persyo, who was malycyous of his condicion and sharpe wyttyd, to th'entent *that* he myght by some meanes attayn to his purpose, whyls *that* Lereano spake *with* the kyng, he callyd to hym .iii. false men lyke to his own condicions & toke theyr othe¹³ that they¹⁴ shuld shew° them.ˣᵛ To *the* which they agreyd.¹⁵ Then he gave to them moche money so that they shuld say and swere to the kyng that they had sene Lereano spekyng *with* Laureola in places suspect° and in tyme dyshonest, which they proferyd to afferme and to swere it to the lesyng° of theyr lyves. I leve to speke of the doloure that Laureola sufferyd, bycause the passyon° shuld not trouble so my wytte°, but that I myght make an [F2r] ende of *that* I have begonne. For I have no lesse payne to remember her sorowe beyng absent then as thought¹⁶ I were present and saw it with myne eyen°.ˣᵛⁱ But I wyll torne to Lereano, who had more sorow for her prysonement° then glory of his victory.ˣᵛⁱⁱ When he knew that the kyng was ryson°, he went to the palayce, & in the presence of the knyghtes of the courte he sayd to the kyng as folowith.ˣᵛⁱⁱⁱ

XXII: Lereano to the kyng

Sir, of ¹ suertie° with better wyll I wold° have sufferyd the chastisement of your justice then *the* shame to have come to your presence if I had not atteygned yesterday the better of the batayll.² The which, yf ye had taken well, I shulde have bene clene° quyte° & delyveryde fro° the false accusacion of Persyo.ⁱ For in the syght of every man I shuld have gyven hym the rewarde that he deservyd.ⁱⁱ It is great dyfference to have power to do a thynge, and to do it in deade. ⁱⁱⁱ Great avauntage ye shewyd [F2v] hym. *The* reason why I can nother° thynke nor imagine, ye commaundyde to desperte°³ us, and specially syn°⁴ our debate tochyd° your selfe so nere as he that shuld desyre to be revengyd for the love of Laureola lyke a pytefull

---

¹² palace] 2 3 *place*
¹³ othe] 2 3 *for*
¹⁴ they] 2 3 *he*
¹⁵] Marginal note 2 3 *A further conspiracio*n
¹⁶ thought] 2 3 *though*

---

¹] 3 *a*
²] Marginal note 2 3 *Leriano oratour to the kynge*
³ desperte] 2 *departe* 3 *depart*
⁴ syn] 2 3 *syns*

father.^{iv} And I beleve well that as now ye be well satysfied of her d[is]charge°⁵ and ignorance°. And, Syr, yf ye dyd it for compassion ye hadde of Persyo, ye ought as justely to have regardyd myne honour as well as his lyfe, seyng° I ame your naturall° subget. And yf ye dyd i[t]⁶ by reasone of the inportunate° suet° of some of his frendes, ye ought as well to have remembryde the servyce that I & myne have done you, syn°⁷ ye know *with* what constauce of hart many of them in dyverce bateyls have loste in your servyce theyr lyves, which none of them have done the .iii. parte.ᵛ Therfore, Syr, I requyre° you that by [ju]stice⁸ ye wyll satysfye the honour that I have wonne *with* my handes.ᵛⁱ ⁹ Syr, kepe your lawes if ye thynke to conserve [F3r] your naturall° subjettes nor, Syr, consent not that so false a man shuld lyve that kepith so evyll pre-emynence of his predecessours, to the entent that his venyme do not corrupte them that be his parte takers°. ᵛⁱⁱ Certaynly I ame culpable in no thyng, but in that I have bene so good a frende to my wrongfull accuser.ᵛⁱⁱⁱ And if for this I have deserved payne, lette me have it, yet my clere° innocency° shall assoyll° me. I have conservyde his amyte°, belevyng he had bene good, and not judgyng his evyll nor falsenes.ⁱˣ If ye suffre hym to serve you, I say he shal be the beste¹⁰ servaunt to make dyscorde and lyes that shal be in all your courte.ˣ Syr, remember in your selfe how ye be bounde to do ryght to evry man. Wherfore determyne° this cause with prudence, and gyve sentence with your acustomed justice.ˣⁱ Syr, the thynges of honour ought to be clere°, and if ye perdone hym for any request though yt be by the pryncipall of your [F3v] realme, or for any other thyng at your pleasur, I wyll not then abyde *the* judgement of dyverce of your me*n* to be taken as clene dyscharged°.ˣⁱⁱ ¹¹ For thought¹² some beleve the trouth by reasone, yet some wyl be troubelyd and say the worste. And though in all¹³ your realme the trouth be not knowen, yet comenly the fame° of the trouth by reasone of ¹⁴ f[a]vour[e]¹⁵ of the partye wyll not be borne farre of, so *that* I can not be clene dyscharged° out of all mennys° fantasyes° yf this man scape° withoute open punysheme*nt*.ˣⁱⁱⁱ Syr, for Godde's sake, sette myne honour with oute any dysputacion°, & as for my lyfe ordeyne at your pleysour.

---

⁵ discharge] 1 *dycharge*

⁶ it] 1 *is*

⁷ syn] 2 *syns* 3 *synce*

⁸ justice] 1 *uistice*

⁹] Marginal note 2 3 *Lerian's request*

¹⁰ beste] 2 3 *metest*

¹¹] Marginal note 2 *The dyversyte of men judging jugment* 3 *The dyversyte of men judg-yng judgme*n*t*

¹² thought] 2 3 *though*

¹³ all] 2 3 Omitted.

¹⁴] 2 3 *the*

¹⁵ favour] 1 *fovour*

XXIII: The auctor

To the sayng° of Lereano the kyng gave good entent° and aunswered that he wold° take counsayll what was best to do, and sayde that in suche a case° delybercion wold° be taken or° any sentence shuld be gyvyn.[i] [1] Of trouth, the kynge's aunswere was not so swete as [F4r] it ought to have ben. For by that I saw, yf the kyng hadde put Laureola at her lybertie, Lereano hadde enduryde no trouble, for he thought to serve her.[ii] For all *that*, he was reputyd° culpable, though his entent were clere° withoute faulte. Thus, the kyng, to eschewe the rumour° and besynes° that was lykely to fall bytwene Lereano's frendes & Persius', commaundyd Lereano to go to a towne of his owne, a .ii. leages fro° *the* court, call[ed][2] Susa, and there to tary tyll he had set a dyrection° in *the* mater.[iii] The which Lereano dyde with a joyful hart, thynkyng that Laureola was clerely dyschargyd°, whiche was *the* thyng he mooste desiryd.[3] But then Persyo, who alwayes travelyde° to offend and to shame his honour and to defende it by malyce, he sente for .ii. of his complyses° or° Laureola was delyverede.[iv] And sayde to them that eche of them a parte shulde go to the kyng, and of them selfe to shew° hym how that the accusacion of Persio was [F4v] trew, and to bere wytnes that they had seen Lereano dyverce tymes speke with Laureola aloone suspyciously.[v] The which wytnes and affyrmacion°, whe[n] the kyng hard it, he was sore° trowbelyd therwith, and examynyd eche of them a parte by subtyle° and sharpe perswasions° to se yf they any thyng swarvyd° in ther sayenges°.[vi] But they were such persons that if a man shulde have wastyde all his lyfe in falsenes, coulde not be lyke them.[4] They were so sure of theyr wordes, the more they were examynyde the surelyer° they fortefyed theyr false lyes, so that therby the kyng gave to theyr false sayenges fayth and beleve. And by reasone of theyr informacion, *the* kyng reputyd° Persyo for trew servant and belevyd that it was more by reasone of his fortune, rather then by his untr[e]w[e][5] quarell that he lost the batayll.[6] O Persyo, better it hadde ben for the to have sufferyd the deth at one tyme, then to deserve so many de[a]th[s]![7] So the kyng in [F5r] purpose° to punysh *the* innocensy° of Laureola, by reasone of the treasone of the false wytnes, ordeynyd° *that* his doughter, Laureola, shuld have the sentence of justyce.[8] The whiche, when it came to the knowledge of Lereano,

---

[1]] Marginal note 2 *The reporte of the kynge's answere* 3 *The reporte of the kynge's aunswere*

[2] called] 1 *callyh*

[3]] Marginal note 2 3 *The examinacion of the fourthe accusacion*

[4]] Marginal note 2 *The examinacions of the wytnes* 3 *The examynacions of the wytnes*

[5] untrewe] 1 *untrw*

[6]] Marginal note 2 3 *The judgement*

[7] deaths] 1 *dethe* 3 *deathes*

[8]] Marginal note 2 *The kingy's order of Laureola* 3 *The kynge's order of Laureola*

he was therwith nere oute of his wytte°. And with great fury and passion° des-
perate°, determynyde° to go to the courte to delyver Laureola and to slee Persyo,
or els to lese his owne lyfe in the quarell. And when I saw hym wyllyng to folow
that fantasye°, wherin was more perell then hope, then I desyryd° hym to worke
sagely. vii And so by reasone of the alterasyon° that he was in, he was in a great
perplexite. 9 And when I saw hym stande in suche a dysmayde trance, I thought
then to serve hym with my counsayll, to th'entent he shuld not do that thyng in
haste wherby to repent hym after.viii And consyderynge the way that I tho[u]ght
moste sure, I sayd to hym thus. [F5v]

XXIV: The auctor to Lereano

Sir, I desyre° you to be dyscrete° to th'entent that I may prayse your wytte°, that
ye¹ may so deale° to remedy° your evyll°, that ye may be joyfull as I desyre and
praysed as ye deserve.² This I say for the sage pacience that thou shuldest shew
in the tyme of thyne adversyte. For though I se well *that* thyne understandyng°
be occupyed *with* passion, yet thou shuldest consyder what thou wylt do and with
what dyscrete° knowledge. Thou shuldest rather folow my symple° counsayll,
then to put to execucion thy foresayde° wyll. Thus, thou shuldest do by thyne
owne naturall intysemente°. Moche have I studyed on that thou oughtest to do in
this thy greate fortune, and accordyng to my power°³ judgement, the fyrst thyng
to accomplysh it for the, to take reste, the lack therof trowbleth the in thy⁴ present case°.ⁱ And after myne opynion thy fyrste determynacion° shal be the laste
to put to execucion, for as thyne enterprice is [F6r] great and weyghty, accordyng therto, demuer° delyberacion shulde be determynyde or° yt were executyd
all wayes in a thyng doughtfull the most surest way wolde° be taken. And yf thou
be disposede to slee Persyo, or to delyver Laureola, fyrste thou muste⁵ consyder
by what wayes thou mayste do it & skape° away with both your honours, for her
honour is more to be estemyd then the⁶ lyfe. For yf thou canste° not accomplyshe

---

⁹] Marginal note 2 *The advysement of the auctor to the partie* 3 *The advisemente of* the
auctor to the parti

---

¹ ye] 2 3 *I*
²] Marginal note 2 *The hole counseyle to delyver Laureola* 3 *The hole counsel to deliver*
Lauriola
³ power] 2 3 *pore*
⁴ thy] 2 *this* 3 *thys*
⁵ muste] 2 3 Omitted.
⁶ the] 2 3 *thy*

thyne enterpryce, thou shalte leve her con̄dempnyd, and thy selfe dyshonouryd. Thou knowyst that men workyth and fortune judgith, and if thynges passe well then they be praysed.[ii] Yf they fortune° evyll, then they be dyspraysed and taken for evyll.[iii] If *thou* delyver Laureola thou shalt be callyde valyant, yf thou assay and fayle then *thou* shalt be reputyd° a fole°.[7] Tary here a .ix. dayes, for then shal be *the* execusion̄ of the sentence agaynst Laureola. In the meane seasone° let us prove° & assay all other remedyes° that [F6v] any hope is in.[iv] And if we fynde no remedy° in that, then execute thyne entent. Though thou lese° thy lyfe therby, yet it shal be to thyne honour and fame°.[v] One thynge thou shuldeste provyde° for or° thou begynne. I putte case° thou haddeste now broken the prisone, & taken oute therof La[u]reola, and caryed her away into thyne owne lande, yet she shulde be condempnyd and reputyd° culpable, and wher so ever thou shuldest sette her yet she shuld suffre payne, the which then shuld be gretter evyll° then *the* fyrst.[8] Therfore the best way, as semeth me, is to do after this maner. I wyll go in thy name to Galleo, brother to the quene, who for parte° desyreth *the* delyverance of Laureola as moche as thy selfe doste°.[vi] And I shall shewe° hym what is thyne entent and desyre° hym (to the entente he sholde bere no charge° nor blame) that he wold° be redy with a certayn number of men the same day that thou shuldest do thyne enterpryce. That [F7r] yf thou fortune° to gette Laureola oute of prisone, then to put her in to his handes in the presence of evry man, in wytnes of his ignorance° and of thy clennes°.[vii] And so he to receyve her tyll the kyng have provyd the trouth in everythyng, and to kepe her in his castell°, wherby this busines may come to a good ende.[viii] But, as I have sayde, this way muste be *the* laste shote ancre°. Therfore, fyrste I wyll go to the court and speke with the cardynall of Gaula and w*ith* other lordes & prelates that I can fynde ther.[ix] And I shall desyre° them to speke to *the* kyng, desyryng° hym to grant Laureola her lyfe.[x] And yf we fynde no remedy° in this, then I wyll desire° the quene that she, with all other ladyes & honest women of her courte and of the citie, to go to the kyng and desyre° perdone for her doughter.[xi] To whose wepynges and peticions, I can not beleve that pitie shal be denyed. And yet if that can not avayll, then I shall cause Laureola [F7v] to wryte to the kyng, her father, certyfyeng° hym of her innocency°. And if all these wayes wyll not serve, then shall I offre to the kyng that thou shalt fynde a persone that shall do deades of armes agaynst those .iii. false witnesses. And if none of these wayes can preuvyll°, then prove thy strength, and therby peradventure° thou shalte fynde *the* pitie in the kynge that thou sekeste for. But yet, or° I deperte, me thynkyth *thou* shuldest wryte to Laureola in strengthyng° of her

---

[7]] Marginal note 2 *The tyme of respyte of the custome of the countre* 3 *The tyme of respyte of the custum of the countre*

[8]] Marginal note 2 *the worste alwayes is to be noted & advoided* 3 *the worst alwayes is to be noted & advoided*

feare with suertye° of her lyfe.[xii] The whiche thou mayste well do. Syn°[9] hevyn dysposith that is wrought upon the erthe, it can be none° other wyse° but that God wyll receyve *the* wepynges[10] of innocentes and thy juste petycions.[xiii]

XXV: The auctor

So Lereano swarvyde° no poynt fro° myne advyse bycause he thought it the moste sure way for the expedicion° of his purpose°.[i] Howbeit his harte was not sure, for he [F8r] doughtyd lest the kyng in his ire shuld have gyven sentence upon Laureola or° the day came. How be it, by the lawes of the lande she shulde have .ix. dayes respyght.[ii] Though his harte fearyd this it was no mervaill°, for they that be true lovers all *that* is contrary to them they lightely° beleve it, and that they desyre most they[1] thinke them selfe therof[2] most uncertayne. How be it he concludyd to write to Laureola with greate dought that she wold° not recyve his letter. The tenour wherof was as folowith.

XXVI: The letter of Lereano to Laureola

Rather wolde° I put my handes to rydde myne owne life then to begyn to write yf I knewe that my workes were cause of your prisone as moch as myne evyll fortune is. *The* which is to me so[1] contrary *that* it can not cause me to dye well wi*th*oute° I may save you.[i] The whiche I purpose° to do. And if I dye in that quarell ye shal be delyveryd [F8v] quite° oute of presone, and then I clene rydde fro° all my mysadventures°. And so the deth of one shal be cause of .ii. liberties. I requyre° you, take me not as your enemy for any thing that ye suffre syn°[2] my merites° are nat the cause, but rather it is myne evell fortune. And ye may well beleve that though your dolours be never so great, yet I fele more torment in *the* thinkyng upon them then ye do in the suffrynge. Wolde° to God that I hadde never knowen you! And yet therby I shulde have lost the sight of you, the which to me is the gretest welth° of this worlde. I shulde have ben ryght happy° and I hadde never sene nor harde

---

[9] syn] 2 *syns* 3 *since*
[10] wepynges] 3 *weping*

---

[1] they] 2 3 Omitted.
[2] therof] 3 *therfore*

---

[1] so] 2 3 Omitted.
[2] syn] 2 *syns* 3 *synce*

of the dolour that ye suffre. And I ame so accustumyd to lyve in hevynes° that I ame fayne to take counsaill for your cause. But in the payne *that* I fele now I take no counsayl, nor I have no rest, nor my harte can not be quyt° for the payne that ye suffre.[ii] Feare not the deth, for my propre° handes shal [G1r] save you therfro. I shall serche all the remedies that I cane fynde to apeace° *the* kynge's ire.[iii] And if *they* faylle, trust in me that for your liberte I shall deale in such wyse° that as long as the world endureth there shal be ³ remembrance° and ensample° of hardy valiantnes°.[iv] For this that I say is no great thyng to be done, for besilde° your excellent valeure ⁴ the cruell justice of your presone causeth my hardynes°.[v] Who can resist my strength syn°⁵ I have it by your meanes? What thing is it that the harte dare not enterprice, your beaute⁶ being fixed therin? Ther is allonely° but one evyll° in your salvasion, the which may be bought *with* an easy° pryce accordyng to your deserte°. That is losynge of my lyfe. And though I so do, it is but⁷ a smalle losse so it may delyver you.[vi] With my good hope strengh° your feblenes. For and ye shuld sette your thoughtes upon al jeoperdes° ye myght sone therby ende your life, wherby .ii. greate inconvenientes° shuld [G1v] ensue.[vii] The fyrst and principall is your deth. The .ii. is I shuld the*n* be prevatyd° fro° the gretest honour that any man myght have, as in that I shulde not then save you.⁸ [viii] Lady, beleve in my wordes and trust my promyse. Do not as some other women do, to take great feare for a small cause. If your femynyne condycion accuse° you with feare, then lete your discrecion° strength you agayne, which ye may well do by myne assurance and bycause this that I say shal be wel provyd. [ix] Therfore, I requyre° you, beleve me. I wryte not to you at length as I wold° do, but I shall prove° to further your lyfe.

XXVII: The auctor

Whyle Lereano wrote his letter I made me redy to deperte. And receyvyd his letter and made all the dylygence° that I coulde, tyll I came to the courte and dyd my devour° that in me was to have spoken with Laureola, to have gyven her some comeforte, but [G2r] I was denyed to se her. Then I was enfourmyde of the chamber wher she laye, wher was a wyndow with a great¹ grate of irone. [i] And

---

³] 2 3 *a*

⁴ your excellent valeure] 2 *the valewe of your excellence* 3 *the valewe of your excelence*

⁵ syn] 2 *syns* 3 *synce*

⁶ beaute] 2 *baute* 3 *bate*

⁷ but] 2 3 Omitted.

⁸] Marginal note 2 3 *A comforte of delyveraunce*

---

¹ great] 2 3 Omitted.

at nyghte I came thyther°, & wrappyd° the letter together and sette it on a spere poynte. & so with moche travaill° I dyd cast the letter in at the wyndowe in to her chamber.[ii] And *the* next mornyng I came thyder° agayne and saw the wyndow open. And I saw wher Laureola stode, but the latyse was so thycke *that* I cowlde have no perfyght syght of her.[iii] Fynally, I aprochyd nerer to the wyndowe. And when she saw me marchyng° for by *the* wyndowe she cast sodenly oute a letter withoute spekyng of any worde bycause of the prease° that was nere hande. And as I was goyng away, she sayd: "Take there the reward of the pite that I have shewed." And bycause her kepers were nere aboute her I durst° make none° aunswere. But her wordes dyd put me in to suche passion°, that who so hadde folowyd me by the [G2v] trace of my wepynge myght well have found me out. The tenour of her letter folowith.

XXVIII: Laureola's letter to Lerea[no] [1]

I can not tell the, Lereano, how to aunswer. And where as every man lawdith° pite and reputith° it for a vertue, and in me it is taken for a vice and accordyng therto I ame chastysed. I do as I ought to do accordynge to pitie & I have as I deserve accordyng to my[2] mysfortune, for surely thy fortune nor thy workes is no cause of my presone. Nor I complayne not of the nor of none° other persone lyvynge, but alonely° upon my selfe, who to kepe the fro° the deth charge° my selfe culpable. Howbeit, this compassyon that I have of the is more paynefull then charge°.[i] I do remedy° as innocent, and yet I ame punyshed as culpable. How be it, moche more pleasyth me this presone beynge withoute errour, then to be at liberte & infectyd ther *with.* And though yt be paynefull to suffre, yet I ame [G3r] easyd agayne that I have not deservyd it. I ame she that amonge all lyvynge creatours° ought leste° to lyve. Without° the kynge save me I hope uppon no thinge but deth. For yf thou delyver me, or any of thyne in what so ever maner it[3] be, I shal be dolorous. And yf thou do not remedye° me, I ame sure to dye. And yf thou delyver me and take me awaye, I shal be condempned as culpable. Therfore I requyre° the to travayll° to save myne honoure and fame° rather then myne[4] lyfe, for the one muste ende and the other wyll endure.[ii] As I have sayde, serche to apeace° the furour of the kynge, my father, for otherwyse I can not be saved without the destruction of myne honour. How be it, I remytte all to thy good counsayle and ad[v]yse.[iii] Thy wysdome can chose the beste waye.[iv] Thou mayste se the rewarde that I have for the favoure that I have shewed the. I ame put in prisone where as murderers were wonte° to be

---

[1] Lereano] 1 *Lerea* 2 3 *Leriano*
[2] my] 3 Omitted.
[3] it] 3 Omitted.
[4] myne] 2 3 *my*

kepte [G3v] and I ame tyed with cheynes°.ᵛ And with sharpe° tormentes, my tendre flesshe is tormented.ᵛⁱ And with force of armes I ame kepte, as though I hadde
the force and power to skape° awaye.ᵛⁱⁱ Thus delicate is my sufferynge and my
paynes so cruell that besyde *the* sentence of deth my father myght otherwyse have
take*n*⁵ vengeance upon me then to suffre me to dye i[n] this cruell priso*n*.ᵛⁱⁱⁱ I have
great mervayle° how of suche a cruell father shulde issue so pacyente° a doughter.
Yf I shulde be lyke hym in condicion, I shulde not feare his justice syn°⁶ he wyll
do it ⁷ unjustely. As to that touched Persio, I wyll make none° aunswer bycause I
wyll not defyle° my tongue as he hath done my fame° and renowne. I had rather
he wolde° revoke and denye his wordes that he hath sayde rather then he shuld dye
for them. But what so ever⁸ I say, determyne thy selfe as thou lyste°. Thou mayest
not erre in that thou wylte do.ⁱˣ [G4r]

XXIX: The Auctour

Ryghte dowtious° I was when I hadde receyved and redde the letter sent fro° Laureola to Lereano, whether I shulde sende it to Lereano or els kepe it styll till I
we[n]t my selfe. As last I determyned° not to sende it for two consyderacyons and
inconveniences°. The one was I feared to put our secretes in perell of discoveryng
by reason of puttyng truste of any meane° messenger.¹ The other was for feare
lest the trouble° that the letter shulde put hym unto shulde cause hym to execute
his purpose in hast before the tyme agreed betwene hym and me, and therby all
myghte have ben lost. So to tourne to my fyrst purpose, the fyrst day I came to
the courte I proved° and tempted° the wylles of suche as I thought wolde° be of
our opinion and as² I fou*n*d none of the contrary desyre, savynge° the frendes
of Persio, to whom me thoughte it but a foly to speake.ⁱ And then I went to the
[G4v] cardynall and desyred° hym *that* it wolde° please hym to make supplicacion
to the king for the life of his doughter, Laureola. The which he grauntyd to do
with no lesse love and compassion then I desyred° it. And so incontinent°, w*ith*
dyvers other prelates and greate lordes together, they wente to the kyng. Then
the cardynall in hys owne name, and in all theyrs, sayd to the kinge as folowith.

---

⁵ take*n*] 2 3 *take*
⁶ syn] 2 *syns* 3 *synce*
⁷] 2 3 *so*
⁸ ever] 2 3 Omitted.

---

¹] Marginal note 2 *her adnisement* 3 *her advisemente*
² as] 2 3 Omitted.

XXX: The cardynall to the kinge [1]

Syr, it is not without reason that noble princes in tyme past ordyned° theyr counsaillors to ordre by them what was to be done wherby they found great profytte.[i] [ii] And though counsaill were stablished° for many goode causes, yet I fynde .vi. reasones that the same[2] law ought to be observed.[iii] [3] The fyrst is bycause that men may moche better order other men's maters rather then theyr owne. For the harte of hym that the mater tochyth° can not be with oute some ire, covetesnes°, affection or [G5r] desire, or some other lyke condicion, so that he shall not determyne° the cause as he ought to do. [4] The .ii. is when maters be pleatyd° and arguyd, the traugth° is the better knowen.[5] The .iii. yf the[6] counsaylours[7] ordeyne° justly and bryng the mater well to passe, the glory and honour is to them that folowyth suche counsayll.[iv] [8] The .iiii. is yf by another manne's counsayll the besynes fayleth and takyth none°[9] effecte, yet he that demaundeth° the counsayll is oute of blame & charge° and they that gave the counsayll muste bere the charge° & faulte.[v] [10] The .v. ys bycause good counsayl often tymes assuryth° thynges that be do[ubt]ous[11].[12] The .vi. is yf a man be fa[u]len in evyl fortune, yet in all adversites good counsayll putteth the pertye° in good hope. [13] Certaynely, Syr, it is but a blynde counsayll° a man to counsayll hym selfe knowynge hym selfe in any furour or passion. Therfore, Syr, blame us not though in the fercenes° of your [G5v] ire we be come to trouble you. For we hadde rather that ye shulde in your ire reprehende us for our comynge to you, then that after ye shulde repent you and condempe us bycause we gave you no counsayll. Syr, thynges done by good deliberacyon and accord procurith profyt and prayse to them that so doth.[vi] And thynges done in hast & with fury, repentance must make amendes. Suche wyse and noble men as ye be when they shulde do any warke, fyrst they shulde determyne° or° they dyspose as well in thynges present, as in thynges to come, and as well in those thy[n]ges that they hope to have profyte by, as in those

---

[1]] 2 3 *for Laureola's lyfe & delyveraunce*

[2] same] 2 3 Omitted.

[3]] Marginal note 2 *vi reasons that counsayl shold be taken* 3 *By treason that counsayl should be taken*

[4]] Marginal note 2 *The firste reson* 3 *The first reson*

[5]] Marginal note 2 *The seconde reson* 3 *The ii. reason*

[6] the] 3 *those*

[7] counsaylours] 3 *unsailours*

[8]] Marginal note 2 3 *The .iii. reason*

[9] none] 3 *no*

[10]] Marginal note *The .iiii. reason*

[11] doubtious] 1 *dotious* 3 *doughteous*

[12]] Marginal note 2 *The .v. reason* 3 *The fyft reason*

[13]] Marginal note 2 *The .vi. reason* 3 *The syxt reason*

thynges that they feare the contrary. And if they fynde them selfe troublyde with any passion°, tyll they be cleryd therfro they shulde gyve no sentence. And yf they debate and delaye ther deades, then they do well. For in all suche weighty maters hast is daungerouse and tariynge is suretie°.vii A wyse [G6r] man that wyl do j[u]stly must thynke on all these thynges, and or° he do anythyng folow reasone and establish the execucion honestly.viii It is the properte° of them that be discrete° to prove° theyr counsailours and not to determyne° upon a lyght° credence°.ix And there as a thyng [s]emyth¹⁴ do[u]btefull holde then the sentence in balance, for all thynges ys not of trouthe that semyth to be true.x The thought of the wyse man now agreeth, & and¹⁵ now demaundeth°, and now ordeyn°, and all wayes cast° in his minde what may fall, and be jelous of his fame, and kepe hym selfe fro erryng. And for feare of fallynge therin wyll remember that is past and take the best therof and ordeyne° for the tyme present with atemperance°, and to remember° what is to come, and in all these to take avysemente°.xi ¹⁶ Syr, all this that we have sayd is that ye shulde remember your wysdome and ordeyne° your deades, not furyously, but lyke a wyse man and [G6v] torne the force of your natural wysdome against the accydent° of your ire. Syr, we have knowledge that ye wyll condemne your doughter, Laureola, to deth yf her¹⁷ bountie° and goodnes have not deservyde ¹⁸ to be justyfyde.xii Then¹⁹ of trouthe, ye are not²⁰ ryghtwyse° judge. Never²¹ trouble your gloryous fame *with* suche a judgement.²² And we put case°, though²³ she had deserved this punyshement, yet in your so doyng ye shal be defamyde and reputyde° rather for a cruell father then a ryghtwyse° kynge.²⁴ Ye gyve credence to .iii. evyll men & of shamefull conversacion°.xiii Certaynly as good reasone hadde it bene to have shortyd° theyr lyves as to have gyven credence to theyr wytnes.xiv They be men sore° defamyd in your courte for they conferme° them selfe to all iniquite.xv They glorifye them selfe in theyr false reasones makyng & in the begylynges²⁵ that they make. And, Syr, why gyve you more fayth to theyr informacion rather [G7r] then to *the* judgemente of God, the which was clerely sene in the batayll bytwene Persio & Lereano? Be not the sheder of your owne blodde, for then of all men ye shal be dyspraised and dispysed. Blame

---

¹⁴ semyth] 1 *femyth* 3 *semeth*

¹⁵ and] 2 3 Omitted.

¹⁶] Margnal note 2 *The wise man's thought* 3 *The wise manne's thought*

¹⁷ yf her] 2 3 *which*

¹⁸] 2 3 *nor she ought not*

¹⁹ Then] 2 3 *Therefore*

²⁰ not] 2 3 *no*

²¹ never] 2 3 *to*

²²] Marginal note 2 *The excedynge to the matter* 3 *The exce kynge to the matter*

²³ though] 2 3 Omitted.

²⁴] Marginal note 2 *Excepton to the wytnessis* 3 *Excepcyon to the wytnesses*

²⁵ begylynges] 2 *begynnyngs* 3 *beginninges*

not the innocent for the counsayll of the envyous. And yf ye thynke that for all the reasons that we have sayde that Laureola ought not to be savyd, yet for that ye ought to do for vertue & bycause ye be bound of your royalnes²⁶. For the service that we have done you, in our most humble wyse°, we requyre° you to have mercy of her lyfe.ˣᵛⁱ And bycause that fewer wordes then we have spoken shuld suffice to your clemency to converte you to pytie, therfore we wyll saye no more, but that ye²⁷ wyll remember how moche better it is that your ire shuld peryshe rather then your noble fame°.ˣᵛⁱⁱ

XXXI: The kynge's aunswere ¹

Syrs, I repute° me well counsaylyd by you if I were not more bound [G7v] to punyshe then to perdone. Ye nede not shew° me the reasone how that great prynces ought to receyve² conusayll, as in that and in other thynges that ye have shewed°, I knew them ryght well. But ye know well, when the harte is chargyd° with passione° then is it locked fro° herynge of any counsayle. And in *that* tyme, the fruteful wordes, to mytigate the passion° of ire, causeth it the sorer° to encrease, bringing to the memory the cause therof.ⁱ Wherfore I say yf I were quyte° for°³ the⁴ unpedyment°, I thynke then I shuld dispose° and ordeyn° sagely for the deth of Laureola, the whiche I will shewe° she hathe deservyd by just causes, determyned° acordyng to honour and justice. And yf her errour shulde be lefte unpunnisshed, I shulde then be no lesse culpable then Lereano.ⁱⁱ As tochyng my dishonour and shame, yf it were publisshed° that I shulde perdone such a case, of my neigbours I shuld be dispraised, and of myne owne subgettes [G8r] disobeyed and of every man smally estemed.ⁱⁱⁱ And also I might well be accused *that* I have evil conserved the generosite° of my predecessours. And this faulte myght be so far exstemed° that it might spotte° & defowle° the fame of myne auncettours° passed, & blemysh *the* honour of them that be present, and steyne *the* blud of them that be to come, for one spotte° in our lignage° myght confounde all our generacion°.⁵ The perdonynge of Laureola shuld be cause of other great evils°, the whiche shulde folow by reason of my perdonyng. Wherfore I hadde rather to

---

²⁶ royalnes] 2 3 *Royalmes*
²⁷ ye] 3 Omitted.

---

¹] 2 *to his counseylloures* 3 *to his counselours*
² receyve] 3 *perceave*
³ for] 2 3 *fro*
⁴ the] 3 *that*
⁵] Marginal note 2 *The honour of the blod is to be estemed* 3 *The honoure of the blod is to be estemed*

cause feare by reasone of my crueltie, then to cause boldnes to do evil by reasone of my pitie. And in my so doing I shal be estemed as a kinge ought to be, by reason of doing justice.^iv 6 Beholde how many reasons there be that sh[ul]de^7 lede° *that* she ought to have sentence. Ye knowe well our lawes hath stablisshed° that a woman accused in such ca[u]ses shuld suffre deth, and ye se well how [G8v] it were better for me to be called a kyng in mynystrynge° justice then to perdone the culpable.^v And it ought well to be noted *that* in stede of conser[v]yng the lawe, if I do breke it my selfe, *the* whiche I ought not to do, then I co*n*demne my self. ^vi The righte waye oughte equally to be kept & observed, for the hart of a juge ought not to be movede for favoure, for love, nor covetyse°, nor for^8 none° other accide*nt*°.^vii Folowing the^9 right justyce is laudable, and yf it be favourable° then it is abhorred.^viii 10 Justice ought never to go oute of° the ryght way syne°^11 it is cause of so moche goodnes.^12 It ca[u]sith feare to them that be evyll and it susteynyth them that be goode. It pacefyeth all differences, it determynyth° al questions, it expelith all stryves° and contensions, &^13 it agreith all debates. It assurith° the wayes°, it honourith the people, it favourith the small° people and of base condicion, it bridilith the myghty men and to the comon weale it is ryght profytable. ^ix [H1r] Then to conserve such a welthe°, and that the lawes susteynyth it, it is ryght that I shuld use justice. Yf ye desire so moch^14 the helth of Laureola and prayse so moche her goodnesse, brynge forth one witnes of her innocensy° as I have .iii. to charge her. Then she shall be perdonyd with reasone and praysed with trouth. Also where as ye say that I shulde gyve faith to the judgemente of God as well as to the wytnes° of other men, it is no mervayll° though^15 I do not so, for I se the wytnes° certayne at myne eye. And as for the judgment is not yet endyd, for thoughe Lereano hadde the better of the batayll, we may judge the myddes° but we know not the ende.^x 16 I will not aunswere to al your alegasyons and sayenges° bycause I wyll make no longe proces° and at the ende sende you away without hope. I desire moche to accept your requestes bycause of your well deservyng therof, and if I do not, yet I requyre° yo[u] take [H1v] it for none° evyll° for ye ought no lesse to desyre the honour of the father then the salvacion of his doughter.

---

^6] Marginal note 2 *The indent is of pytie and cruelte* 3 *The indent is of pyty and crueltie*
^7 shulde] 1 *shlude* 3 *shuld*
^8 for] 2 3 Omitted.
^9 the] 2 3 Omitted.
^10] Marginal note 2 3 *The duty of a judge*
^11 syne] 2 *syns* 3 *synce*
^12] Marginal note 2 *The pyte of justcye* 3 *The pity of justice*
^13 &] 2 3 Omitted.
^14 the helth of Laureola and prayse so moche] 3 Omitted.
^15 though] 1 *thought* 3 *thoughe*
^16] Marginal note 2 *The ende is to be regardyd* 3 *The ende is to be regarded*

XXXII: The Auctor

The desperate° aunswere of *the* kyng was to the herers great hevynes°.[i] And when I saw that this remedy° was to me contrary then I sought for a nother way, trustyng that shulde be more profitable.[1] And *then* was I thought to go to the quene that she shuld desyre° the kyng for the salvacyo*n* of her doughter Laureola. So I wente to her, who was partaker° of her doughter's sorow, and I founde her in an hall aco*m*panyd with many noble ladyes and other who were suffycyente to have atteygnyde° theyr desyres, other juste or unjuste, though the m[att]er[2] hadde ben never so greate. Yet theyr desyres ought not to have ben refused bycause of *the* auctorite° of the quene, who knelyd downe and spake wordes to the kyng, as wel leyeng charge to hym for his ire as also wordes [H2r] of pitie to apeace° hym.[ii] And she shewed° hym the moderacyon that a kyng ought to have, and reprehendyd the percevera*n*ce of his ire. And shewyng° hym how he was a father, and allegyd reasones ryght dyscrete° to note and full of sorow, sayng that if he wolde° nedes° execute his cruell judgemente to do it rather upo*n* her selfe (seyeng° great parte of her yeres were passyd) then uppon Laureola in her yonge age, aprovyng° that by her owne deth the fame of the judge shulde be savyde, and the lyfe of her that is judgyd, and the mynd of the desyrer° fulfylled.[iii] [3] But the kynge styll was indurate° in his fyrst purpose°. All the quene's rasones could not serve, nor yet her bytter wepynges. And therwith the quene went in to her chamber with small strength, sore° wepyng and as redy to dye. And when I sawe that the quene could gette no grace of the kyng, I went to the kyng withoute any feare of his fersnes° and sayd how he ought [H2v] to gyve his sente*n*ce with clere° justice, for Lereano shulde fynde a man to fyght agaynst all those .iii. false wytnesses or elles to do it his owne proper° person and to pay them accordynge to theyr desertes[4]°, and then God shall shew where the ryght is.[iv] Then the kyng aunswered me that I shuld leve myne ambassade° for Lereano, sayeng how the heryng of his name encresyd his passyon° and ire. And when the quene knewe there was no remedy to save the lyfe of Laureola, she went to the prisone and kyssed her dyverce tymes, and sayde as folowith.

---

[1]] Marginal note 2 3 *Another remedye for to delyver Laureola*

[2] matter] 1 *mttaer*

[3]] Marginal note 2 *Note here the love of the mo*[ther] *toward the* [d]o[u]ghter 3 *Note here the love of the mother towarde the doughter*

[4] desertes] 2 3 *deserte*

XXXIII: The quene to Laureola[i]

O bountie°, by malice accusyd! O vertue, by ire condemnyd! O doughter, borne of thy mother to sorow! Thou shalte dye withoute justice and I must wepe by reason.[ii] [1] Thyne unhappe° hath more pusance° to condempne the then thyn innocency° to save the. Without the I shall lyve accompanyed with doloures, the whiche in thy stede thou [H3r] shalt leve me. Thy deth shal ende .ii. lyves, the one is thyne without cause, and myne by good reasone and ryght.[iii] To lyve after *thee* shuld be to me a sorer° deth then that thou shalte receve, for it is farre greatter tormente to desyre the deth then to suffre it. Wolde° to God thou myghtest[2] be called the doughter of the mother *that* shuld dye, rather then to be she *that* I shuld se dye. Of every man thou shalt be bewailed as long as the worlde endureth. All that of the have any knowledge wyll sette litle by this realme, *the* whiche thou shuldest enheryte accordyng to thy desertes°. For all that *thou* art fallen in to thy father's displeasour, yet all suche as knowith the[3] affyrmyth that there is none° in all this land that deserve thy merytes°.[iv] Suche as be blynde desyre to se *thee*, the dome° desyreth to speke with the, the powre[4]° and *the* ryche to serve *thee*.[v] All the world is wel content with the. *Thou* arte behatyd *with* no creature, but alonely° with Persio. Yf I may lyve a seasone° [H3v] he shall receve for his demerites° juste rewarde. And thouhe I have noone° other strength but to desyre his deth and to be revengyd of hym yf I coulde, the evill will I bere hym shuld then soone be utteryd.[vi] Yet this can not satysfye me, for I can not heale the dolour of the spotte° of the execucion of the vengeans.[vii] O my dere doughter, thy honesty hath provyd thy vertue! Why doth not the king gyve more credence to thy presence then to the wytnes of thy false enemyes? In thy wordes, deades and thoughtes, all wayes thou hast shewyd a vertuous harte. Why then shulde God suffre the to dye? I can fynde none° other cause but by reason of my synnes that I have commyttyd, rather then for any meryt° of thy ryghtwisnes[5]°. I wold° my deades myght be comparyd to thyne[6] innocency°.[7] Dere doughter, lyfte up thyne harte to hevyn! Take no sorow to leve that must nedes ende for that thyng that is permanent. I assure the [H4r] our Lord God wyll that thou shalt suffre as a marter, to th'entente *that* thou shalte joye in his beatitude.[viii] In me have none° other hope, but that and I were worthy to go thyther°, as thou arte suer° to go, I wolde° shortely bere the company. Thynkyst thou not that it is a harde trouble to me to remember how

---

[1]] Marginal note 2 3 *The quene's lamentacion for & to Laureola*
[2] myghtest] 2 3 *myght*
[3] the] 2 3 *and*
[4] powre] 2 3 *poore*
[5] ryghtwisnes] 2 *unrightwysnes* 3 *unryghtwysenes*
[6] thyne] 2 3 *thy*
[7]] Marginal note 2 3 *The token of vertue*

many supplicacions hathe ben made to the kynge for thy lyfe, and yet they can not obteyne.[ix] And at this houre, a sharpe knyfe may rydde and make an ende of thy lyfe and therby leve the father in faulte, and the mother in sorow, and the doughter withoute helthe° & the realme withoute an[8] herytour°. O the lanterne° of myne eyen°! I say to the these feareful wordes to the entent they shuld breke thyne harte a sonder°, for I hadde rather thou shuldeste dye in my power by sorow then to se the dye by justice. For though I shuld shede thy bludde, yet my handes shulde not be so cruell as is the condicion of thy father.[x] O virgyne [H4v] immaculate![xi] Syn°[9] I can not accomplysh my desyre, and that I muste [10] deperte fro° the, yet receyve the dolorous laste kyssynge and blyssyng° of thy sorowfull mother. And thus I wyll go fro° thy syght and fro° thy lyfe, & most desyring to go fro° myne owne lyfe.

XXXIV: The Auctor

When the quene hadde endyde her wordes she wolde° not abyde the aunswere of *the* innocent, her doughter, Laureola, bycause she wolde° not receyve doble sorow. Thus the quene, and suche lordes as were in her company, departed with the grettest lamentacions[1] that ever was made.[i] And when she came[2] in to her chamber she sent to Laureola a messenger advysing her to wryte to *the* kyng, her father, thynkyng that he wolde° take more compassion by reasone of her piteous wordes, rather then by the peticio[n]s of any other that travellyde° for her liberte.[3] Who, at the commaundement of her dolorous mother [H5r] toke penne and[4] inke [5] and wrote with greater turbacion° then hope of remedy°. [ii] Her letter specyfyed as folowith.

---

[8] an] 3 *any*
[9] syn] 2 *syns* 3 *since*
[10]] 3 *nedes*

---

[1] lamentacions] 2 3 *lamentacion*
[2] came] 3 *come*
[3]] Marginal note 2 *The quene's counceil to her doughter* 3 *The quene's council to her doughter*
[4] and] 2 3 Omitted.
[5]] 2 3 *and paper*

XXXV: The letter of Laureola to the kynge [i][1]

Dere father, I understande that ye have gyven sentence upon me to dye and that the terme of my lyfe shal be accomplyshede° within these .iii. dayes. & I knowe well the innocentes ought no lesse to feare theyr fortune then suche as be culpable to feare the lawe. And syn°[2] it is so that my mysfortune hath brought me in to this parell° that I ame in, and not for any defaute° that I have done, the which lyghtly° ye m[y]ght[3] [4] know[5] if the furour of your ire wolde° suffer you to se the trouth. Ye are not ignorante of the vertue that the auncyante° cronicles & historyes manyfestith° of the kynges and quenes fro° whome I do procede. Then why was I borne of suche a blodde that wyll byleve rather the false informasion then [H5v] the bounte° naturall? [6] Yf it pleace° you to slee me, for your pleasur ye may well do it, but as tochyng justice ye have no cause therto. The deth that ye will gyve me, though[7] I refuce° it for feare, yet by reasone of obedience I do consent therto, as she that lovyth better to dye[8] under your obedyence rather then to lyve in your dyspleasure. Howbeit, I requyre° you, or° ye determyne° take good advyse, for as sure as God is true I never dyd thyng to deserve to suffre any payne°. But Syr, I say to you, it is as convenient° the pitie of the father as the rygoure of justice. Withoute dought I desyre as well my lyfe because it tocheth° your honour so nere as I do bycause it perteyneth to my selfe, for at the ende I ame your doughter. Considre, Syr, whosoever usith crueltie serchith for his owne [9] perell. More surer it is to be belovyd for usynge of pitie and clemence rather then to be fearyd by crueltie.[ii] [10] He that wyll be fearyd muste feare. [iii] Cruell [H6r] kynges are of every man behatyd. And suche, some tyme in serchynge to be avenged losyth them [s]elfe[11] for theyr subgettes rather desyre trouble & change of the tyme then the conservacion of theyr astates°. For good people feare suche condicions in a prince. And suche as be evell feare theyr cruell justice so that therby, often tymes, theyr owne servantes study to put them downe° and to slee them[12], usynge with them the same condicion of cruelte suche as they usyd them selfe before and

---

[1]] 2 3 *her father*
[2] syn] 2 *sens* 3 *sence*
[3] myght] 1 *mdght* 3 *might*
[4]] 2 3 *have*
[5] know] 2 3 *knowen*
[6]] Marginal note 2 *The obedyence that she ought to her father* 3 *The obedience that she ought to her father*
[7] though] 1 *thought* 3 *thoughe*
[8] to dye] 2 *todaye*
[9]] 2 3 *a*
[10]] Marginal note 2 *The condet of cruelte*
[11] selfe] 1 *felfe*
[12] them] 3 *hym*

gave them ensample°. Syr, I say this bicause I desyre to susteyne your honour and
your lyfe. Small hope your subgettes shall have in you so cruell against me. They
shall feare the same and therby have you in a mervelous° suspecte.° iv And he that
is not sure, can make no suretie°. O how frely delyveryd fro° suche occasions are
those prynces whose hartes are endeued° with clemencye and ¹³ pitie! Theyr nat-
urall° subgettes careth not to dye in [H6v] theyr quarels to save them fro° perell.
They will wake all nyght and defende them on *the* day.¹⁴ More hope and strength
these benynge° and pitefull kynges have, by reasone that they be belovyd of theyr
people, then in the strenght of the walles of theyr stronge forteresses. And otherwyse, if the kynge be behatyd of his subgiettes, if he hadde nede, they¹⁵ that
come most slackest to save hym shall¹⁶ have moste thanke of the people.ᵛ Therefore, Syr, regarde° well what hurte and dau*n*ger crueltie causeth and what profyt
gentlenes° and pitie procureth. Howbeit, if ye thynke the opinyon of your furour
better than good counsaill and naturall prudence, then unhappy° is that doughter
to be borne to bryng her father's lyfe in to co*n*dicio*n* of sclaunder°, provyd with
suche cruell deades. Thus no man shall trust in you, nor ye shall trust no man, for
if men procure your deth ye can be in no suretie°.ᵛⁱ And the thyng that most gre-
vith me is in [H7r] gyvyng sentence agaynst me ye do justice against your owne
honour, the wiche all wayes shal be recordyd, more for the cause then for justice
in it selfe. My blode shall occupye but a small place, but your crueltie shal sprede
over all the yerth°. Ye shal be callyd the cruell father and I the doughter innocent.
For syn°¹⁷ God is juste he shall clere my trouth, for I shal be lefte w*ith* oute faulte
when I have receyvyd the payne° of dethe.

XXXVI: The Auctor

When Laureola had endyd her letter, she sent it to the kynge by one of her kepers,
who loved and favoured her in suche wyse° *that* he wolde° gladly she had bene at
her libertie, for he was as moche moved t[o]¹ pytie her as to obey the kinge's co-
maundement.ⁱ And when the kynge hadde receyved *the* letter and redde it, he
co*m*maunded streygthly° that the berer therof shulde avoyde his presence. And
when I saw that, then newly [H7v] agayne I cursed my mysadventure° *&* thought
that my tormente was so great that it occupied my harte in dolour, yet my mynde

---

¹³] 2 3 *great*
¹⁴] Marginal note 2 *Howe pyte causeth love* 3 *How pity causeth love*
¹⁵ they] 3 Omitted.
¹⁶ shall] 3 *that*
¹⁷ syn] 2 *syns* 3 *synce*

---

¹ to] 1 *te*

forgat not to do *that* I ought.ⁱⁱ And though I hadde more space° to endure payne
rather then to fynde remedy°, yet then I wente and spake with the Lorde Gawlo,²
her uncle, and shewyd° hym how Lereano was determynyd to take Laureola per-
force° out of presone.ⁱⁱⁱ ³ Wherfore I desyred° hym to be redy with a certayne nombre of men that when Lereano hadde taken her oute of preso*n*, then he wold° delyver her to his power to sette her in savegarde°, because that if Lereano shulde
cary her away with hym it shulde veryfy° the wytnes° of the false accusers. And
bycause that *the* deth of Laureola was as dere to hym as to the quene his suster, he
aunswered me & sayde how he was content therwith.ⁱᵛ And when his wyll and my
desyre were confyrmable° together then I depertyd secretly, bycause that or° any
brute° were [H8r] made *the* dead myght be executyd sode*n*ly. And when I came to
Lereano, I shewyd° hym all that I hade done and of the small effect therof. And
then I delyvered hym Laureola's letter. And what for the compassion of the wordes
therin and with the thoughtes that he determyned to do, his harte therwith was
so oppressyd° *that* he wist° not what aunswere to make me. He wepte for compassion, an[d]⁴ coulde not refrayne° his ire, and was sore° discomefortyd° by reasone
of his evyll fortune, and yet he hopyde° accordyng to justice.ᵛ When he thought to
reskew° Laureala he was joyfull. And agayne, when he doughtyde to brynge it
aboute his harte changyde. Fynally, leveng al doubtes & knowyng the aunswere
of Galleo, then he began to study what waye to accomplishe his enterprice.ᵛⁱ And
lyke a wyse knyghte, well provydyde°, whyle I hadde ben in the courte he had as-
semblyd together of his own serva*n*tes .v.C. men of armes° [H8v] without knowl-
edgyng° of any of his kynne or frendes.ᵛⁱⁱ Some, peradventure°, wolde° have agreyd
with hym with discrete° consideracion suche as were made privy°.ᵛⁱⁱⁱ Some of them⁵
sayd *the* kyng dyd evil. And some ⁶ sayd⁷ it was a jeopdous° enterprice and perilous
to accomplysh.ⁱˣ Therfore, to exchew° al such inco*n*venie*n*ts°⁸ he thought to execute his dead° alone *with* his owne men. So the day before that Laureola shuld
have bene judged, Lereano callyd before hym all his servantes and sayde to them
how the good vertuous men were more bounde to feare theyr shame then the perell of theyr lyves. Also sayenge how yet lyveth the fame of them that be passyd by
reasone of theyr deades that they have done.⁹ And he desired them that for cov-
etyse° of worldly goodes, *the* whiche shall have an ende, that they shulde not for
that lose the glory of them that liveth perpetually.ˣ And he desyred them to have

---

² Gawlo] 2 3 *Galleo*

³] Marginal note 2 *Extremyte the laste remedy* 3 *Extrmyte the laste remedye*

⁴ and] 1 *any*

⁵] 2 3 *wold have*

⁶] 2 *wold*

⁷ sayd] 2 3 *say*

⁸ inco*n*venie*n*ts] 3 *inconveniente*

⁹] Marginal note 2 3 *The comforte of Laureola to his servauntes*

in theyr memory the rewarde of well [I1r] dyeng. & he shewyd° the*m* what foly-
shnes it was to feare deth. And in theyr so doyng he promysed them great gyftes
& rewardes. And when he hadde made to them a long sermon then he declaryd
the cause that he sent for them. And all they with one voice° proferyd to lyve and
dye with hym. And when Lereano saw theyr good wylles he thought hym selfe
then well accompanyd, and so depertyd in the nyght and came in to a valey nere
to[10] the citie.[11] Ther he taryed all the nyght and infourmyd his me*n* what they
shulde do. He apoyntyd one capitayne with a .C. men of armes° that they shuld go
streyght to the lodging of Persyo and to slee hym, and as many as dyd resyst them.
Then he apoyntyde other .ii. capitayns[12] with eche of them .l. footemen to go up
[13] the two principall streates goyng to the presone where as Laureola was, co*m*-
maundyng them that when they came to the preson then[14] they to[15] torne[16] theyr
faces to the citie warde° & [I1v] kepe[17] & defende that no person shulde entre in
to the castell° untyll suche tyme as he with other .iii.C. men came to take oute
Laureola. And the capitayne that he hadde co*m*maundyd to sle Persio, he char-
gyd° hym that when he had done to come and mete with hym at the preso*n* and
they to defende the passage yf any came[18] to entre in to the castell° whyle he were
taking oute of Laureola. And all this thus agreyd & co*n*cluded, when the gates
were opened in the mornynge sodenly he and all hys men entered in to the citie
and every capitayne toke hede to his charge. The capitayne that had the charge to
sle Persio executed his co*m*maundemente, for he slew Persio & all other that were
in his way to lette° hym. Ther Persio endyd his myserable lyfe.[19] And Lereano
went to the preson and what with the furour of his ire & with the vertue of his
force fought so fercely with the kepers of the presone, and slew so many that he
could not get forewarde [I2r] for dede° bodyes, but with moche payne°. But as in
al perels the bountie° encrea[s]th[20] by force of armes, so by clene force he came in
to the preson wher as Laureola was and there he toke her with as greate seremony
and honour as thought hit°[21] hadde bene in tyme of peace.[xi] He knelyd downe to

---

[10] to] 2 3 Omitted.

[11]] Marginal note 2 *The hole appoyntme*nt *of Leriano's company for to delyver Laureola*
3 *The hole appointmente of Leriano's company for to delyver Laureola*

[12] capitayns] 3 *capytayne*

[13]] 2 3 *to*

[14] then] 2 3 *that*

[15] to] 2 3 Omitted.

[16] torne] 2 3 *tourned*

[17] kepe] 3 *kept*

[18] came] 2 3 *come*

[19]] Marginal note 2 3 *The sleynge of Persio*

[20] encreaesth] 1 *encreafeth*

[21] hit] 2 3 *it*

the yerth° and kyst hir hande, lyke the doughter of a kynge.[22] And with that present turbacion° she stode without strenght so that she coulde not move her selfe.
Her harte dismayd, her colour faylyd, litle parte of any[23] lyfe was lefte in her. Then
Lereano tooke and caryed her oute of prisone and then mette with Galleo, her
uncle, accordynge to his promyse, who came thyther° with a certayn number of
men. And there in the presence of every man Lereano delyveryd Laureola in to his
handes, and still his men fought against them that came againste hym.[xii] [24] But he
set Laureola upon an hakeney that Galleo had ther redy and agayne [I2v] kyste
her hande, and then went to ayde his men that were styll fyghtyng. And still he
regardyd° after Laureola till he hadde loste the syght of her. So Galleo, her uncle,
ledde her to a castell° of his owne not farre thence.[xiii] And when *the* brute° of this
dead came to the heryng of the kynge, he callyd for his armure and sownyd°
trompettes and causyd all the men of his courte to be armyd, & many of the citie.
And when Lerea[n]o saw that of necessite it was tyme for hym to get oute of the
towne in to the feldes° then he comfortyd his men with swete and hardy woordes.[25]
And allwayes in his reculynge° he defendyd° the multitude of his enemyes with a
valiante harte.[xiv] And to kepe an honest maner in his reculynge° he went in good
order and not with so great haste as the case° requiryd. Thus lesyng°[26] some[27] of
his men and sleyng of[28] many of his enemyes, he[29] came thither° where he had left
al theyr horses. So suche order as he had sette before [I3r] was well and truely
kepte. And so without perel he & his lept upon theyr horses, the which was hard
to have ben done if he had not wysely providyd the remedy° therof before hand.[xv]
Then the horsemen° put before them theyr fotemen° and toke the way to Suria,
fro° whence they[30] cam.[xvi] And when Lereano saw .iii. bandes° of the kynge's
aproche nere hym then he wente oute of the waye and conductyd so wisely his
company by wayes of avauntage that he scapyd° with as great honour in his
reculynge° as he hadde wonne in the fightynge. So he enteryde agayne in to the
towne of Suria withoute losse of any of his men, which was greate mervayll° for
the kyng was ther in propre° person with .v.M. men of armes°, who [31] was inflamyd with ire and so beset the towne about in purpose not to depert thence till he

---

[22]] Marginal note 2 The *delyvering of Laureola* 3 *The delyverynge of Laureola*
[23] any] 3 Omitted.
[24]] Marginal note 2 3 *Laureola was by Leriano delivred in to her uncles custody*
[25]] Marginal note 2 *Leriano reculynge* 3 *Leriano reculing*
[26] lesyng] 2 3 *Leriano*
[27] some] 2 3 Omitted.
[28] of] 2 3 Omitted.
[29] he] 2 3 Omitted.
[30] they] 3 *the*
[31]] 3 *who*

had taken vengeance of Lereano.[xvii] [32] When Lereano saw how he was besegyd°, he sette his men lyke a wyse man of warre to the walles. [I3v] Where as was most feblyst parte there he sette most defence, and where as he myght best issue out in to the feld there he sette such men as were mete° for that purpose, and there as he fearyd other crafte or treasone there he sette such as he trustyd best.[xviii] Thus he usyd hym selfe lyke a wyse capitayne. The kyng, thynkyng to bryng his enterprice to an ende, commaundyd to fortefy his campe and to provyde for all thynges necessary perteynynge to a campe royall, as engy[n]s,° bastides° and bulwerkes° to beat the citie with artilery, and made greate dykes° that none° shuld issue oute.[xix] [33] When the kynge saw so longe tariynge at this siege his ire encreasyde, for he hadde thought to hade taken Lereano by reasone of famyne and for all that he saw the towne ryght stronge. Yet he determynyd° to sawte° it, the whiche he provyd° with suche fercenes that they within had great nede to put to° theyr strength and[34] dilygence to resiste. Then Lereano [I4r] went & visytyd his men with a .C. men, suche as were deputyd° for that purpose. And every where he saw any fyghtyng he ever encoragyd them, and where as he saw valiantnes° he praysed them, and where he saw an[35] evyll order he founde remedy°.[36] Fynally the kynge caused to sowne° the retrayte[37] with losse of many of his knyghtes, & specially of the yonge lusty courteers who ever sekyth for perells to wynne therby glory. Lereano, at the same assaulte, was hurte in the face and also loste many of his princpal men. This assualte past, the kyng gave other .v. assaultes within the space° of [38] monethes so that in maner men beganne to fayle on bothe parties so that Lereano was doubteous° of that enterprice.[xx] How be it, in his wordes and countenance, nor in his deades, nothynge of feare coulde be aspied° so that *the* corage to[39] of the capitayne incoragyd° all the other capitayns. And then to gyve corage to his men suche as were lefte, he sayde to [I4v] them as folowith.

---

[32]] Marginal note 2 *The besegynge of Leria[n]o in Suria* 3 *The beseging of Leriano in Sura*

[33]] Marginal note 2 *Thyges necessa for a syege* 3 *Thinges necessary for a siege*

[34] nede to put to theyr strength and] 3 Omitted.

[35] an] 2 3 *any*

[36]] Marginal note 2 *The gode comforte of a capytayne* 3 *The good comfort of a captaine*

[37] retrayte] 2 *certaynte* 3 *certayne*

[38]] 2 3 *.iii.*

[39] to] 2 3 Omitted.

XXXVII: Lereano[1] to his company°

Certaynly, Syrs, as ye be but few[e][2] in no*m*ber so our strength is not greate. I have doubte in our enterprice accordyng to our evyll fortune, but in that vertue is estemyde more then is greate nomber, and consyderynge your noble deades passed, I thynke I shuld have more nede of good fortune then of greate no*m*ber of knyghtes, [3] wherfore alonely° in you is[4] all my hope.[i] And syne[5]° our helthe is in our handes, as well for the sustentacion° of our lyves as for the glory of good fame, we ought valia*n*tly to fyght. Now *the* case° is offeryd us or els to leve the profyt of our enherytance to them that wold° disheryte° us.[ii] Thus we shulde be unhappy° if for feare & faynte corage we shuld lese° our herytage. Therfore lette us fyght to delyver our blude fro° shame and dishonour, and my name fro° enfamy.[iii] This day, lette us make an ende of our lyves or els conferme our [15r] honours. Lette us defende our selfe and not [6] be shamyd, for greater is the rewarde of vyctory then the occasions of perel. This paynefull lyfe that we lyve in, I know not why we shulde so moche desyre it. The daies therof are but shorte and longe in travayll°, *the* which for feare increseth not nor for hardynes° shorteth not. For when we be borne our tyme is lymyted, the whiche we shal not passe, thereby feare is subdued & hardynes° lawded. We can not put our fortune in a better state then to hope of an honourable deth. O glorious fame![iv] [7] O covetyse laudable! The averise° of honour wherby is ateyned greatter deades then this of ours is! Lette us not feare the great company that is in the kinge's campe, for at the fyrste encounter the weke shall fyrst fyght and overcome them, & they shall abashe° the multitude & the small nombre wyll enforce° them selfe by vertue.[v] Many thynges dryveth us to be hardy. Bountie° and vertue byndeth us [15v] and justice enforseth° us. Necessitie shall rewarde us, wherfore we ought not to feare for theyr is nothynge that shulde cause us to dye. Syrs, all these reasones that I have sayde is[8] but superflew° to enforce° our strenght syn°[9] we have it naturally. But I will say to you that in every tyme our hartes o[u]ght to be occupied in noblenes, & our handes in deades of armes, and our thoughtes in good workes & good wordes amonge company, as we do now. I receve equal glory as wel for the amorous good wyll that ye shew me, as for the deades of armes that ye have done. And bycause I se our enmyes prepayre them to fight, we be constrayned to leve our talkyng, & every man to gette hym to his charge and defence°.

---

[1] Lereano] 2 *Laureola*

[2] fewe] 1 *fewr*

[3]] Marginal note *The wordes of Leriano to comfort his men* 3 *The wordes of Leriano to comfort hys men*

[4] is] 2 3 Omitted.

[5] syne] 2 *syns* 3 *sins*

[6]] 2 3 *to*

[7]] Marginal note 2 *The lyfe is not to be estemyd* 3 *The lyfe is not to be estemed*

[8] is] 2 3 *be*

[9] Syn] 2 3 *Syns*

XXXVIII: The auctor

Lereano was au*n*swerd of his knightes *with* greate constance° and corage of harte, whereof he thought hym selfe ryght happy° that he hadde suche [I6r] men in his company.[1] So every man went to his defence° where as they were apoyntyd. And then anone they hard the trompettes blowe, and wi[th]in[2] shorte space° there came to the walles a .l.M. men and began fresly° to gyve assaulte. Then Lereano shewed his vertue and by reasone of theyr defence the kynge thought they within hade loste never a ma*n*. This assaut endured fro° *the* myddes°of the day tyll it was nyght, the which depertyd° them.[i] There were slayne & hurt of them withoute a .iii.M., and as many of them within, so that Lereano hadde lef[t][3] no mo°[4] with hym but .C.l. persones, and yet by his contenance he semyd as though he ha[d][5] loste never a man. How be it, he was inwardly sory for them that he had loste. All that nyght he buryed the dede bodyes and praysed and lawdyde the valiantnes of them that were lefte alyve, and gyving no lesse glory to them that were dede then to them that were alyve.[ii] The next day, at the relyefe° [I6v] in the morenynge, Lereano determynyd° that .l. of his menne with hym shulde issue oute and syt[6] upon a lodgyng that joynede to the walles perteynynge to a kynnesman's of Persyo's. Lereano dyde this bicause the kynge shuld not thynke that he lacked men. And this he dyde with ferme boldnes and so brente° the sayde lodgynge and sleu° many such as made defence. And, as God wolde°, in the same busynes there was taken one of them that hadde accusyde Laureola.[iii] [7] [8] He was brought to Lereano and was put to payne° till he was causyd to shewe° all the trouth of the hole mater. And so he confessed the hole circu*m*stance of the mater. And when Lereano was enfourmed of the trouth he sent hym to the kynge, besechynge hym to dyscharge Laureola fro° all blame and to do justice upon them for the payne that they have caused Laureola to endure. And when the kyng knew the certaynte° he was ryght gladde and thought it was reason that [I7r] he requiryd.[iv] And to make shorte proces°, the kinge dyd justice upon *the* .iii. falce wytnesses accordynge to theyr desertes°.[v] [9] Then incontynent°, he reised up° the siege and reputyd° his

---

[1]] 2 3 Marginal note *The good answere of his men*

[2] within] 1 *wihtin*

[3] left] 1 *lefet*

[4] mo] 2 3 *more*

[5] had] 1 *has*

[6] syt] 2 3 *set*

[7]] Marginal note 2 *The takyng of one of the thre wytnes and the ende of the so*nge 3 *The taking of .i. of the .iii. wytnes & the ende of the songe*

[8]] 2 *&* 3 *and*

[9]] Marginal note 2 *The ponyshm*ent *of the .iii. wytnes* 3 *the ponishment of the .iii. wytnes*

doughter, Laureola, discharged & Lereano withoute fawte°. And so went to his citie of Suria & then sente for Laureola by *the* grettest lordes of his court. And she was brought with equall ho[n]our acordynge to her deservynge°, and was joyfully recevyd of the kyng & of the quene, who wepte for joy.[vi] And there the kinge discharged her fro° blame, and the quene kyst her, and all other servyd her[10]. Thus the payne passed was turned to great joy present. Then the kyng sent to Lereano co*m*maundyng hym not to come to his court till he had apeased *the* kynnesmen & frendes of Persio, the which co*m*maundement he receyved wi*th* greate sorow bycause he mighte not se Laureola. And when he saw none° other remedye°, he felte hym selfe in a strange maner.[vii] And seynge° hym selfe depertyd°[11] [17v] fro° her, he lefte the workes of chyvalry and retourned agayne to his olde amorouse thoughtes and trowbles.[viii] Desyryng to know what case° Laureola was in, he desyrede° me to fynde some honest maner how he myght se & speke wi*th* her. And yet his desyre was so honest that he desyryd not to speke with her in suche wyse° that any suspecte° shulde be layde to her, of the whiche he deservyde to have had great thanke. And I, who was glade to folowe his desire, deperted fro° hym and went to Suria. And when I came there and had kyste Laureola's hande, then I shewyd° her Lereano's desyre. And she aunswered me and sayde that in no wyse° she wolde° speke with hym for dyverce causes that she alledgyde. And though she was not content to grau*n*t me at that tyme, yet ever after, as often as I myght speke with[12] her I made styll my supplycacion. And fynaly, at laste, she aunswerede me & sayde ons for all that if I spake any more to her [18r] in that mater she wolde° be utterly displeasyd with me. And when I harde her aunswere and saw her displeasure then I went to Lereano with[13] greate hevynes° and dolour. And when I had shewyd° hym how it was then he began newly to complayne and sorowe for hys mysadventure°, so that withoute doubt he was in the condicion to have dispayred.[ix]

[And beyng in case° as a man that was not well advysed, for to augment his sorowe, hopynge therby to abbrydge his myserable and most payneful lyfe, beynge assured that musycke to a sorowfull persone is as paynful as it is pleasaunte to one that delyghteth in myrthe, toke his harpe colored all blacke, played this dytie folowynge.

O fortune moste envyous unto prosperyte,
O fortune most plentyfull of cruell displeasuer,
O fortune mercyles and lackynge of pytie,
O fortune mutable unperfyte° and unsure,

---

[10] her] 3 *he*
[11] depertyd] 3 *departe*
[12] with] 3 *to*
[13]] 2 3 *a*

O fortune spytefull not letynge joy to endure,
O fortune most false with thy subtyll trayne,
Why doste thou deale[14] *or falsly or*[15] *me procure,*
Up for to ryse and throwe me downe agayne.

Farewell hope, welcome dispayre,
Farewel rest, welcome unquyetnes,
Farewell pleasure that dyd me repayre°,
Farewell myrth for I am comfortles,
Farewell joy, welcome distresse,
Farewell helth that dyd me sustayne,
Farewell that hope that me redresse,
And welcome dispayre that hath throwen[16] *me downe agayne.*

O death unkynde why doste thou refrayne
To come unto me to ease my harte,
And life I say where doste thou remayne
So longe within me to abyde this smar[t],[17]
Why dost thou not from me departe
But sufferest me styll to abyde this payne,
And that I it s[u]ffre the cause thou arte
To let me ryse and throwe me downe agayne.

And therwithall semed halfe deed so that he almost lacked lyfe to conclude. I perc-
eyvyng hym redy[18] *to sownd for the anguyshe that he suffered.]*

And when I saw that yet to entertayne hym I sayde & counsaylyd hym to[19] write
agayne to Laureola, recordynge therin what he[20] hadde[21] done for her and mar-
vaylynge° of her change, seynge° she had rewardyd hym[22] before with her[23] wri-
tynge°. Then he aunswered and sayde how he was well content to write but not to
recite therin any thyng that he had done for her, the which he sayd was nothynge
accordynge to her deservynge°. Nor also he sayd he wolde° make no remembrance
in his letter of any rewarde *that* he had receyvyd of her, for he sayd: "The lawe of

---

[14] deale] 3 *steale*
[15] or] 3 Omitted.
[16] throwen] 3 *this men*
[17] smart] 2 *smarre*
[18] redy] 3 *reade*
[19] And when I saw that yet to entertayne hym I sayde & counsaylyd hym to] 2 *To comforte hym I coun̄seyled hym & sayd* 3 *To comfort hym I coun̄seld him and said*
[20] he] 2 3 *you*
[21] hadde] 2 3 *have*
[22] hym] 2 3 *you*
[23] her] 2 3 Omitted.

love defendeth° [I8v] any suche thynge to be wryten. What satisfacion shulde I receve therby for the greate perell that myght fall yf the letter were sene? Thus not tochynge those maters I wyll wryte to Laureola." The tenour of his letter folowith.

XXXIX: The letter fro°¹ Lereano to Laureola ⁱ

Fayre Lady Laureola, accordyng to your vertuous pytie, synne°² ye know my passion°, I can not beleve but *that* ye wyll consente to my demaunde°.ⁱⁱ Syn°³ I desyre nothynge that shall be to your dishonour, seinge° ye knowe myne evill°, why do you dought? Withoute reason I dye. Ye know that great payne occupyeth so myne harte that I feale the evill° and can not shewe it. Yf ye take it for good that I shuld dye, thynking to satisfye me with the passion° *that* ye gyve me, syn°⁴ it procedeth fro° you hit°⁵ is the grettest welth° that I can hope for, and justely I shall take it for the ende of my reward. Yf ye judge me uncourteise in *that* [K1r] I shulde not be content with that ye⁶ do to me, gyvinge me cause of so gloriouse thoughts, yet blame me not, for⁷ though the wyll ⁸ be ⁹ satisfyed, the understanding° ¹⁰ maketh quarell.ⁱⁱⁱ And yf my dolour do pleace° you bycause I never dyd you service that might atteyne to the heighnes of your deservyng.ⁱᵛ When I remembre these thynges & many mo°, I thynke *that* bycause that ye wyll not graunte my¹¹ supplycacion bycause I can do nothynge that shuld deserve it, yet hardynes° hath causyd me to hope upon mercy, not according to my deserving°, but according to your bountie° that may gyve it.¹² And I thynk that your vertue, compassyon & pitie shulde ayde me bycause they be agreable° to your condycion. When a man hathe any busynes with a greate personage°, thynkyng to attayn to have grace, fyrste he must wynne the good wylles of the ser[v]auntes, wherby a man lightely° shall come to his entent. But as for me, I can fynde no remedye°. I [K1v] ha[v]e done my devour° to serche for ayde, whome I have found alwayes ferme°& stable. For all they have requyred° you to have mercy upon me. *The* sowle bycause he suf-

---

¹ fro] 2 3 *of*
² synne] 2 3 *syns*
³ syn] 2 *syns* 3 *sins*
⁴ syn] 2 3 *syns*
⁵ hit] 2 3 *it*
⁶ ye] 3 Omitted.
⁷ for] 2 3 Omitted.
⁸] 3 *not*
⁹] 2 *not*
¹⁰] 2 3 *of me*
¹¹ my] 2 3 *me*
¹²] Marginal note 2 3 *The feldes of noblenes*

feret, and¹³ the lyfe bycause it susteyneth, the harte bycause it endureth, the understandynge° bycause it feleth.¹⁴ And syn°¹⁵ ye wyll gyve no reward for all these in that they desyre and by reasone have deservyd, I ame the moste unfortunat of all other unhappy°.ᵛ The water refressheth the yerth°, but my wepynges can not molefye° your endurat° hardnes.ᵛⁱ The water gyveth liquor° to the feldes, herbys and trees, but my wepynge can not entre in to your harte. As¹⁶ I fynde my selfe disposyd, dyspayre shuld rydde my lyfe yf I myght be alone. But alwayes I ame accompanyd with the thoughtes that ye gyve me and with *the* desyre *that* ye ordeyne me. Also the remembrance° of that I wolde° do comforteth me, remembrynge how they kepte me company. In suche wyse° that whatsoever [K2r] cause I have desperacion yet it kepeth me fro° dispayryng. Yf it be your plesure that I shall dye, let me have some knowledge therof. Then I shall not be all unhappy° for then I shall passe it the more wyllyngly, and at the ende it shal be to me the more ease bycause it is for your gyfte.ᵛⁱⁱ And syn°¹⁷ ye wyll not se me, I must be enforsed° to go that trace°.ᵛⁱⁱⁱ

XL: The auctor

Thys letter I bare to Laureola. W*ith* moche payne she receyved it. And to dispache° her fro° Lereano honestly she wrote agayne in this maner, with full determynacyon never to receyve agayne fro° hym other letter or message. The tenour of her letter folowith.

XLI: The letter fro° Laureola to Lereano ⁱ

Lereano, the displeasure that I have of thyne evyll° shulde be satisfactio*n* for thy love, yf thou knew how greate it is. And this alonely° take for thy remedy° withoute demaundynge° of [K2v] any other, though it be but a small payment for that thou hast deserved agaynst me. For as I am bound to do, yf thou wylt demaunde° of my goodes and ryches as thou dost desyre° agaynst myne honour, I wolde° gladly gy[v]e it the.¹ I will not aunswere every article° of thy letter, for

---

    ¹³ hand] 2 3 *and*
    ¹⁴] Marginal note 2 *The servauntes that oughte to be sued unto* 3 *The servauntes that ought to be sued unto*
    ¹⁵ syn] 2 *syns* 3 *since*
    ¹⁶ As] 2 3 *And*
    ¹⁷ syn] 2 *syns* 3 *synce*

---

    ¹] Marginal note 3 *Leriano request*

I, considerynge that I do thus wryte to the, the bloud rynneth fro° my harte and
my reason banyssheth fro° my judgement. Ther is no cause that thou hast wryten
of that causeth me to consent to be sory for thyne evyll°, but it is alonely° by reason of my bounte°. Yet I have no doubt but that thou enduryst moche evyll°, for
the perell that *thou* hast bene in beareth wytnes of that *thou* hast suffred.[ii] Thou
sayst thou dyddest me never service. That thou hast done for me I shal never
forget, but alwaye desyre to satisfye it. But not as thou desiryst, but accordyng
to myne honestye. The vertue, [2] pitie and compassion that thou thynkyst shulde
ayde the agaynst [K3r] me bycause they ar agreable to my condicio*n*, how be it,
in this case° they are enmies to my fame° & therfore thou findest them contrary.
When I was take*n* thou savyddest[3] my lyfe, & now *that* I am quyte° thou wold-
est° co*n*demne° me w*ith* thy desyre. Rather I ought to seke thy payne with myne
honour, then to remedy° the with myne owne faulte & shame.[iii] [4] Beleve not that
the people lyve so holily but & they knew *that* I spake w*ith* the they wold° judge
our clere° entensions to the worste, for the worlde is so dyverce that men wyll
rather defame bountie° then to prayse vertue. Thus thy demau*n*de° is excussyd,
therfore take no hope therein though thou shuldest dye as thou sayst. For better
is honest crueltie then pitie culpable. Herynge this, peradventure, thou wylte say
I ame moveable° bycause I began to shew the some mercy, as in wrytynge to the,
and now determyned° not to remedy° *thee*. Thou knowest[5] wel under what maner
I dyd wryte to the, and for what [K3v] entent. And though it hadde ben for any
othere cause, yet as conveniente is the mutacion in thynges that be hurtefull as is
ferme° stedfastnes in thynges that be honest.[iv] [6] I require° the, strenght° thy selfe
lyke a valiant knyght and remedy° thy selfe discretly°. Put not thy life in perell
and myne honour in disputacio*n* syn°[7] thou so moche desyrest it. What shal be
sayde if thou dye? That I do rewarde service done to me with takynge awaye theyr
lyves, to the which I wyll shew *the* contrary. Yf I outelyve the kynge, my father,
for then shall I gyve the what parte of *the* rea[l]me[8] that thou wylte desyre. And
I shall encrease thyne honour, & double thy rentes°, and enhaunce thyne astate°
& all that thou wylte ordeyne no thy[ng]e[9] shal be denyed. And thus by thy lyfe
I shall be judgyd a good rewarder. And if thou dye I shal be reputyde° of evyll
co*n*dicions.[10] And if it were for none° other thynge but for this, thou shuldest en-

---

[2]] 2 3 *of*
[3] savyddest] 2 *savyd* 3 *saved*
[4]] Marginal note 2 3 *The remembraunce of a good torne*
[5] knowest] 2 *knwest* 3 *knewest*
[6]] Marginal note 2 *Mutab[i]lite is somtime condemned* 3 *Mutabylite is somtime con-*
demned
[7] syn] 2 3 *syns*
[8] realme] 1 *reame*
[9] thynge] 1 *thygne* 3 *thing*
[10]] Marginal note 2 3 *Laureola rewarde by promyse for his des[]erte*

forse° thy selfe, but for the trouble [K4r] that thy payne putteth me unto. I wyll
say no more to the, bycause thou shalte not think that in thy demaund° I shuld
gyve the counsayll or put the in any hope.ᵛ Wold° to God that thy desyre were
honest. Thus I co[un]sayll¹¹ the on the one parte and satysfye the on the other.ᵛⁱ
And at this poynte I send to the this letter on the purpose° never to aunswere nor
to heare the speke more.

XLII: The auctor

When Laureola had wryten this letter she sayd to me with a determynate° aunswere that this shulde be the last tyme that I shuld apere before her presence,
sayeng that her comnyng°¹ with me causyd moche suspect° and that in my goyng
& comynge ther was more perell to her² then hope to me of any remedy°.ⁱ Then I,
seynge° her determynate° will, it semyd to me that my travayle° was more payn-
full to me then remedy° to Lereano. So³ I went fro° her *with* more wepyng then
wordes. And after I had [K4v] kyst her hand I wente out of the place° with
sobbynge and gulpynge in my throte, that I was nere strangeled to kepe in my
wepynge and to th'entent to cover my passio*n*°.ⁱⁱ And when I was oute of the citie
alone, then I began to wepe in suche wyse° that I coulde not retayne° my voyce
fro° brayng° so that I thought it was better for me to dye in Masedonia then to
returne into Castile. *The* which desire was resonable, for by the dethe myne evyll°
adventure⁴ shulde make an ende, and with ⁵ lyfe my sorow shulde encrease. Thus
all the way wepyng and syghyng⁶ feylede° me not. & when I came to Lereano, I
delyveryd hym the letter fro° Laureola. And when he hadde redde it, he sayd he
wolde° nother° take strength nor receyve any counsayll syn°⁷ it was so good reason that he shulde dye. Then he sayde to me that alwayes he wolde° take me for
more then his fre*n*de bicause of the good counsayll that I had gyvyn hym. Then
with voyce and colour mortal [K5r] he began to complayne, not blamynge his
wekenes nor dispraysynge his fall, for every thynge that myght shorte*n* his lyfe
he praysede.ⁱⁱⁱ He shewyde hym selfe frende to dolour and toke recreacion *with*
tormentes. He lovyd sorowes. All the[s]e⁸ he callyd his welthe°, to be messengers

---

¹¹ counsayll] 1 *conusayll* 3 *counsail*

---

¹ comnyng] 2 *commu*nynge 3 *communing*
² to her] 3 Omitted.
³ So] 3 Omitted.
⁴ adventure] 3 *sorow*
⁵] 3 *my*
⁶ and syghyng] 3 Omitted.
⁷ syn] 2 *syns* 3 *sins*
⁸ these] 1 *thele*

to Laureola.⁹ And bycause they shuld be entreatyde accordynge as fro° thence as they came, he¹⁰ fyxyd them in his harte, he joynyde them to his understandynge° and conveied them with his memory. He desiryde° them to make a shorte ende of that they hadde to do to the entent that Laureola myght be servyde. And thus beynge without hope of any welth° and trobled with mortall paynes could not susteyne hym selfe no le*n*ger, but perforce° co*n*streynede° to lye downe upo*n* his bedde, where he wolde° nother eate, drynke, nor slepe nor take any thyng for sus- te*n*tacion of his lyfe, ever calyng hym selfe happy° to come to the case° to do some service to Laureola as by his dethe to brynge her [K5v] oute of all trouble.ⁱᵛ ¹¹ So anone it was publyshed° abrode°, in the realme and in the courte how Lere- ano was lyke to dye.ᵛ The[n] his kynne & frendes came to comforte hym. And to torne° his purpose they sayde and dyde as moche as they coulde imagyne to prevayle his lyfe. & bycause his infyrmite was to be curyd by holsome° reasones, every ma*n* sharpyd° theyr wyttes° to do the best they coulde.ᵛⁱ And there was a knyghte callyd Teseo, a greate frende of his, he considerynge that his sekenes° was for love, though he knewe not for whome it was, he sayd and shewyde° to Lereano all the evyls of women that he coulde devise.ᵛⁱⁱ And to conferme° his owne reasones, he alegyd as many thynges as he coulde in the defamyng of wom- en, thynkyng therby to have restoryd Lereano to his helthe.ᵛⁱⁱⁱ When Lereano hadde well harde° hym, and consyderyde that Laureola was a woman, he re- bukyde greatly Teseo for spekynge of suche wordes.ⁱˣ And though [K6r] as then his disposicion was not moche to speke, yet he enforcyd° his tonge°, and with the passion of greate [yre]¹², sayde as folowith.

XLIII: Lereano¹ ² agaynst Teseo and agaynst³ all evell spekers agaynst women ⁱ

Frend Teseo⁴, yf another man that owed the not so good love as I do hard° my wordes it wolde° cause the to receyve payne° accordynge to thy deserte°.ⁱⁱ Howbeit my reasons shal be to the suche an ensample to cause the to kepe thy tonge°. And it shal be a chastisement in stede of thy payne°, in the which I shall folow the

⁹] Marginal note 3 *The priv̇ate messạnger to Laureola from Leriano*
¹⁰ he] 2 *she*
¹¹] Marginal note 2 3 *That was to sle hym*
¹² yre] 1 *iri*

¹ Lereano] 2 3 *Leriano's*
²] 2 3 *argumentes*
³ agaynst] 2 3 Omitted.
⁴ Teseo] 3 *Theseo*

condicion of a true frende. For yf I shewyd the not thy fault by quyke° reasons, peradventure° thou woldest utter forth agayne in other places suche like wordes as thou ryght now sayd.ⁱ ̓ⁱ It shal be most for thy profyt to amend thy self by my contradictions rather then to shame thy selfe with perseverance. The entent of thy wordes was [K6v] as a frende, the whiche I well considre. Thou sayedest them bycause I shulde abhorre them that hath brought me in to the case° that thou seist° me in. And by reason of thy sayeng evyll of women thyne entension was therby to gyve me remedy° of my lyfe, and therby thou hast gyven me the soner deth.ⁱᵛ For the shamefull wordes that thou hast sayd putteth me to suche torment bycause it is a woman that hath put me to this payne. Therfore by reasone of a⁵ herynge of thy wordes I shall lyve the lesse season°, wherby I shall receve a great welth°. For the receyvynge of this dolorous deth were better to be shortely then to susteyne *the* lyfe any lenger. For it is a thyng delectable to suffre and with a swet rest to make an ende of this lyfe, the whiche swete ende shal be by reason that these, my last wordes, shal be in the prease° of women and my wyl is somewhat to satisfye her, in whome res[ty]th⁶ al the cause.ᵛ & to begynne to shew the thyne errour, I [K7r] wyll alledge .xv. poyntes agaynste all them that erreth in spekynge evell of women, and .xx. other reasones I shall lay° wherby we are bound to say well of all women, with dyverce other samples° of theyr bountie° & goodnes. And as to the fyrst, let us found° our reasone⁷ how that all thynges made by the hande of God are necessarily good. For accordyng to the warkeman° the warke° ought to procede.ᵛⁱ Then knowynge that women are His creatures, they that speke evyll of them offende not allonely° them, but also they blaspheme the Workeman, the which is God.ᵛⁱⁱ *The* .ii. cause is *that* before God & man ther is not a more abhomynable synne, nor harder to be perdoned, then is ingratitude.⁸ For where can ther be a greatter synne then to put out of knowledge and to forgette the welth° that is to come to us by reasone of the Vyrgyn Mary and dayly cometh.⁹ She¹⁰ delyvered us fro° payne and causeth us to meryte the glory of heven. She¹¹ saveth us, she¹² susteyneth [K7v] us, she¹³ defendeth us, she¹⁴ gydeth us, she¹⁵ gyveth us lyght of grace.ᵛⁱⁱⁱ Then seynge° she was a woman, then all other

---

⁵ a] 2 3 Omitted.

⁶ restyth]1 *resith* 3 *resteth*

⁷] Marginal note 2 *Ols exeatura bona est. The fyrst cause that women be good* 3 *Ols exatuea bona este The fyrst cause* that *women be good*

⁸] Marginal note 2 3 *The .ii. cause*

⁹] Marginal note 2 3 *Judgement*

¹⁰ she] 2 3 *her sede*

¹¹ she] 2 3 *her sede*

¹² she] 2 3 Omitted.

¹³ she] 2 3 Omitted.

¹⁴ she] 2 3 Omitted.

¹⁵ she] 2 3 Omitted.

for her sake ought to be crowned with lawde° and prayse. The .iii. is bycause it is defended° to all men, accordynge to vertue, to shew any strength agaynst the weke sex femynyne. And this is observed amonge brewt° bestes°, wherfore men shulde folow the same. Yet some suche as lyst° to speke evyll say though that women can make but small resystence with theyr handes, yet they have no lesse[16] liberte with theyr tonges°.[ix] [17] The .iiii. is [18] man ought not to say evyll of women withoute he dishonour hym selfe, bycause he was creatyde° and noryshede° in the wombe of a woman and is of her substance. And also bycause of *the* honour and reverence that every child ought to do to his mother.[19] The .v. is bycause of the disobedience to God, who sayde with His owne mouth that father & mother shulde be honouryde.[x] Therefor suche as [K8r] do otherwy[s]e[20] deserve[21] sore° punishement & payne°.[22] The .vi. is bycause noble men are bounde to occupye them selfe in vertuous deades, as well in woordes as in workes. Then yf fowle° wordes defowle° clenlynes, then in perell of slander and defamy° is the honour of suche persons that wasteth theyr lyfe in suche vayne wordes.[23] The .vii. is when that the ordre of chyvaylry was fyrste stablysshed, among other thynges, whoso-ever shuld take the ordre of knighthod, he shuld be bound to kepe° & defend all women and to gyve them all reverence and honeste°. And who so doth the con-trary breketh the lawe of noblenes.[24] The .viii. is to defend honour fro° perell.[25] The auncyent° noble men, with greate deligence and study, kepte and observed alwayes such thynges as perteyned to bountie°.[xi] And they reputed° that so great that they had no greater feare of any thynge in the worlde then they had to leve[26] behynde them to[27] remembrance° of infamy and [K8v] reproche, *the* which they kept not.[xii] *They* preferreth turpitud° & fowlnes before vertue, putting spottes° in theyr fame by reason of theyr evyll tonge°.[xiii] For oftentymes a man is juged to be accordyng to his wordes. The .ix. & most princypal is for the condemnacion° of *the* sowle. Al thi[n]ges[28] wrongfully taken may be satysfyed, but *the* fame° robbyd and taken away the satisfaccion thereof is doughtfull°, *the* which is more com-

---

[16]] 3 *by*
[17]] Marginal note 2 3 *The .iii. cause*
[18]] 2 3 *a*
[19]] Marginal note 2 3 *The .iiii. cause*
[20] otherwyse] 1 *other wife* 3 *otherwise*
[21] do serve] 2 3 *deserve*
[22]] Marginal note 2 3 *The .v. cause*
[23]] Marginal note 2 3 *The .vi. cause*
[24]] Marginal note 2 3 *The .vii. cause*
[25]] Marginal note 2 3 *The .viii. cause*
[26] leve] 3 *lefte*
[27] to] 2 3 *the*
[28] thinges] 1 2 *thiges*

pletly determynyde in our beleve°.xiv 29 The .x. is to eschew hatryd. For suche as
bestowe theyr tyme in evyll spekynge agaynst women, they make them selfe not
onely enemyes agaynste them, but also t[o]30 them that be vertuous.31 For lyke as
vertue & vice are contrary and have dyfferente32 propreties, so the evyll speker
can not be withoute hate, and evyll wyll and many enemyes. The .xi. 33 bicause
of the hurtes *that* by suche malicious deades are encreasyde. For wordes gevith
lycence, and are joyned to the herynge of the rude° people as well as to them *that*
be [L1r] discrete°.xv And herynge of suche tayles, suche as be but of small speryte°
wyll reprove the evyl speker, & cause them to repente theyr wordes, & entreate
them evyll, ye34 & peradventure° sle them the causes may toche so nere.xvi The
.xii., to eschew the murmuracions°, the whiche every man ought to dought°. For
a man beyng defamed and called an evyll speker in every place, as well within
houses° as abrode° in *the* feldes, men wyll speke shame of hym & murmure as his
vice.xvii 35 The .xiii. is for *the* perell that may ensue. For when suche be taken for
evyll spekers they are behated of every man. And some, peradventure°, to please
theyr ladies, wil set ther handes upon them that speke evyll of any woman.36 The
.iiii.37 [i]s38 for *the* beautie and grace *that* is in 39 women40, the whiche is of suche
excelence that though they had all suche other vices in them as the evyll spekers
do slaunder them withall, yet it were better to prayse one thynge of trouth then to
dysprayse all with [L1v] malice.xviii 41 The .xv. and the last is for the great welth°
and goodnes that women be causers of. For of them are borne emperours, kynges,
lordes42, and all other noble men, and all other vertuous men doynge deades worthy of prayse. And also of them procedeth wyse men who seketh to know what is
good, in whose beleve° we be saved.xix 43 44 Also of women cometh these inventyve
persons, who maketh cities and stronge buyldynges of perpetuall excellence.xx &
by them are brought forthe such men as seke for all thynges necessary for the sus-
tentacion° of the humayn lynage°.

29] Marginal note 2 3 *The .ix. cause*
30 to] 1 *the*
31] Marginal note 2 3 *The .x. cause*
32 dyfferente] 2 3 *difference*
33] 2 3 *is*
34 ye] 3 *yea*
35] Marginal note 2 3 *The .xii. cause*
36] Marginal note 2 3 *The .xiii. cause*
37 .iiii.] 2 3 *.xiiii.*
38 is] 1 *s*
39] 3 *a*
40 women] 3 *woman*
41] Marginal note 2 3 *The .xiiii. cause*
42 lordes] 3 *lorde*
43] Marginal note 2 3 *The .xv. cause*
44] 2 3 *And*

XLIV: The other[1] .xx. reasons that Lereano shewed°, wherby that men are bound to love women

Now Teseo, syn°[2] thou hast hard° the causes wherin thou arte culpable and all other that folow such aronyous° opinyon, lette us leve all prolixite and here .xx. reasones wherby I wyll prove that men are bounde to women. [L2r][3] The fyrst is bycause by[4] theyr meanes *the* symple° & rude° persones dispose them selfe to at-tayne to vertue and to prudence. And not alonely° they cause the symple° to be discrete°, but they cause them that be discrete° to be more subtile°. For if they be luryd° with the passion of love they study then so moche for theyr libertie. & in sufferynge of theyr dolour they study & imagyne to speke reasones so swete and so mete° for theyr purpose, *that* often tymes for compassyon therof they are dely-verd.[i] [5] & such as be symple° and rude° of nature, yf they be enteryd in to love, though they begynne rudely° yet they quycken° so theyr understandynge° that often tymes they come therby to wysdome. Thus[6] they have by women though[e][7] theyr naturall reasone fayle. The .ii. reason is that by reason of justice they cause men to have the vertue of sufferance°. For such as be in the trayn° of love and suf-fre payne out of mesure they take it in maner for a comeforte, [L2v] justifyinge *that* they suffer it ryghtwysly°. And yet they make us not alonely° joy for this ver-tue, but also [8] other as naturall.[ii] [9] For they that be stedfast lovers, to be praysed of them that they serve, they seke all *the* wayes they can to pleace°. For which cause they lyve justly, not excedynge in any thynge in that is honourable nor mete° to be done bycause they wolde° not be famyd° to be of evyll condycions, or to use any evyll customes.[iii] The .iii. cause is they make us worthy in the vertue of atemperance°. Bycause they[10] shulde not abhorre us, nor that we shuld not be be-hatyd of them, they cause us to use atemperance° in eatynge, and drynkyng, and slepyng and in all other thynges that perteynith to the vertue of atemperance°, as well in spekynge as in all other warkes°, so that we woll not excede in no poynte frome hones[ty]e[11].[iv] [12] The .iiii. is they that lacke strength, women do gyve it to

---

[1] other] 2 3 Omitted.

[2] syn] 2 *syns* 3 *sins*

[3]] Marginal note 2 *.xx. reasons whiche men ought to love women* 3 *.xx. reasons which men ought to love women*

[4] by] 3 Omitted.

[5]] Marginal note 2 *Pruden* 3 *Prudenc*

[6] Thus] 2 3 *This*

[7] thoughe] 1 *thought*

[8]] 2 3 *for*

[9]] Marginal note 2 3 *The .ii. reason is justice*

[10] they] 3 *the*

[11] honestye] 1 *honeslie*

[12]] Marginal note 2 *The .iii. reason is temperance* 3 *The .iii. reason is temperaunce*

them. And suche as hath strength by the meanes of women, it [L3r] doth encrease. They cause us to be strong to suffre, they cause hardynes° to enterprice°,
they cause the harte to hope. When they putte theyr lovers to any jeopedy° they
cause them to be in glory. They cause us to repute° feare a great vice, for we esteme more *the* prayse of our lover then the price of longe lyfe.ᵛ ¹³ For theyr sakes
they begynne & make an ende of many greate enterprices, puttyng theyr strength
in the state as they deserve, wherfore we may well j[u]dge *that* we be bounde to
them.ᵛⁱ The .v. is they endue° us with no lesse vertuos theogecals° then they do
with vertuos cardynals°.ᵛⁱⁱ ¹⁴ And to speke of the fyrst, the which is faith, yf any
man be in dought° of his beleve°, if his mynde be ones° set in love then he shall
truely beleve in God and laude his puyssance° to create suche a creature as his
lover is with so excellent beawtye.ᵛⁱⁱⁱ And they wyll be so devoute that the apostels
in holynes shall have of them none° advauntage.ⁱˣ The .vi. reasone is bycause they
engender [L3v] in our sowles the vertue of hope. So though *the* subgiettes to the
lawe of love endure moche payne, yet alwayes they hope in theyr beleve°, they¹⁵
hope in theyr stedfastnes, they hope in *the* pitie of them that cause theyr payne,
they hope in the condycion of theyr lover who distroyeth them, they hope in the
adventure. Seynge° they have so moche hope upon them that gyvith them theyr
passion°, then they must nedys have hope in God who offerith and promyseth
perpetuall comforte and reste.ˣ ¹⁶ The .vii. reason is they cause us to deserve charyte, the propretie therof is love. This restith in our wyll, this we put in our
thoughtes, this we drawe in to our memory, this we ferme° in our hartes.¹⁷ And
though it be so that we use this love towardes our loveres, yet it redoundithe° to
the soverayne° utilyte and welthe° in tyme to come, so that *with* quyke contricion
it shall brynge us to God. For love at *the* pynche of deth° causith us to do almesse°
deades, and commaundith [L4r] to say masses, and occupieth us in¹⁸ charytable
warkes°, to th'entent to delyver us fro° our¹⁹ cruell thoughtes.ˣⁱ And bycause that
women naturally are devoute, and bycause we wolde° be pertakers° of theyr
deades, it enforsith° us to do suche good warkes° as we do. The .viii. reason, bycause they make us contemplative. For the prisoners of love do²⁰ gyve themselfe
to contemplacion in remembrynge the beaute, grace and excellence of them that
they love. And so moche they thynke upon theyr passions°, that often tymes they
remember God & set so theyr hartes upon hym that they thynke them selfe well

---

¹³] Marginal note 2 3 *The .iiii. reason is fortitude*
¹⁴] Marginal note 2*The .v. reason is fayth* 3 *The .v. reason ys fayth*
¹⁵ they] 2 3 *the*
¹⁶] Marginal note 2 3 *The .vi. reason is hope*
¹⁷] Marginal note 2 3 *The .vii. reason is charyte*
¹⁸ in] 2 3 *to*
¹⁹ our] 3 Omitted.
²⁰ do] 2 3 *to*

worthy to receyve theyr payn*e*s & torme*n*tes.[xii] [21] Thus it may be knowe*n* clerly
thet women helpe &[22] ayde men to wynne the glory perdurable°. The .ix. reasone
is they make our hartes contryte. Notw*ith*standynge that some be sore° peyned°
bycause they ca*n* not attayn to theyr wylles and desires, then with wepynges and
syghynges they desire of theyr ladyes [L4v] some remedye°.[xiii] And the accos-
tumyng° of this doyng bryngith them to go *con*fesse theyr synnes w*ith* wepyng
and waylynge in suche wyse° that they deserve perdone and absolucio*n* of theyr
synne.[23] The .x. is the good counsayle that women gevith us.[24] Often tymes it
falleth[25] that we fynde i[n][26] theyr redy° cou*n*sayll that we have long studyed for
before and sought for with great dylygence.[xiv] And by theyr peaseable° counsaylls
withoute sclaunder° they have withstande many evylls° & savyde many lyves.
They conserve the peace, they resfrayne° ire, & apeace° furiousnes, and sette
amyte° betwene enemyes. The .xi. is men be honouryd by them.[xv] They cause
greate maryages w*ith* great ryches and rentes°.[27] Some, peradventure°, wyll say
that honour restith not in ryches but rather in vertue, I say therto they cause as
well the one as the other. I presume that ther be greate vertue in us, yet the greate
honours and prayse that we desyre to have *com*myth by them.[xvi] Bycause of [L5r]
women, we esteme more shame then our lyves. For theyr sakes we study to do al
warkes° of noblenes. The .xii. reasonne is they[28] seperate fro us° all averise, the
which is the rote° of all evyll, and causith us to be accompanyd with lyberalyte,
wherby lyghtly° we get the good wyll of every man.[29] They cause us lyberally to
spend that we have wherby we are praysed & fast° tyed to every man w*ith* good
love, so that in what so ever necessite we fale° in, we shall receyve ayde and service. And not alonely° they profyt us as in causynge us to use lyberalyte as we
ought to do, but therby they cause us to be moche set by° and made of.[xvii] And
what surer thynge can be then to have the good wyll of the people? The .xiii. reasone is wome*n* encrease and kepe our goodes and rentes°. And that we have go-
ten, they conserve it with greate dylygence.[30] The .xiiii. is the clennes° that they

---

[21]] Marginal note 2 *The viii. reason is conte*mplacion 3 *The .viii reason is contempla-
cyon*

[22] &] 3 Omitted.

[23]] Marginal note 2 *The ix. reaso*n *is co[n]tricion & confession* 3 *The .ix. reason is contricion & confessyon*

[24]] Marginal note 2 *The .x. reason is theyr good counsayll* 3 *The .x. reason is their good
counsayle*

[25] falleth] 2 *faylleth*

[26] in] 1 *i*

[27]] Marginal note 2 3 *The .xi. is p*romocion *that co*me *by them*

[28] they] 3 *the*

[29]] Marginal note 2 *The .xii. reason is our liberalite* 3 *The .xii. reason ys our lyberalyte*

[30]] Marginal note 2 *The .xiii. is theyr circu*msicion 3 *The .xiii. reason ys theyr circum-
sycyon*

procure us to use, as well in our persones as in our habylymentes° and in [L5v] every thynge that we medle with.³¹ The [xv]³² is for *the* good bryngynge up of chyldren, the which is a princypall thyng whereof men have greate nede. For if we be well brought up we shall use all curtesye and eschew the contrary. Therby we shal honour the small° and serve the great. & not alonely° they cause us to be well brought up but also to be belovyd, for yf we entreate every man as he de-servyth they shall entreate us accordyng to our desertes°.³³ The .xvi. is they cause us to be galante° and freshe° in our aperell°. ³⁴ For theyr sakes we study how to aperell° us and what we may were°.ˣᵛⁱⁱⁱ And for theyr sakes we aray us by good in-dustry° and crafte to brynge our personages° in to a³⁵ dewe° forme, *the* which some tyme peradventure° nature denyeth. Then to hyde that deformyte, crafte must be usyde and occupyed° devysyng the aperell° accordynge, some tyme long, some tyme shorte, some tyme streyght, some tyme wyde, as best may become the persone. ˣⁱˣ [L6r] These galantes°, for love of women, devyse new entayles°, and cuttes with discrete borders° and dyverse other new invensions.ˣˣ The .xvii. rea-sone is often tymes they cause musyke° to be hadde of all instrumentes, & many of them occupy the same so that we joy of theyr swete armony°.ˣˣⁱ For theyr sakes are songe° these swete romanses in as subtyle° wayes as can be devysed.³⁶ The .xviii. is they cause our force and strength to encrease, for when men come before ladyes and gentle women, they enforce° them to cast stones, barres° and dartes, and to wrestyll, rynne° and leape. And the syght of the women uttereth° theyr feates with more force then yf the³⁷ women were absent. & all this is to th'entent to atayne *the* love of theyr lady.³⁸ The .xix. is they quykken° the inwarde° spirite° as well as the body. For if we know that our lover take pleasure in any thynge, other in synginge, daunsynge or playeng upon any instrumente, they wyll then applye them selfe [L6v] to lerne it and to travayle° theyr sprytes° there aboute.ˣˣⁱⁱ And though they were but dull° before, yet with suche diligence they wyll at-tayne to the perfection of *the* arte therby to gyve recreacion° to theyr lover.³⁹ The .xx. and the last reason is bycause we be women's chyldren. By the whiche respect

---

³¹] Marginal note 2 *The .xiiii. is theyr clennes* 3 *The .xiiii. reason y[s] thyr clen[n]es*

³² *xv*] 1 Omitted

³³] Marginal note 2 *The .xv. is oure educacion* 3 *The .xv. reason ys oure educacyon*

³⁴] Marginal note 2 *The .xvi. is the cause of our aparell* 3 *The xvi. is* [the] *ca[u]se of our aparell*

³⁵ a] 3 Omitted.

³⁶] Marginal note 2 *The .xvii. reason is they cause musyke* 3 *The .xvii. reason is the cause of musyk*

³⁷ the] 3 Omitted.

³⁸] Marginal note 2 *The .xviii. reason is they increase our strengthe* 3 *The .xviii. reason is the incres our strengthe*

³⁹] Marginal note 2 *The .xix. is the qcken our lyvely spurites* 3 *The .xix. is the quicken our litel spyrytes*

we are most bounde to women rather then for any other cause sayd before or to be sayde.[40] For pleasure of women are ordyned these justes° royall, and pompeous° tourneis°, and these bankettes° and joyfull feastes. For them is begonne° thynges of gentlenes°. There is no cause why they shulde be by us dipray[sed][41].xxiii O trespas of grevous chastiment°! What woman is there in all the worlde that wyll not have compassion of the cryes & lamentacions that we shew them, or of the paynefull wordes and syghes that we utter before them, or of the swerynges and promyses that we make to them?xxiv [42] Or what is she that wyll not beleve the stedfast fayth that we promyse? [L7r] What harte can be withoute frute, herynge the commendable prayses that we gyve them by ferme° harte and wyll, and by none° adulasion nor malyce?xxv What woman is she of so ferme° and stable a mynde that can defende her selfe yf she be contynually pursued? Consyderynge the deades of armes wherwith they be fought withall, though they make but small defence, it is no mervayll°. And yet suche as can not defend them selfe ought to be praysed & namyd° pitefull rather then to be reputed° culpable.xxvi

XLV: The profe by ensample° of the bounte° & goodnes of women shewed by Lereano[i]

To th'entent that lawdable° vertue of *the* sex femenyn shuld be declared accordyng to theyr desertes°, I purpose° to alledge certayne ensamples°. Howbeit my desyre was to have restyde° with this that I have sayde, to th'entent that my ignorante[1] and rude° tonge° shulde not have troubled° theyr clere° bounte° by [L7v] reason of my[2] unwysedome°.ii Howbeit my prayse can not encrease theyr goodnes nor my disprayse can not abate theyr propertye°.iii [3] If I shuld make rehersall° of the chast virgins, tyme past and present, I hadde nede to have the devyne° revelasion for ther be and have ben so many that no humayne wytte° can comprehende them. And to be breve° I shall shew° of some as I have redde, as well Crystened° as Gen-tyls° & Jewes°. I wyl make ensample by the few to comprehende the vertue of the mo°. As for suche as be auctorysed° to be sayntes, I wyll not speke of them for .iii.

---

[40]] Marginal note 2 *The .xx. and last reas*on *is byca[u]se we be theyr fleshe and blode* 3 *The .xx. & last reason ys bycause we be thyr fleshe and bloude*

[41] dispraysed] 1 *disprayede*

[42]] Marginal note 2 3 *The paynes of a lover*

---

[1] ignorante] 3 *ignoraunce*

[2] my] 3 *the*

[3]] Marginal note 2 *The enamples of Leriano in the comm*en*dacion of women* 3 *exam*ples *of Leryano in the com*mendacyon *of women*

causes. The fyrste bycause it is manyfeste° and openly knowen, then it were but symplenes° & waste to reherce° it. The.ii. cause is *the* chyrch gyveth them unyversall prayse. The .iii., bycause I ame not worthy to put in my rude° wordes theyr excellent goodnes & specially of our Blessed Lady.[iv] [4] All the doctours° and devoute contemplatyves° coulde never speke nor prayse her as she is worthy, [L8r] nor reche to the lest parte of her excelle*nt*°[5], wherfore I wyll come lower and declare of them that I may spek more liberally. I wyll begynne at the chaste Gentiles°. Lucresia, chefe crowne of the nacion romayne°, wyfe to Colatyne, knowynge herselfe enforsed° & defowled° by Traquyne, she sayde to her husband, Colatyne:[v] "Dere spouse, know for trouth that a strange° man hath defowled° thy bedde.[6] Howbeit, though my body be enforced°, my harte is innocent. Though I be fre fro° *the* trespace, I can not be assoyled° fro° *the* payne. And to th'entent that no lady nor other woman hereafter by myne ensample° shuld erre," and so with speking of those wordes with a sharpe sword she ryd her owne lyfe. Also Porcia, who was doughter to the noble Catone, and wyfe to the noble & vertuos Bruto[7], and when she knew the deth of her husband, she tooke such grevous sorow, that to the ende of her lyfe she dyd eate hote° coles to make sacrefice of her selfe.[8] [vi] Penolope, wyfe to [L8v] Ulixes, she knowyng that he went in to warre agaynst the Troyans, knowyng that yonge men of Italy were sore° enamored upon her beautie, in the absence of her husband dyverce desyred to mary with her.[9] [vii] And she, desyrynge to kepe her chastitie & to defende her selfe agaynst them, sayd how she wold° make a webbe° as Ladies used in those dayes, & when it was finished she promysed her wowers° then to accomplish theyr desyres. And when she hadde graunted this, by her subtile° wyt° as moche as she made in the day she brake° it agayn in *the* nyght. And by that meanes she drave° of the seasone° .xx. yere. And then Ulixes came home alone, olde & in greate povertie, yet the [c]hast[e][10] Lady receved hym a[s][11] though he hadde come in[12] greate prosperytie.[viii] Also Julia, doughter to Cesar,[13] fyrst emperour, beinge wyfe to Pompeye, she loved hym so entierly that on a day she fyndynge his clothes bloudy, belevynge that he hadde bene dede, fell sodenly to the erth [M1r] and dyed for sorow.[14] [ix]

---

[4]] Marginal note 2 *whiche wyl not speke of Sayntes* 3 *which wil not speke of Saints*

[5] excell*ent*] 2 *excelence* 3 *excelle*nce

[6]] Marginal note 2 *Lucres* 3 *Lucres*

[7] Bruto] 3 *Brito*

[8]] Marginal note 2 *Porcia* 3 *Porcys*

[9]] Marginal note 2 *Penol[o]pe* 3 *Penolope*

[10] chaste] 1 *hast* 3 *chast*

[11] as] 1 *ad* 2 3 *&*

[12] in] 2 *i to* 3 *into*

[13]] 2 3 *the*

[14]] Marginal note 2 3 *Julia*

Atrenisa, amonge other mortayll creatures worthy to be praysed, she beinge
maried to Mansall, Kynge of Icaria, she loved hym with so ferme° a harte that
when he was dede she gave hym sepulture within her owne brest.[15] [x] She brente°
his bones, and *the* asshes of them she dranke litle and litle°. And the seremonies
made of his obsequy, thinkinge that she wold° go to hym, slew her selfe with her
owne handes. Argea, doughter to Kynge Adastro and wyfe to Polymytes, sonne
to Egisto, Kynge of Thebes.[xi] When Polimites was slaine in a batayll by the
handes of his brother, she knowinge therof (withoute fearing of her enemyes, or
of any other wylde bestes, nor fearynge the emperou[r]'s[16] law) wente oute of
Athenes in the nyght in to the felde, and found oute amonge the dede bodies her
husbande's body, and caryed it in to the citie, and caused it to be brent° accordyng
to the custome with bytter wepynge, puttynge the asshes in [M1v] to a cofer of
golde, and then promysed her lyfe to perpetuall chastite.[17] Ipola of Grece, say-
lynge by the see, by her evyll fortune she was taken by her enemyes and they
wolde° have enforsed° her.[xii] And she, to conserve her chastite, went to the one
side of the shyp and wyllyngly fell over the boorde in to the see and there was
drowned. Howbeit the fame of her dead° was not greatly laudable.[18] [xiii] No lesse
worthy of prayse was the wyfe of Amede[19], Kynge of Thesale.[xiv] She knoweng by
the aunswere of the god Apollo, that her husb[an]d[20] shulde receyve the deth
withoute voluntaryly some other personne wolde° dye for hym, and so wyllyngly
to save the kynge, she disposed her selfe to dye.[21] Now of the nacion[22] of the Jues°.
Sara, wyfe of Father Abraham, when she was taken and in the power of Kynge
Pharao, defendynge her chastitie with the armes of prayer°, desyred° God to delyver her oute of his handes.[xv] [23] And when the kyng thought to have fulfylled his
[M2r] e[v]yll dead°, God heryng her petecion, the kynge waxyde° seke° in suche
wyse° that then he knew well it was for his wanton desyre.[xvi] Then he commaydyd
to delyver her quyte° *with*oute any spotte° of unclennis°. Delbora, enduyd° with so
many vertues, deservyd to have the spirite of prophesye.[24] [xvii] She shewyd not
alonely° her bounte° in artes femenyne, but also in stronge° batayles,[25] feyghtynge°

---

[15]] Marginal note 2 *Artrenisa*

[16] emperour's] 1 *emperous*

[17]] Marginal note 2 *Argea*

[18]] Marginal note 2 *Ipola drownd her selfe to save her chastite* 3 *Ipola drownde her selfe to save her chastitye*

[19] Amede] 3 *Emede*

[20] husband] 1 *husbnad* 2 *husbande*

[21]] Marginal note 2 3 *The wyfe dyed to save her husbande* 3 *The wife dyed to save her husband*

[22] nacion] 3 *nacions*

[23]] Marginal note 2 3 *Sara*

[24]] Marginal note 2 *Delbo* 3 *Delbora*

[25]] 3 *of*

agaynste her enemyes with a valyante and a vertuous harte. And she was of suche
excellence that .xl. yere[26] she rulyd the people of the Jues°. Hestere, brought in
captyvyte in to Babilone, for her vertue & fayernes she was take*n* to wyfe° to
Kyng Assuara, who at that tyme rulyd a .C.xxvii. provy[n]ces.[27] [xviii] And by her
merites & prayers delyvered the Jues° fro° theyr captyvyte.[xix] Also the mother of
Sampson, desyrynge to have a sonne, deservyd by her vertue that an angell shewyde the natyvyte of Sampsone.[28] [xx] Elisabeth, wyfe to Sacarias, as she was the
very servant of God, for her [M2v] deservynge° she had a sonne sanctified or° he
was borne, which was Saynte John.[29] [xxi] Now of olde stories of Cristen° women, I
can not wryte them at lenght, but to be breve° to shew° some of a latter tyme of
the nacion of Castile. Don Marya Coronell, by whome beganne *the* lynage° of the
Coronelles, bycause her chastite was praysede and her bountie° not hyd, she was
accusyde of a cryme wherfore wyllyngly she brente° her selfe, havyng lesse feare
of the deth then to be founde culpable.[30] [xxii] Also, Done Isabell, mother to the
Mayster of the Order of Calatrane, Done Rod[r]igo, and mother to .ii. erles° of
Urenia, Done Alonso & Don John.[xxiii] She beyng a widowe fell in to a sikenes
and the phisycions to procure her helth sayd how she coulde not lyve withoute°
she maryed or had the company° of a man.[xxiv] Then her chyldren knowynge what
case° she was in, desyryd° and counsayled her to take an husbande. She aunswerd
and sayd: "By the grace of God that shall I [M3r] never do, for I had rather dye
to be called mother to suche chyldren as ye be then to lyve and to be called wyfe
to another husband." And with this chaste consyderacyon and by the pleasoure of
God, when she dyed ther were mysteries° sene of her salvacion.[31] Also Don Maria Gracia, the blessed woman borne in Toledo of the gretest lynage° in all the
citie, she wolde° never mary, kepynge her vyrginite .iiii. score[32] yere, a[t][33] whose
deth were sene dyverce myracles, the whiche yet in Tolledo be had in perpetuall
remembrance°.[xxv] [34] O what may a man say of the pure vyrgyns of gentiles°?[xxvi]
Atrisalya[35] Sybela, borne in the citie of Babilone, for her merites she prophesied
by divyne revelacion many thinges to come after, always conservinge her vyrgi-
nytie tyll she dyed.[xxvii] Pallas & Mynerva, fyrst sene about the ryver of Tritonia,

---

[26] yere] 2 3 *yeres*

[27]] Marginal note 2 3 *Hester*

[28]] Marginal note 2 3 *Sampson mother*

[29]] Marginal note 2 3 *Elisabeth*

[30]] Marginal note 2 *The constaunce to be noted in acordyng a dreme* 3 *The constance to be noted in a cordynge to a dreme*

[31]] Marginal note 2 *She had rather dye of a sycknes then to mar[ye] agayne* 3 *She had rather dye of a sycknes then to marye againe*

[32] .iiii. score] 2 *xixx* 3 *xlxx*

[33] at] 1 *as*

[34]] Marginal note 2 *A mayd of .lc. yeres* 3 *A mayde of .lx. yeares*

[35] Atrisalya] *Arrisalia*

newe inve*n*ters of many offices perteynynge to the femynyne sex, and also to men, alwayes lyvyng as vyrgins.ˣˣᵛⁱⁱⁱ And so ended Atalanta, [M3v] she that fyrst strake° the porke of Calydonia°, in virgynite and noblenes she co*n*tynuyd.ˣˣⁱˣ Canulla, doughter to Macabeo, Kyng of *the* Bostos, she dyed³⁶ no lesse then other dyd in kepyng of her virgynite.ˣˣˣ Cala[u]dea Vesta, Clodya Romayne, they kepte the same law till theyr dethe.ˣˣˣⁱ Yf it were not to length my trouble, yf I shuld lyve this .M. yere, I coulde not resite° the ensa*m*ples° that I could reherce°. Therfore, Tesio, accordyng as thou haste harde°, thou, and suche other as do blaspheme the nature femenyne, are well worthy of juste punysion. The which I counsaill the not to abide to receyve it of another, but rather punyshe thy selfe. Yf thou do it of malyce, condemne the shame therof!ˣˣˣⁱⁱ

XLVI: The auctor

All suche as were present had great marvayll° of his wordes, seynge° by his spekynge to be so nere the deth as he was. For when he had ended his wordes his tonge° began to fayll and [M4r] his syght nere lost. Then his servauntes began to crye and wayle, and his frend¹ begane to wepe, and his subjectes cryynge oute in the streates so that all joy was turned to sorow.ⁱ And the Lady, his mother, beynge absente, for his sekenes° was kept fro° her knowledge, howbeit she gyvynge more credyte to her feare then to that was shewyd° her, with boldnes of maternall love, she deperted fro° her owne howse and came to Susa. And when she entered the gate, every persone that she saw gave her evydence of dolour with wordes of extreme passyon, rather then with wordes well ordered.ⁱⁱ She, herynge how her sone, Lereano, was in the extremyties° of deth, her strenght fayled her so that she fell downe to the erth in a trance°. & so longe she laye that every man thought that *the* mother and the sonne shulde take theyr sepulture at one tyme. ⁱⁱⁱ Howbeit, with harde remedy° she came agayne to her selfe, and then went to her sone. And when she saw hym [M4v] in that astate°, with greate wepynge and passyon° of deth she sayd as folowith.

---

³⁶ dyed] 2 3 *dyd*

---

¹ frend] 2 3 *frendes*

XLVII: The complaynte of Lereano's mother[1]

O Lereano![i] The myrth, comforte, rest and supporte of myne olde dayes![ii] O swete companyon to my wyll! This day I ame lyke° to leve callyng the any more sonne, nor thou to call me mother. Of this I have greate feare by the sygnes that I se of thy shorte dayes. Often tymes I hadde suche dremes where with I have bene in greate feare all the nyght durynge. Other tymes, when I have ben in my oratory prayng for thy helth, my harte hath faylede me and a colde sweat hath taken me in suche maner that of along tyme I wyst° not what to do. Also *the* bestes° have c[er]tified[2] me of thyne evyll°, for on a day as I came out of my chamber ther came to me a dogge and made sodenly suche a howlyng that for feare ther of I lost the strength of my body and could not speke nor could [M5r] not remove° oute of the place that I was in.[3] And therby I gave more credence to my suspecte° then to thy messengers, and to satysfie my selfe I ame come to se the. O the lyght of my syghte and lyfe! O blyndnes of the same if I se *thee* dye! & I can se none° occasio*n* of thy deth, *thou* beyng in age to lyve![iii] *Thou* hast alwayes ben fearefull of God, & lover of all vertues[4], and enemye to all vyces, fre*n*de to fre*n*des and belovyde. Thynke for certane this day *the* force of thyne evyll fortune takith away the ryght of reaso*n* syn°[5] thou dyest or° thy tyme withoute any infyrmytie. Happy° be they that be of low and base co*n*dicio*n* and rude° of wytte°, for they feale no thynge, but take every thynge as it comyth.[iv] And unhappy° be they that by subtyll° wytte° and sharpe understa*n*dyng° know every thynge.[v] Wolde° to God thou werte one of the rude° and dull°, for I had rather to be callyd mother to a rude° persone havynge thy lyfe then to have thy deth beyng never so wyse.[vi] O cruell deth, [M5v] enemy to all mortal creatures! Thou wilt perdone no synners[6], nor assoyll° the innocentes! [7] Thou arte suche a traytour that no man can make defence agaynst the. Thou thretenyst age and takest awaye yough°. The one thou sleyste° by malyce and *the* other for envy. Though thou tary longe, yet thou wylte° not forget to come at laste.[vii] Thou governyst thy selfe with oute law or reasone. It had ben better for the to have co*n*servyd my sonne, beyng of .xx. yeres, rather then to leve me his mother of .lxx. yeres of age.[viii] Why doste° thou turne *the* ryght upse down°? I have lyved longe inough and he is yong yet for to lyve. Perdon me *that* I thus say to the, for thou by thy cruell warkes° causyste dolours, yet agayne thou gyvist comforte, takyng away them shortely that thou

---

[1]] 2 *at his death* 3 *at hys deathe*
[2] certified] 1 *cretified* 2 *certyfied*
[3]] Marginal note 2 *Sodayne toke*ns *ar to be noted* 3 *Sodayne tokens are to be noted*
[4] vertues] 3 *vertuous*
[5] syn] 2 *syns* 3 *since*
[6] synners] 3 *sinnes*
[7]] Marginal note 2 The *properte of deth* 3 *The propertye of death*

levist behynde them that thou takest away.[ix] For the which, yf thou wylte° so do
with me, I were moche bosid°[8] to the that I myght go with my sonne Lereano,
but yf he myght lyve and I to dye, it [M6r] shulde be my comeforte. O sone!
What shall become of my age remembryng the ende of thy yough°? Yf I lyve it
shal be rather to wepe and bewayll my synnes, then by reasone[9] to have any wyll
or desyre to lyve.[x] [10] With what thyng coulde I receyve more cruell payne then
to lyve long? Thyne evyll° is very great that ther canne be found mo°[11] remedye°.
What avaylyth now the strength of thy body, or the vertue of thyne harte, or the
hardynes° of thy corage? All these thynges that shulde avayll *thee* faylythe. Yf for
the price of love thy lyfe myght be bought, I wolde° desyre deth to do his offyce°
upon me and to delyver the quyte° fro° hym. But thy fortune wyll not suffer it,
nor I can not. Therfore sorow shal be my drynke, and my mete, and my thought,
my slepe, untyll the tyme that the force of dethe and my desyre shall brynge me
to my sepulture.[xi] [M6v]

XLVIII: The auctor

The wepyng that Lereano's mother made encreasyde the payne of all them that
were presente. And allwayes Lereano had Laureola in his remembrance°. Of that
was past he had but small memory, and consyderyng that he shulde joy but a
shorte space° with the syght of the[1] .ii. letters that Laureola hadde sente hym, he
wiste° not how to order° them.[i] [2] When he thought to breke° them, he[3] thought
he shuld offende therby Laureola in castynge away suche wordes of so worthy
price as was wrytin in them. And when he thought to put into any of his servauntes' handes, he fearyd lest they shulde be sene wherby perell myght folow.
Then in all these doubtes he toke the sureste way. He callyd for a cup of water and then brake° the lettres into small peces, and so sette° up in his bed and
dranke up the water with the peces of the letters. And so he satisfyde therby his
wyll. And then drawynge to his enden warde°[4], he cast his syght upon [M7r]
me & sayde: "Frende, now all myne evylles° be endyd." And therwith gave up

---

[8] bosid] 2 3 *bounde*

[9] by reasone] 2 3 Omitted.

[10]] Marginal note 2 *Death doth make al thin to fayle* 3 *Deathe doth make al thinges to fayle*

[11] mo] 2 3 *no*

---

[1] the] 3 Omitted.

[2]] Marginal note *what was don with the .ii. leters* 3 *what was don wyth the .ii. letters*

[3] the] 2 3 *he*

[4] enden warde] 2 *endewarde* 3 *endwarde*

his lyfe in witnes of his true fayth. ⁵ Then what sorow I felte and what I dyd is lyghtly° judged.ⁱⁱ The wepynges that was there made of his deth are⁶ of⁷ suche esteme⁸ that me thynke it cruelty to wryte it.ⁱⁱⁱ Then his obsequyes and buryals were done most honourably, accordyng to the deser[t]es°⁹ of his vertues.ⁱᵛ & as for my selfe, with a better wyll I wolde° have depertyd this lyfe then to have taryed on the yerth° alyve. So with sighes I went my way, and depertyd wyth wepyng, and with lamentacion I sore° complaynyde, and with suche thoughtes I wente to my lodgynge.ᵛ And when I saw that the consentynge and desirynge of my deth could not remedy° hym that was passyd, nor could be no comforte to my selfe, then I determyned° to deperte and to go into myne owne countrey. And yet fyrst I purposed° to go to the courte to here and se what was sayd for *the* deth of Lere-ano [M7v] and to se how Laureola toke the mater. Thus I thought to go thyther°, what for this cause & for other buysnes that I had ther to do with some of my frendes. Also I purposyd° to speke with Laureola, if I myght, to know if I myght se in her any repentance, and to se what true lovers wolde° say of her crueltye usy-de against hym that deservyd hygh reward.ᵛⁱ And also I was glad to deperte fro° the place wher as Lereano dyed, to put parte of my sorow out of my mynde. So I came to the courte more accompanyed with sorow then with any desire to lyve, remembryng how he that made me begynne this mater was in his sepulture. At the palayce I was receyvyde with moche hevynes° of many that knew the deth of Lereano. Then I resyted° to suche as were his frende¹⁰ the secretenes° of his deth. Then I went in to *the* hall where I was acustumed to speke with Laureola, to se if I myght se what chere°¹¹ she made. And I, who by reasone of sore° wepynge [M8r] had nere lost my syght, I lokyd all aboute but I culde not se her. Yet when she saw me, lyke a dyscrete° Ladye, suspectynge that I wolde° have spoken with her, wenynge° that I hadde not seen her she turned towarde her chambre. And as she came by me, I spied well it was she who hadde brought Lereano fro° his lyfe & me almoste withoute knowledge°. Then I, with sore° wepynge and payneful sighes, began to speke to her in this maner.

---

⁵] Marginal note 2 *Leriano's deth* 3 *Leriano's deathe*
⁶ are] 2 3 *were*
⁷ of] 2 3 Omitted.
⁸ esteme] 2 3 Omitted.
⁹ desertes] 1 *deserdes* 2 *deserts*
¹⁰ frende] 2 3 *frendes*
¹¹ chere] 2 3 *there*

XLIX: The auctor to Laureola

Lady, moche more it[1] hadde bene better for me to have lost my lyfe then to have knowen your cruelnes and small pytie.[2] I say this bycause I had rather with reason ha[v]e praysed your gentlenes° with seinge° you to have satisfied the servyce that hath bene done to you by Lereano then to prayse your beautie & great deservynge°, gyvyuge dethe to hym that so often tymes, with so good will to do your[3] servyce, hath desyred to dye. But syn°[4] your mynde was to [M8v] gyve hym the deth ye have not begyled hym nor me, for ye have payed hym therwith.[i] Ye have bleryd° the clennes° of your lynage°. Remembre that suche as be of so hygh blud as ye be are as[5] moch bou*n*d to satisfy the lest servyce that is done to them, as wel as to kepe and defend theyr honour.[6] And certaynly I say that yf ye had sene his deth, all the dayes of your lyfe ye wolde° wepe. Remembre now what charge of conscience ye brought hym in, for when he died where as he shulde have had most memory upon hys sowle and what shuld have ben done with his body, he then remembred more the letters that ye had[7] sent hym, the whiche he toke, and tare° in peces, & drank them in water because they shuld never be sene, and bycause he wold° cary with [h]ym[8] some thynge that had bene yours. To the entent that ye shulde have more compassio*n* of his deth then ye had of his lyfe, I shew° you for certayne, thus I saw hym dye bycause ye shewyd hym [N1r] no compassion.[ii] Now ye[9] shew your selfe to be sory that[10] in the[11] absence of your small love was clene forgoten. O how many now do wepe for his deth and yet they know not the cause! But as to me (fro° whom the secretnes°[12] was not hiden) then moche more it muste nedes° greve me, remembrynge how in your handes restyd his lyfe, and seynge° your crueltie and his small remedy°. Ye caused hym to dye & cause his mother to lyve in sorow bycause she can not dye. And as for me[13] lyvynge, I ame alwayes dyeng. And I beleve ye covytte° not gretly your owne lyfe to remembre what ye have done, but that ye know well there be but few persons that know

---

[1] it] 2 3 Omitted.

[2]] Marginal note 2 *After Leriano's deth* 3 *Leriano's deathe*

[3] your] 2 3 *you*

[4] syn] 2 3 *syns*

[5] as] 3 *so*

[6]] Marginal note 2 *Nobyly it ought rather to recompens the*n *to forget* 3 *nobylyte ought rather to recompens them to forget*

[7] had] 3 *have*

[8] hym] 1 *gym* 3 *him*

[9] ye] 2 *you*

[10] that] 2 *than*

[11] the] 2 3 *suche*

[12] secretnes] 3 *secretes*

[13] me] 2 3 *my*

what ye have done. I thynke ye feare but litle the fame° of your evyll name, for ye
se clerely how I ame lyke to dye, therfore ye feare not *that* I shuld publishe° youe
crueltie. [iii] Thynke not that I ame in feare to say thus to you. For yf I trouble you
with the qualitie, content you then with the quantite [N1v] syn°[14] I have so greate reason to speake and not to ende properly.[iv] And for this, my boldenes, yf I
deserve any punyshement cause me to be slain, for ye shal better reward me with
deth then to suffre me to lyve in this case°.

L: The auctor

Sore° troubelyd stode Laureola. Yet for all that every I sayd her face shewyd no
alterasion of her hart.[i] Howbeit, lyke a discret° Lady, refreynynge wepynge, dis-
simuled° her sorow. And not blamy[n]ge my boldenes, with an hevy° chere° she
aunswered me as foloweth.

LI: Laureola to the auctor

I wolde° I had as moche wisdome to satisfye the as I have reasone to discharge°
my selfe. And yf it were so, thou shuldest fynd me as wel discharged° as I re-
pute° the dylygent. Thou sayest thou woldest° thou haddest as moche case°[1] to
prayse my pytye as thou hast cause to blame my crueltie, and on that condicion
thou desyryst no lenger to lyve. Tho[u] [N2r] blamyst me, sayng how I thought
to sle Lereano and that[2] begylyde hym and weryde° the. I wolde° thou knewyste
I never thought to gyve hym the deth for doyng as thou sayst. What is it that
I have done? I never brake any promise. What do I owe the or hym that thou
dyddest trawayll° for? Or what dyde I to satisfye thyne entension? I dyde put
hym without doubte, and the *with*oute charge. If I had ben belevyd then myne
is but a small charge. Thou saist I ought to regarde the clennes° of my lynage°.
Lokyng profoundly theron hath causyde me to do as I have done. Thou knowyst
well all women are more bounde to regarde theyr honors rather the*n* to accom-
plysh° any amorous wyll or appetight. Then syn°[3] all women are bounde to this,
how moche more then by reasone are those bou*n*de that be dysce*n*dyd of a blude
roiall? Thynk not that I receyve any pleasure for the deth of Lereano, nor beleve

---

[14] syn] 2 *syns* 3 *sins*

---

[1] case] 2 3 *cause*
[2] that] 2 *hathe* 3 *hath*
[3] syn] 2 *syns* 3 *sins*

not that it ca*n* so moch greve *thee* as it sorowith [N2v] me. How be it, the feare
of my honour & the feare of my father dyd more in me then the evyll wyll that
I bare hym.[4] Nor thynke not that the knowledge of his service was forgoten, but
that I gave hym great thank. And yf *with* any reward I myght have payed hym,
savynge my honour, it shuld have ben done and cost hym nothyng.[i] Then both
he and thy selfe shulde as moche have praysede as now thou blamyste me for unkyndnes in his lyfe. Without the losse of lyfe I could not rewarde hym accordyng
to his desire. I wyll thou know that his deth causith me to lyve alwayes dyenge.[ii]
Now shalte thou se how moche it sorowith me and how moche he pleasyde me.
Now thou shalt judge what love I bare hym, and know yf I dyd well to suffer
hym to dye. Thou knowist well that with his lyfe he myght have wonne that by
his deth he dysparyd and lost it. But syn[5] I can not now paye nor rewarde hym,
I shall satisfye the & make the bere[6] witnes yf I [N3r] rewarde not service as I
ought to do.

LII: The auctor

She endyd her wordes with suche hevynes° that she coulde scante make an ende
for sorow. Then she went fro° me, subbyng° and sore° wepyng, wherby her tonge°
was sore° troubelyd, & chaunged colour. And so went in to her chamber with
sore° inwarde lamentacio*n* for feare she shuld have ben hard°. Then I we*n*t to my
lodgyng *with* [1] great sorow that often tymes I was desperate° of my lyfe. With
myne owne deth I wold° have ben revengyd if I coulde, not puttynge my selfe in
dyspayre. And thus beynge alone, withoute pleasure as well as withoute frendes
to speke unto, for werynes° I layd me downe. And as though I had sene Lereano
before me presente, I sayd to hym as folowith.[2]

LIII: The auctor to Lereano

O Lereano, enemye to thy adve*n*ture°and frende to thy myshape°! Who can be
cause of thy lyfe with this [N3v] ambassade° as I was cause of thy deth *with* my
message? For now if thou knewyst the repentance of Laureola, thou woldest°

---

[4]] Marginal note 2 3 *Feare*
[5] syn] 2 *syns* 3 *synce*
[6] bere] 2 3 *here*

---

[1]] 2 3 *so*
[2]] Marginal note 2 3 *The aucour dremeth*

change the glory celestyall for thy lyfe temporal, for by thy deth thou hast lost thy desyre.[i] If thou haddest savyd thy lyfe, without doubte, thou shuldest have wonne that by thy deth thou hast lost.[ii] Dyd I nat say to the when thou lay a dyenge that by thy deth thou shuldest lese° all and by thy lyfe thou myghtest attayne to thy desyre? O unhappy° *that* I am *that* I were not in *the* place where as I myght shew° the all that Laureola hath sayd to me, and of the thought that she takith for le-synge° of thy lyfe! Though *with* the deth thou hast wonne the desire of thy will, by that she shewith now thou oughtest to thynke thy deth well bestowyd°. Great joy I shuld rece[v]e if I knew that thou dyddeste here me and beleve me, for thou maist se that alonely° her repentance suffyseth to pay *thee* thy reward. Yf thou haddeste lyvyde, thou shuldeste [N4r] have had no cause to have be*n* in trouble°. Now thy payne shal be withoute hope of sufferance°. Now thou nediste not to be troubl[ed][1] with thy lyfe nor take no joy of thy deth. O what welth° shuld it be for me if God wold° suffer° me to lese° my lyfe to recover thyne! Why doth God leve me here without the? Who can lese° the and lyve after? Wold° to God that the good will that I have in[2] thy lyfe that[3] thou[4] myghtest[5] pay me with my deth. [iii] *The* which I hope thou shuldest do if thou haddest as good wyll to se me as I have desire to serve *thee*. Thus I wyll leve any further to trouble the.[iv]

LIV: The auctor's dreme

Thus I was so wery° that I left my talkynge, and as he that wyst° not what he dyd, I fell in[1] a slombere.° And amonge other thynges[2] I beganne to dreme, wherby I had more payn then pleasure. I drempt that[3] I saw Lereano before me aparelled° after this[4] maner. He had[5] on his hedde [6] a bonet° of scarlet with [N4v] a grene ryband° of an evyll colour, with a worde°[7] enbrowdered° saieng thus[8]: "Hope is

---

[1] troubled] 1 *troubly*
[2] in] 2 3 *to*
[3] that] 2 3 Omitted.
[4] thou] 2 3 Omitted.
[5] mightest] 2 *myghte* 3 *myght*

---

[1] in] 2 3 *on*
[2] amonge other thynges] 2 3 *anone*
[3] I drempt that] 2 3 *For I thought*
[4] this] 2 3 *a wonderous new*
[5] he had] 2 3 *For*
[6]] 2 3 *he had*
[7] with a worde] 2 3 *whereon was*
[8] saieng thus] 2 3 *this sentence*

dead with his colour[9] slayne by your[10] unkyndnes."[i] And[11] when he came nere me, sawe he had on a[12] shyrte [13] wrought with blak sylke with a border of letters, sayenge[14]: "Encreasyng my stedfastnes, at the ende I found deth."[15] Also he[16] had a[17] doblet° of yeolow° saten, enbrowdered° with this worde[18]: "My passion° with my joye satisfied, in doynge that I have done[19]."[ii] Also he had on[20] a jaket of blake velvyt° with[21] a border of saten of the same colour, and theron a wrytynge° that sayd[22]: "In my stedfastnes, shewed is myne evyll° and your trespace[23]."[iii] Also he had a[24] gerdell° of golde[25] with letters reportynge[26]: "More r[ic]her[27] was my[28] dethe then lyfe, if ye wolde° be servyd therwith[29]."[iv] He had also a[30] dager, *the* [31] knyves° [32] and pomell° of asure, *with* letters sayeng[33]: "Ryght sore°[34] was the passion° that ye gave me, and yet ye never repentyde it[35]." Also he had a[36] sworde

---

[9] with his colour] 2 3 *&*

[10] your] 2 3 Omitted.

[11] and] 2 3 *but*

[12] sawe he had on a] 2 3 *I marked hys*

[13]] 2 3 *wheron was*

[14] with blak sylke with a border of letters, sayenge] 2 3 *these wordes*

[15] Encreasyng my stedfastnes, at the ende I found deth] 2 *Death is founde & gyven for stedfast[n]es* 3 *Death is founde & given for stedfastnes*

[16] Also he] 2 3 *and his*

[17] had a] 2 3 Omitted.

[18] with this worde] 2 3 *thus*

[19] My passion with my joye satisfied, in doynge that I have done] 2 *Passion for joy my love hath satified* 3 *Passion for joy my love hath satiffied*

[20] Also he had on] 2 3 *&*

[21] with] 2 3 *&*

[22] and theron a wrytynge that sayd] 2 *reportyng* 3 *reportinge*

[23] in my stedfastnes, shewed is myne evyll and your trespace] 2 *Your trespase my stedfastnes full well hath veryfied* 3 *Your trespas my stedfastnes ful wel hath veryfied*

[24] Also he had a] 2 3 *His*

[25]] 2 *enamuled* 3 *enamiled*

[26] letters reportynge] 2 *this wrytynge* 3 *this writing*

[27] richer] 1 *rather* 2 3 *better*

[28] my] 2 3 Omitted.

[29] if ye wolde be servyd therwith] 2 3 *you to serve*

[30] He had also a] 2 3 *His*

[31] *the*] 2 3 *and*

[32]] 2 3 *the haftes*

[33] *with* letters sayeng] 2 3 *ingraven with this texte*

[34] ryght sore] 2 3 *Yet unrewarded*

[35] ye gave me, and yet ye never repentyde it] 2 *dyd me sterve* 3 *did me serve*

[36] Also he had a] 2 3 *And his*

with the sheth &[37] gyrdell° of sylke, [38] enbrowderyde° *with* this [N5r] worde°[39]:
"Gyvyn to my lyfe[40] such torment that [41] diyng and[42] lyvyng I[43] was content."
Also[44] his hosen°, one white [45] a nother blew, *with* this word[46]: "Chastite jelus° of
my lyfe & could not be sufferyd° to serve[47]."ᵛ And[48] over all this he had a cappe[49]°
of [50] blacke enbrowderyd°[51] with darke[52] tawny°, with a worde° that sayd[53]: "[54]
Hevynes° [55]can not so travayll° me that it shulde[56] cha*n*ge my stedfastnes."ᵛⁱ [57]
His slippers were[58] enbrowdered° *with* smal letters that[59] sayde: "Myne evyls° are
at an ende for my servyce, and denyed me is the benyfyte[60]."ᵛⁱⁱ And on his gloves
was writen: "Thus begynnyth and endeth the name that most deservyth[61]."ᵛⁱⁱⁱ So
when I had at length regarded° his aparell° and [62] the stedfaste thoughtes that by

---

[37] with the sheth &] 2 *and scabbarde of velvet a* 3 *and scabbard of velvet a*

[38]] 2 *the hyltes and pomel sylver, and on both sydes* 3 the *hiltes and pommel silver, & on bothe sydes*

[39] this worde] 2 3 *letters of golde that sayde*

[40] Gyvyn to my lyfe] 2*Your letters dowtfull to my lyfe gave* 3 *Your letters doutful to my life gave*

[41]] 2 3 *rather*

[42] and] 2 3 *then*

[43] I] 2 3 Omitted.

[44] Also] 2 3 Omitted.

[45]] 2 *&* 3 *and*

[46] this word] 2 *letters of purpull colour sayeng* 3 *with letters of purpull colour sayinge*

[47] Chastite jelus of my lyfe & could not be sufferyd to serve] 2 *My lyfe caused jelousnes in your chastyte, but to serve you, suffred I coulde not be* 3 *My lyfe caused jelousnes in your chastite, but to serve you, suffred I could not be*

[48] And] 2 3 *But*

[49] cappe] 2 3 *cloke*

[50]] 2 *the newest fashyon, the coloure* 3 *the newest fashion, the colour*

[51] enbrowderyd] 2 3 Omitted.

[52] darke] 2 3 *sadde*

[53] with a worde that sayd] 2 *sayeng* 3 *sayinge*

[54]] 2 3 *My*

[55]] 2 3 *and payne*

[56] so travayll me that it shulde] 2 3 Omitted.

[57]] 2 3 *And*

[58] were] 2 3*of red velvet*

[59] that] 2 3 *and*

[60] Myne evyls are at an ende for my servyce, and denyed me is the benyfyte] 2 *Endyd be myne evyls, and my servyce payde with unkyndnes* 3 *Endyd be myne evylles, and my servyce payed with unkyndnes*

[61] Thus begynnyth and endeth the name that most deservyth] 2 *Love beganne my payne, and death endyd it agayne* 3 *Love began my payne, and deathe endyd it againe*

[62]] 2 3 *consyderyd*

lykelyhod he enduryd, I[63] behelde[64] his face and[65] I saw his jesture°[66] so beautefull
that it semed he had never taken thought. And with an[67] amorous [68] semblant°,
after he had curtesly salutyd° me with the same voyce as he was wonte to speke,
me thought he began to say in this maner. [ix] [N5v]

LV: Lereano [1] to the auctor

O thou, my true frende! Thou hast thought that my presence hath bene longe fro°
the so that I could not tell what *thou* dyddest nor hard° what thou hast spoken.
Thynke not so, for I shall never be so farre fro° the, but that I shall always be
joyned with the. For though by adventure° in my lyfe I deperted fro° the, never
in the deth I shall deperte fro° the. I shall always be jo[yn]ed[2] with the. And
all that thou hast sayd of Laureola and of me, I was present and hard° it. God
knowith, if I myght, I wold° have spoken to the, but I could not, nor feare wold°
not leve[3] me. For[4] I certifie° the that this that I do, though my speche be short
yet it tormenteth me, and therfore acordynge to the trust that I have in thy great
vertue, I wyll not put the to the payne° with long wordes. Therfore I wyll goo to
the effect of thy wordes and to my aunswere. Thou sayest thou woldest° gladly
put me agayne in to life [N6r] as thou puttedest me to deth. Beleve nat that thy
message gave me the deth, nor I in the begynnynge can not be excused fro° coming to this[5] ende.[i] Thou sayst thou woldest° that I were in the dysposicion that I
myght joy me for the repentynge of L[a]ureola[6]. I can not thanke the therfore bycause I can not make *thee* a recompence, for the gretest service[7] that I could make
is not so greate, but the lest deservynge° that I h[av]e[8] receyved of the is moche
gretter. As for her rewardes, I desyre them not, for I can have as now no joye of

---

[63] I] 2 3 *and*
[64] behelde] 2 3 *beholdynge*
[65] and] 2 3 Omitted.
[66] jesture] 2 3 *countenaunce*
[67] an] 2 3 Omitted.
[68]] 2 3 *and demure jesture and*

---

[1]] 2 *beynge deed* 3 *being dead*
[2] joyned] 1 *ionyed*
[3] leve] 2 3 *let*
[4] for] 2 3 *but*
[5] this] 3 *hys*
[6] Laureola] 1 *Loureola*
[7] service] 1 *seriuce* 2 *serurce*
[8] have] 1 *huae*

them, though I desyre them never so moche. And though now with her repentynge she thynk to satysfie me, yet her cruelnes was so trobelous° that though she
dyd more, yet I can not be rewardyd. Thou sayst I shuld thynke my dethe well
enployede syn°⁹ I have wonne by her that without her I lost.ⁱⁱ Now wold° I do it
if lyfe were lefte with me, for though I myght joy therwith what profyt shuld it
be to me to beleve [N6v] this without° I myght se what she doth? And I beleve if
she myght se me agayne to lyve° she wolde° gyve me more payne and lesse hope.
But the best to be delyveryd fro° hope is deth, for it is better to suffer a good deth
then to endure with an evyll° lyfe. Beleve not but and I had belevyd that I shuld
have servyd her better lyvyng then to dye, I wold° not have dyed yet, but syn°¹⁰
that with my lyfe I could not prevayll, I thought then with deth to remedy° me.ⁱⁱⁱ
Thynke not that I was so farre withoute wytte° that I knew not that it was good
to lyve to serve her though I coulde have no joy of her. But I could never know by
her aunswere that she was content with my servyce, as *thou* knowist ryght well.
But she dyd let me dye, for I desiryd lyfe to leve me. Also *thou* seist° that *thou*
desirest to recover° me & to lese° thy lyfe. I beleve *thee* and I thanke *thee* therof,
though I can do none° other thyng. *Thou* desirist me to pray for thy deth bycause
we myght lyke frendes joy together [N7r] syn°¹¹ we could not in our lyfe. Be not
of *that* beleve, for I had rather her° spekynge of thy lyfe withoute syght of the then
to know thou shuldest be with me dede. Howbeit by thy deth thou shuldest but
change thy lyfe, for thy fame° shuld never dye but ever° lyve. Thus I wyll leve the,
not bicause I wyll go farre fro° the. Wherfore I requyre° the take it for none° evyll°
that I speke no more to the, for though I wolde°, I can not.

LVI: The auctor

When Lereano had made an ende of his wordes I thought to have aunswerd hym,
but¹ then in my dreme me thought I saw² Laureola entre³ into my chambre as vy-
syble as though I had bene⁴ wakyng°.⁵ Me thought she was in a strange⁶ aparel°

---

⁹ syn] 2 *syns* 3 *since*
¹⁰ syn] 2 *syns* 3 *sins*
¹¹ syn] 2 *syns* 3 *synce*

---

¹ but] 3 Omitted.
² I saw] 2 3 Omitted.
³ entre] 2 3 *entred*
⁴ bene] 2 3 *sene her*
⁵] 2 3 *but*
⁶ she was in a strange] 2 3 *her*

⁷ and with a new companyon⁸. ⁹ ⁱ And in *the*¹⁰ regardynge° of so new a vision¹¹ I left ¹² aunswerynge¹³ Lereano and began to marke the maner¹⁴ of her ¹⁵aparell°. ⁱⁱ And I so regarded° her that I left lokyng upon¹⁶ Lereano.¹⁷ She hadde¹⁸ [N7v] upo*n*¹⁹ her hed° a fresh° ²⁰ atyer°, frete°²¹ & enbrowdered° with letters sayeng: "My cruell condicion gyveth no deth to servyce, nor yet rewarde²²." Her smocke°, wrought with whyte sylke, tyed with²³ letters ²⁴ sayeng²⁵: "Thy deth is so fastened to my lyfe that I can not scape° without deth²⁶." Her kertell° of blacke saten with a folyage° of ²⁷ tawny° ²⁸ w*ith* letters²⁹ sayeng: "Thy stedfastnes myght have gyven me suche payne, that at the ende it myght have wonne me³⁰."³¹ Her gyrdell° was

---

⁷] 2 3 *was straunge*

⁸ with a new companyon] 2 *not comely for one suche of her astate and condycion* 3 *not commely for one such of her astate & condicion*

⁹] Marginal note 2 3 *The forme of Laureola when she appered*

¹⁰ *the*] 2 3 Omitted.

¹¹ of so new a vision] 2 *the noblenes of the thynge* 3 *the noblenes of the thynge*

¹²] 2 3 *to*

¹³ aunswerynge] 2 3 *answere*

¹⁴ the maner] 2 3 *and take hede*

¹⁵] 2 *newe* 3 *new*

¹⁶ and I so regarded her that I left lokyng upon] 2 3 *so that I loked no more of*

¹⁷] 2 3 *for*

¹⁸ hadde] 3 Omitted.

¹⁹ up*on*] 2 3 *on*

²⁰] 2 *and a newe* 3 *& a new*

²¹ frete] 2 *fcet* 3 *set*

²² My cruell condicion gyveth no deth to servyce, nor yet rewarde] 2 3 *My unkyndnes hathe not slayne you, nor my cruelnes*

²³ tyed with] 2 3 *the*

²⁴] 2 3 *therof*

²⁵ sayeng] 2 *sayde* 3 *saide*

²⁶ Thy deth is so fastened to my lyfe that I can not scape without deth] 2 *Your lyfe better then death shulde fayle my stedfastnes* 3 *Youre life better then deathe should fayle my stedfastnes*

²⁷] 2 *sadde* 3 *sad*

²⁸] 2 *embrowdred* 3 *embrodred*

²⁹ letters] 2 3 *this*

³⁰ stedfastnesmyght have gyven me suche payne, that at the ende it myght have wonne me] 2 *death hath lost that thy lyfe myght have atteyned* 3 *death hath loste that thy life might have atteyned*

³¹] *Her gowne of blacke velvet, with borders of tyssue embrowdred with letters. Thy lyfe shulde have clered that thy death hath atteyned* 3 *Her gowne of blacke velvet, wyth borders of tyssue embrodered wyth letters. Thy life shoulde have clered that thy deth hath atteyned*

wrought with thredes°[32] of [33]gold, reportynge[34]: "More rather shulde have bene my glory with thy lyfe then with thy deth[35]."[iii] Her mantel° was of .ii. colours, the one parte red the other blew, with a wrytynge° that sayde: "Now joye can not enjoye me without great thought."[36] She had a tabard° of blew russet° with letters sayeng: "With thy deth my memory is certayne so that lyvynge, my glory is dede[37]."[iv] Also,[38] on her gloves was wryten thus[39]: "With that I began, I make an ende though I deserve no deth[40]."[v] Her slyppers [N8r] were enbrowdered° with this word: "I have more payne for thy payne then for myne own, yet more deserveth my shame[41]." So when I had well regarded° her aparell°[42] and marked well the sygnificacions of[43] the wrytynges°, I saw how w*ith*[44] moche sorow and smal

---

[32] was wrought with thredes] 2 3 Omitted.

[33]] 2 3 *beten*

[34] reportynge] 2 *sette with perle in letters sayeng thus* 3 *set with perle in letters saying thus*

[35] More rather shulde have bene my glory with thy lyfe then with thy deth] 2 *Thy lyfe myght enjoyed thy desyre* 3 *Thy life might enjoyed thy desyre*

[36] Her mantel was of .ii. colours, the one parte red, the other blew, with a wrytynge that sayde: Now joye can not enjoye me without great thought] 2 *Then her tablet of golde, hangynge with a lace of white & blacke ingraven thus. Space myght have quenched your great fyre* 3 *then her tablet of golde, hanginge with a lace of white and blacke ingraven thus. Space might have quenched your great fyre*

[37] letters sayeng: With thy deth my memory is certayne so that lyvynge my glory is dede] 2 *with these wordes graven on both sydes. Yf pytie myght revyve the agayne, thou shulde not leve thus in vayne. Her mantell was of two coloures, one parte red, the other blewe, with a wrytynge that sayd: Yf the servyce myght be without suspeccion, agaynst the to serve me, I wolde have made no excepcion. Her petycote of crymsen sylke embrowdred with letters of whyte sayeng: Thy stedfastnes and payne, causeth my hevynes. And her slyppers of tawnye velvet, and upon them leters that sayde: Thy evylles be ended, but myne be endles* 3 *with these wordes graven on bothe sydes. Yf pity might revive the again thou should not leve thus in vaine. Her mantel was of .ii. coloures, one parte red, the other blewe, with a writing that saide: Yf the service myght be without suspeccion, againste thee to serve me, I wolde have make no excepcyon. Her peticote of crimsen silke embrodred with letters of white sayig: Thy stedfastnes & paine causeth my hevynes. And her slippers of tawnye velvet & upon them letters that sayd: Thy evils be ended, but mine be endles.*

[38] Also] 2 3 *And*

[39] thus] 3 Omitted.

[40] With that I began, I make an ende though I deserve no deth] 2 *Thy payne begynneth my payne, and wolde deth shuld ende it agayne* 3 *Thy paine begineth my paine & wold deth shuld end it againe*

[41] Her slyppers were enbrowdered with this word: I have more payne for thy payne then for myne own, yet more deserveth my shame] 2 3 Omitted.

[42] So when I had well regarded her aparell] 2 *All these well noted* 3 *Al these wel noted*

pleasure [45] (by semblant° more lykely to dye then to lyve) she[46] turned[47] her face towardes Lereano, wher as[48] he stode, and[49] began to say in this maner[50].

LVII: Laureola to Lereano

Frende Lereano, never thynke that the force of thy[1] strenght, for so litle an incon-venience° that I sh[u]ld consent to lose. For as thou hast sayd to be desyrous° to serve me, more honour *thou* shuldest have done me in lyvynge then I to gyve *thee* deth.[i] For surely thy wekenes nor thy payne[2], nor yet thy love, coulde not make me beleve that thou shuldest have died. Therfore, thou maist clerely se what evyll° thou hast done.[3] Yf *thou* thynk that I dyd was to mocke the or to prove° [N8v] the, what errour then I have done to thy purpose? Yf true lovers cane not suffre how shall they come to theyr desyrs?[ii] He that can not suffre can not joy, nor but seldome attayne to his glory.[iii] There is no vertue but in sufferynge of payne therby to have joye of theyr good adventure°. Thou oughtest more to be blamed, beynge discrete°, for that thou hast done, then to be praysed for a trew lover.[iv] And beleve surely that yf I had not ben surer of thy fayth I wolde° have gyven no credence to thy stedfastnes, nor yet have gyven the none° occasion at the begynnynge to have come to this ende. And more to shew° the the trouth then to rewarde the of thy payne, I make the sure yf I had beleved that *thou* shuldest have died, I wold° rather have taken the deth my selfe then to have consented to thy deth, for it shuld have bene greate conscience° to me to have s[uff]ered[4] the to dye. For the trust that I had in that thou dydest for my servyce caused me in maner° [O1r] to beleve thy wrytynge°, but then agayne the suretie° *that* I thought

---

[43] well the sygnificacions of] 2 *and dyd perceyve* 3 *& did perceve*
[44] I saw how *with*] 2 *me thought as I dyd conjecture, they answered as directly to the wry-tynges that I sawe upon Leriano, as though one had spoken and the other had answered, but she havynge* 3 *me thought as I did conjecture, they answered as directly to the wrightinges that I sawe upon Leriano, as though one had spoke and the other had answered, but she havyng*
[45]] 2 3 *and*
[46] she] 2 3 Omitted.
[47] turned] 2 *tournynge*
[48] as] 2 3 Omitted.
[49] and] 2 3 Omitted.
[50]] 2 *&c*

---

[1] thy] 2 *the* 3 *y*
[2] payne] 2 3 *paynes*
[3]] Marginal note 2 3 *The infidelyte in some women*
[4] suffered] 1 *sffuered* 2 *sufferyd*

had ben in thy wysdome and dyscrecion° caused me to doubte it.ᵛ And in this⁵ maner, I gave more credence to thy discrecion° then to thy determyned deth. Lereano, it ought to have suffysid the to remember in what case° myne honour stode in, and perell of my lyfe, and to have ben content to know that I ought° the my favour, for thy evyll° grevyd me worse then myne owne, though I shewyd it not to the. If thou wylte denye this, remember what I was and how small necessite I had of thy service. Ones° writyng to the shuld have sufficyd, though I dyd not put the in no suretie° for thou knewist⁶ well that my wrytyng procedyd of no feare, but of myne owne good wyll. & thou canste not denye whan of my message thou dyddeste dispaire and dyed, dyd I not put the in hope when I sayde that if I lyvyd lenger then my father then ⁷ shuldest se how I wold° rewarde thy deservyng?ᵛⁱ So that thou shuldeste not blame [O1v] me for any unkindnes, I will speke no more syn°⁸ I shall no more se the, and bycause I can receyve no more passion° then I do for thy deth. Therfore, I make short my wordes though my payne be large, makynge the sure I shall rewarde thy sowle, syn°⁹ by myne unhap, by reasone of thy¹⁰ deth, I can not rewarde thy body.

LVIII: The auctor

When Laureola spake these wordes to Lereano I stode in a¹ strange maner, ryght sore° abasshyde° to se her greate pite. And joynynge her wysdome, and knowyng her wyll, and heryng of her amorous reasones, these over came my strength. Though she spake not² to me, yet I praysede moche her sayeng°, though it avaylyd but lytle. Howe be it, me thought her reasones were so just *that* Lereano coulde make none° aunswere to satisfye them. Not for the small confydence that I hadde in his wisdome, but bycause of the trouble of his spirytes° in seynge° present before hym the creature [O2r] whome he most desiryd. Yet me thought he cast up his eyen° to hevyn, and with great curtesye he aunswere³ her in this maner.

---

⁵ this] 3 Omitted.
⁶ knewist] 3 *knowest*
⁷] 2 3 *thou*
⁸ syn] 2 3 *syns*
⁹ syn] 2 3 *syns*
¹⁰ thy] 3 *my*

---

¹ a] 2 3 Omitted.
² not] 3 Omitted.
³ aunswere] 2 3 *answered*

LIX: Lereano to Laureola

O dere Lady, yf I had the wisdome to shew° you the case° and quarell° of myne evyll° as well as I have reasone to suffer it, I coulde then as well aunswere you as if I myght lyve to serve you. Ye say ye coulde never beleve *that* the force of my dethe coulde overcome my strength. Have no mervayl° thereof, for without my desyre I coulde fynde no thyng to defende me. But of that ye blame me, ye deserve the payne°, for ye myght have gyvyn me remedy° & ye consentyd that I shuld dye. And where as ye say I erred bycause I wold° not defend my selfe, affermynge that I shuld have sought all the wayes therto. Yf ye dyd it to prove° or to mocke me, judge what ye say and beholde what case° I was in. & ye shall say that a harte full of sorowe [O2v] never takyth good newes for certayne, and of evyll newes it makith no doubte. And all this that ye have sayd, I beleve it trew of your owne parte, knowyng your great cruelte and my small hap°.[i] Thynke not that the small travayll° that I toke was in defendyng of my lyfe, but that it was to serve you. For it had ben more payne for me to have defendyd my selfe fro° the dethe then to suffre it.[ii] Remembrynge my selfe that I had no desire to lyve, but alonely° to serve you, and when I saw that I erryde and that ye wolde° not of my service ly-vyng, then I thought to serve you with my deth. And thynke not *that* I joy so litle of my deth, but that I thynke it well enployed syn°[1] ye have now discoveryd your pitie, the which in my lyfe allwayes ye denyed. Ye say the hope that ye gave me shuld have suffisyd me°. I denye it not accordyng to *that* ye be, for one loke of you had ben sufficient for any[2] service that I could have done. For where as the lesse hope aperyd [O3r] certayne, then moche more was your deservyng°, and of my deservyng° I was in doubte for the gretter that *the* reward was the lesse I belevyd[3] it, and therfore I dyd as ye have seen.[iii] And where as ye speke of is honour and lyfe, ye know well for certayne, if ye forgette it not, what small charge° it was to you.[iv] And the experience which gre[v]id me, ye know your selfe. *The* warkes° are witnes. Also, ye say that at the begynnynge ye were withoute any charge°, and after what perell I saw you in, and that I was redy to have gyven occasion to have brought you in to suspect°. I begyled you not, for afterwarde I shewed your clennes°. Ye never sayde in your wrytynge° anythyng for certayne, but alwayes I was in doubt of any rewarde. And the lesse I hopyd the more I feared, and thus ye may se that by your owne excuse ye condempe° your selfe.[v] And syn°[4] I can not serve you, I will not trouble you nor speke no more, save I desire° of you, in [O3v] rewarde of my true faith, to let me kysse your hand bycause with that glory I may joy in my deth, seyng° I co[u]ld not in my lyfe, nor ye wolde° not suffer° me. And

---

[1] syn] 2 *syns* 3 *sins*

[2] any] 2 3 *my*

[3] belevyd] 2 *deservyd* 3 *deserved*

[4] syn] 2 3 *syns*

thus I wyll deperte fro° you, besechyng you as ye saye to have reme*mbra*nce° of my sowle syn°[5] ye have forgoten my body. Nor I desire no more to trouble you, nor to be inportunate° with any mo° wordes. Thus I make an ende, desirynge° you of⁶ perdone. & if any thynge may presume to avayll for the ryches of my service, that ye wyll remember my trouth and good wyl, the which I sette be fore your eyen°, to th'entent that of my deth ye shulde have some compassion syn°[7] ye had none of my lyfe.

LX: The auctor

When this mater was thus passed betwene them I stode and behelde the curtesy that Lereano made and the small thought° that he shewed of his deth, for then he knowyng[1] that she was no lesse sorowfull for his deth then hymselfe [O4r] selfe was. Therfore to th'entent not to trouble her he sufferyd the payne, and wolde° speke no more of his deth. And as moche as it pleased me to se them together, as moche it greved me the remembrance° of the deth of Lereano. And accordynge to ther reasones, they joyed me so that I wolde° theyr reasons shulde nev[e]r[2] have endyd, for then I knew well that Lereano receyved glory to se her and Laureola receyved no payne to se hym, though he were dede.[i] I desyre that theyr speche shuld never have endyd, nor theyr syght depertyd a sounder°. But alwayes the thynges of pleasour seldome endurith longe.[ii] And [3] I thus lay dremyng, at last me thought I harde° a hevy° voice that said: "Come away Lereano and tary no longer!" And then w*ith* a dolorous sygh, Lereano, with his bonet° in his ha*n*d, we*n*t to Laureola and kyst her hand and she, to gyve him some glory, sufferyde hym, the which in his lyfe tyme she wold° never do. And so kyssyng her had he sayd: [O4v] °O *thou* deth! *Thou* hath slayne my memory, yet to my deth is give*n* glory!" & ther w*ith* he vanished away. And whe*n* I saw I could se hym no more, the*n* I regarded° Laureola to se what co*n*tena*n*ce she made.[iii] I saw her sta*n*d in greate hevynes°, her eyen° bathed in water & her beautie fadyd of colour, pale and wanne, and had lost her spech. And I, seynge° her in suche maner of disposicion°, hadde compassio*n* to se her then Lereano that was dede°.[iv] What with the[4] syght of the one and of the other was in suche perell and so disperate°, that to say the

---

[5] syn] 2 3 *syns*
[6] of] 3 *to*
[7] syn] 2 *syns* 3 *sins*

---

[1] knowyng] 2 3 *thought*
[2] never] 1 *nevr*
[3]] 2 3 *as*
[4] the] 2 3 Omitted.

truth I desyred rather to have folowed Lereano dede° then to have folowyd Laureola lyvynge, who with great hevynes°, as moche as she myght, dyssimuled° her payne that she enduryd for the deth of Lereano. & discretly she dyd refrayne her wepynge and sayd to me as folowith.

LXI: Laureola to the auctor

Frende, truely with a better harte and wyll I wyll contynew° this [O5r] lyfe rather thenne to goo oute of thy chamber, without it were that I beleve in my goynge away my sowle shall departe.[i] For surly° yf I had beleved to have sene Lereano *in* that case° as I have sene hym now, I wolde° never have come hither to se hym, but rather have suffered payne with his absence then glory to se hym, seing° I can not remedy° hym. I had thought never to have had suche payne for hym, for the more that the greatnes of astate° withstode & denyed. Yet for all that, I thought to have done the contrary or° my lyfe had departed. For with great travayll° I thought to have suyd° to the kyng, my father, for his libertie.[ii] It was not by my consent that he was co*m*maundyd not to come in to *the* courte where as he myght have place° to have sene me. Yet for al *that* he neded not to have dyed, for the tyme myght have come *that* he shulde have hadde no cause to have disparyd. For though[1] I, by my crueltie, had consentyd to have [p]ut[2] hym [O5v] to passion°, yet I myght as[ ]well agayne have rewarded hym by my bountie° and pitie as to have denyed hym. I wyll as now make no quarell to my wyll, syn°[3] his servyce & good warkes° I thought to have rewardyd, but I quarell with the bautie that God hath gyven me and so myght Lereano have done, for that more begyled hym then other condicio*n* or wyll. But bycause the tyme is short and the passion° great, I wyll no more say, but I make the sure that thought[4] Lerea[n]o were not worthy of astate° nor lynage° to have had me to his wyfe, yet he shuld not have bene in dispayre therof. But syn°[5] I can not as now rewarde his warkes° and good servyce, I desyre° the not to depart fro° the courte thou[gh][6] thy desyre be in to thyne owne natural° countrey, & so doinge thou shalt know by the rewardes that I shal gyve the what honour I bare° to Lereano lyving.[iii] [O6r]

---

[1] thought] 2 3 *thoughe*
[2] put] 1 *out*
[3] syn] 2 3 *syns*
[4] thought] 2 *thoughe* 3 *though*
[5] syn] 2 *syns* 3 *since*
[6] though] 1 *thouhg* 3 *thoughe*

LXII: The auctor

When Laureola had endyd her wordes[1] she[2] was so hevy° and so full of wepyng *that* in a maner h[er][3] payneful lyfe grevyde me as sore° as the dethe of Lereano. And to all this that she hadde sayd, I wolde° have aunswerde her and thankyd her of her great bountie° to me shewyd as well as for the curteyse of her meke° speche. And so me thought, as I was movyd sodenly. With a great sighe she depertyde fro° me, and with a loude voyce sayd: "I can no more sorow *that* deth which is ever° certeyne then the losse of the lyfe of hym that is dede." Then I lokyd all aboute and saw how I was left all[4] alone, and therwith awoke out of my dreme. [i] Then was I so sorowfull that I wist° not what to do nor thynke of my dreme. And when I saw no man to speke unto I was so pensyve that often tymes with myne owne handes I thought to have ryde my lyfe, therby thynkynge to have founde that I had lost. And when I remembryd that with my deth I could [O6v] not recover the lyfe of the dede°, then I thought it a great errour to lese myne own sowle without the joyeng of his body. And as it is a sure xperience°[5] that musyk° encreasith payne to hym *that* is in sorow, so lyke wyse[6] it encreasith pleasur in the harte of them that be contente and in joye. Then I toke an harpe and songe° as folowith.[ii]

Harte take no payne in this lyfe for it may be overcome, for it canne not endure longe. Bicause we be mortall the evyll° that shewith her force is redy to take the deth. Synne° that lyfe is most evyll°, then I counsayl the shew no strength against *the* overcome, for who that sleith the lyfe with deth is pleasyd.[7]

Therfore that lyfe is good, that takith deth after the best sorte.[iii] He that dyeth lyvyng hath not moche to suffre, but he that lyveth dyenge, his evyll° & payne is stronge. Who can not suffre evyll° when they be satisfyed with evyll°? And though they be mortall yet the sorow is equall.[8] [iv]

---

[1] wordes] 3 *worde*

[2] she] 3 Omitted.

[3] her] 1 *hre*

[4] all] 3 Omitted.

[5] xperience] 2 3 *experie*nce

[6] wyse] 3 Omitted.

[7] Harte take no payne in this lyfe for it may be overcome, for it canne not endure longe. Bicause we be mortall the evyll that shewith her force is redy to take the deth. Synne that lyfe is most evyll, then I counsayl the shew no strength against *the* overcome for who that sleith the lyfe, with deth is pleasyd.] 2 3 Omitted.

[8] Therfore that lyfe is good, that takith deth after the best sorte. He that dyeth lyvyng hath not moche to suffre, but he that lyveth dyenge, his evyll & payne is stronge. Who can not suffre evyll when they be satisfyed with evyll. And though they be mortall yet the sorow is equall] 2 3 Omitted.

Thus[9] I make an ende of my songe.[v] And then [O7r] without any more stu-
dyng that° I had to do, I commaunded to sadell my horse for I thought it was
tyme for me to deperte to go in to my owne country. And thus I departed fro°
them that I mette in the streate, more accompaned *with* sorow and wepynge yes°
then with any other consolasion of pleasoure. My hevynes° so encreased and my
helth so payred° that I never thought to come alyve in to my countrey. & when
I was well entered on my way, there came so many thynges to my fantasye° that
thynkyng on them I was nere oute of my witte°. Howbeit, at last remembrynge°
my selfe that it was no profyt to muse on them, I traveled° my self as moch as I
myght to brynge them out of my remembrance°. So I traveled° my body in this
journey and my sowle in sundry thoughtes, and fynally I arryved at my[10] owne
poore mansion°.[vi] And thus I bydde fare well & adew° all true lovers and all *the*
readers an herers of this proces°, desyryng° them [O7v] where they fynd faulte to
amend it. And I shall pray to God for theyr prosperyte, and at theyr ende to send
them the joyes of paradyce.

Amen. Finis[11].

Prynted at London, in Paul's Churcheyarde, by Johan Turke, at the sygne of
the Byble.[12] [O8r]

---

[9] Thus] 2 3 Omitted.

[10] my] 2 3 *myne*

[11] Finis] 2 3 *Thus endeth this Castell of love*

[12] Prynted at London, in Paul's Churcheyarde, by Johan Turke, at the sygne of the
Byble] 2 *Imprynted by me, Robert Wyer, for Richard Kele* 3 *Imprinted at London, in Crede
Lane, by John Kynge.*

Linguistic Notes and Commentary

Notes to Title Page

[i] The English title page appears to be based on the French heading at the beginning of the prologue, which translates as "This book was translated from Italian into French and treats the love of Lereano and Laureola, daughter to the king of Macedonia." As in the English title page, the first line identifies the book as a translation, naming the source and target languages. The English, however, has additional information as it names the text, the translator, and the person for whom the translation was executed. The second sentences of the French and English texts are identical, which suggests that the title page may have been translated by Berners from the French and later adapted for publication. The fact that Elizabeth Carew is referred to as Nicholas's late wife can establish that the title page was altered after 1542, the year of her death, probably in preparation for publication. On Elizabeth and Nicholas Carew, see section 1 of the introduction. On the French translator and his use of the Italian source see section 2 of the introduction.

Berners uses the term "castell" instead of "prison" to translate "cárcel" and "prison." This is not a mistranslation as later, in Chap. II, he translates the noun as "prison." While "prison" may be the more usual translation of "cárcel" (Sp) and "prison" (Fr), Berners may have chosen "castell" because of its phonetic similarity to the Spanish term. Moreover the term may denote "prison" as well as "castle." The *OED* defines "castle" as "A large building or set of buildings fortified for defence against an enemy; a fortress, stronghold" (3a) and the figurative or allegorical definition is, "Stronghold, fortress" (4). The use of the term "castell" may have been used to align Berners's text with other similarly named works such as the c.1320 translation of Grosseteste's *Castel off loue*, the late fifteenth-century morality play, *The Castle of Perseverance,* Thomas Elyot's *Castel of Helth* (1533) and *The Castle of Knowledge* (1551). The term also exploits the figurative connotations of the medieval castle: see R. D. Cornelius, *The Figurative Castle: A Study in the Medieval Allegory of the Edifice* (Bryn Mawr: Bryn Mawr University Press, 1930).

[ii] None of the other language versions mentions Macedonia at this point in the text. By mentioning the country on the title page of the English edition, the text is aligned with the Greek romances which were very popular in the mid-sixteenth century.

Notes to Prologue

[i] Elizabeth Carew was Berners's niece: Berners's sister, Margaret Bryan (née Bourchier) was Elizabeth's mother. Berners's translation is the first secular, English translation made for a woman that does claim to be edifying and that is presented to a female patron, audience, dedicatee, or single reader for her pure enjoyment. See Alexandra Barratt, "Carried Forward: Translations for Women to 1550," Australian and New Zealand Association for Medieval and Early Modern Studies Fifth Biennial Conference, Auckland, New Zealand, 2–5 February 2005, unpublished conference paper.

This initial line is directly translated from French, as is the majority of the prologue. There are a few lines in the French and English prologues which correspond to the Spanish, but even in those instances Berners follows the slight alterations in the French. These lines will be indicated below, but unless otherwise stated the English and French agree against the Spanish.

[ii] While Berners states that *Castell* is translated from the Spanish text, he uses the Spanish and the French equally. See section 3 of the introduction.

[iii] The French has an addition here which Berners translates as "and founde . . . ymagynacyons."

[iv] In this segment the English follows the French word for word in its amplifications of the Spanish, adding "sperit," "quycke intellygence," and "vertue and prudence."

[v] "seguridad" (Sp, reassurance) is amplified to "seureté et hardyesse" (Fr, surety and boldness): Berners preserves the French addition with "suertie and hardynesse." Berners also follows the French in omitting the verb "buscava" (Sp, searched)

[vi] Berners follows the French in omitting a large passage from the Spanish. See "It may be that . . . completing my task" in Keith Whinnom, trans., *Prison of Love, c. 1492, Diego de San Pedro, Together with the Continuation, c. 1496 by Nicolas Núñez* (Edinburgh: Edinburgh University Press, 1979), 3–4.

[vii] The final line of the Spanish prologue is similar, translating as: "And so I beseech your lordship, before condemning my inadequacy, to weigh my motives, so that I may receive the thanks appropriate not to my [reasoning] but to my good intentions" (*Prison of Love,* trans. Whinnom, 4).

[viii] These verses are added to the second and third editions, as discussed in section 5 of the introduction.

Notes to I: The Auctor

[i] On Auctor and the medieval concept of *auctoritas* see A. J. Minnis, *Medieval Theory of Authorship: Scholastic Literary Attitudes in the Later Middle Ages* (London: Scolar Press, 1984); Joseph F. Chorpenning, "Rhetoric and Feminism in the *Cárcel de Amor,*" *Bulletin*

of Hispanic Studies 54 (1977):1–8; John Dagenais, "Juan Rodríguez del Padrón's Translation of the Latin *Bursarii*: New Light on the Meaning of 'Tra(c)tado'," *Journal of Hispanic Philology* 10 (1985): 117–39; Keith Whinnom, "*Autor* and *Tratado* in the Fifteenth Century: Semantic Latinism or Etymological Trap," *Bulletin of Hispanic Studies* 59 (1982): 211–18.

[ii] This is probably a reference to Ferdinand and Isabel's campaigns against Granada which began in 1482: see *Prison of Love*, trans. Whinnom, 101 n. 4; Carmen Parrilla, ed., *Cárcel de amor* (Barcelona: Crítica, 1995), 4.1.

The English doublets "done and finyshyd" and "fiers and furious" are derived from the French added doublets; the Spanish employs single terms.

Berners specifies that the way taken is a straight way, which is based on the French addition "ung estroit" (a strait). This detail is important in the allegorical context: a straight, rather than a twisty path, symbolises that he is heading in the right direction. On allegory in *Cárcel* see Bruno Damiani, "The Didactic Intention of the *Cárcel de Amor*," *Hispanófila* 56 (1976): 29–43; Bruce Wardropper, "El mundo sentimental de la *Cárcel de Amor*," *Revista de la Filología Española* 37 (1953): 168–95.

Despite the translations of these French additions, Berners does not follow the French for the whole sentence: the French also has the doublets "esclairer & illumoner" (light up and illuminate) for the Spanish "esclarecer" (illuminate), which Berners translates as "illuminyd"; and "sallir et venir" (Fr, to leave and to come) for "salir" (Sp, to leave), which Berners translates as "walkyd."

Auctor is a much-studied character in Spanish criticism, see Haydée Bermejo Hurtado and Dinko Cvitanovic, "El sentido de la aventura espiritual en *Cárcel de amor*," *Revista de Filología Española* 49 (1966): 289–300; Chorpenning, "Rhetoric and Feminism"; Frederick A. de Armas, "Algunas observaciones sobre *La Cárcel de amor*," *Revista de Estudios Hispánicos* 8 (1974): 107–27; Peter N. Dunn, "Narrator as Character in the *Cárcel de amor*," *Modern Langauge Notes* 94 (1979): 188–99; Elena Gascón Vera, "Anorexia eucarística: la *Cárcel de amor* como tragedia clássica," *Anuario Medieval* 2 (1990): 64–77; Alfonso Rey, "La primera persona narrativa en Diego de San Pedro," *Bulletin of Hispanic Studies* 58 (1981): 95–102; Esther Tórrego, "Convención retórica y ficción narrativa en *Cárcel de amor*," *Nueva Revista de Filología Hispánica* 32 (1983): 330–39; Wardropper, "El mundo sentimental," 168–95.

[iii] On savage men in medieval and early Renaissance literature see: R. Bernheimer, *Wild Men in the Middle Ages: A Study in Art, Sentiment and Demonology* (Cambridge, MA.: Harvard University Press, 1952); A. D. Deyermond, "El hombre salvaje en la novela sentimental," *Filología* 10 (1964): 97–111; idem, *Tradiciones y puntos de vista en la ficción sentimental* (México: Universidad Nacional Autónoma de México, 1993); Timothy Husband and Gloria Gilmore-House, *The Wild Man: Medieval Myth and Symbolism* (New York: Metropolitan Museum of Art, 1980); Harold Livermore, "El caballero salvaje: ensayo de identificatión de un juglar," *Revista de la Fililogía Española* 24 (1950): 166–83; Martín de Riqueur, *Historia de la literatura catalana*, vol. 3 (Barcelona: Ariel, 1964). See also *Prison of Love*, trans. Whinnom, 101–2 n 5; and Parrilla, *Cárcel de amor*, 4.2.

In the English text his shield is described as "bryght." The sources use the expressions "muy fuerte" (Sp) and "moult fort" (Fr, very strong). The term "bryght" may have been chosen specifically to alliterate with "bare" since the initial clause is formed of three alliterating pairs: "hande he," "bare bryght," and "schilde stele."

"shynynge" is a mistranslation or alteration of "una imagen femenil" (Sp) and "ung ymage de femme" (Fr, the image of a woman). Parker argues that this image, used to ensnare men is an image of Venus, while Sharrer posits that it is a conflation of Venus and the Virgin Mary. See Alexander A. Parker, *The Philosophy of Love in Spanish Literature, 1480–1680* (Edinburgh: Edinburgh University Press, 1985); Harvey L. Sharrer, "La *Cárcel de amor* de Diego de San Pedro: La confluencia de lo sagrado y lo profano en 'la imagen femenil entallada en una piedra muy clara'," in *Actas del III congreso de la Asocicion Hispanica de Literatura Medieval, I*, ed. Maria Isabel Toro Pascua (Salamanca: Biblioteca Española del Siglo XV, Departamento de Literatura Española e Hispanoamericana, 1994), 983–96. There is a woodcut depicting Desire with his shield in Bernardí Vallmanyà, *Lo carcer de Amor* (Barcelona: Johann Rosenbach, 1493).

ⁱᵛ The French and English texts have added terms to emphasise the suffering. The English "dolorous playntes and sorowfull passions" is clearly based on the French "douloureux plaings et appassionnes gemissements" rather than the Spanish "lastimero gemido" (a piteous moan).

Numerous critics have drawn parallels between Lereano's and Christ's passion. See Wardropper, "El mundo sentimental," 168–93; Joseph F. Chorpenning, "Leriano's Consumption of Laureola's Letters in the *Cárcel de amor*," *Modern Language Notes* 95 (1980): 422–25; E. Michael Gerli, "Leriano's Libation: Notes on the Cancionero Lyric, Ars Moriendi, and the Probable Debt to Boccaccio," *Modern Language Notes* 96 (1981): 414–20.

ᵛ "Frende" is used to translate "caminante" (Sp) and "viateur" (Fr, traveller). The same translation is used below. Berners also adds the term "friend" repeatedly as a form of address used by Lereano and Auctor. See section 3 of the introduction. Cf. Aristotle, *Ethics* VIII, 1156b, and Cicero, *De amicitia* on the value of male friendship. This notion of male friendship accrued in importance in Tudor England as can be seen by the popularity of Erasmus's commentary on Cicero's text, first printed in 1518 (Balet: Lugduni, 1518). See also R. Hyatte, *The Arts of Friendship* (Leiden: Brill, 1994), and for a feminist approach to this topic, see Lorna Hutson, *The Usurer's Daughter* (London: Routledge, 1994).

ᵛⁱ Berners does not translate the French additions of "que avoye encommencé" (who had begun) and "faire et acomplir" (to do and accomplish).

ᵛⁱⁱ Berners adds the term "pacient" to refer to the captive Lereano, which accurately denotes his condition of suffering. It also follows the amorous tradition of describing the lover as a patient needing the Lady to act as a physician and cure him with her pity or love.

ᵛⁱⁱⁱ The phrase "my spirites began to respyre" is a translation of the French addition "et que peuz respirer mes esprits"; it is not present in the Spanish.

ⁱˣ The terms "empachado" (Sp) and "empesché" (Fr) denote "ashamed" or "embarrassed," and not "determined" as in the English. The description of Auctor as ashamed as a result of his initial doubt is reminiscent of Launcelot's hesitation to jump into the cart and Guinevere's reaction to his hesitation in Chrétien de Troyes's *Le Chevalier de la Char-rette*. Interestingly, as Malory does in the *Morte Darthur*, Berners omits this detail.

The French doublet "chemin & voye" (route and way) is not preserved in the English; Berners writes "way," based on "la vía" (Sp, the way).

[x] The French doublet "tourne & revolte" (turn and revolve) is omitted. Instead, Berners uses "revolvyde," based on the Spanish "rebolví."

[xi] The French has two short additions which Berners does not preseve, indicating that he was probably using the Spanish here.

[xii] The name "God of Love" is used which corresponds to the French "du Dieu d'Amours," instead of the Spanish "Amor" (Love).

[xiii] The doublet "broyle and enflame" is added based on the French "bruslé et enflambé"; the Spanish has the single term "quemo" (burn).

[xiv] On the symbolism of the ascent see Barbara E. Kurtz, "Diego de San Pedro's *Cárcel de amor* and the Tradition of the Allegorical Edifice," *Journal of Hispanic Philology* 8 (1989): 123–38, and idem, "The Castle Motif and Medieval Allegory of Love: Diego de San Pedro's *Cárcel de amor*," *Fifteenth-Century Studies* 11 (1985): 37–99.

[xv] The doublets "regard or note" and "ouerage & newelte" are based on the added French doublets rather than the Spanish single terms; this indicates that Berners was using the French here.

[xvi] After "of nature" the French adds "que jamais semblable n'avoie veue" (that I never saw one like it). Yet, in this line the English still is closer to the French: the phrase "stone clere and stronge of nature" is based on the French "tant forte & tant clere de la nature" (so strong and so clear of nature), rather than the Spanish "tan fuerte de su condición" (so strong of condition).

On literary-architectural models for this prison see ed. Parilla, 6.16; Chandler R. Post, *Medieval Spanish Allegory* (Cambridge, MA: Harvard University Press, 1915; repr. Westport: Greenwood Press, 1974); Joseph F. Chorpenning, "The Literary and Theological Method of the *castillo interior*," *Journal of Hispanic Philology* 3 (1979): 121–33; Kurtz, "Castle Motif."

[xvii] The English follows the French text in omitting the possessive "nuestra" (Sp, our) before "human," but Berners does not follow the French for the whole sentence: the order of the colours differs in the French where they appear as tawny, grey, and then black.

[xviii] The sources have a line which translates as "on which stood an eagle, whose beak and wings shone brightly in the rays of light, which reached them from within the tower." This is omitted from Berners's translation. The English makes no mention of the eagle until the next chapter when the symbols composing the allegory are described.

[xix] The reading "mer[v]ayled" is based on the catchword, which provides the "v." In the main body of the text the letter is inverted and presented as "n."

[xx] The doublet "obscure et tenebreuse" (Fr, dark and gloomy) is added to the French, but not translated by Berners. He is following the Spanish in this sentence.

ˣˣⁱ The initial phrase is based on the French "Et prenant cueur" (and taking heart), rather than the Spanish "Y forçada mi fortuna" (Sp, In defiance of my fortune). The whole sentence is not based on the French: "by reason of . . . in" is omitted from the French and so Berners must have been using the Spanish here.

ˣˣⁱⁱ The French doublet "usance & coustume" (habit and custom) is translated rather than the single Spanish term "usança" (Sp, habit).

ˣˣⁱⁱⁱ The French text omits "descanso" (Sp, rest): Berners must have preserved the term from the Spanish.

ˣˣⁱᵛ The sense is that there are chains descending from the images, which are high up, and that these chains hold the prisoner.

ˣˣᵛ The use of terms which are phonologically similar produces confusion in the English and French translations. The Spanish "adornavan" (to decorate, to adorn) becomes "ordonnoient" (Fr, to determine) in the French translation; Berners translates as it "ordeyned."

The adjective "sharpe" and the phrase "his hed to the" are added to the English text, which heightens the gory violence of the scene.

ˣˣᵛⁱ "súpitamenta" (Sp) and "subitemment" (Fr, suddenly) are mistranslated as "subtilly."

ˣˣᵛⁱⁱ Berners follows the French in adding "grande" (Fr), which he translates as "great."

ˣˣᵛⁱⁱⁱ "rest & solacious comfort" is derived from a combination of Spanish and French terms: "descanso" (Sp, rest) and "soulagement et confort" (Fr, relief and comfort).

The sense is unclear in the English. The Spanish and French mean, "he saw that the time had come to repay the little debt he owed me with his words."

Notes to II: The prisoner

ⁱ "and quyet judgement" is based on the Spanish "sosiega tu juizio" (calm your mind). The phrase is omitted from the French, indicating that Berners was using the Spanish. This is further supported by the fact that Berners does not replicate the French error of "ce que tu veulx dire" (what you want to say): the Spanish reads "a lo que quiero dezir" (Sp, what I want to say).

ⁱⁱ The English and French texts indicate that Auctor should help if it is in his power; but in the Spanish it depends on is if he thinks it is right or good to help: "si por bien lo tovieres." Berners is using the French text here.

ⁱⁱⁱ His name may be based on Sir Leriador from *Merlin*: see Parrilla, *Cárcel de amor*, 9.8.

The names used in the different languages differ: Guerro (Eng), Guersio (Sp and Fr); and Colerea (Eng), Coleria (Sp), Collerial (Fr).

With Lereano's speech we have moved into the literal realm, but the allegorical world will be re-invoked as Lereano elucidates the symbolism of his prison. The allegorical world dissolves completely once Auctor departs from the prison to go to Laureola. On the movement between the literal and allegorical worlds see Parrilla, *Cárcel de amor*, 9.10.

iv The name Laureola has antecedents in the Arthurian characters of Laurette au Blanc Chief and Laurette de Brebaz. It also recalls Petrarch's Laura: see Parrilla, *Cárcel de amor*, 9.11; Alan Deyermond, *Tradiciones y puntos de vista en la ficción sentimental* (México: Universidad Nacional Autónoma de México, 1993).

The added doublet "voulut et ordonna" (Fr, wanted and ordered) is omitted from the English text: Berners bases his translation on the single Spanish term "ordenó" (Sp, arrange).

v This seems to be a reference to the Aristotelian theory that feelings of love derive from man's sensual side, the *motus primus sensualitas*, and that man's rational side can prevent him from acting on his feelings. Here Lereano explains that while his feelings derived from his senses, he does not want to avoid love and so he has confirmed his love with his reason: see Parrilla, *Cárcel de amor*, 9.12.

vi His faith is his love for Laureola, Parrilla, *Cárcel de amor*, 9.13.

vii The notion of four, rather than three divisions of the soul derives from Nicolás de Cusa: see Parrilla, *Cárcel de amor*, 10.14. Cf. Enrique Moreno Báez, ed. *Cárcel de amor* (Madrid: Cátedra, 1989).

viii "considering . . . suffre it" is a direct translation from the Spanish; it is omitted from the French.

ix The phrase "to be persecuter of wyll and desyre" is based on the French phrase "perseverer de vouloir et desirer," rather than the Spanish verb "querer" (Sp, to desire).

x The French added doublet "tristesse et ennuy" (Fr, sadness and worry) is not preserved. Berners uses the single term "hevyness" based on "tristeza" (Sp, sadness).

These colours are traditionally associated with the pains of love: Parrilla, *Cárcel de amor*, 10.16.

xi Berners has created the doublet "ease nor rest" by taking a term from each of the French and Spanish texts: "descanso" (Sp, rest) and "aise" (Fr, ease).

xii While the English omitted the earlier reference to the eagle in Chap. I, it still includes this line which presupposes that we were aware of the eagle.

xiii The doublet "mountyth and ascendyth" translates the French "saillent & montent." The Spanish has "llegar" (to attain).

xiv The English preserves the Spanish reading "me pueda entrar" (could enter into me), rather than the French, which translates as "could not enter into that place."

xv Berners follows the French, which has contracted the Spanish. The Spanish translates as "Torment performs the same task in accordance with the wishes of the first, for it was Desire who put him in that post."

Note that we have seen that Desire brought Lereano, not Torment.

xvi This is a traditional image of suffering from lyric poetry. See Parrilla, *Cárcel de amor*, 11.19 for analogous examples.

xvii "& pensyfenes . . . solicitude" is added. It is partially based on the added French doublet "soucy & penser" (worry and thought).

xviii "poore" is added based on the French addition of "povre" (poor).

xix The French doublet "tuer & occire" (kill and slay) is replaced by "slee," which translates the Spanish "matarme" (kill me).

xx The correct translation of the Spanish is "the spoon of doubtfulness with which I eate." Berners's translation is closer to the French "le soucy avecques quoy je mange" (Fr, the worry with which I eat).

xxi It should be understood that the water is drawn from *his* heart. In Spanish and French a determinate article is often used instead of a personal pronoun to refer to parts of the body when the person to whom the body part belongs is obvious. By following his sources here, the English is slightly confusing. Berners executed a similar translation above, writing "the harte."

Berners makes slight changes to create the compound terms "meat of doubtfulnesse" and "*the* cup of tribulation," which are highly effective. For example, the latter is based on the Spanish and French which translate as "the tribulation, and with it, something from which to drink."

xxii The English adds the doublet "advertysed & knowe" based on the French "advertie et sache." The Spanish has the single verb "sepa" (know).

xxiii In this line the English and French share several additions, showing that Berners was using the French text in this instance.

Notes to III: The aunswer of the auctor to [Lereano]

i Berners preserves the additions of "occuper et oster" (Fr, occupy and get rid of) and "bien" (Fr, well).

ii This phrase is confusing; the sources both translate as "how be it, to comfort my weary troubled mind, thou hast forced thy will to speak."

iii The term "doughtes" is added to the English, possibly because Berners read the French addition "d'obtenir" (Fr, to obtain) as a *faux-ami*. In the same sentence "perfight judge" is based on the Spanish "perfeto de juizio" rather than the French "parfaict de sens et de bon jugement" (Fr, perfect in knowledge and with good judgement). This indicates that both sources were used to form the English sentence.

ⁱᵛ The French adds four doublets here, only one of which is preserved by Berners.

ᵛ Berners slightly changes the sentence: the Spanish and French translate as "I am happy to know who you are . . ."

ᵛⁱ The French and English translators have slightly misunderstood their source here, and both change the sentence from the past to the present tense. The Spanish means "I had seen them many times before: since they are perceptible only to a captive heart, when my heart was a prisoner I recognised them and now that it is free they confused me."

To create the doublet "captyvyte and prison" Berners takes a term from each of the French and Spanish texts: the first term derives from the Spanish "cativo" (captive) and second from the French "emprisonné" (imprisoned).

Parrilla explains that Auctor's heart was imprisoned even though he was not in love, because San Pedro is using the notion of captivity metaphorically to refer to a state of bad fortune: Parrilla, *Cárcel de amor*, 12.4.

ᵛⁱⁱ Here the English stays close to the Spanish, with the exception of the addition of the doublet "rudnes and dulnes," which is derived from "grossesse & rusticité" (Fr, rudeness and rustic simplicity) rather than "rudeza" (Sp, rudeness).

That Auctor speaks a different language seems to be an unnecessary and somewhat implausible detail as he is clearly, and without difficulty, able to speak to all the Macedonians despite his Spanish origins. This detail may be intended to recall the similar situation of the lover, Eurialo, in Eneas Silvius Piccolomini's *De duobus amantibus*, with which *Castell* has much in common. Alternatively, it may be provided as a realistic detail lending support to Auctor's status as a foreigner: see Parrilla, *Cárcel de amor*, 12.6.

ᵛⁱⁱⁱ The English doublet "inconvenientes and daungers," translates "inconveniens et dangiers" (Fr), rather than the single term, "inconvenientes" (Sp).

ⁱˣ In this sentence, the French adds "prompte et affectionée" (prompt and caring) to qualify "servant," which is not present in the Spanish and which is not preserved by Berners.

ˣ Because of the linguistic parallels between the French and English in this line, such as "promyse / prometz," "accomplish / acompliray," "power / pouvoir," and "commandements / demendes," it seems as though Berners's source is the French text. Also the English and French expand the Spanish considerably; the Spanish translates as "I will gladly do what you demand."

ˣⁱ The French adds the doublet "deliberation et deliverance," but Berners preserves the single Spanish term "deliberación."

ˣⁱⁱ Berners omits the added doublet "peines et fatigues" (Fr, pains and troubles), and he follows the Spanish translating "trabajos" as "travyls."

ˣⁱⁱⁱ The Spanish has a different reading; it says that Lereano should temper his distress with hope. Berners's translation corresponds to the French.

Notes to IV: The Auctor

[i] Berners follows the French in omitting "a la sazón" (Sp, at that time) before "the kyng," but does not follow its omission of "Macedonia" nor its use of the place name "Syrie."

[ii] The string of verbs "resorte, goo, come, or abyde" is based on a combination of the two sources: the French has "aller et estre" (go and abide) and the Spanish has "ir, estar o aguardar" (go, come, or abide).

[iii] The French doublet "propre et naturelle nacion" (own and native nation) is not preserved.

[iv] It is at this point in the narrative that Auctor begins to occupy the dual role of narrator and character, see Parrilla, *Cárcel de amor*,13.3; Tórrego, "Convención retórica," 330–9; Deyermond, *Tradiciones y puntos de vista*; Peter N. Dunn, "Narrator as Character in the *Cárcel de amor*," *Modern Language Notes* 94 (1979): 188–99; Patricia E. Grieve, *Desire and Death in the Spanish Sentimental Romance (1440–1550)* (Newark: Juan de Cuesta, 1987); James Mandrell, "Author and Authority in *Cárcel de amor*: The Role of El Auctor," *Journal of Hispanic Philology* 8 (1984): 99–122; Alfonso Rey, "La primera persona narrativa en Diego de San Pedro," *Bulletin of Hispanic Studies* 58 (1981): 95–102.

[v] In the Spanish, Auctor speaks of Spain; in the French he talks about unspecified places he has been; the English combines the two sources and Auctor narrates tales about both.

[vi] This line means "she treated me as if I were one of her servants."

Notes to V: The Auctor to Laureola

[i] In the sources Laureola says that it is *no* less goodness for the great to pardon those who have done them disservice than for lesser men to take vengeance when they have been wronged. By omitting the negation from the Spanish and French, by moving "the great" and "lesser men" to object from subject positions, and by using an impersonal subject, the meaning of the sentence is altered although most of the original terms are preserved.

[ii] This sentence, dependent on the previous sentence, is very confused. It is divided into two parts discussing "the one" and "the other" respectively, but since their referents are undefined and their actions are mistranslated, this translation is problematic. The Spanish and French make the point that the lesser will become greater by taking care of their honour, and that the great demonstrate their nobility by showing mercy.

[iii] According to Aristotelian thought, pity is a natural female condition (*De Animalibus* IX, 1). This concept is frequently used in defences of, and diatribes against, women. Pity is a desired female virtue, but it is associated with the emotive, rather than rational,

side of the soul and so it is frowned upon. Here the notion is being exploited by Auctor in order to manipulate Laureola: Parrilla, *Cárcel de amor*,14.2.

ⁱᵛ The already confusing sentence is made even more confusing by Berners. The Spanish and French text write that he found courage in thinking of her nobility, since she cannot be so high-born and still lacking in magnanimity. The same terms are used in the English but to a very different effect.

ᵛ The French translator adds the redundant phrase "moy trouver devant ta pressence" (finding myself before you) and the doublet "souffrir et endurer" (to suffer and endure); Berners, however, follows the Spanish and does not translate the additions.

ᵛⁱ The French adds the doublet "piller et prendre" (to pillage and to take) which Berners does not translate.

ᵛⁱⁱ The adjective "swete" is moved to before the noun "prison," while in the Spanish and French it is after "prison" as it qualifies the next clause and not the prison. By moving the adjective he alters the sentence: in the sources the prison is not sweet; it is as sweet toward his will as it is bitter to his life.

ᵛⁱⁱⁱ Berners translates the verbs "secutar" (Sp, execute) and "excuse" (Fr, to excuse) as "executeth." He preserves the Spanish reading and avoids the error made by the French translator. He also does not translate the added French doublet "moleste et trouble" (disturb and trouble).

ⁱˣ Berners does not preserve the added French doublet "pleurs et larmes" (cryings and tears).

ˣ The French adds two doublets, which Berners does not translate.

ˣⁱ The added French doublet "te feisse et rendre certaine" (to make and render you sure) is not preserved.

ˣⁱⁱ Berners changes the verb to judge from a past ([Sp] te juzgué; [Fr] je te jugeay) into a present-tense verb, thus altering the meaning conveyed in this sources. In the French and Spanish, Auctor is contrasting his earlier state, whereby as the result of Lereano's feelings, he judged Laureola to be cruel with his present state whereby knowing her he judges her to be piteous.
    The phrase "& not *with*out reason" is an addition based on the French, "et non sans raison."

ˣⁱⁱⁱ "noble" is added based on the French addition of "excellent."

ˣⁱᵛ This line shows the proximity of the English to the Spanish. There are several additions in the French which Berners does not preserve.

ˣᵛ The French text has an addition at the end of the sentence, which Berners does not preserve: "en te improperant le nom d'homicide" (in your appropriating the name of murderer).

^{xvi} The doublet "passio*n* & adversite" is based on the French addition of "passion & adversité." The whole line is not based on the French; the doublet "charge et obligation" is omitted.

The Spanish text indicates that Lereano's passion and adversity are his service to her, not that he serves her despite these hardships. Berners's change is based on the French translation.

^{xvii} The Spanish and French do not indicate that Lereano causes her to act like God; they write that he gives her the occasion or opportunity to do so. This is an important alteration because the true lover would never force his lady to do anything. The image of the woman as having creative and redemptive powers appears frequently in the *novelas sentimentales* and derives from the conflation of religious and amatory language in these texts: see Parrilla, *Cárcel de amor,* 15.10; E. Michael Gerli, "Leriano's Libation," *Modern Langugae Notes* 96 (1981): 414–20.

^{xviii} In the English, Lereano is removed from the subject person and the verb is conjugated in the first person singular, so that Auctor is asking for Laureola's pity rather than Lereano asking to be pitied. The confusion arises from a misunderstanding in the French, where the Spanish "te supplica" is translated as a first rather than a third person singular. Berners may err as the result of following the French or he may make the same error coincidentally.

^{xix} The French text has the doublet "marrié et doulente" (sad and doleful) which Berners does not preserve.

The French adds a phrase which translates as "do not believe that I ever wanted to ask you" after "grevable," which Berners omits.

^{xx} In the Spanish, Auctor's pain is specifically the pain he feels for Lereano's sake. In the French, however, Auctor says that his pain is so great that no harm can come to him which can equal the pain of him who causes him pain. This makes little sense. Berners alters his sources, drawing an analogy between the pain of the two men.

^{xxi} The French adds three doublets, two of which are not preserved. The third is transformed into the expression "delivered quyte."

Notes to VI: The aunswer of Laureola to the auctour

ⁱ The English translation is unclear. The term "ryve," the obsolete form of "rife," makes little sense in this context since it is unlikely that Laureola is trying to say that cruelty is as common as pity, and because in the sources she states the opposite. The sense of the Spanish and French is "although in similar cases clemency is less due than harsh justice, if I were to impose the latter upon you it would have two beneficial results."

ⁱⁱ Berners translates the added French doublet "mansuetude et benignyté" as "mekenes and benignite." Also indicating his use of the French text here, Berners uses the term "punish," similar to the French "punition," rather than "chastisement" which corresponds

to the Spanish word "castigo." However, he omits the French doublet "raison & justice" only preserving the single term "justice"; it appears as "derecho" in the Spanish.

ᶦᶦᶦ Berners omits the added French doublet, writing "fole hardynesse" based on "el atrevimiento" (Sp).

ᶦᵛ The French doublet "notice et cognoissance" (notice and knowledge) is omitted; Berners follows the Spanish in using the single term "knowledge."

ᵛ Rather than "ought to think," the Spanish phrase means "it would not be unreasonable to think." Berners seems to have made this error because he was looking at the French, "se doibt aussi penser." He does not adhere to the French for the entirety of the sentence, however. He translates "grandeza" (Sp, royal rank, status) as "dignyte," avoiding the French mistranslation of "hardiesse" (Fr, boldness), and he does not preserve the added French doublet "timeur et crainte" (trepidation and fear).

ᵛᶦ The verb "entend" is likely based on the Spanish "entendes" rather than the French "laborer."

ᵛᶦᶦ The French and Spanish texts mean "Although you are a stranger by birth, you will be a naturalised Macedonian in your grave."

ᵛᶦᶦᶦ In both sources Laureola says, "let your hope be short-lived" and not "let your life be short."

Notes to VII: The Auctor

ᶦ After "Spain" the French text adds "ma region naturelle" (my native region), which Berners omits.

ᶦᶦ Berners writes "duryng my lyfe," while his sources denote a loss of life.
The French addition "et le tout considerant" (and all considering) is not translated by Berners.

ᶦᶦᶦ The French doublet "imaginations et suspitions" (fantasies and suspicions) is omitted.

ᶦᵛ This line appears to be based on the Spanish; Berners does not preserve the French additions.

ᵛ The single term "wherto" is used to abbreviate "a cuál de mis pensamientos" (Sp, to which of my thoughts). In abbreviating the Spanish, Berners is following the French text.

ᵛᶦ The additions of "lieu convenable" (Fr, convenient place) and "crainte & timeur" (fear and trepidation) are not preserved; Berners follows the Spanish text.

ᵛᶦᶦ The English sentence is based on the French: "doubtfull" is added based on the French addition of "dubitation"; and "con la desvergüença de quien dize" (Sp, "if the speaker shows no embarrassment" [*Prison of Love,* trans. Whinnom, 16]) is omitted from the French and English. Yet, the sentence is not an exact translation of the French; Berners does not preserve the doublet "grandesse et auctorité" (Fr, greatness and authority).

viii The French text conveys the opposite of the Spanish and English, indicating that Laureola remained as angry as she was previously: "tant de yre et de courroux." It is clear that Berners was following the Spanish text as he does not share the French text's error. He also does not translate the French doublet "pertinent et convenable" (pertinent and convenient).

ix The Spanish includes the adverb "menos," which is completely illogical in this context: see *Prison of Love,* trans. Whinnom, 103 n.15. The French text omits the term, as does Berners. With the exception of this omission, the English sentence is closer to the Spanish that to the French: Berners does not preserve the French addition "pourquoy osoye parler et dire" (why would I dare speak and say), nor the doublet "ses semblant et gestes" (her demeanour and gestures).

x Berners translates the Spanish term "lugar" with the doublet "tyme & place." He may have been influenced by the French "lieu et commodité propice" (favourable place and convenience), or he may have been aware that the term "lugar" (Sp) can denote both "time" and "place."

xi This sentence is based on the Spanish; the Spanish is abbreviated in the English translation, which is especially interesting as the French amplifies the sentence. The French adds "du mal que suffroit" (the evil that she suffered) before "Lereano" as well as the doublets "dur et aspre" (firm and sharp) and "toutes & quantesfois" (all and many times), which Berners does not translate.

xii The phrase "And when I . . . thynges" corresponds to the French and Spanish lines which translate as "And so as I was alert to anything that might be an advantage, I saw in her. . ." The differences are slight, but their implications are important when trying to decide whether or not Laureola loved Lereano. The Spanish and French texts imply that he perceives the signs only because he is looking for them, and therefore it is possible that he imagined them because he desired to note them. In the English text, however, the implication is more that the signs are really there notwithstanding his wish to see them.

xiii Berners omits the French doublet "jamais allegre ne joyeuse" (Fr, never happy nor joyous). He writes "not be mery" based on "no muy alegre" (Sp, not very happy).

xiv Berners says that she feigns her illnesses, while in the French and Spanish she complains of illnesses.
Berners does not preserve the French addition of "qua*n*t estoit seule" (when she was alone), nor the doublet "desplaisante & ettedieuse" (Fr, displeasing and hateful).

xv While Berners writes "she wolde sodeynly . . . blushe," his sources translate as "she would become distracted in her speech, and turn red . . ." He adds the simile "redde as a rose."

xvi The phrase her "voyce wolde change" would have been more accurately translated as "her voice would become husky": the sources use the terms "ronca" (Sp, husky) and "enrouée" (Fr, hoarse, husky).

These are all the traditional literary and medical symptoms of love. See Parrilla, *Cárcel de amor*, 17.10; Deyermond, *Tradiciones y puntos de vista*; June Hall Martin, *Love's Fools: Aucassin, Troilus, Calisto and the Parody of the Courtly Lover* (London: Tamesis, 1972), and on the scholastic and intellectual theorising of love in contemporary Spain see Pedro M. Cátedra, *Amor y Pedagogía en la Edad Media (Estudios de doctrina amorosa y práctica literaria)* (Salamanca: Universidad de Salamanca Prensa, 1989).

xvii This is a rare instance where Auctor functions as an omniscient narrator.

xviii The French adds the doublet "signatz & semblans" (signs and semblances), which Berners does not preserve.

It is likely that Berners was looking at the French here and confused "despeche" (Sp, mission) for the verb "depecher" (Fr, to hurry), which he translates as "spedde."

xix The French adds a doublet which Berners does not retain.

xx Berners gets the term "reasons" from the Spanish "razones": it is omitted from the French.

The English sentence is incoherent. The Spanish and French lines are accurately translated as, "And although he was in a fitter state to dictate his will than to write a love letter, he wrote the following." The terms which translate as "will" seem to confuse Berners: "memorial de su hazienda" (Sp) and "testament et ordonnance de derinère voulenté" (Fr). The use of the verb "remember" indicates that Berners may have been influenced by the Spanish term "memorial."

The phrase "he tooke ink and paper" is translated from the French addition "print il encores plume & papier." A similar addition occurs in Chap. XXXIV.

Notes to VIII: The lettre fro Lereano to Laureola

i This line is based on the Spanish: the term "reason" is made plural in French, but Berners preserves the singular noun from the Spanish; and the added French doublet "sans timeur ne crainte" (without trepidation nor fear) is not preserved.

ii The French adds the doublets "penser & savoir" (to think and to know) and "entendement & memoire" (mind and memory), which Berners does not translate. Further indicating Berners's adherence to the Spanish in this sentence, the French translates "el seso" (Sp) as "mon sang," but Berners accurately translates the Spanish, writing "my witte."

iii Berners adds the doublet "feare & doubte" based on the French "craignisse et doubtoise."

iv The doublet "grace or merite" is added based on the French addition "si aucune grace t'avois merité" (if I deserved any grace from you).

^v The French text alters the line to read "at this present hour"; the Spanish translates as "these my presente reasons." The French text also adds the doublet "admorties & destainctes" (destroyed and abolished), which Berners does not translate. He keeps the Spanish "destruiste," writing "destroyed." The English is a direct translation of the Spanish.

^{vi} Berners's translation is inaccurate. The Spanish and French sentences mean "if you counted my pain as service, no matter how much you would pay me I would still think that you were in debt."

^{vii} Berners translates "pensé escrevirte" (Sp, thought to write to you) as "so bolde to write to you." His translation is based on the French text which reads "je ose et pense à t'éscripre" (I dare and think to write to you). Berners does not preserve the French doublet, but still retains the sense.

^{viii} The French text omits the links between the terms so that Laureola's beauty is the cause of all the other things, while in the Spanish and English versions her beauty instigates a chain of events. This is reinforced by the use of *gradatio*, which is employed by the Spanish and English texts. By repeating the term "causeth" Berners emphasises the interdependence of the clauses.

^{ix} "wyll" and "good" are added by Berners. The term "good" derives from the French word "bonne," and Berners adds "wyll" independently. In so doing he changes the meaning of his sources which translate as "live without your (good) hope." The French also adds a doublet to this sentence, but it is not preserved by Berners.

^x The term "defamyd" is based on the French addition "difamée en ton renom" (defamed in your renown); however, the French doublet "meurdrière et homicide" (murderer and one who commits homicide) is not preserved. Berners follows the Spanish in using the single term "murtherer," which corresponds to "matadora" (Sp).

^{xi} The French text has several additions in this sentence, none of which are preserved by Berners. Berners's line is dependent solely on the Spanish.

^{xii} The French translation uses only one of the time-place substantives of the Spanish text: of "tiempo" (Sp, time) and "lugar" (Sp, place) the French preserves "temp." Only one term actually is needed to preserve the sense of the Spanish text since San Pedro uses the words synonymously, but by only using one term the antithetical construction of the Spanish text is blurred. The English text uses both "time" and "place" and preserves the parallel antithesis. Yet the whole sentence is not based on the Spanish: the doublet "tary not, nor be not slowe" is derived from the French "ne soyes delayante ne tardive" (Fr, do not be delaying or tardy), rather than the Spanish "no lo tardes" (do not delay).

"redeme" is used to convey "remediar" (Sp) and "remedier" (Fr, to remedy). This may be a compositor's error, although redeem may be used to convey something similar to "remedy" in the sense of "to restore, to set right again" (*OED* 11b). It is also possible that "redeme" is being used, and paired with the term "repent," in order to stress the Christian context of Lereano's love and his presentation as a martyr for his love.

Notes to IX: The auctor

[i] Berners combines the Spanish "discreción" with the French "prudence" to create the expression "prudent discretion."

"gravity of his passions" is a direct translation of the French "la gravité de ses passsions." The Spanish has an adjective-noun construction "grave passions" (Sp, acute passions).

The French doublet "scavoir & certi[fi]er" (to know and certify) is not preserved. Berners uses "to knowe," following the Spanish "saber."

[ii] The added French doublets "escript et envoye" (write and send) and "scavoir et estre seur" (to know and be sure) are omitted.

[iii] The French has two additions that Berners does not preserve; he follows the Spanish.

[iv] Berners does not translate the numerous French additions in this line.

Notes to X: The auctor to Laureola

[i] This sentence is based on the French. Berners translates all the French additions, including the invocation to Laureola; the doublet "dolour & payne"; and the adjective "poore." Moreover, while the Spanish text clearly states that the captive is Lereano, the French text is ambiguous and the prisoner may be either Auctor or Lereano. As a result, Berners contradicts the Spanish and states that Auctor is the captive.

[ii] By inverting the terms "dolour" and "oppress" some confusion is created in the English text. It should not say "his dolour is oppressyd" but rather "he is oppressed by his dolour." The French is even more confused as it indicates that Laureola will be rewarded by his dolour. There are many additional mistranslations in the French text which Berners does not preserve, showing that he was using the Spanish text here. First, in the French text Auctor tells Laureola to have confidence in her virtue; he does not say that Lereano has faith in it. Second, Auctor says that he wants to put all of his words, and not all of his pains, in her presence. Further, Berners does not preserve the two added French doublets.

[iii] There is an odd omission in the French text which may have arisen as the result of an eye-skip; the text in between the two instances of the term "desea" in the Spanish text is omitted from the French. This corresponds to the portion of the English text between "desyreth" and "desyre." As the result of this omission Berners was obliged to use only the Spanish text, with which he has difficulties: it translates as "Because you are its cause, he calls his pain happiness, and so as not to suffer it he desires to lose his mind; and to praise your beauty he desires his wit and that of all the world."

[iv] The Spanish and French translate as "he honours himself because you are destroying him."

^v The French addition is not preserved by Berners.

^{vi} The doublet "dydde ordeyne and devise" is based on the French added doublet, "ordonées et composées."

^{vii} This sentence is based on the Spanish: the French omits "& as God . . . erth" and so Berners must have translated it from Spanish. Also the French adds "et le consoles" (and console him) after "aunswere," which Berners does not translate.

^{viii} The added French doublet is not translated: Berners uses the term "mynysh" corresponding to "afloxarás" (Sp).

^{ix} The French doublet "debitoire et obligée" (debtor and one who is obliged) is omitted from the English translation. The Spanish "deves" is translated as "bounde."

Notes to XI: Th'aunswere of Laureola to the Auctor

ⁱ Berners translates "he dubdado" (Sp, I doubted) and "pensé et ésté en doubte" (Fr, I thought and doubted) as "thought is dought." Berners seems to have been confused by the French addition of "pensé." But although this suggests that he was looking at the French, he does not preserve the addition of "deux choses" (Fr, two things) nor the two other added French doublets which occur in this sentence.

ⁱⁱ The French omits "Yet I . . . to do," so it must be translated directly from Spanish.

ⁱⁱⁱ Berners does not translate the added French doublet.

^{iv} The differences between the translations and the Spanish text are considerable in this sentence. The English and French claim the opposite to the Spanish text; they write that life is more to be esteemed than virtue, rather than the converse.

^v The antithesis between Lereano's life (or death) and Laureola's kindness (or lack thereof) is absent in the French and English texts. These translations do not establish any connection between the two characters, and thus the statement in Berners's text that Lereano's life should end with death is ridiculous. The meaning of the original is lost.

Following the French translation, Berners adds "daunger" to create the doublet "daunger or blottyng of myn honour," which is based on the French "denigrer ne maculer."

^{vi} A more accurate translation than "for al peple . . . spot" is "for all people watch them so closely that they sooner notice a small spot."

^{vii} In this sentence Berners preserves many terms from the Spanish including, the polyptoton of "aplaze" and "plazer" as "pleaseth" and "pleasour"; however, he muddles the sense. The line should read "you have much for which to be grateful to me since I communicated my thoughts to you. This I have done because, although your request troubles me . . ." Instead of following the Spanish, he closely adheres to the French, which translates "agradecerme" (Sp, grateful) as "plaisir" (Fr, pleasure); then to make sense of the line Berners adds the clause "which is contrary," but the sense of the Spanish is lost.

The triplet "charge, blame, & sclaunder" is created by Berners by adding the Spanish "cargo" to the French doublet "scandale et blasme."

[viii] Berners follows the Spanish here by keeping Lereano as the subject: he translates "sus porfias" (Sp) as "his hope," while the French changes the subject to Auctor, writing "tes pertinacitez" (Fr, your obstinacies, obstinate arguments). Berners was also looking at the French sentence. He adds "hope" based on the French addition of "d'esperance." Moreover, the doublet "pacyence & sufferyng" is created by translating and joining the French "pacience" (Fr, patience) and the Spanish "sofrimiento" (Sp, suffering).

[ix] This sentence is unclear. It should say "For two reasons I blame myself for 'comoning' so long with the."

[x] The Spanish translates as "the nature of our conversation much annoys me." Berners's translation does not capture the exact meaning.

[xi] In the English translation, Laureola threatens Auctor twice, while in the sources Laureola utters only one threat. This may be the result of Berners using both the Spanish and French texts, and taking a phrase from each without considering the total effect.

Notes to XII: The Auctor

[i] "then I . . . the way" is a mistranslation of the Spanish, "me dava mayor desvío" (Sp, she gave me great confusion). It seems as though Berners mistook "desvío" (Sp, confusion) for "de vía" (of the way). Lending further support to the suggestion that this sentence is based on the Spanish, Berners does not translate the added French doublet "timeur et crainte" (Fr, trepidation and fear).

[ii] Berners follows the French in removing Laureola from the subject position; the Spanish translates as "In receiving the letter she satisfied me." He does not, however, translate the added French doublet, indicating that he was also looking at the Spanish.

Notes to XIII: The Auctor to Lereano

[i] Berners mistakes the term "dicha" (Sp, fortune) for "dicho" (Sp, words or saying). The French text reads "fortune," so it appears as though Berners did not look at the French. He also omits the three French additions to this sentence, which further indicates that Berners was using the Spanish for this sentence.

[ii] This line is omitted from the French, and so its source must be the Spanish text. Berners misunderstands the verb in his source and so conjugates it in the first person singular when it should be in the third person singular (feminine), indicating that Laureola had good reason to help.

ⁱⁱⁱ The doublet "newe and dyverce" is created by taking a term from each of the Spanish and French: "nueva" (Sp, new) and "muable" (Fr, changeable).

The French conjugates "to understand" in the second person singular rather than as the first person singular, as in the Spanish. Berners preserves the Spanish reading.

ⁱᵛ "I was joyfull . . . wordes" is translated from the Spanish; it is omitted from the French.

ᵛ While these comments on mutability are presented as though they pertain to humanity in general, the accusation of mutability is frequently levelled against women. Cf. Parrilla, *Cárcel de amor*, 23.6; and on women's "inconstant and weak minds," see Juan Luis Vives, *On the Education of A Christian Woman*, ed. and trans. Charles Fantazzi (Chicago and London: University of Chicago Press, 2000), 118.

ᵛⁱ The initial clause has been misunderstood by Berners: his sources translate as "what will *you* say?"

ᵛⁱⁱ The final phrase of the Spanish and French, which creates an opposition between the time to speak and the matter of the speech, is omitted from the English text. A complete translation of the Spanish and French line would read "I shulde want tyme to speke it *before matter to speak*."

"grevous case" is omitted from the French, indicating that Berners must have translated this expression from the Spanish.

ᵛⁱⁱⁱ This line is unclear: the Spanish and French mean "use your reason to reduce your passion."

ⁱˣ "as a monument to thy faith" would have been a better translation than "in stede of thy true fayth." The second half of the sentence also does not accurately reflect the originals; they translate as "you would be better to live and suffer than to die and to be rid of your pain."

ˣ "crowne of lawde & prayse" is added based on "gran corona" (Sp) and "courage de grande louenge" (Fr). Berners omits the term "gran/grande" (great) and takes "corona" (crown) from the Spanish. He omits "courage de" (courage of) from the French and preserves "louenge" as "lawde," and he then adds "& prayse" to form the doublet.

Berners amplifies the second part of the sentence considerably; the long phrase "*that* thou enforcest . . . sake" translates the brief Spanish expression "para sofrirlo" (to endure it). The French amplifies the Spanish slightly but not to the same extent as Berners.

ˣⁱ The English doublet "stronge & vertuous" is an addition based on the French.

ˣⁱⁱ "be tempt and provyd" is based on an added French doublet.

ˣⁱⁱⁱ The doublet "wepynges & complaynt" is based on an added French doublet.

"that ardent . . . his flames" does not convey the sense of the originals. The Spanish means "instead of killing your anguish I awaken it," and the French translates as "while trying to extinguish the flame I light it."

Notes to XIV: Lereano to the auctor

[i] This sentence is omitted from the French; Berners must have used the Spanish text. Berners's translation does not convey the same meaning as the original, which would be accurately translated as "because Laureola extracts these tears from my heart, they are sweet nourishment for my soul."

[ii] By changing the structure of the sentence the meaning is obscured. The Spanish and French sentence mean: "if you, whose judgement is free, cannot understand the things passed between you and her, how should I, whose wits are alive only so that I can praise her beauty, know them?"

[iii] The French translation abbreviates the passage, omitting the initial question and the final clause of the second question so that it translates as "I could not have any greater good in my misfortune than the desire of her." Berners must have been using the Spanish here.

[iv] The verb "to serve" is in the future tense in the Spanish; Berners follows the French in conjugating the verb in the past tense.

[v] The phrase "al my wyttes" is added by Berners since he does not seem to understand that the subject of the sentence is "the which," i.e. "the aforementionned regret." The sentence in the Spanish and French translates as "The which, considering what she is, is past the order of reason."

[vi] Berners seems to have been using the French here: the term "apruevo" is omitted from the French and English; it should come after "I know." The French adds a doublet, however, which Berners does not preserve.

[vii] Two French doublets are added, but Berners follows the Spanish, using the single terms "travayll" and "desyre."

[viii] The term "transitory" derives from the French "transitoire." It does not occur in the Spanish.

Notes to XV: The letter of Lereano to Laureola

[i] The addition of "but one . . . me," changes the question of San Pedro's text to a statement. In making this change, Berners is following the French text.

[ii] This sentence primarily is based on the French. The Spanish text translates as "you may ask how so quickly, in the year or a little more that I have been your servant . . ." Berners's translation is slightly different, corresponding to the French: while San Pedro specifies the duration of his service, Berners omits this detail, following the French omission; "to put . . . then myne," is based on the French addition; the added doublet is also derived from the French. However, by making "force" singular rather than plural, he is following the Spanish.

ᶦᶦᶦ "that ye are cause therof" is based on the French "de telles choses eusses esté cause" (Fr, of these things you were the cause), rather than the Spanish "que a tal cosa dieras lugar" (that you would allow this to happen).

ᶦᵛ The French text adds "aucun" (none) before "dommage," which alters the meaning of the line. Berners does not follow this addition.

ᵛ "for all . . . of love" is added based on the French "et guerdon de toy ne puis avoir" (and as I cannot receive a reward from you). Berners also follows the French by omitting the Spanish which translates as "so that I could be all yours." He replaces it with "yet I desyre to serve you."

ᵛᶦ A more accurate translation of the Spanish and French would have been "How can anyone wish to serve or love you if you destroy your own things?"

ᵛᶦᶦ The French mistranslates the Spanish here by writing a line which translates as "you would be an enemy to all if you would want to remedy and save me." Berners wisely follows the Spanish.

ᵛᶦᶦᶦ The doublet "deth & perdycyon" derives from an added French doublet.
Berners does not convey the same meaning as his sources, which translate as "This you ought to do, so that you will not be condemned. So that some good may come from my destruction, I wish that I could cause you to repent."

ᶦˣ Berners omits the added French doublet "peine et ennuy" (pain and trouble).

ˣ The French has several additions, which Berners does not preserve. His translation is very close to the Spanish.

ˣᶦ The added French doublet is not preserved.

ˣᶦᶦ In the phrase "ye have the power to slee me" the term "me" is an addition based on the French addition "me" before "tuer." As a result of the addition, the sentence refers specifically to Laureola's power over Lereano, rather than her power to kill all men, as in the Spanish.

ˣᶦᶦᶦ This last phrase, "for without . . . therof," does not accurately reflect the Spanish text; Berners erred in translating the term "esperiencia" (Sp, experience) because he mistook it for "esperar" (Sp, hope). Therefore, the translation should read "without my experience, your beauty has already made that known." The French text correctly translates the Spanish term as "experience."

ˣᶦᵛ The initial portion of the Spanish phrase, which translates as "If by chance it pleases you because you think," is omitted from the French and English. The whole sentence does not follow the French: Berners does not translate the added French doublet "douleurs & peines" (suffering and pains).

Notes to XVI: The auctor

ⁱ The term "satysfyed" is derived from the Spanish "satisfaziendo": it is omitted from the French.

ⁱⁱ The French adds "cha*n*gée" (changed) before "sore" which Berners omits.

ⁱⁱⁱ "yet the . . . trouble" is unclear. The sources translate as "and her confusion did not prevent her from watching mine." Moreover, "I demaundyd of her" should read "she demanded of me."

^{iv} The French translation adds that Laureola withdraws to her "chambre." Berners does not preserve the addition.

^v The term "vertuous" is added, based on the French "vertueuses."
Berners follows the French in omitting several terms from the Spanish.

^{vi} The term "eloquence" is added in the English. For an excellent overview of the importance of eloquence in this period, see Brian Vickers, ed., *English Renaissance Literary Criticism* (Oxford: Clarendon Press, 1999), 1–55.
The syntax of the English is so confusing that it makes little sense. The Spanish translates as "she told me that she had written to him, since it seemed to her inhuman not to save at such small cost a man such as he. And since, because of my pleasure at what I heard, I was inattentive to the way she phrased it, I shall not attempt to reproduce the sweetness and modesty with which she discoursed. Anyone who heard her would have recognized that she was quite unstudied in such matters" (*Prison of Love*, trans. Whinnom, 26–27). The French is almost identical to the Spanish.

^{vii} The English translation is problematic; rather than write "my answer," as in the sources, Berners writes "her answere."

^{viii} The syntax makes this sentence difficult to understand: it can mean either that she took his letter, or that he took hers. The Spanish and French sentences mean "after kissing her hands, I received her letter."

Notes to XVII: The letter fro Laureola to Lereano

ⁱ The French text errs in conjugating "to wait" in the first person singular, rather than the second person singular. Berners avoids the French error and follows the Spanish.

ⁱⁱ Berners has misunderstood his sources which translate as "But alas for me, this explanation will only serve to satisfy myself."

ⁱⁱⁱ The French adds the doublet "doubte et timeur" (doubt and fear), which Berners does not retain; he writes "feare" based on "miedo" (Sp).

ⁱᵛ "assoyled" is used to translate "asuelto" (Sp, resolved or distinguished) and "absoulz et delivrée" (Fr, absolved and freed). While the English does not preserve the French doublet, it retains its mistranslation.

ᵛ Here the English text follows the French. They both omit a phrase from the Spanish. The Spanish translates as "with my reply you are in the midst of your most proud pleasures." Also, rather than translate the Spanish "de quien los causó" (of her that has caused them), Berners translates the French with "of her that hath sent it." The verb "sene" is added, also based on a French addition, and "send" corresponds to the French "envoyer," rather than to the Spanish "causar" (Sp, to cause). Berners was also looking at the Spanish; he forms the doublet "fame and renoun" by combining "fama" (Sp, fame) and "renommée" (Fr, renown).

ᵛⁱ Berners makes "the favours" the object of the verb "to publysh," following the French. In the Spanish text it is a reflexive verb and the favours desire to publish themselves.

ᵛⁱⁱ "spotted or defamyd" is based on an added French doublet.

Berners writes "I reporte me to thy selfe," altering his sources: "tú lo conosces" (Sp) and "tu le cognois" (Fr, you know it). His translation implies that Laureola is submitting herself to Lereano's judgement, rather than implying that he agrees with her.

ᵛⁱⁱⁱ Berners follows the French here by conjugating the verb "to use" in the present, rather than in the past tense.

ⁱˣ This sentence is poorly translated; the Spanish translates as "In God's name, I require you to unfold my letter in your faith, because if you are as true as you say then my letter will not be lost, nor will it be seen by anyone." The French is an accurate translation up to "faith." The final part of the French sentence is so muddled that it is impossible to translate. While Berners's translation is not perfect, unlike the French it is readable. It appears to be based on the Spanish.

ˣ "then arte thou begyled in that beleve" is an addition. It echoes the proverb "He that beguiles another is oft beguiled himself." See Morris Palmer Tilley, *A Dictionary of the Proverbs in England in the Sixteenth and Seventeenth Centuries. A Collection of the Proverbs Found in English Literature and the Dictionaries of the Period* (Ann Arbor: University of Michigan Press, 1950), D179; Bartlett Jere Whiting, *Proverbs, Sentences, and Proverbial Phrases; from English Writings Mainly Before 1500* (Cambridge, MA: Harvard University Press, 1968), B211.

ˣⁱ The Spanish "hazer la vida otro tanto" is difficult to understand and neither of the translators had particular success with it. The French omits the phrase, and Berners writes "thus wyll . . . dayes." The translation provided by Whinnom is "life should treat me as justly as I have acted" (*Prison of Love*, 29). He is unsure of his translation, however, admitting that it "is little more than a plausible guess" (*Prison of Love*, 103 n. 17).

Notes to XVIII: The auctor

[i] The French text erroneously substitutes the first person construction for a third person singular pronoun, which refers to Laureola. Such a reading makes no sense in this context. Berners does not follow the French error. He also does not translate the two added French doublets.

[ii] Green is the colour of hope: see Parrilla, *Cárcel de amor*, 29.7.

[iii] The adverbial expression "a sobre ora" (Sp, on top of) and the adjective "verdad" (Sp, truth) are omitted from the French and English translations.

[iv] The French text errs by making "he" rather than "I" the subject of the verb "to come." Berners does not follow the error; he adheres to the Spanish. The French also adds a doublet that Berners does not translate. The sentence is not entirely based on the Spanish; the phrase "Pues yo, que no levava espacio" (and I, who had no time) is omitted from the English and French translations, suggesting that Berners was looking at his French source. Furthermore, the French and English replace Auctor with Rest as the subject of the sentence.

[v] The Spanish line translates as "and when I came to where that happy man lay." Berners is following the French text here.

[vi] In this sentence the French has many small additions which are not preserved by Berners. The French also omits the phrase "Contentacion cleryd his eyen," so Berners must have translated it from Spanish.

[vii] Again the French amplifies this line slightly. Berners does not follow its additions; his translation is closer to the Spanish.

[viii] The Spanish text specifies that Lereano thinks it is a small reward for Auctor's service, "parecíale poco precio"; while in the French Auctor thinks it is too great a reward for his service, "qui estoit beuacoup plus grande remuneration." Berners follows the Spanish in writing that the reward is too small, but the subject of the verb "to think" is ambiguous.

[ix] "accordyng to his degre" is omitted from the French and so Berners must have taken this phrase directly from Spanish.

[x] The italicised text which follows was added to the second and third editions, as explained in section 5 of the introduction.

[xi] The phrase which translates as "and as he was already acquainted with these old ceremonies," is omitted from the English and French texts. Similarly, later on Berners omits Auctor's scathing reference to battle scenes as tedious elements pertaining to the "old stories" and the old style of literature. These, and other minor alterations, give the impression that Berners is more interested in ceremony and chivalry than San Pedro. The next line offers further support of this hypothesis. See also Chap. XXXI.

[xii] Like the changes made in the previous line, by adding the term "nobly" and the phrase "and his duetie done to the kyng," Berners demonstrates a concern for royal ceremony not shared by San Pedro. Berners's latter addition is based on the longer addition in the French, which translates as: "where the king was lodged, to whom he did reverance and he was made very welcome by the king." The sentence is not wholly based on the French: in the French Lereano does not kiss Laureola's hand, and so this detail must be derived from the Spanish.

The narrator's comments raise the question of whether or not there really are things to be noted. He ushers in the possibility that he may only be seeing signs because he is looking, rather than because they are actually there. This ambiguity is furthered by his subsequent comments.

[xiii] Berners omits the final clause of the French which specifies that Persio "suspected that there was love between them two."

The English text says that Persio's father is named Gania, while he is called "Gavia" in Spanish and "Gany" in French. This discrepancy between the French and Spanish is probably the result of the printer confusing a "u" or "v" for an "n." The "n" in the English text may indicate that Berners got the name from the French text or that the English compositor turned the letter by mistake.

In the French "Persio" is named "Persco." Berners preserves the Spanish name.

Persio is of the same social standing as Lereano and so would also not be of a social class high enough to marry the princess. Barbara Weissberger argues that their desire for Laureola is combined with a desire for social ascendancy: see "The Politics of *Cárcel de amor*," *Revista de Estudios Hispanicos* 26 (1992): 307–26.

[xiv] Berners erroneously translates "escudriñan" (Sp, examine, inquire) as "disordereth," following the French variant reading of "désordonnent." The French and English use a third person plural pronoun, while the Spanish uses a third person singular pronoun.

The sources would be more accurately translated as "to what he imagined, which was everything."

The verb "regarded over" is here used to denote "to consider" (*OED* 9a). Interestingly, the only other recorded usages of this meaning of "regarded" derive from other works by Berners.

[xv] Persio's jealousy is mentioned in the French and English texts. The Spanish does not include it here, and so Berners must be using the French text.

The accusation of Laureola and her imprisonment and rescue which follow parallel the story of Guinevere and Lancelot in *Le Mort le roi Artu*, where Guinevere is accused of infidelity and saved by Lancelot: see E. Michael Gerli, "Toward a Poetics of the Spanish Sentimental Romance," *Hispania* 72 (1989): 474–82.

[xvi] In the French text the king does not sleep on the problem; this detail must have been translated directly from the Spanish. The doublet "vertue and auctoryte" originates in the Spanish and is not preserved by the French, further indicating Berners's indebtedness to the Spanish.

ˣᵛⁱⁱ The French text postpones this line about Laureola being in prison, including it later. Berners translated this line directly from Spanish.

For different explanations of the king's reaction see Parrilla, *Cárcel de amor*, 31.20.

Laureola's real prison parallels the allegorical prison in which Lereano was held captive at the start of the romance. Later when she is freed from the prison, Lereano returns to captivity. Their opposing movement from freedom to captivity suggests the impossibility of their union since for one to be free the other must relinquish his or her own freedom.

ˣᵛⁱⁱⁱ The French text expands this sentence considerably, but Berners does not preserve the additions. Also, Berners follows the Spanish in making the king the subject of the phrase; the French changes the subject to Persio.

ˣⁱˣ The French adds an extra sentence after "& vertue" that is not in the Spanish and which Berners does not preserve.

ˣˣ The French adds a doublet that Berners does not preserve.

On the historical practice of exchanging challenge letters, see Parrilla, *Cárcel de amor*, 31.24.

Notes to XIX: Persius' writtyng to Lereano

ⁱ This letter has many similarities with actual challenge letters exchanged in fifteenth-century Spain. See section 5 of the introduction.

ⁱⁱ The doublet "renome and fame" is created by taking a term from each of the Spanish and French texts: "fama" (Sp, fame) and "renomé" (Fr, renown).

ⁱⁱⁱ The doublet "dread and feare" is based on the added French doublet.

ⁱᵛ The French sentence is very muddled; Berners does not follow its errors and so must have used only the Spanish here.

ᵛ The term "mal" (Sp, Fr), which Berners translates as "evyl" makes the sentence difficult to understand. A better translation would have been "you have *little* profited by the unblemished honour that you inherited."

The French adds two doublets to this sentence, only one of which is preserved by Berners.

ᵛⁱ This sentence is based on the Spanish. Berners does not preserve the added French doublet nor the French alteration: the French translates "mayores" (ancestors) as "filz" (sons), which is its exact opposite. Berners follows the Spanish with "progenitours."

ᵛⁱⁱ The sources write of "an honourable death," but Berners describes "an honourable lyfe."

ᵛⁱⁱⁱ Berners does not mention the blood obligation—"obligación de tu sangre" (Sp, the obligation of your blood), "obligation que ton sang a envers lui" (Fr, the obligation that your blood has towards him)—but rather speaks of his "duetie to thy kyng." This supports the idea that Berners is more concerned with chivalry than his sources, as observed in the notes to Chaps. XVIII and XXXI.

The French adds "ton souverian seigneur" after "kyng," which Berners does not preserve.

ⁱˣ "the kynge's doughter" is added by Berners, based on the French addition "sa fille unique" (his only daughter). The French has several other additions in this sentence that Berners does not preserve.

ˣ The French adds a doublet here, which Berners does not preserve.

ˣⁱ Berners writes "ensample" for the Spanish "exemplo." He does not follow the French addition of "allegue & exemple" (allegation and example).

ˣⁱⁱ Berners's translation is not accurate. The Spanish translates as "I am bold enough to act thus because of my confidence in your falseness and in my truth. Choose the weapons in whatever manner you desire . . ." The French is the same as the Spanish except that it concludes as follows: ". . . choose the arms and the manner."

Notes to XX: The aunswer of Lereano

ⁱ The French and Spanish begin with a direct address to "Perseo," which functions as a salutation to the epistle.

ⁱⁱ Berners's translation is based on the French; the Spanish translates as "you would have avoided such perils by knowing my intention."

ⁱⁱⁱ The French and English translations both use present instead of past tense verbs, which accentuates Persio's hypocrisy.

ⁱᵛ In the Spanish text the adjective "cierto" (true) qualifies "amigo" (friend), indicating the depth of Lereano's and Persio's friendship. The adjective is omitted from the English and French texts. The whole sentence is not based on the French, however, as Berners omits the added doublet "tenois et reputois" (Fr, held and reputed). He follows the Spanish by using the single verb "I thoughte."

ᵛ Berners alters his sources; the Spanish and French imply that Lereano used to confide in Persio, and that he may have told him of his love for Laureola.

The expression which Berners renders as "or I may . . . to thyself" is based on the French. It is a mistranslation of the Spanish which means, "Oh! Enemy to thyselfe! This I can say according to reason . . ."

ᵛⁱ In the English text the adjective "serpentyne" is added to qualify "tonge," based on the French expression "ta langue serpentyne."

ᵛⁱⁱ Lereano is the subject of the sentence in the English text; it explicitly states that he will accomplish all the acts mentioned. The construction is passive in the Spanish and

French, implying that all will be done without Lereano's agency. As a result he appears to be less heroic than in the English text.

The French doublet "mensonges et faulseté" (lies and falsehood) is not preserved by Berners; he translates the single Spanish term "mentira" as "falsehodde."

[viii] Berners adds the noun "wordes" to "unmesurable" following the French addition.

[ix] The English is hard to understand. The Spanish and French lines translate as "I wish only to say something about the central issue, for there lies the cause of our quarrel."

[x] The phrase "clenlynes of honeste" is based on a combination of the Spanish and French terms: "limpieza" (Sp, cleanness) and "l'honnesté" (Fr, the honesty).

[xi] Berners mistranslates his sources here. The Spanish translates as "Well, when the intention is free of sin, he who judges is blameless," and the French translates as "It is such that when the intention is free of sin, the verdict will always be reasonable."

Technically, Lereano is telling the truth; he never "spoke" to her, he only ever wrote to her.

[xii] The added French doublet is not translated, but "and shame and rebuke to the" is added by Berners based on the French addition "et vituperation de toy."

[xiii] The technical terms in these final lines prove difficult for Berners. The Spanish translates as "Let the weapons which it is for me to choose be for combat on horseback, according to our custom; ourselves armed at all points, and the horses with bardes, crannets, and chamfrons; our lances shall be of equal length, and each shall have a sword, without any other of the usual weapons. With these, in defence of what I have said, I shall slay you, or force you to retract, or drive you from the field" (*Prison of Love*, trans. Whinnom, 33). The French translates as "the weapons that I [or you] have to choose are these: we will be armed at all points, on horses barded with chamfrons, with lances, and swords of equal length. With which, defending myself, I say that I will kill you, I will make you unsay what you said, or I will drive you from the field, victorious over what you said."

Notes to XXI: The auctor

[i] "welth & prosperite" is based on the added French doublet "bien et prosperité" (wealth and prosperity). The remainder of the sentence is based on the Spanish: Berners does not preserve the other French addition, and he translates the Spanish phrase "she gave hym a torne," which is omitted from the French.

[ii] Berners omits the final portion of the Spanish line which contains the term "reuto" (challenge) which provided him with difficulties earlier in Chap. XX. The French line does not agree exactly with the Spanish or the English.

[iii] The narratorial intrusion "como es escrito" (Sp, as is written) is omitted from Berners's and the French text. This whole sentence is not based on the French, however, as Berners does not translate the added French doublet.

To "assure the field" is to approve the challenge by fixing a place for the battle (Parrilla, *Cárcel de amor,* 34.1).

[iv] After "stage" the French text adds a sentence, which Berners does not preserve.

[v] The French and English translations both omit the Spanish clause which should occur before "so they." The French translation adds details about Lereano's and Persio's state of mind and about their form of riding as they meet, which are not preserved by Berners.

Berners adds "so they after . . . kyng," which supports my hypothesis that Berners has more respect for the idea of kingship than the authors of the continental versions. See Chaps. XIX and XVIII.

[vi] Berners adds the gory detail "so that it fell to the erth, sworde and all," based on a longer French addition. He also omits San Pedro's dismissal of "cuento de istorias viejas" (Sp, tales of old stories). While for San Pedro the battle scenes are "old stories," not worthy of textual space, for Berners they are an integral part of the tale. Whinnom and Deyermond, amongst others, have seen this reference as proof that San Pedro sees his text as a part of a new literary tradition (i.e. the *novela sentimental*), distinct from the romance, where battle scenes play a small (or even non-existent role): see Keith Whinnom, ed., *Obras Completas, II* Cárcel de Amor, Diego de San Pedro (Madrid: Clásicos Castalia, 1971), 117; Deyermond, *Tradiciones y puntos de vista.* In fact, this absence of jousts and duels is one of the features which is used to differentiate the romance from the *novelas sentimentales. Castell* is one of the few *novelas* that contains a battle scene: see Julio Rodríguez-Puértolas, "Sentimentalismo 'burgués' y amor cortés: la novela del siglo XV," in *Essays in Narrative Fiction in the Iberian Peninsula in Honour of Frank Pierce* (Oxford: Dolphin, 1982), 121–39.

[vii] Berners includes a few slight additions, which make his sentence somewhat confusing. The sources translate as "so that you do not pay with your life for the falseness of your tongue."

[viii] Berners expands his sources, writing "and gave hym many sharpe & hevy strokes," again showing his interest in battles.

[ix] Throwing down his baton would signal the end of the fight: cf. Shakespeare *Richard II* (I.iii). In ending the duel prematurely, the king demonstrates a lack of faith in divine justice, as the Cardinal and Laureola point out to him in Chaps. XXX and XXXV, respectively.

[x] The added French doublet is not preserved by Berners. He writes, "condiscendyd" based on the sole Spanish verb, "otorgó."

ˣⁱ Barbara Weissberger, "The Politics of *Cárcel de amor*," *Revista de Estudios Hispanicos* 26 (1992): 307–26, posits that the king's favouritism for Persio is a commentary on, and reflection of, the tensions between nobility and crown towards the end of the fifteenth century in Spain.

ˣⁱⁱ The French text omits the idea of "seremonyes," which Berners preserves from the Spanish "iguales en cerimonia, aunque desiguales en fama" (Sp, equal in ceremony although unequal in reputation/worth). Berners was not only looking at the Spanish here; he retains the added French doublet, translating it as "fame & honour."

ˣⁱⁱⁱ The French adds a sentence that Berners does not translate.

ˣⁱᵛ The French amplifies the text again here; Berners does not preserve the additions, remaining close to the Spanish text.

ˣᵛ The French text expands the description of Persio, but Berners's translation is taken directly from the Spanish. Berners follows the French in omitting the Spanish narratorial intrusion, and the final clause confirming their agreement is added by Berners based on the French addition.

ˣᵛⁱ The phrase "and saw it with myne eyen" is added based on the French addition "de la veoir en ma pensée" (seeing it in my mind).

ˣᵛⁱⁱ The verb "to turn" is omitted from the French; Berners must have translated it directly from the Spanish.

ˣᵛⁱⁱⁱ The French text replaces "de su corte" (Sp, of his court) with "& autres courtisans" (Fr, and other courtiers). Berners follows the Spanish.

Notes to XXII: Lereano to the kyng

ⁱ Berners does not translate the addition to the French text.

ⁱⁱ The doublet "quyte and delyvered" is based on the French "quicte & delivré," which translates "libre" (Sp, free).

ⁱⁱⁱ The sentence "It is great . . . in deade" recalls the proverb "There is a great difference between word and deed" (Tilley, *A Dictionary of the Proverbs*, D333). See also Whiting, *Proverbs, Sentences, and Proverbial Phrases*, D136.

ⁱᵛ The verb "desire" is conjugated in the second person singular in the sources, but Berners conjugates it in the third person singular. As a result he needs to refashion the sentence to make his reading fit. The sources translate as "even if you desired to be revenged on Laureola."

ᵛ This sentence is confusing since Berners omits "You never assembled an army in which they did not form a third part" from the sources, but retains the clause "the .iii. parte," which makes no sense.

^{vi} The French adds a doublet, but Berners follows the Spanish in using the single verb "wonne."

^{vii} Again, Berners does not retain the French doublet; he follows the Spanish, writing "conserve."

^{viii} In the English and French texts Lereano refers to Persio as his "wrongfull accuser," while in the Spanish he is "del culpado" (the guilty).

^{ix} The French adds several short phrases, which Berners does not translate.

^x The French elaborates on the Spanish "leal cizañador" (Sp, loyal mischief-maker), and Berners follows the French with "the beste servaunt to make dyscorde and lyes."

^{xi} Three French doublets occur in this line that are not preserved; Berners adheres to the Spanish.

^{xii} The sources translate as "I will never be exonorated in the minds of all people."

^{xiii} The Spanish and French texts ask a rhetorical question: Berners rewrites his sources so that they form a statement.
The French adds a phrase which Berners translates as "so *that* I can . . . fantasyes." However, his sentence is not entirely based on the French; he omits the added adverb "integrallement" (Fr, entirely) and the doublet "reste et demeure" (Fr, stay and remain).

Notes to XXIII: The auctor

ⁱ The French adds a doublet before "delyberacion," which Berners does not preserve.

ⁱⁱ The last half of this sentence and the next are very confused. The Spanish and French translate as "even if the king were to liberate Laureola, the king himself would not be free of anger, because the king knew that Lereano had intended to serve her and the king thought that intention was blameworthy even if Lereano's intentions were not really worthy of blame." The problem occurs because Berners makes Lereano the grammatical subject of the sentence when in the sources the king is the subject and Lereano is the object.

ⁱⁱⁱ The French errs in using a feminine subject in the clause "commaundyd Lereano to go to"; Berners follows the Spanish text, avoiding the French error.
The city "Susa" is called "Size" in the French; Berners follows the Spanish, which also has "Susa."

^{iv} The French omits the final verb, which Berners preserves as "was delyverede."

^v Berners omits the reference to the king's doubts which occurs before "how that the accusacion." As a result the king seems to be acting in greater haste in the English than in the sources.

ⁱᵛ The English doublet "subtyle and sharpe" is based on the Spanish doublet, which is not preserved in the French.

ᵛⁱⁱ "fantasye" is based on "fantasie" (Fr) rather than "consejo" (Sp, advice).

ᵛⁱⁱⁱ Berners changes the verbs to first person singular conjugations from third person singulars. The sources translate as "he desired to serve himself of my advice."

Notes to XXIV: The auctor to Lereano

ⁱ This sentence seems to be based on the Spanish: "fortune" translates "fortune" (Sp, fortune), rather than "desfortune" (Fr, misfortune); and Berners omits the added French doublet, writing "trouble" based on the single term "desvia" (Sp, confusion).

ⁱⁱ The French adds "seront tenues et louées pour bonnes" (will be held and praised as good), but Berners follows the Spanish, writing "be praysed."

ⁱⁱⁱ The doublet "dyspraysed and taken" is added based on the Spanish "avidas." The term is omitted from the French.

ⁱᵛ "Prueva" (Sp, prove) and "essaye" (Fr, try) are translated by the doublet "prove & assay." Berners combines the two languages.

ᵛ The doublet "honour and fame" is based on the added French doublet.

ᵛⁱ The orthography of the name "Galleo" differs slightly in the sources: they call him "Galio" (Sp) and "Gallio" (Fr).

ᵛⁱⁱ For the Spanish "cargo y de la vida" and the French "infamie et de mort" Berners writes "charge nor blame." He does not choose between the Spanish "vida" (life) and the French "mort" (death) but provides an alternative reading.

Berners appears to be using the Spanish here. The French changes the pronoun from "he" to "she," writing "qu'elle soit sauvée" (Fr, that she will be saved). Berners does not preserve the error. In addition, the French text omits "y tu limpieza" (Sp, and your cleanness). Thus "and of thy clennes" must be derived from the Spanish.

ᵛⁱⁱⁱ Berners alters the grammatical subject; the line should read "till the truth has been proven to the king."

Berners follows the French in omitting the name of the "castell" in which she will be kept. It is called Dala in San Pedro's text.

ⁱˣ In the Spanish text the Cardinal is of "Gausa" and in the French he is of "Gausee." Berners writes "Gaula."

ˣ The French doublet "supplier et interceder" (to implore and to intercede) is not preserved.

ˣⁱ Again here the French adds the adjective "unique" to "doughter," stressing Laureola's status as sole heir, and Berners does not preserve the addition.

^{xii} The doublet "doubte et timeur" (Fr, doubt and fear) does not occur in the English or Spanish; Berners writes "feare" based on "miedo" (Sp, fear).

^{xiii} The French doublet "justes et raisonables" (just and reasonable) does not occur in the English or Spanish; Berners writes "juste" based on the Spanish "justas."

Notes to XXV: The auctor

ⁱ "más sanamente" (Sp, very honourably) is omitted after "purpose" from the French and English translations. Berners does not adhere to the French completely. He omits the verb "to walk" which occurs in the French, creating a journey metaphor: "je marchoye par le chemin" (I was walking along the way).

ⁱⁱ "How be it . . . dayes respyght" is added based on a French addition.

Notes to XXVI: The letter of Lereano to Laureola

ⁱ The English sentence is a bit confusing since it omits the verb "no poder" (Sp, not to be able) or "ne ma peu" (Fr, I could not do).

ⁱⁱ In this sentence Berners mistranslates both instances of "consuelo" (Sp, comfort) and "console" and "consolations" (Fr, console and consolations) as "counsel." The sources translate as "I am now so used to living in sadness that I take comfort in that same sadness because it is caused by you."

ⁱⁱⁱ Berners amplifies the sentence by adding terms on either side of "remedies." In so doing he is following the French.

^{iv} In the Spanish, Lereano is not saying "if thou faylest trust in me," but the converse: "if you lack faith in them [the remedies] you can have faith in me." Berners's error may arise from the subtle alteration in the French line, which translates as "and if in that I lack faith, you can have faith in me."

^v The Spanish line begins, "If this does not seem to you to be a great thing." The French completely mistranslates the Spanish, and writes the opposite: "what I say seems to me to be a great thing." Berners conveys the general sense of the Spanish, avoiding the errors of the French text.

^{vi} This line poses problems for Berners. An accurate translation is "and not only is my life a little thing to lose, all that I could desire to lose is nothing."

^{vii} Rather than "ye myght . . . your life" the Spanish means "you may fall into a decline." Berners may have been influenced by the French which translates as "because if you give in to those thoughts it may cause you to lose your life."

viii The French omits "as in that . . . save you"; Berners must have translated it from "no podiendo salvarte" (Sp, not being able to save you).

ix The doublet "te socoure et do*n*ne fortesse" (Fr, to succour you and give you strength) is omitted; Berners writes "strength you agayne" based on "te dé fortaleza" (Sp, give you strength).

Notes to XXVII: The auctor

i The French specifies that he was told "d'une sienne femme" (Fr, by one of her women), but Berners does not preserve that addition. The comparison "no menos fuerte que cerrada" (Sp, no less strong than close together) is replaced by the term "great," and the English translation is closer to the French phrase "une grille de fer moult fort" (Fr, a very strong iron grate).

ii The added French doublet is omitted; Berners writes "moche travaill" based on the Spanish "mucho trabajo."

iii Berners's line is closer to the Spanish; the French alters this sentence to: "and the next day as I was out walking, the window being open, I saw that Laureola was looking at me. However, because of the thickness of the lattice I could not see her well."

Notes to XXVIII: Laureola's letter to Lerea[no]

i The end of the phrase causes difficulties for Berners. It translates as "though the pity I felt for you carries its penalty" (*Prison of Love,* trans. Whinnom, 42). Berners's mistranslation was probably influenced by the French "ay . . . plus pensé que chargé" (Fr, I thought more than I blamed).

ii Berners creates the doublet "honoure and fame" by combining his sources: "fama" (Sp, fame) and "ho*n*neur" (Fr, honour).

iii The doublet "counsel & advyse" is from the French "conseil & advis" (counsel and advice). The Spanish has "consejo" (counsel).

iv Berners follows the French by making "wisdom" the subject of the sentence: in the Spanish Lereano is the subject. The whole sentence, however, is not based on the French; after "best waye" the French has an addition, which Berners does not preserve.

v The French text adds "grosses" (thick) to describe the chains, but Berners does not preserve the addition. The French also adds the doublet "les homicides et criminelz" (murderers and criminals), but Berners follows the Spanish and writes "murderers."

vi "my tendre flesshe" is based on the French addition "ma te*n*dre chair."

[vii] Berners and the French omit the Spanish phrase, which translates as "because I spared you."

[viii] The French begins this sentence with the addition "My patience is so diminished," which Berners does not preserve.

[ix] The French alters the final words to "because in things that are deliberated there can be no error." The Spanish says that if he acts according to justice he will not err in his judgement. Because Berners omits "judgement" from the previous sentence and adds "as thou lyste," the final line makes little sense.

Notes to XXIX: The Auctour

[i] The French omits "So to tourne . . . purpose"; Berners must have translated it directly from the Spanish.

Notes to XXX: The cardynall to the kinge

[i] The sources pose problems for Berners. They do not say that the king is forced or ordered to do anything, but rather that he asks for advice.

[ii] On the importance of counsel, see section 4b of the introduction.

[iii] "yet I fynde" derives from the French addition "je treuve" (I find).

[iv] The doublet "glory and honour" is based on the French doublet "la gloire et honneur." The Spanish has the single term "gloria."

[v] The Spanish, which translates as "because of the contrary of this," is omitted from the French and English texts. Yet the whole sentence is not based on the French; the French text adds the doublet "l'advis et oppinion" (Fr, advice and opinion), which Berners does not translate. Berners follows the Spanish in using the single term "counsayll" to translate "el parecer" (Sp, the opinion). Also, "and they that gave . . . faulte" and "charge & faulte" are both omitted from the French, so Berners must have translated them directly from the Spanish.

[vi] The French adds the doublet "faictes et ordonnées" (done and ordained); Berners follows the Spanish by using a single term: he translates "obradas" as "done." The French uses the terms "meure deliberation" (mature deliberation) to translate the Spanish doublet "deliberación y acuerdo." Berners preserves the Spanish doublet with "good deliberacyon and accord." This sentence appears to be based on the Spanish.

[vii] Cf. Seneca, *De clementia* II, iv, 1, "Quod sapiens casus providet et in expedito consilium habet" (qtd. in Parrilla, *Cárcel de amor*, 45.3). As Parrilla explains, while much of the Cardinal's speech has precedents in Seneca, these ideas on counsel had become

commonplace in late fifteenth-century Spain, and as I show in the introduction (section 4b), they were equally well known in Tudor England.

ᵛⁱⁱⁱ Berners adds the term "must" based on the French addition "doit," making the verb "to think" an imperative.

ⁱˣ "prove theyr counsailours" is omitted from the French text. This phrase must have been translated directly from Spanish.

ˣ "for all thynges . . . true" is proverbial, based on "Things are not as they seem" (Tilley, *A Dictionary of the Proverbs*, T199). See also Whiting, *Proverbs, Sentences, and Proverbial Phrases*, T119.

ˣⁱ The phrase "and be jelous . . . erryng" is difficult to understand. It translates the Spanish and French phrases which mean "And because he is jealous of his reputation he keeps himself from error."
"now agreeth" is omitted from the French. It must have been translated directly from Spanish.

ˣⁱⁱ The sources translate as "Unless goodness deserves to be put to the sword" (*Prison of Love*, trans. Whinnom, 45).

ˣⁱⁱⁱ "& of shamefull conversacion" is added, based on the French addition "et de mauvaise conversation."

ˣⁱᵛ Berners erroneously translates "pesquisar" (Sp, inquired into) and "d'avoir esgard" (Fr, to have regard, to consider) as "shortyd." He may have confused the Spanish verb "pesquisar" with the adjective "pequeño" (Sp, small). The corresponding phrase in Spanish and French translates as "considered their lives."

ˣᵛ After "courte" the French has an addition, which Berners does not preserve.

ˣᵛⁱ After "done you" the French text adds "et continuellement faisons" (and continually do); Berners does not translate the addition.

ˣᵛⁱⁱ The French adds the doublet "fame et renommée" (fame and renown), but Berners uses the single term "fame" based on the Spanish "fama."

Notes to XXXI: The kynge's aunswere

ⁱ Berners does not retain the French doublet "l'accroissent et augementent" (increase and augment); he translates the Spanish "acrecientan" (increase) as "encrease."
Melibea's words to her father in *La Celestina*, XX are almost identical to the king's words in *Cárcel* (Parrilla, *Cárcel de amor*, 46.1). In fact, there are numerous verbal echoes between *Cárcel* and *Celestina*: see Dorothy Sherman Severin, "From the Lamentations of Diego de San Pedro to Pleberio's Lament," in *The Age of the Catholic Monarchs 1474–1516: Literary Studies in Memory of Keith Whinnom*, ed. Alan Deyermond and Ian Macpherson

(Liverpool: Liverpool University Press, 1989), 178–84, and in the notes to Parrilla, *Cárcel de amor.*

[ii] The French adds the expression "certes non" (certainly not) after "Lereano," which Berners does not preserve.

[iii] Berners creates the doublet "dishonour and shame" by taking a term from each of his sources: "desonra" (Sp, dishonour) and "vergongne" (Fr, shame). Berners translates "publicado" (Sp) as "yf it were publisshed," while the French uses the doublet "sceu & divulgé" (knew and divulged).

[iv] The preceding lines echo Seneca, *De clementia* II, iii, 1, 4, (Parrilla, *Cárcel de amor,* 47.5).

[v] The charge of adultery rests solely on Laureola, and there is no punishment for Lereano. This is discussed by Pamela Waley, "*Cárcel de amor* and *Grisel y Mirabella*: A Question of Priority," *Bulletin of Hispanic Studies* 50 (1973): 340–56; Whinnom, *Obras Completas, II*; and Parrilla, *Cárcel de amor,* 47.6.

[vi] The beginning of the phrase is based on the French, "which should not be done," and the the end on the Spanish "for he condemns himself who condones evil" (*Prison of Love,* trans. Whinnom, 47).

[vii] "The righte . . . observed" is omitted from the French. Berners's line is a direct translation of the Spanish.

[viii] The phrase "And yf it . . . abhorred" means that if justice is not impartial then it is abhorrent. The sources translate as, "and when it is partial it is abhorrent."

[ix] "and of base condicion" is added based on the French addition "de basse condition."

[x] The phrase "it is no . . . eye" is omitted from the French; Berners translated it directly from Spanish.

Notes to XXXII: The Auctor

[i] The French expands "grave tristeza" (Sp, great sadness) to "very great dolour and sadness"; Berners preserves the Spanish with "great hevynes."

[ii] "yet theyr . . . the quene" is rather confused. The Spanish translates as "much less that favour, for the king had no less reason to grant it than the queen to request it" (*Prison of Love,* trans. Whinnom, 48), and the French translates as "and much lesser things ought not to have been refused to the authority of the queen." The English is closer to the French than to the Spanish, as they both omit all reference to the king and claim that the queen's authority is the reason why her request ought not to be refused.

[iii] "in her yonge age" is added based on the French addition "pour l'age tendre."
    The last three things listed—the fame of the judge, the life of her that is judged, and the goods of the supplicant—are "savyde" in Berners's text, while in the Spanish and

French text they are killed: "mataría" (Sp) and "tueroit" (Fr). Also, "and the mynd . . . fulfylled" is not an accurate translation; the sources mean "the good qualities of her who supplicated."

ⁱᵛ The Spanish and French, which Berners translates as "and to pay . . . desertes," mean "although he demeaned himself in so doing."

"and then God . . . ryght is" is omitted from the French; Berners must have translated it directly from the Spanish.

Notes to XXXIII: The quene to Laureola

ⁱ The queen's lament for Laureola parallels Lereano's mother's lament in Chap. XL–VII. On the rhetorical organisation of the *planctus*, see Jeanne Battesti Pelegrin, "Tópica e invención: los lamentos de las madres en la *Cárcel de amor* de Diego de San Pedro," in *La literatura Hispánica Reyes Católicos y Descubrimento. Acta del Congreso Internacional de la literatura hispánica en la época de los reyes Católicos y el Descubrimento*, ed. Manuel Criado del Val (Barcelona: PPU, 1989), 237–47.

ⁱⁱ The French changes "muerta" (Sp, die) to "plai*n*te" (Fr, lament). Berners follows the Spanish with "dye."

ⁱⁱⁱ Berners forms the doublet "good reasone and ryght" by taking one term from each of his sources: "derecho" (Sp, right) and "raison" (Fr, reason).

ⁱᵛ The sources translate as "There was room for you in your father's anger, yet all who know you say that the whole earth was too small to constrain your virtues" (*Prison of Love*, trans. Whinnom, 50). Berners did not understand this line; he translates the key terms but rearranges them.

ᵛ The Spanish and French say that the poor desire riches to serve her. Berners does not convey the sense of the original. By adding "and" and by changing the object "riches" to the subject "the rich," the meaning is altered.

ᵛⁱ The sources mean "to take revenge on him I will borrow strength from the hatred I bear him." Berners misunderstands the second part of the line: he adds "yf I coulde," and substitutes "shuld then soone be utteryd" for the verb "to borrow from."

ᵛⁱⁱ Berners is confused by the end of this sentence. The sources translate as "for executing vengeance on him will not assuage the pain of my grief" (*Prison of Love*, trans. Whinnom, 50).

ᵛⁱⁱⁱ Rather than "joye in his beatitude," the sources mean "joy as do the blessed."

ⁱˣ The French alters the Spanish by adding "without delay I should have plucked you out of this that is such a hard trouble to me" at the start of the sentence. Berners's translation follows the Spanish.

ˣ The expression "luz mía" (Sp, my light) is expanded by Berners, based on the French "O lumière des yeulx miens" (Fr, Oh, light of my eyes!).

[xi] The address to the Virgin Mary is an addition. Unlike the other references to the Virgin Mary, which are removed from the second and third editions, as discussed in section 5 of the introduction, this one is retained in subsequent editions.

Notes to XXXIV: The Auctor

[i] Berners writes "lordes" based on the French "seigneurs"; the Spanish has "señoras" (ladies).

[ii] Berners qualifies "hope" as "hope of remedy," based on the French addition, "d'ésperance de obtenir grace" (hope to obtain grace).

Notes to XXXV: The letter of Laureola to the kynge

[i] The whole French chapter is in verse, as are Chaps. XXXIX and XLI. In these chapters the French follows the Spanish quite closely with the exception of slight changes in word order to make the text fit the verse scheme of pentametre couplets. The verse format appears not to have interested Berners. In these three chapters he relies almost exclusively on the Spanish text. In the notes that follow (as well as those for Chaps. XXXIX and XLI), I will not indicate the alterations, additions, and omissions made by the French translator, except for instances where it is possible that Berners may have been influenced by them. Unless otherwise stated it should be assumed that the French agrees with the Spanish, or that the difference had no bearing on Berners's translation.

[ii] Berners adds the term "pitie" to create the doublet "pitie and clemence." This may be based on the French doublet "clemence et douleur," or it may have been an independent alteration, as he makes the same change below with no help from the French.

[iii] Proverbial (Tilley, *A Dictionary of the Proverbs*, M515). This proverb does not appear in Whiting, *Proverbs, Sentences, and Proverbial Phrases*.

[iv] The sources translate as "you will have given them a lesson in rebellion."

[v] Berners has clearly misunderstood his sources; they translate as "When they go out in the streets, he who is the last to bless and laud them is the first to think he has erred."

[vi] Cf. Seneca, *De clementia* III, x, 4 (Parrilla, *Cárcel de amor*, 52.6).

Notes to XXXVI: The Auctor

[i] In the final portion of the sentence Berners understands all the terms but he does not seem to understand how they are related, and so he slightly muddles the sense. The sources mean "they would have given her freedom if they were as obliged to their pity as they were loyal."

[ii] The French mistranslates "dolor" (Sp, dolour) as "doulceur" (Fr, sweetness), but Berners follows the Spanish with "dolour."

[iii] The spelling of "Gawlo" is unique to Berners; the sources have "Galio" (Sp) and "Gaullo" (Fr).

[iv] The doublet "he aunswered me & sayde" is based on the Spanish "respondióme" (Sp, he answered me). The verb is omitted from the French.

[v] In the expression "evyll fortune," "fortune" derives from the Spanish "fortuna," and "evyll" is from the French "malheurté" (misfortune). The French errs in writing "*la mienne* malheurté" when the pronoun should be "his" rather than "my." Berners does not follow the French error and translates the Spanish "su" as "his."

[vi] "enmudecía" (Sp, became mute) is replaced with "changyde" by Berners, following the French alteration of "se changeoit" (Fr, changed)

[vii] This sentence may be based on the Spanish: the term "provydyde" derives from the Spanish "proveido" rather than the French "advisé" (advised).

Like a perfect knight, Lereano resorts to violence only when all other means fail. See Parrilla, *Cárcel de amor*, 53.6 and Whinnom, *Obras completas, II*.

[viii] Berners mistranslates his sources. The Spanish translates as "The which was determined with sage consideration" and the French translates as "and that done wisely." Also, the English phrase "suche as were made privy" alters the sources which mean "because if he would have communcated this to his relations."

[ix] This sentence is altered by Berners. The Spanish and French translate as "some so as not to disobey the king, would have said it was a bad thing; others, wanting to keep secure their property, would have told him to abandon it; and others, because of the danger involved, would have told him not to undertake it."

[x] Berners adds the phrase "And he desired them," based on the French addition "les pria."

[xi] "in tyme of peace" is based on the Spanish "en tiempo seguro"; the French omits the term "seguro."

[xii] The French adds "liberalement" (freely) after "delyveryd." Berners does not preserve the addition.

[xiii] The French omits the name of the fortress, "Dala," from the Spanish, and mistakes the last term "dicha" (Sp, fortune) for the verb "decir" (Sp, to say), as its past partici-

ple is also dicho/a. Berners also does not include the name "Dala," but he does not follow
the French mistranslation; he substitutes the final clause for "a castell . . . thence."

xiv The sources translate as "he remained always bringing up the rear."

xv The French doublet "peril n'y empeschement" (peril nor obstacle) is not translated.
Berners writes "without peril" based on the Spanish "ni peligro."

xvi In the Spanish text Lereano sends the footmen ahead, but in the French and English the horsemen send the footmen ahead. Berners was probably using the French here.
"Suria" is "Susa" in Spanish and "Suze" in French.

xvii Prior to this line, the French adds an entire sentence, which Berners omits.

xviii "man of warre" is based on "homme de guerre" (Fr, man of war) rather than
"guerrero" (Sp, warrior).

xix "as engyns . . . issue oute" is original to the English, further indicating Berners'
interest in military operations. The Spanish and French translate as "he ordered that his
outposts be advanced to the siege-lines of the town, and he manned them with his best
men" (*Prison of Love*, trans. Whinnom, 57).

xx Berners does not convey the sense of his originals. The Spanish translates as "so
that he lost two thirds of his men" (*Prison of Love*, trans. Whinnom, 57) and the French
as "with the loss of a great many of his knights."

Notes to XXXVII: Lereano to his company

i The change in the verb tense of "tener" (Sp, to have) from a conditional to an indicative in the English, coupled with the omission of the term "alguna," makes Lereano's doubt seem much stronger. In San Pedro's text the line means "I may have some
doubt . . ." Despite these changes Berners's text is much closer to the Spanish than the
French; the French writes the complete opposite: "j'auroye aucun doubte" (Fr, I would
have no doubt).

ii This sentence provides difficulties for Berners. The Spanish and French lines
translate as "Now we have the opportunity to hand down to our heirs the noble reputation which we inherited" (*Prison of Love*, trans. Whinnom, 58).

iii In the Spanish "vergüença" (Sp, shame) qualifies both "your blood" and "my
name." The French separates the two terms and Berners follows the alteration. Berners
and the French associate "shame and dishonour" with "blood" and "enfamy" with "name."
The French also adds "aujourd'huy" (today) after "d'infamie," which Berners omits.

iv In the phrase "o gloriosa fama" (Sp, or glorious fame) Berners interprets "o" to be
the "O!" of an invocation rather than an "o" (or) signifying choice. The French omits "o"
altogether, indicating that Berners was using the Spanish.

ᵛ Berners mistranslates his sources, which translate as "Do not fear the large companies recently arrived from the king's camp [Fr, for in the first battles] the weakest will fight. Fools are frightened by a large host, but wise men gain courage from a virtuous few."

Notes to XXXVIII: The auctor

ⁱ The French adds "obscure" to qualify "nyght," but Berners does not follow the addition.

ⁱⁱ "the valiantnes . . . alyve" is an amplification of the Spanish "los bivos" (the living) based on the French addition, which translates as "and increased the courage of the living."

ⁱⁱⁱ Berners follows the French in omitting "de los damnados" (of the damned) from after "of them."

ⁱᵛ Berners muddles his sources, which translate as "as just reason demanded of him."

ᵛ The French has a chapter break here, which Berners does not retain.

ᵛⁱ This line is omitted from the French, and so Berners must have translated it from the Spanish.

ᵛⁱⁱ "strange manner" is based on "estraña manera" (Sp, strange manner); the French alters it to "extrême douleur" (Fr, extreme dolour).

ᵛⁱⁱⁱ The doublet "thoughtes and trowbles" is created by taking a term from each of the sources: "las congoxas" (Sp, the thoughts) and "passions" (Fr, passions, troubles).

His mission completed, Lereano reverts back to his old ways. He has proven himself to be a perfect knight, and so now returns to being the perfect lover.

ⁱˣ The sentence is a bit muddled. The Spanish and French mean "and when I told him that his misfortune had begun anew."

The italicized text which follows is added to the second and third English editions.

Notes to XXXIX: The letter fro Lereano to Laureola

ⁱ Like Chaps. XXXV and XLI, the French chapter is in verse. The subsequent notes will follow same guidelines as outlined at the beginning of Chap. XXXV.

ⁱⁱ The Spanish provides difficulties for Berners; it translates as "you can consent to my suffering without any cause."

iii Berners translates "ufano" as "gloriouse." "Pride," with its pejorative connotations, would have been a better translation. It is possible that Berners was influenced by the French "glorieux."

iv Berners slightly muddles this sentence; the Spanish means "If it pleases you because I never did you any service [it is because] the services never could have attained the highness that you deserve."

v The English "syn ye wyll gyve no reward" seems closer to the French "Puis donc a tant tu nyes grace" (since that you so deny a reward) than to the Spanish "no niegues galardón" (do not deny a reward).

vi "The water ... hardnes" translates the Spanish "Water makes the earth grow green again, but my tears have never given fresh life to my hopes of you" (*Prison of Love*, trans. Whinnom, 63). The English may have been influenced by the French "Certes les eaues la terre reverdissent / Mais non jamais mes lermes amolissent / Ton ésperance" (water makes the earth green, but my tears will never mollify your hope). The added French verb "amolissent" (mollify) seems to have been used by Berners, but the substitution of "endurat hardnes" for "hope" is original to him, as is the substitution of "refressheth" for "make green."

vii The Spanish translates as "the first part of my life was spent in innocence; and the knowledge stage of life was spent in sorrow; at least the end will be in rest."

viii "I must ... trace" mistranslates "será forçado que veas," which means "will inevitably come to your knowledge" (*Prison of Love*, trans. Whinnom, 63).

Notes to XLI: The letter fro Laureola to Lereano

i The French chapter is in verse and so the same guidelines regarding the notes apply as in Chaps. XXXV and XXXVIII.

ii Berners translates "estrecho" (Sp, the extremity) as "the perell." This is probably based on the French "le peril."

iii The Spanish "onra" (honour) is translated by its opposite: "faulte & shame." This alteration may have been inspired by "la mienne coulpe" (Fr, my own fault).

iv The Spanish translates as "it is as proper to prove inconstant in ill-advised conduct as to prove steadfast in honourable matters" (*Prison of Love*, trans. Whinnom, 64). Berners seems to comprehend the Spanish text, but his translation is difficult to understand.

v Berners alters the meaning of the sentence. The Spanish means "you may not say that you asked me for hope and I gave you counsel."

vi The Spanish would be more accurately translated as "so that you could have seen how as I now offer you counsel on one hand, I would have satisfied your desire on the other."

Notes to XLII: The auctor

[i] The French translates "mucha" (Sp, much) as "non petit" (Fr, not little); Berners follows the Spanish writing "moche." The French uses the conjunction "et" instead of the personal pronoun "elle," but Berners does not replicate the error, writing "she" before "sayd." He seems to have been using the Spanish here.

[ii] The expression "sobbynge and gulpynge in my throte" translates "un nudo en la garganta" (Sp, a lump in my throat). The French also translates this phrase creatively: "un si gros souspir en l'estomach" (a very great sigh in my stomach). Berners and the French may be playing on the proverb, "A coeur dolent la bouche souspire" (Fr), "Sighes in the mouth, sorrow at the heart." See Cotgrave under "souspir": Randle Cotgrave, *A Dictionarie of the French and English Tongues* (London: Islip, 1611; repr. with introduction by William S. Woods, Columbia, SC: University of South Carolina Press, 1950).

[iii] The French omits the term "mortal"; Berners must have translated it from the Spanish.

[iv] "bien ni esperança" (Sp, good nor hope) is translated as "foy ne esperance en bien aucun" (Fr, faith nor hope in any good) and as "hope of any welth" by Berners. The English is closer to the French than to the Spanish.

The French translates "enojos" (Sp, trouble) with a doublet, but Berners follows the Spanish, only using the single term "trouble."

Lereano here prepares himself to die for love.

[v] Rather than "was lyke to dye" the Spanish and French translate as "was allowing himself to die." Berners may have made this alteration due to implications of suicide in the originals, see section 3 of the introduction. On Lereano and suicide, see Damiani, "The Didactic Intention," 37 n.31; Wardropper, "El mundo sentimental," 176; Samuel Gili Gaya, ed., *Cárcel de Amor* (Madrid: Espasa-Calpe, 1967), xii–iii, who interpret his death symbolically, and not as a suicide. Or, for a different perspective, see Barbara Matulka, *The Novels of Juan de Flores and their European Diffusion* (New York: Columbia University Press, 1931), 34, 158; Otis H. Green, *España y la tradición occidental. El espíritu castellano el la literature desde el 'Cid' hasta Calderón*, 4 vols. (Madrid: Gredos, 1969), 3: 204–24; and María Rosa Lida de Malkiel, *La originalidad artistica de la Celestina* (Buenos Aires: Eudeba, 1962), 239 ff., who designate his death a suicide and discuss its implications for the *novela* and the characterisation of Lereano. Despite Berners's omissions and the critics' rationalisations, Lereano's death is a suicide. He is a martyr to his love, and so resembles the women he praises in Chap. XLV for taking their own lives.

[vi] "to comforte . . . purpose" is omitted from the French. The French also substitutes "& bycause . . . reasones" for a phrase meaning "and those with the role of curing illnesses." The English translation is based on the Spanish.

[vii] "Teseo" is "Tefeo" in Spanish and "Theseus" in French.

[viii] While Lereano will be given many pages in which to defend women, Teseo's dispraise of women is given no textual space.

The defaming of women was a medically recognised cure for love as described in several treatises such as Ovid, *Remedia Amoris*, 299–303, 312. See also Pedro M. Cátedra, *Amor y Pedagogía en la Edad Media* (Salamanca: Universidad de Salamanca Prensa, 1989), 215; Michael Solomon, *The Literature of Misogyny in Medieval Spain: The Arcipreste de Talavera and the Spil* (Cambridge: Cambridge University Press, 1997); and Françoise Vigier, "Remèdes à l'amour en Espagne aux XVe XVIe siècles," in *Travaux de l'Institut d'études Hispaniques et Portugaises de l'Université de Tours*, ed. A. Redondo (Tours: Tours University Press, 1979), 2: 151–84.

[ix] The French omits "a woman" and adds "éstoit frustré" (was frustrated) in its place; Berners retains the Spanish reading.

Notes to XLIII: Lereano agaynst Teseo and agaynst all evell[ ]spekers agaynst women

[i] This and the subsequent two chapters form part of the pro-woman side of the woman debate in fifteenth-century Spain. On the debate see Elena Gascón Vera, "La ambegüedad en el concepto del amor y de la mujer en la prosa castellana del siglo XV," *Boletín de la Real Academia Española* 59 (1979): 119–55; Gerli, "Leriano's Libation," 414–20; María Eugenia Lacarra, "Representaciones femininas en la poesía cortesana y en la narativa sentimental del siglo XV," in *Breve historia feminista de la literatura española (en lengua castellana). II. La mujer en la literatura española: modos de representación. Desde la Edad Media hasta el siglo XVII*, ed. Iris M. Zavala (Madrid: Anthropos, 1995), 159–75; Jacob Ornstein, "La misogonia y el profeminismo en la literatura castellana," *Revista de Filología Hispánica* 3 (1942): 219–32; Nicholas G. Round, "Renaissance Culture and its Opponents in Fifteenth-Century Castile," *Modern Language Review* 57 (1962): 204–15; Antony Van Beysterveldt, "El amor caballeresco del *Amadís* y del *Tirante*," *Hispanic Review* 49 (1981): 407–25. Lereano's arguments are largely derived from *Triunfo de las donas* by Juan Rodríguez del Padrón and *Tratado en defensa de virtuosas damas* by Diego de Valera. On this indebtedness see José Francisco Gatti, *Contribución al estudio de la Cárcel de Amor: la apología de Leriano* (Buenos Aires: n.p., 1955) and Nicholas G. Round, "The Presence of Mosén Diego e Valera in *Cárcel de amor*," in *The Age of the Catholic Monarchs 1474–1516*, ed. Deyermond and Macpherson, 144–54.

[ii] Berners errs in the use of the possessive phrase "in my wordes." The words are Teseo's and so the correct pronoun should be "thy."

[iii] Berners does not translate the added French doublet.

[iv] The Spanish and French translate as "in the way in which you have afforded me relief, nevertheless you have certainly done so" (*Prison of Love*, trans. Whinnom, 67). Berners mistakes the terms "vía" (Sp) and "voye" (Fr, way) for the verb "to live" (Sp, vivir; Fr, vivre). As a result the final clause actually denotes the opposite of the originals.

[v] Berners is somewhat confused by this sentence. The Spanish and French translate as "So, then, you have brought relief to my suffering and grateful ease to my dying, for

my last words shall be in praise of women, so that she shall have proof of my fidelity, she who possessed all the qualities to inspire my devotion, but not the inclination to reward it" (*Prison of Love*, trans. Whinnom, 67). Berners preserves some of the terms of the originals, but he does not preserve the sense, especially not at the beginning of the sentence. This sentence seems to be based on the Spanish. The French uses the verb "partir" (Fr, to go) to translate "padecer" (Sp, to suffer from) and omits the adjective "dulce" (Sp, sweet). Berners does not follow the French alterations.

[vi] Proverbial: "As is the workman so is the work" (Tilley, *A Dictionary of the Proverbs*, W855).

[vii] The French omits "nor harder"; Berners translated it from Spanish.

[viii] The English textual variants are discussed in section 5 of the introduction.

[ix] The English does not convey the sense of the originals, which translate as "and if by chance those men who abuse them thought they would receive physical opposition, then they would be less free with their tongues."

[x] Exodus 20:12.

[xi] "tenían" (Sp, they held) becomes "craignoient" (Fr, they feared) in the French, probably as a result of a misreading or misprinting of the *n* for an *m*: "temian" means feared. Berners does not follow the error and translates the Spanish with the doublet "kepte and observed."

[xii] Berners omits "lo que no me parece" (Sp, it does not appear to me to be so) from the Spanish text and substitutes it for "*the* which they kept not," which is directly based on the French "chose q*ue* ne gardent."

[xiii] The doublet "turpitud & fowlnes" is formed by taking a term from each of the originals: "fealdad" (Sp, ugliness) and "turpitude" (Fr, turpitude).

[xiv] The verbs "tomadas" (Sp, taken) and "robada" (Sp, robbed) are omitted from the French. Berners preserves them as "taken" and "robbyd," indicating that he was using the Spanish.
The final phrase poses difficulties for Berners. It translates as "which is completely determined by our faith."

[xv] Berners mistranslates his sources, which mean "are as free to reach the ears of the uneducated as those of the wise."

[xvi] Berners mistranslates this sentence. The Spanish and French translate as: "when those who understand little hear these ugly tales about women, they repent of having married, lead them a wretched life or abandon them, or perhaps even murder them" (*Prison of Love*, trans. Whinnom, 69). Berners writes of repenting words rather than of repenting marriage.

[xvii] The Spanish means "and wherever his vicious tongue is mentioned." The French translates it as "with approbation, his vice is murmured of." Berners's version is closer to the French.

^{xviii} Berners translates "beautie & grace" from the added French doublet; the Spanish uses the single noun "la hermosura" (the beauty). Although Berners adds the doublet, he neglects to accord the verb with the plural subject as in the French. This indicates that while he copies the doublet from the French, for the remainder of the sentence his eyes are on the Spanish text with its singular verb.

^{xix} The French translation adds the doublet "scavans & saiges" (Fr, wise [men] and sage), based on the Spanish "sabios" (Sp, wise). Berners follows the Spanish, writing "wise." The French also adds the term "hommes" (men) before the doublet. While Berners omits this doublet, he emulates this addition and adds "men" to go with the adjective "wise," thus combining his sources.

The English has "good" for "Dios" (Sp) and "Dieu" (Fr, God). This is probably a compositor's error, although "good" also makes sense in this context.

^{xx} Berners seems to have confused the terms "fuercas" (Sp) and "forteresses" (Fr, fortresses) for the adjective "forças" (Sp) or "fortes" (Fr, strong).

Notes to XLIV: The other .xx. reasons that Lereano shewed, wherby that men are bound to love women

ⁱ The sources mean "their wit spurred by their sufferings."

ⁱⁱ Berners writes that the women make the men have sufferance, but in his sources they make the men accept (suffer) the virtue of justice.

ⁱⁱⁱ "bycause . . . customes" elaborates the sources: "por no infamarse de buenas costumbres" (Sp) and "pour fuyr l'infamie des mauvaises costumes" (Fr, to avoid the infamy of good/bad customs). The Spanish uses the adjective "buenas" (Sp, good) which makes no sense in this context. Berners follows the French in correcting this error.

^{iv} The French adds the doublet "horreur et fascherie" (horror and offence), but Berners preserves the Spanish reading by translating "aborrecibles" (Sp) as "abhorre."

^v The Spanish means "they hold affronts as vice" not "they cause us to repute feare a great vice." Berners's sentence is based on the Spanish: the French alters this clause to "they take pleasure in affronts and adverse things" so that it denotes the opposite.

Berners slightly confuses this line. The Spanish and French translate as, "When lovers are put in any danger, they see it as a chance to win glory."

^{vi} The second use of the pronoun "theyr" which occurs before "stre*n*gth" seems to refer to "women's," but in the sources "the" (la) is used and the implication is that the strength is the men's. Also, "as *they* deserve" is "as *it* deserves" in the sources.

^{vii} The Spanish and French translate as "The fifth reason is because they endow us with the theological virtues, no less than with the cardinal virtues that I have already mentioned."

ᵛⁱⁱⁱ Berners changes the doublet "ecelencia y hermosura" (Sp, exellence and beauty) into the adjective-noun construction "excellent beawtye," emulating the French expression "excellent beaulté."

ⁱˣ "catolicos" (Sp) "catholicques" (Fr, Catholic) is omitted from the English text after "devoute."

ˣ "they hope" is omitted from the French; Berners translates it from Spanish.
"perpetuall comforte and reste" is created by combining terms from the two sources: "d[e]scanso" (Sp, rest) and "perpetuel reconfort" (Fr, perpetual comfort).

ˣⁱ "commaundith to say masses" signifies "we command masses to be said."

ˣⁱⁱ The sources mean "that when we desire to meditate upon the the Passion of Christ, our hearts are so tender and torn that we are able to feel His wounds and torments as if they were our own" (*Prison of Love*, trans. Whinnom, 71–2). Part of the confusion in the English text arises because Berners misunderstands the pronouns.

ˣⁱⁱⁱ While the Spanish says that the lovers look to God for pardon, Berners follows the French in writing that the male lovers ask pardon from their beloveds.

ˣⁱᵛ The French adds "ce que à nous est de besoing" (of which we are in need) after "counsayll," which Berners does not preserve, suggesting that he was using the Spanish.

ˣᵛ Berners's line implies that they honour men, not that they cause men's honour to be increased, as in his sources.

ˣᵛⁱ Berners misunderstands the term "presunciones" (Sp, aspirations) to mean "I presume," and so does not accurately convey the Spanish which means "They inspire in us such virtuous aspirations" (*Prison of Love*, trans. Whinnom, 72). Berners definitely was using the Spanish here as the French translation differs significantly.

ˣᵛⁱⁱ The sources mean "they deposit our goods in the safest place."

ˣᵛⁱⁱⁱ Berners translates "desvelamos" (Sp) and "eveillons" (Fr, we wake) as "study."
The French adds "port & gestes" (demeanour and gestures) to translate "traer" (Sp, to wear). Berners follows the Spanish with "were."

ˣⁱˣ Berners discusses neither the hair nor legs of the man, as do the Spanish and French. He replaces this point with a list of different types of clothing that the man may wear: "some tyme long . . . wyde."

ˣˣ Berners interprets "los galanes" (Sp) "les gentilz" (Fr) to mean the gallant men, but in his sources it is an adjective describing the "entretalles" (Sp, garments) and "entailleurs" (Fr, tailors).
Berners follows the French in omitting the Spanish phrase, which translates as "for sure, they are the cause of great goods" after "invensions."

ˣˣⁱ Berners changes the questions of the Spanish into statements in this and the next line. The same alteration is made in the French, suggesting that Berners was using the French here.

xxii The French omits "play an instrument" and so Berners must have translated that detail from the Spanish.

xxiii The French makes the subject of the sentence "us/we" which Berners does not retain.

xxiv Berners translates "vertemos" (Sp, we pour, spill) and "que espandons" (Fr, that pour, spill out) as "we shew them." He has confused the Spanish "verter" with "ver" (Sp, to see) and has not used the French to help him. Further indicating that he is using the Spanish in translating this sentence, "the syghes . . . before them" is omitted from the French, and so it must be based on the Spanish.

xxv "no harán fruto" (Sp) "ne feroient fruct" (Fr, will not increase) is translated by Berners as "be withoute frute." He does not seem to understand that the expression is being used metaphorically to signify increase. The last question is muddled completely by Berners: it translates as "Whose chaste will cannot be moved by our steadfast perseverance?"

xxvi The terms "menos" (Sp) and "la moindre" (Fr, the least) in the originals seem to confuse Berners. He writes "though they . . . defence" rather than "even if it were only a minority of them who sucessfully fended us off" (*Prison of Love*, trans. Whinnom, 74).

Notes to XLV: The profe by ensample of the bounte & goodnes of women shewed by Lereano

i Gatti, *Contribución al estudio*, and Round, "The Presence of Mosén Diego e Valera" demonstrate that almost all the examples of virtuous women which follow also appear in Diego de Valera's *Tratado en defensa de las virtuosas mujeres*.

ii The doublet "ignorante and rude" is created by taking a term from each of the sources: "rude" (Sp) and "ignorante" (Fr).

iii "segund su propiedad" (Sp), "selon la proprieté" (Fr, according to its/the quality) is misunderstood by Berners. He understands "propiedad/proprieté" to mean "goodness" rather than "quality," possibly as a result of mistaking the source terms for their *faux-ami* "propriety."

iv The French adds "la Vièrge Marie" (the Virgin Mary), which Berners omits.

v During the war against Ardea, Collatinus (Lucrecia's husband) and his friends decided to test their wives' virtue. Lucrecia did not fall prey to any of their tricks, but she was subsequently raped by Tarquinius. She told her father and husband of the attack and then killed herself, preferring to die than to live with an unchaste body. See Livy, *History of Rome*, I.57.6–60.4; Ovid, *Fasti* 2.686–852; Chaucer, *Legend of Good Women*, legend v; and Shakespeare, *Rape of Lucrece*.
    "enforsed & defowled" is created by combing a term from each text: "forçada" (Sp, enforces) and "ont souillé" (Fr, they dirtied).

The French omits "Colatyne . . . Colatyne" which must have occurred as a result of an eye-skip. Berners translated this portion of the text directly from the Spanish.

[vi] Portia was married to Brutus and she committed suicide after his death. See Cicero, *Epistulae ad Brutum*, 1.9.2, 17.7; Valerius Maximus, *Facta et Dicta*, 3.285, 4.6; and Plutarch, *Alcibiades* 6.63, 7.87, 9.88.

[vii] Penelope avoided the advances of suitors for three years while waiting for the return of her husband, Ulysses, by saying that when the shroud that she was weaving for Laertes was finished she would select a new husband. She delayed making a decision by undoing at night what she had woven during the day. See Homer, *Odyssey*, 1, 19, and 21; Ovid, *Heroides*, epistle 1; and Boccaccio, *De mulieribus claris*, 38.

[viii] The French omits "& in greate . . . receved hym." Berners translated this passage from Spanish.

[ix] Julia was the daughter of Julius Caesar and Cornelia. She was married to Pompey and lived 82–54 B.C.E. See Valerius Maximus, *Facta et Dicta*, 4.6.4, and Boccaccio, *De mulieribus claris*, 81.

[x] Artemisia was the queen of Halicarnassus, in Caria. The tomb she built for her husband was considered one of the seven wonders of the world (355 B.C.E.). See Valerius Maximus, *Facta et Dicta* 4.6.1, and Boccaccio, *De mulieribus claris* 55.

[xi] Argia was the daughter of Adrastus and Amphithea and married Polyneices. See Statius, *Thebaid*, 2.201ff and 11.425f; Virgil, *Aeneid*, 6.480; Hyginus, *Fabulae*, 69, 70.

[xii] "enforsed her" replaces the more euphemistic expressions in the Spanish and French which translate as "taken of her a greater part than was due to them." For her story see Valerius Maximus, *Facta et Dicta*, 6.1.1.

[xiii] "Howbeit . . . laudable" makes little sense. The sources translate as "the waves had the power to drown her, but they could not drown her reputation of chastity."

[xiv] Amede's wife is Alceste. For her story see Euripides, *Alcestis*; Valerius Maximus, *Facta et Dicta* 4.6.1; Ovid, *Ars Amatoria*, 6.57; and Boccaccio, *Genealogia deorum gentilium*, 746–47; Chaucer, *Legend of Good Women*, Prologue.

[xv] On Sara, see Genesis 12: 10–20.

[xvi] "God heryng her petecion" is omitted from the French; Berners translates it directly from Spanish.

[xvii] On Deborah, see Judges 4–5.

[xviii] The story of Esther can be found in the biblical book of the same name.

[xix] The French adds "de mort qu'il attendoient" (of the death that awaited them) before "fro theyr." Berners does not translate the addition.

xx On Samson, see Judges 4.

xxi See Luke 1.

xxii The French uses the title "la noble matrosne" to translate "Doña" throughout this chapter; Berners follows the Spanish with "Don." The French omits "and her bountie . . . wherfore," and so Berners must have translated this from Spanish.

She was married to don Juan de la Cerda and when he was condemned to death by King Pedro I, she retired to the convent of Saint Agnes of Seville, which she had founded earlier in her life: see Báez, *Cárcel de amor*, 96; Parrilla, *Cárcel de amor*, 75.15.

xxiii She was the mistress of Don Pedro Girón and mother to his children. See Báez, *Cárcel de amor*, 98; Parrilla, *Cárcel de amor*, 75.16.

xxiv Berners follows the French in several small omissons, possibly indicating that he was using the French text here.

xxv She founded a religious community in Toledo. After her death in 1404 its members adopted the rule of St Jerome and became cloistered monks.

xxvi The invocation is omitted from the French. Berners must have translated it from the Spanish.

xxvii The French confuses her name "Atrisilia" for "à Thessalie" (Fr, in Thessaly) and calls her simply "Sibille." Berners probably got the correct name from the Spanish.

This is probably the Sybil, named Erythrea or Herophile, referred to by Isidore of Seville, who prophesied the Trojan War and was originally from Babylon. See Báez, *Cárcel de amor*, 101; Parrilla, *Cárcel de amor*, 76.18; and *Prison of Love*, trans. Whinnom, 103 n. 26.

xxviii Berners uses the conjunction "and" in between "Pallas" and "Mynerva" but the Spanish and French have "o" (Sp) and "ou" (Fr, or). Berners does not realise that they are two names for the same individual. As a result, the terms "invenrers" and "vyrgins" are made plural by Berners since he has two subjects for his sentence.

Pallas Athena is one of the Olympian gods in Greek mythology and Minerva is her Latinised name. This story is in Valerius Maximus, *Facta et Dicta* 5.4.6: see Parrilla, *Cárcel de amor*, 76.20.

xxix The French text indicates that she was the first to "naviga le port de Callidoyne" (Fr, navigate the port of Callidoyne). Berners did not follow this error, and so must have translated this passage from the Spanish.

Atalanta was a virgin huntress. She participated in the famous Caledonian boar hunt, which led to the death of the sons of Theseus. See Homer, *Iliad*, 9.543–99; Ovid, *Metamorphoses*, 8.290–327; Hyginus, *Fabulae*, 99.

xxx Camilla was dedicated to Diana. She was in Turnus's army against Aeneas, where she fought in a company of warrior-women. Helped by Diana, she slew many of the enemy, but was finally killed by Arruns, who had the assistance of Apollo. See Virgil, *Aeneid*, 7.803–817 and 11; Ovid, *Heroides*, epistle 11; Dante, *Inferno*, 1.107, and 4.124.

ˣˣˣⁱ The only known source for Claudia Vesta is Diego de Valera, *Epístolas*. She was a vestal virgin. When a Roman tribune tried to stop a triumphal procession in honour of her father, she ran out of her temple and attacked the tribune to avenge her father's honour.

Claudia Romana is Cloelia, who was the hostage of the Etruscans. She escaped from them by swimming across the Tiber and she then freed all the other hostages. The leader of the Etruscans was so impressed with her bravery that he allowed her to return to Rome, where a statue of her was erected on the Sacred Way: Valerius Maximus, *Facta et Dicta*, 3.2.2, 5.4.6; Pliny, *Naturalis Historia*, 34.6x.13; Livy, *History of Rome*, 2.13.6–7; Virgil, *Aeneid*, 8.650.

ˣˣˣⁱⁱ The Spanish and French here confuse Berners. They translate as, "Assuredly, if it were not tedious to go on, I should not, for a thousand years from now, lack examples of their virtue to relate to you" (*Prison of Love*, trans. Whinnom, 78). Also the end of the sentence translates as "for by the malice which you display you condemn yourselves to infamy" (*Prison of Love*, trans. Whinnom, 78).

Notes to XLVI: The auctor

ⁱ The French omits "his servauntes" and so Berners must have translated it from the Spanish.

ⁱⁱ "with wordes of extreme passyon" is a translation of the French "voix appassionnées." The Spanish "con bozes lastimeras" refers to "wailing" or "crying" or any non-verbal expression of sorrow, which can be opposed to "wordes well ordered."

ⁱⁱⁱ "shulde take theyr sepulture" is based on the French "donneroient sepulture" (give them their sepulchre), rather that the Spanish "enterrar" (to bury).

Notes to XLVII: The complaynte of Lereano's mother

ⁱ On the *planctus*, and on the parallels of this letter with Melibea's father's lament in *La Celestina*, XXI, see Severin, "From the Lamentations," 178–84; Luis Miguel Vicente, "El lamento de Pleberio: Contraste y parecido con dos lamentos en *Cárcel de Amor*," *Celestinesca* 12 (1988): 35–43.

ⁱⁱ "rest" derives from the Spanish "descanso"; the term is omitted from the French. The whole sentence is not based on the Spanish, however, as Berners also adds "comforte," based on the French addition of "confort."

ⁱⁱⁱ The French omits "O the lyght . . . same." Berners translated this from Spanish.

ⁱᵛ The sources translate as "for they feel things only in the degree to which they understand them" (*Prison of Love*, trans. Whinnom, 80).

ᵛ The French adds the possessive "tu" in the phrase "O bienheureux les malades de ta condition" (Oh, fortunate are those who suffer of your condition), which implies that only those of Lereano's condition are fortunate. This contradicts the point she is trying to make in the Spanish. Berners does not replicate the French error, and he preserves the Spanish reading. Further suggesting that Berners was using the Spanish here, the French adds an invocation at the beginning, which Berners does not translate.

ᵛⁱ Berners does not translate the added French doublet.

"beyng never so wyse" is a mistranslation of the Spanish and French which mean "and known as the son of that lonely woman."

It was thought that only nobles could experience true love: see Whinnom, *Obras completas, II*; Wardropper, "El mundo sentimental"; Parrilla, *Cárcel de amor*, 78.5.

ᵛⁱⁱ This line is based on the Spanish. The French mistranslates the line, confusing the verb "olvidas" (Sp, forget) with "oblige." As a result the French means the opposite of the original, translating as "you may be late but you never oblige."

ᵛⁱⁱⁱ In the Spanish she is sixty years old, but she is seventy in the English and French texts.

ⁱˣ The sources pose problems for Berners. They translate as "you carry off those you have left behind to join those you have already taken" (*Prison of Love*, trans. Whinnom, 80).

ˣ Berners manages this difficult line very well. He does not seem to understand his sources completely, but he is able to offer a coherent sentence nonetheless. The Spanish and French translate as "If I live much longer it shall be because my sins weigh heavier than the reasons for ceasing to live" (*Prison of Love*, trans. Whinnom, 80).

ˣⁱ The English substantives "drynke," "mete," "thought," and "slepe" are all verbs in the Spanish. In transforming them from verbs to nouns, Berners is following the French. However, he also uses the Spanish for this sentence, as he preserves all the possessives before the nouns ("my") as in the Spanish. They are omitted from the French which only has the single possessive "mien" (mine) at the end, after "slepe."

Notes to XLVIII: The auctor

ⁱ In the Spanish and English texts two letters are mentioned, while the French text indicates that there are three letters. The French is, in fact, correct since Laureola sent Lereano three letters.

ⁱⁱ The Spanish and French translate as "easy to imagine," not as "is lyghtly judged."

ⁱⁱⁱ The French adds the doublet "pleurs et plaintz" (Fr, cries and complaints), but Berners does not preserve the doublet, translating "lloros" (Sp) as "wepynges."

ⁱᵛ This is the last line of the French text; the remainder of *Castell* is based solely on the Spanish.

The French adds "La funeraille pompe" at the start of the sentence, which Berners translates as "his obsequyes and buryals." The Spanish makes no mention of his funeral.

ᵛ Rather than translate "llegué aquí a Peñafiel" (I arrived here in Peñafiel) Berners writes "I wente to my lodgynge" so that the story can continue. San Pedro's text ends here and Núñez's text begins with a prologue which is not translated by Berners. See *Prison of Love*, trans. Whinnom, 83–4 for an English translation of Núñez's prologue. The remainder of the Spanish is by Núñez.

ᵛⁱ Berners does not quite understand the Spanish. It translates as, "and so that I might say to Laureola, if I found her to be repentant, how badly she was accounted by all true (female) lovers for using such cruelty against one who deserved her favour." Berners misunderstands the original conditional verb (to speak). Furthemore, in the English text, Auctor says that he wants to see what true lovers say, while in the Spanish he knows what they have said and he wants to convey that information to Laureola.

Notes to XLIX: The auctor to Laureola

ⁱ The Spanish translates as "And, since you did not ever intend to act otherwise" (*Prison of Love*, trans. Whinnom, 85). The change in verb tense from imperfect subjunctive to perfect alters the sense. The Spanish text means that she should not have acted thus, not that she did act in this way.

ⁱⁱ Berners changes the Spanish so that Laureola is accused of being the cause of Lereano's death; she is not thus charged in the Spanish.

ⁱⁱⁱ In the Spanish he is saying that he would like to make her deeds known, but he will not be able to because he is on the brink of death.

ⁱᵛ Berners translates "aína" as "properly," but it means "quickly."

Notes to L: The auctor

ⁱ Berners misunderstands this line. The Spanish translates as "She was very calm," and not as "Sore troubelyd stode." Also, Berners contradicts his source when he writes "her face . . . her hart." The Spanish means that she did show her emotions.

Notes to LI: Laureola to the auctor

ⁱ "and cost hym nothyng" should read "and cost *me* nothing," because in the Spanish text the honour mentioned is Laureola's.

ⁱⁱ Berners uses the expression "to lyve always dyenge" to mean "a living death."

Notes to LIII: The auctor to Lereano

[i] Berners omits the Spanish phrase which translates as "if by fortune you have it" after "celestyall," and he replaces "which you lost when you killed yourself" with "for by thy deth, thou hast lost thy desyre." Both these Spanish phrases cast doubt on whether or not Lereano was saved, and so by omitting them Berners evades the issue.

[ii] The Spanish "If you had not so incontinently taken your life" (*Prison of Love*, trans. Whinnom, 87), is altered to "if thou haddest savyd thy lyfe," omitting the mention of Lereano's death as suicide. On similar omissions of comments pertaining to suicide, see section 3 of the introduction.

[iii] Berners offers a literal translation of the Spanish, but it is difficult to understand. The Spanish translates as "Please God that you repay the love I have for you, and had while you were alive, by praying for my death" (*Prison of Love*, trans. Whinnom, 88).

[iv] The final clause, expressing Auctor's wish to die is omitted; it translates as "wishing I could similarly leave my life." Berners routinely omits all references to suicide.

Notes to LIV: The auctor's dreme

[i] In the source the hat is "of vivid purple silk" (*Prison of Love*, trans. Whinnom, 88), but Berners says that it is "of scarlet." Purple symbolises penitence or nostalgia, but red symbolises joy and so by changing the colour, Berners alters the symbolism: Parrilla, *Cárcel de amor*, 89.3; *Prison of Love*, trans. Whinnom, 104 n.38.

The Spanish is mistranslated as "of an evyll colour." It means "so dark that it could scarcely be perceived as green" (Whinnom, *Prison of Love*, 88). Green symbolises hope: Parrilla, *Cárcel de amor*, 89.3.

The verses which follow are *letras de invenciónes*. These are either octosyllabic rhyming couplets, or three octosyllabic lines, or two octosyllabic lines plus a half line of four syllables. *Letras* are epigrammatic and are usually engraved or embroidered on objects: see *Prison of Love*, trans. Whinnom, 104 n.36; Keith Whinnom, *La poesía amatoria de la época de los Reyes Católicos* (Durham: Durham University Press, 1981), 46.

[ii] The motto means "My suffering to my joy / is matched / since it is she who causes it" (*Prison of Love*, trans. Whinnom, 89). Berners understands the individual terms but is unable to accurately convey their relationship to each other.

Yellow is representative of despair and suffering, *Prison of Love*, trans. Whinnom, 104 n.38.

[iii] Whinnom and Parrilla suggest that Núñez is playing with the different meanings of black: while it represents fidelity in heraldry, it is indicative of suffering and mourning in artistic symbolism, and it symbolises falsehood or guilt in religious symbolism, see *Prison of Love*, trans. Whinnom, 104 n.39; Parrilla, *Cárcel de amor*, 90.7.

iv "rather" must be a printer's error. It should read "richer" based on the Spanish "rico." This is not a mistake Berners would have made.

Gold is representative of riches: *Prison of Love*, trans. Whinnom, 104 n.40.

v Berners omits to mention that Lereano is wearing French hose, "calças francesas." He makes a similar omission in Chap. LVI.

Blue symbolises chastity and white represents life: *Prison of Love*, trans. Whinnom, 104 n.42; Parrilla, *Cárcel de amor*, 90.11.

vi Tawny symbolises sadness: *Prison of Love*, trans. Whinnom, 104 n.43; Parrilla, *Cárcel de amor*, 90.12.

vii This is an echo of Lereano's last words: "Frende, now all myne evylles be endyd" (Chap. XLVIII).

viii "con eles y aes" (Sp, with Ls and As) is omitted. As a result, the motto makes little sense. The Ls and As are the initial and final letters of her name, respectively. Berners omits a similar phrase in Chap. LVI.

ix "me thought" is added, which adds an extra layer of doubt within the already fictional world of the dream.

Notes to LV: Lereano to the auctor

i The Spanish translates as "nor I, according to the beginning I had, could not have avoided arriving at this end."

ii The pronouns in the Spanish mislead Berners. He thinks that the feminine pronouns refer to Laureola when they refer to Lereano's death. The Spanish translates as "since by it I won what without it I could not win" (*Prison of Love*, trans. Whinnom, 91).

iii Berners omits the verb "dexándome" (letting myself) from before "to dye," again omitting a reference to Lereano's suicide; see section 3 of the introduction.

Notes to LVI: The auctor

i There is no further explanation of who this new companion is. She may be a personification of Laureola's new feelings of love for Lereano.

ii The following description of her clothing parallels that of Lereano's attire in Chap. LIV. The symbolism of the colours is also the same and so I refer readers to the notes to Chap. LIV for an explication of the colours.

iii The terms of the motto are preserved by Berners, but he alters their sense. The motto means "My fortune would be richer, if life would allow me to die" (*Prison of Love*, trans. Whinnom, 92).

ⁱᵛ The adjective "francesa" (French) used to desribe the tabard is omitted here. A similar omission occurs in Chap. LIV.

ᵛ "escritas en ellos unas eles y oes" (with Ls and Os written on them) is omitted here, just as the similar phrase was omitted from Chap. LIV. As a result of the omission the motto makes no sense in its English translation. The Spanish motto means "With this beginning and this ending perished one who did not deserve to die" (*Prison of Love*, trans. Whinnom, 93). L and O are the letters which begin and end Lereano's name.

Notes to LVII: Laureola to Lereano

ⁱ Berners makes "to give yourself death" into a first person verb, "I to gyve *thee* deth," omitting another reference to suicide. See section 3 of the introduction.

ⁱⁱ The Spanish sentence ends with "who will be there to suffer them?"

ⁱⁱⁱ Proverbial. See Tilley, *A Dictionary of the Proverbs*, P420. See also Whiting, *Proverbs, Sentences, and Proverbial Phrases*, S864.

ⁱᵛ The Spanish "for anyone can enjoy and profit from good fortune should it befall him" (Whinnom, *Prison of Love*, 93), is abbreviated to "therby to . . . adventure." As a result the meaning is obscured.

ᵛ Berners interprets the pronoun "lo" at the end of "creerlo" as referring to "thy wrytynge," but it refers to her belief regarding whether or not he would die.

ᵛⁱ "and dyed" replaces "y dexaste morir" (Sp, and allowed yourself to die). See section 3 of the introduction on the omission of references to suicide.

Notes to LIX: Lereano to Laureola

ⁱ Berners muddles this line. It translates as "Thus I believed all the messages they brought from you" (*Prison of Love*, trans. Whinnom, 95).

ⁱⁱ The Spanish translates as, "And do not imagine that I made little effort to save myself in order to go on serving you" (*Prison of Love*, trans. Whinnom, 95). Berners implies that that effort Lereano took was not to save his life, but rather to serve Laureola.

ⁱⁱⁱ Berners omits the verb "I could recall" from the line "I could recall only your great worth, and I doubted that I could be worthy of you" (*Prison of Love*, trans. Whinnom, 95). As a result, according to Berners, Laureola's "deservyng" increases.

ⁱᵛ The English is a bit confusing; the Spanish line means "of the peril in which your honour and life were placed."

ᵛ Berners turns all the third person verbs into first person verbs and as the result the line makes no sense. His translation bears little resemblance to his original, which means "for once your innocence had been proved no one could ever have made any accusation that would not have been rejected as false, for everyone knew what fate the other false accusers had met with; and he who was most prone to gossip would have been most shunned and feared. And so you see that your excuses cannot exonerate you" (*Prison of Love*, trans. Whinnom, 96).

Notes to LX: The auctor

[i] The construction of the Spanish phrase confuses Berners. The Spanish does not mean that "Laureola receyved no payne," but that she was unhappy to see him dead and that she did feel pain.

[ii] Proverbial. See Tilley, *A Dictionary of the Proverbs*, P414 and H474. Whiting, *Proverbs, Sentences, and Proverbial Phrases* takes this instance from *Castell* for P267.

[iii] In the Spanish text a new chapter begins here.

[iv] In the phrase "hadde compassio*n* . . . dede," Berners omits "más" (more) from before "compassio*n*," and as a result the English makes little sense. The Spanish line means that he had more compassion for her than for Lereano, who was dead.

Notes to LXI: Laureola to the auctor

[i] In the Spanish text, Laureola says she would more willingly die than leave his room; Berners writes the opposite.

[ii] The comparison "más trabajo y menos olvido" (Sp, with more travail and less forgetfulness) is lost and the meaning of the line is somewhat changed. In the Spanish, Laureola says that she thought that she might have tried harder and more frequently to get the king to have mercy on Lereano.

[iii] The past tense of the verb "to bear" in the English text makes it seem as though Laureola already honoured Lereano, but the Spanish verb is a subjunctive indicating a possible, not a definite, event. It translates as "I should have bestowed on Lereano had he lived" (*Prison of Love*, trans. Whinnom, 98).

Notes to LXII: The auctor

[i] A new section begins here in the Spanish.
Her voice wakes Auctor in accordance with the dream vision convention whereby something within the dream wakes the dreamer. This is made more explicit in the Spanish where her voice is described as so loud "con que pudo recordarme" (Sp, with which she could wake me).

ⁱⁱ There follow two poems, a *canción* and a *villancico*, in the Spanish which Berners transforms into prose. The canción is 12 lines long in the rhyme scheme abba cddcabba. The villancico is in two stanzas, the first of eight lines and the second of seven. The rhyme scheme is abbcbcbb deeddbb.

ⁱⁱⁱ The Spanish becomes an incoherent statement in the English translation. It means "What good is life / if death / is a happier fate?" (*Prison of Love,* trans. Whinnom, 99).

ⁱᵛ The final verse translates as "He who can tolerate his pain, / or complain of it to the one who caused it, / can live content with his suffering, /even though it will kill him. / But even in the extreme agony/ of death, / what dying man can be regarded as unfortunate?" (*Prison of Love,* trans. Whinnom, 100). Berners makes several errors in translating this passage and it is not entirely clear.

ᵛ The Spanish text begins a new chapter here.

ᵛⁱ Berners replaces the Spanish, which translates as "in Peñafiel (as San Pedro said) where I remain kissing the hands of your greatnes" with "at my owne poore mansion."

Glossary

The glossary contains all words or expressions from *Castell* that may cause difficulty for the modern reader, including words with spellings which make them hard to recognise; terms which are now obsolete; and terms which have changed their meaning since the sixteenth century. For words which fall into the first category, the modern spelling is provided as a definition. Regarding the latter two types of words, the definition is based on the definitions supplied in the *OED*.[1] Where the word or expression to be defined is not included in the *OED*, my definition is based on the context in which the term is found in *Castell* and verified against Berners's French and Spanish sources.

    The term to be defined is listed in bold the left-hand column. It is followed by two sets of parentheses: the first gives the chapter number(s) of *Castell* in which the term appears; the second indicates its grammatical part of speech. The definitions are given in the right-hand column, preceded, where applicable, by the *OED* definition number on which the definition is based. Where more than one inflection of a verb is listed, the definition of the infinitive is provided. Infinitives are also provided for definitions derived from the *OED*, as that is the form in which they appear in the dictionary. If the singular and plural forms of a noun are both glossed, the definition will be given in the singular. The definition will also be in the singular form if it is based on an *OED* definition, following the form of the definition in the *OED*. An asterisk before the term to be defined indicates that it precedes the first recorded usage in the *OED*.

---

[1] http://dictionary.oed.com

A

a sonder (xxxiii) **a sounder** (lx) (*adv.*)	asunder
abashe (xxxvii) **abasshyd** (xv) **abashyde** (xviii) **abasshyde** (lviii) (*v., adv*)	1. to put out of countenance, confound, discomfit
abrode (xlii, xliii) (*n.*)	1a. broadly, widely, at large
accomplysh (li) (*v.*)	1. to fulfil a desire
accomplyshede (xxxv) (*v.*)	3. to complete
accostumyng (xliv) (*vbl. n.*)	accomplishing
accuse with (xxvi) (*v.*)	to cause
accydent (xxx) **accident** (xxxi) (*n.*)	II. a non-essential feature
adew (lxii) (*sentence substitute*)	adieu
adorned (prol.) (*v.*)	II.5. embellished
adventure (i, x, xlii, liii, lv, lvii) (*n.*)	chance, fortune
advertyse **advertysed** (ii) (*v.*)	4. to notify, warn
advyse (i) (*n.*)	4. deliberation
advysed (vii) (*v.*)	3. to consider, think over, ponder
affeccyant (prol.) (*n.*)	affection
* **affyrmacion** (xxiii) (*n.*)	4. an assertion or declaration
agaynst (xviii) (*prep.*)	19. in anticipation or preparation
agreable (xxxix) (*adj.*)	4. conformable, suitable

allonely (ii, xv, xxvi, xliii)
alonely (iii, vi, viii, x, xiv, xvii, xviii, xx,
  xxviii, xxxiii, xxxvii, xli, xliv, xlv, liii,
  lix) (*adv*)
	only

almesse (xliv) (*n.*)	alms
alteracion (i) **alterasyon** (xxiii) (*n.*)	alteration
ambassade(s) (vi, xi, xviii, xxxii, liii) (*n.*)	1. the mission or function of an ambas- sador or 3. the message borne by an ambassador
amyte (xx, xxii, xliv) (*n.*)	friendship
aparel(l) (liv, lvi) **aperell** (xliv) (*n.*)	clothing

aperell (xliv) **aparelled** (xviii) (*v.*)	to dress
aparel (xviii) **-lled** (vi) (*v.*)	to prepare
apeace (xxvi, xxviii, xxxii, xliv) (*v.*)	to appease
apleynge (prol.) (*v.*)	applying
appetyght (xiv) (*n.*)	desire
aprovyng (xxxii) (*v.*)	1. to prove, demonstrate
ardent (xiii) (*adj.*)	5. glowing with passion, animated by keen desire; intensely eager
armes of prayer (xlv) (*n.*)	weapons of prayer
armony (xliv) (*n.*)	harmony
aronyous (xliv) (*adj.*)	erroneous
article (xli) (*n.*)	III. the separate portions of anything written
asoyled (ii) **assoyll** (xxii, xlvii) **-led** (xvii, xlv) **-leth** (v) (*v.*)	to absolve
aspied (xxxvi) (*v.*)	espied
assautes (iii) (*n.*)	assaults
assurance (xix) (*n.*)	1. a formal engagement, guarantee
assure (i) **-yng** (xxi) (*v.*)	7a. to promise
assure (xvi) **-yth** (xxx) (*v.*)	8. to give confidence to, encourage
assuryd (xxi) **-ith** (xxxi) (*v.*)	1. to render safe from danger
assyngned (xxi) (*v.*)	3. to set a place apart for a purpose
assysted (ii) (*v.*)	attached
astate (lxi) (*n.*)	rank
astate (xlvi, lxi) (*n.*)	state, condition
astate(s) (xxxv, xli) (*n.*)	estate(s)
astonyd (i) (*v.*)	1. stunned
aswage (xiii) (*v.*)	to assuage
atemperance (xxx, xliv) (*n.*)	temperance

attcyne (prol.) **attayne** (i) **attaigne** (ii) **atteygnyde** (xxxii) (*v.*)	attain
atyer (lvi) (*n.*)	4. a head-dress; tiara
auctorite (vii, xxxii) (*n.*)	authority
auctorysed (xlv) (*v.*)	authorised
auncettours (xxxi) (*n.*)	ancestor
auncyante (xxxv) **auncyent** (xliii) (*adj.*)	ancient
avayleable (i, iv) (*adj.*)	1. of avail, effectual
averise (xxxvii) (*n.*)	avarice

B

bandes (xxxvi) (*n.*)	1a. a troop
(under his) baner (xviii) (*n.*)	1b. on his side
bankettes (xliv) (*n.*)	banquets
bardyd (xx) (*v.*)	to be wearing 1. protective coverings for the breast and flanks of a war-horse
bare (lxi) (*v.*)	bore
barres (xliv) (*n.*)	2a. a thick rod of iron or wood used in a trial of strength, the players contending which of them could throw or pitch it farthest
base lute (xviii) (*adj.* + *n.*)	a lute tuned to a bass range, see http://www.grovemusic.com under "lute"
bastides (xxxvi) (*n.*)	1b. a temporary hut or tower erected for besieging purposes
begonne (xliv) (*v.*)	begun
behovable (vii) (*adj.*)	14. useful, advantageous
behoveth (i) (*v.*)	3a. to be incumbent or proper
bek (ii) (*n.*)	beak
beleve (xvii, xliii, xliv, xlv) **byleve** (vii) (*n.*)	belief
benynge (xxxv) (*adj.*)	benign

besilde (xxvi) (*prep.*)	beside
besegyd (xxxvi) (*v.*)	besieged
bestes (xliii, xlv, xlvii) (*n.*)	beasts
bestowyd (liii) (*v.*)	5. to devote for a specific purpose
besynes (xxiii) (*n.*)	7b. ado, commotion
besynes (iii, v, viii, xiii) **beisynes** (i) (*n.*)	business
* **bleryd** (xlix) (*v.*)	2. to morally stain; to defile
blynde counsayll (xxx) (*n.*)	ignorant advice
blyssyng (xxxiii) (*vbl. n.*)	blessing
bonet (xliv, lx) (*n.*)	1. a cap
boord (ii) (*n.*)	board
borne (xxxvii) (*v.*)	born
bosid (xlvii) (*v.*)	bound [?]
bountie (iii, vi, xi, xviii, xix, xx, xxx, xxxiii, xxxv, xxxvi, xxxvii, xxxix, xli, xliii, xlv, lxi, lxii) **bountye** (xiii) (*n.*)	1a. goodness in general, worth, virtue
brake (xlv) (*v.*)	9a. to demolish, destroy
brake (xlviii) **breke** (xlviii) (*v.*)	2a. to rend or tear
* **brayng** (xlii) (*vbl. n.*)	1. loud or harsh crying; hoarse shouting
brennynge (i) **brent(e)** (i, xxxviii, xlv) **brynneth** (ii) (*v.*)	to burn
breve (xlv) (*adj.*)	brief
brewt (xliii) (*adj.*)	brute
brute (xxxvi) (*n.*)	2. report noised abroad, rumour
bulwerkes (xxxvi) (*n.*)	1. a substantial defensive work, a rampart, a fortification
burest (xviii) (*n.*)	duress [?]

C

canste (xxiv) (*v.*)	can
cappe (liv) (*n.*)	cape
case(s) (prol., i, ii, iii, vi, vii, viii, xi,xiii, xv, xviii, xxiii, xxiv, xxxvi, xxxviii, xli, xliii, xlv, xlix, li, lvii, lix, lxi) (*n.*) **(come to the) case** (xx, xlii) (*vbl. phrase*)	I.1a. a thing that happens, an event, occurrence, hap, chance. A situation have the chance
cast (xxx) (*v.*)	42. to consider, ponder, deliberate
castel(l) (title pg., i, ii, xxxvi) (*n.*)	prison
castell (xxiv, xxxvi) (*n.*)	castle
certaynte (xxxviii) (*n.*)	1. truth
certyfyeng (xxiv) **certifie** (xv, lv) **-ed** (xlvii)(*v.*)	3a. to assure
charge (xxiv, xxviii, xxx, xlix, li, lix) (*n.*)	IIa. a lot of trouble or blame
charge (xxviii)(*v.*)	accuse of being
chargyd (i, xxxi) (*v.*)	II. to burden
chargyd (xxxvi) (*v.*)	14a. to command, to give a charge
chastiment (xliv) (*n.*)	1. chastisement
chere (vii, xlviii, l) (*n.*)	2a. countenance, 3a. disposition, mood, as showing itself by external demeanour
cheynes (ii, xxviii) (*n.*)	chains
chylde (i) (*n.*)	shield
clene (xviii. xxii, xxxvi) (*adj., adv.*)	V14. total, complete
clenlynes (xx, xliii) (*n.*)	the quality of moral purity
clennes (xxiv, xliv, xlix, li, lix) (*n.*)	2. moral purity; chastity, innocence
clere (xviii, xix, xx, xxii, xxiii, xxxii, xli, xlv) (*adj.*)	9a. evident 15.a. unsullied, innocent
clere innocency (xxii) (*adj.+ n.*)	obvious innocence
clerenes (i, ii, xviii) (*n.*)	1. brightness, fairness, beauty
*** clowdy** (ii) (*adj.*)	4c. dim, obscure
comfortable (v) (*adj.*)	to be in agreement with, conformable
comon (vi, xi) **-ed** (xx) **-ing** (xi) **comnyng** (xlii) (*v.*)	6. to confer, talk with, 4b. possibly with sexual connotations

had the company (xlv) (*v.*)	2. sexual connection
complyses (xxiii) (*n.*)	accomplices
condemnacion (xliii) **condmnacion** (xvii) (*n.*)	condemnation
condemp(n)e (prol. xxxiii, lix) (*v.*)	to condemn
condiscendyd (xxi) (*v.*)	II. to concede, comply, or agree
conferme (xxx) (*v.*)	to conform
conferme (xxxvii, xlii) (*v.*)	to confirm
confyrmable (xxxvi) (*adj.*)	conformable
conscience (lvii) (*adj.*)	8. remorse
constreynede (xxi, xlii) (*v.*)	3b. to assume by straining any behaviour or expression of feeling
constance (xxxviii) (*n.*)	constancy
* **consumyd** (i) (*v.*)	6c. to burn away
contemplatyves (xlv) (*n.*)	1. a person devoted to religious meditation; one who leads the 'contemplative life'
contentacion (i, xviii) (*n.*)	3. contented or satisfied condition
continance (vii) (*n.*)	countenance
contrary (ii) (*adj.*)	1d. different, other
contynew (lxi) (*v.*)	to continue
convenient (xxxv) (*adj.*)	3. agreeing with the nature or character of a thing or person
convenient (vii) (*adj.*)	4a. suitable to or for a purpose
conversacion (xxx) (*n.*)	6. behaviour, mode or course of life
course (i) (*v.*)	curse
covenable (iv) (*adj.*)	3. suitable, convenient
covetesnes (xxx) **covetyse** (xxxvi, xxxvii) (*n.*)	covetousness
covytte (xlix) (*v.*)	to covet
creatours (xxviii) (*n.*)	creatures
creatyde (xliii) (*v.*)	created
credence (xxx) (*n.*)	belief
cristen (xlv) (*adj.*) **crystened** (xlv) (*n.*)	Christian
curtes (i) (*adj.*)	courteous

D

dangerous (x) (*adj.*)	1b. difficult to please, particular
dead(es) (xxxvi, xlv) (*n.*)	deed(s)
deale (xxiv) (*v.*)	19. to conduct oneself, behave, act
dede (xxxviii, lx, xlii) (*adj.*)	dead
defamy (xliii) (*n.*)	defamation
defaute (xxxv) (*n.*)	default
defence (xxxvii, xxxviii) (*n.*)	a position one is required to defend
defended (xliii) -**eth** (xxxviii) (*v.*)	2. to prevent, 3. to prohibit
defendyd (xxxvi) (*v.*)	II4. to fight against
defoilyst (xix) **defowle** (xxxi, xliii) -**ed** (xlv,	3. to destroy the moral purity 4. to
defoyll (xix) **defyle** (xxviii) (*v.*)	violate the chastity of, debauch
degre (xviii) (*n.*)	4a. rank, position
deliberyd (i) (*v.*)	deliberated

demaund(e) (i, v, xli)
  -**eth** (xxx)
  -**yd** (i, ii, xvi)
  -**ynge** (xli) (*v.*)
	3. to ask

demaund(e) (ii, viii, xi, xxxix, xli) (*n.*)	6. a request, a question
* **demerites** (vi, xxxiii) (*n.*)	1. merit, desert
demuer (xxiv) (*adj.*)	2. sober or reserved in demeanour
depertyd (xxi, xxxviii) **desperte** (xxii) (*v.*)	2. separated, parted
deputyd (xxxvi) (*v.*)	1. to appoint a person to a particular office or function
deruall (xviii)	devall [?] 1 to move downwards, sink, fall, descend
deserdes (xlviii) **deserte** (ii, xx, xxvi, xli, xliii)	1. deserving; becoming worthy of
desertes (xxxii, xxxiii, xxxviii, xliv, xlv) (*n.*) **deservyng** (xviii, xxxix, xlix, lvii, lix) **deservynge** (xxx, viiii, xlv, lv) **deserving** (xxxix) (*vbl. n.*)	reward or punishment

desire (i, xv, xxiv, lix)
desyre (v, xvi, xxi, xxiv, xxix, xxxii, xli, lxi)
  -ed (v, xxxvi, xxxviii, xlv)
  -yd (xxiii, xlv)
  -yng (xxiv, lixlxii)
  -iryde (xliii) (*v.*)

6. To express a wish to a person; to request, pray, entreat

desperate (xv, xxiii, xxxii, lii)
disperate (lx) (*adj.*)

in despair, hopeless

desyrer (xxxii) (*n.*)

a person who desires

desyrous (iii, lvii) (*adj.*)

1. having desire or longing

determynacion (xx, xxiv) (*n.*)

2. judicial or authoritative decision or settlement

determynate (xlii) (*adj.*)

A. determined

determyne (i, ii, xxii, xxx, xxxv)
  -ed (v, vii, xviii, xx, xxi, xxix, xxxi, xli, xlviii)
  -yd (xviii, xx, xxi, xxxvi, xxxviii)
  -yde (xxiii, xxiv)
  -yth (xxxi)
  -de (i)
  -eth (ii) (*v.*)

II. to end a dispute or doubtful matter; to conclude, settle

devour (xxvii, xxxix) (*n.*)

1. duty

devyne (xlv) (*adj.*)

divine

dewe forme (xliv) (*adj.* + *n.*)

6. proper bodily shape

dewe (vi) (*adj.*)

due

arte diabolycke (iii) (*n.* + *adj.*)

diabolical arts

discharge (xx, li)
  -ing (x)
  -ed (li)

9a. to remove anything of the nature of a charge, obligation, etc.

dyscharge (xxii)
  -ed (xxi) (*v.*)

discomfortyd (xxxvi) (*v.*)

1. to deprive of courage or strength of mind, 2. to deprive of comfort or gladness; to distress, sadden

discover (ii, xvi)
  -ed (v)
  -est (xx)
  -yd (i) (*v.*)

3a. to disclose, reveal

discret(e) (i, vii, xx, xxx, xxxvi, xliii, xliv, l, lvii) **dyscrete** (xxiv, xxxii, xlviii) (*adj.*)	1. Showing discernment; judicious, prudent
discrecion (ix, xxxvi, lvii) **dyscrecion** (xvi, xviii, lvii) (*n.*)	3. the faculty of discerning. 6. discernment; prudence, sagacity
discrete borders (xliv) (*n.*)	well-wrought borders
discretly (xli) (*adv.*)	in a discreet manner, see "discret"
disheryte (xxxvii) (*v.*)	disinherit
disordereth (xviii) (*v.*)	1. to upset
dispache (xl) (*v.*)	5. to rid oneself promptly of a thing
dispose (xiv, xxxi, xliv) **-ed** (xlv) (*v.*)	5. to make fit or ready; to prepare
* **disputacion** (xli) **dysputacion** (xxii) (*n.*)	3. doubtful or disputable condition
dissimuled (vii, l) **dyssimuled** (lx) (*v.*)	1. to dissemble
* **dyverce** (xiii) (*adj.*)	2. differing from itself under different circumstances at different times; changeable
doblet (liv) (*n.*)	1a. a close-fitting garment, with or without sleeves, worn by men from the 14th to the 18th centuries. Rarely applied to a similar garment worn by women
doctours (xlv) (*n.*)	2a. an eminently learned man
domage (xv) (*n.*)	damage
dome (xxxiii) (*n.*)	dumb
doste (xxiv, xlvii) (*v.*)	does
doubteous (xxxvi) **doughtfull** (xliii) **dowtious** (xxix) (*adj.*)	doubtful
dought (xi, xliv) (*n.*), (xliii) (*v.*)	doubt
dought (xi) (*adj.*)	doubtfull
doughtes (iii) (*adv.*)	doubtless
drave (xlv) (*v.*)	22. to prolong, defer
drawe (i) (*v.*)	37. to withdraw
dull (xliv, xlvii) (*adj.*)	1. slow of understanding; not sharp of wit; obtuse

dulnes (iii) (*n.*)	dullness, in the sense of dull, above
durst(e) (viii, xxvii) (*v.*)	to dare
dykes (xxxvi) (*n.*)	I.1 a ditch or trench used for defence
dylygence (xxvii) (*n.*)	2. speed, haste
(set a) dyrection (xxiii) (*vbl. phrase*)	4. orderly arrangement or disposition of matters

E

easy (xxvi) (*adj.*)	14. not oppressive or painful
egle (ii) (*n.*)	eagle
enbransing (i) (*v.*)	embracing, surrounding

enbrowdered (liv, lvi)
   -yd (liv)
   -yde (liv) (*v.*)
	embroidered

endue (xliv) **-eued** (xxxv) **-ewed** (prol.) **-uyd** (xlv) (*v.*)	to endow
endurat (xxxix) **indurate** (xxxii) (*adj.*)	2. morally hardened, rendered callous; stubborn, obstinate
enforsed (xlv) **enforced** (xlv) (*v.*)	9. to overcome by violence; ravish

enforcyd (xlii)
   -est (xiii)
 enforsed (xxxix)
   -yd (xviii) (*v.*)
	10. to compel, constrain, oblige

enforce (xiii, xiv, xvi, xxxvii)
 enforse (xli)
   -seth (xxxvii)
   -sith (xliv) (*v.*)
	2. to strengthen in a moral sense; to encourage

enforce (xxxvii, xliv) (*v.*)	3. to strengthen in a physical sense
engyns (xxxvi) (*n.*)	5a. a large machine or instrument with a mechanism used in warfare
enlumyne (ii) (*v.*)	to illuminate
enployed (iii) (*v.*)	to employ
ensample (vi, xix, xxvi, xxxv, xlii, xlv) (*n.*)	example
entaillid (i) (*v.*)	engraved
entayles (xliv) (*n.*)	2. the cut or fashion of a garment

entend (xxiii) (*n.*) ententyve (ii) (*adj.*)	10. the act of listening to something attentive
enterprice (xliv) -ysed (prol.) (*v.*)	1. to undertake something
entre (i, xviii) (*n.*)	entry
erles (xlv) (*n.*)	earls
ever (lv, lxii) (*adv.*)	I. always
evell (xii, xxvi, xxxv) evels (xv) evil(s) (ii, xxxi) evill (ii, xxxix) evyl(s) (i, ii, v, viii, x, xviii, xxx, xlii, xliii, liv) evyll(s) (ii, v, ix, x, ix, xiv xv, xvi, xxi, xxiv, xxvi, xxxi, xxxvi, xxxvii, xli, xlii, xliii, xliv, xlv, xlvii, xlix, li, liv, lv, lvii, lix, lxii) evylles (xlviii) (*n., adj.*)	6. a calamity, disaster or misfortune
excellent (xlv) (*n.*)	excellence
exchew (xxxvi) (*v.*)	to eschew
expedicion (xiii) (*n.*)	4. the action of issuing or sending out official documents
expedicion (xxv) (*n.*)	1. the action of expediting, helping forward, or accomplishing
exstemed (xxxi) (*v.*)	esteemed
extremyties (xlvi) (*n.*)	7. a condition of extreme urgency or need
eyen (i, ii, xiv, xvi, xviii, xxi, xxxiii, lviii, lix, lx) eien (ii) (*n.*)	eyes

F

fabricate (i) (*v.*)	fabricated
fale (xliv) (*v.*)	fall
fall (vi) (*v.*)	VII. to pass suddenly into a certain condition
fame (xi, xvii, xix, xxi, xxii, xxviii, xxx, xli, xliii, xlv, xlix, lv) (*n.*)	2a. reputation
famyd (xliv) (*v.*)	to have the reputation of

fantasye(s) (xxii, xxiii, lxii) (*n.*)	4a. imagination
fare (xiii) (*n.*)	fear
fast(e) (i, ii, xliv) (*adv.*)	2a. with firm grasp or attachment
faute (xv) **fawte(s)** (xi, xx, xxxviii) (*n.*)	fault
favourable (xxxi) (*adj.*)	3. showing undue favour, partial
fawchon (i) (*n.*)	1. a broad sword more or less curved with the edge on the convex side
fayre (xv) (*adv.*)	far
(loste his) fealyng (xviii) (*vbl. phrase*)	2a. to faint
felde(s) (xxxvi, xliii) (*n.*)	2a. the country as opposed to a town or village
ferme (ii, xxxix, xliv, xlv) (*adj.*)	firm
ferme (xliv) (*v.*)	enclose
fercenes (xxx) **fersnes** (xxxii) (*n.*)	fierceness
feyghtynge (xlv) (*v.*)	fighting
feylede (xlii) (*v.*)	failed
first movynge (ii) (*n.*)	first stirring
fole (xxiv) (*n.*)	fool
fole hardynes (vi) -**sse** (vi) -**ines** (vi) (*n.*)	foolhardiness
* **folyage** (lvi) (*n.*)	2. the representation of leaves, used for decoration
footemen (xxxvi) **fotemen** (xxxvi) (*n.*)	2. foot-soldiers
for (xxxi) (*prep.*)	of
force (vii) (*adj.*)	forceful
force (i) (*n.*)	strength
foresayde (xxiv) (*adj.*)	aforesaid
fortune (xxiv) (*v.*)	4d. to have a certain fortune, to fare
found (xliii) (*v.*)	3. to begin or prepare to do something
fowle (xliii) (*adj.*)	foul
frequentation (v) (*n.*)	2. familiar intercourse with a person
fres(s)h(e) (prol., xliv, liv) (*adj.*)	I.1a. new
fresly (xxxviii) (*adv.*)	freshly, newly

frete (lvi) (*v.*)	1. to adorn with ornamental, interlaced work, gold, silver, jewels, or flowers
fro (i, ii, iii, iv, v, vii, ix, xi, xii, xiv, xv, xvi, xvii, xx, xxii, xxiii, xxv, xxvi, xxviii, xxix, xxxi, xxxv, xxxvi, xxxviii, xxxix, xl, xli, xlii, xliii, xliv, xlv, xlvi, xlvii, xlviii, lv, lix, lxii) (*prep.*)	from
frowardenes (xiii) (*n.*)	froward condition; untowardness

G

galante (xliv) (*adj.*)	gallant
galantes (xliv) (*n.*)	gallant men
generacion (xxxi) (*n.*)	3a. offspring, progeny
generosite (xxxi) (*n.*)	1. goodness of race; nobility of birth or lineage
Gentiles (xlv) **Gentyls** (xlv) (*n.*)	2. heathen, pagan
gentylnes (i) **gentlenes** (v, xix, xxxiii, xliv, xlix) **gentlnes** (v) **gentlenesse** (prol.) (*n.*)	3. good breeding, courtesy
gerdell (liv) **gyrdell** (liv, lvi) (*n.*)	1a. a belt worn round the waist
gloryfye (xiii) (*v.*)	1. to glory
(good) gree (viii) (*n.*)	1c. goodwill
go oute of (xxxi) (*v.*)	to swerve from
grevous (ii, xiii) (*adj.*)	2a. bringing serious trouble or discomfort; causing hurt or pain
grevously (vii) (*adv.*)	see grevous, above

H

habylymentes (xliv) (*n.*)	clothes
hap (lix) (*n.*)	1. chance or fortune (good or bad)
happy (prol., ii, iii, x, xiv, xxvi, xxxviii, xlii, xlvii) (*adj.*)	2a. lucky, fortunate
hard(e) (xlii, xliii, xliv, xlvi, lii, lv, lx) (*v.*)	heard

hardynes(se) (prol., xxvi, xxxvii, xxxix, xliv, xlvii) (*n.*)	1. boldness, daring; audacity
(shew grettest) harte (xiii) (*vbl. phrase*)	11a. to show courage or spirit
hastyde (i) (*v.*)	made haste
heate (xi, xviii) (*adj.*)	11a. fervour, ardour, passion, rage
hed(de) (i, ii, lvi) (*n.*)	head
helth (xxxi) (*n.*)	5a. well-being, welfare, safety
helthe (xxxiii) (*n.*)	life
her (lv) -**yng** (xlv, lviii) -**ynge** (xliv) (*v.*)	to hear
here (i) (*n.*)	hair
heres (xxi) (*n.*)	hearers, auditors
heyre (prol.) **herytour** (xxxiii) (*n.*)	heir
hevy (xxi) (*adj.*)	8. having great momentum; striking or falling with force or violence
hevy (ii, l, lx, lxii) (*adj.*) -**ynes** (ii, v, xiv, xxvi, xxxii, xxxviii,xlviii, lii, liv, lx, lxii) -**ines** (ix) (*n.*)	27a. sorrowful, sad, grieved the state or quality of being heavy, as in hevy, above
history (xxi) (*n.*)	1a. relation of incidents (true or imaginary); a narrative, tale, story
hit (i, xxxvi, xxxix) (*pron.*)	it
hole (xviii) (*adj.*)	3a. free from disease; healthy
holsome (xlii) (*adj.*)	2. conducive to health
honeste (xx, xliii) (*n.*)	honesty
hoopes (i) (*n.*)	hopes
hopyde (xxxvi) (*v.*)	hoped
horsemen (xxxvi) (*n.*)	1b. a mounted soldier
hosen (liv) (*n.*)	hose
hote (xlv) (*adj.*)	hot
house(s) (i, xviii, xliii) **howse** (ii, xviii) (*n.*)	a place, generally

I

ignorance (xxii, xxiv) (*n.*)	innocence
imagynacion (xviii) **ymagynacyons** (prol.) (*n.*)	5. mind
*** importunat(e)** (x) **inportunate** (xxii, lix) (*adj.*)	2. burdensome; grievous, grave
in maner (lvii) (*prep.phrase*)	10. almost entirely, very nearly
incontinent (xxix) **incontynent** (xxxviii) (*adv.*)	immediately, without delay
inconvenience(s) (xxix, lvii) **inconvenyence** (prol.) **inconvenient(e)s** (iii, viii, xxvi, xxxvi) (*n.*)	that which is inconvenient
incoraged (xxxvi) (*v.*)	encouraged
in dead (xx) (*prep. phrase*)	in deed
indurate (xxxii)	stubborn
industry (xliv) (*n.*)	2. an application of skill, cleverness, or craft
indyght (xviii) (*v.*)	1. to inspire a form of words which is to be repeated or written down
innocency (xxii, xxix, xxxiii) **innocensy** (xxiii, xxxi) (*n.*)	innocence
instaunce (title pg.) **insance** (prol.) (*n.*)	insistence
in truste (prol.) (*prep. phrase*)	trusting
intyerly (xv) (*adv.*)	entirely
intysemente (xxiv) (*n.*)	1. incitement, instigation
inwarde (xliv, lii), **inwardes** (ii) (*adj.*)	inner

J

jelus (liv) (*adj.*)	jealous
jeobarde (xi) **jeopedy** (xliv) **jeoperdy(e)** (xviii, xxii) **jeoperdes** (xxvi) (*n.*)	jeopardy
jeopdous (xxxvi) (*adj.*)	full of jeopardy
jesture (liv) (*n.*)	1a. bearing, carriage, deportment

jewes (xlv) **jues** (xlv) (*n.*)	Jews
justes royall (xliv) (*n.*)	royal jousts
justyfyde (xxx) (*v.*)	1. to bring to justice

K

kative (x) (*n.*)	captive
kepe (xliii) (*v.*)	14. to guard, protect
kepe thy tonge (xliii) (*vbl. phrase*)	hold your tongue, keep quiet
kertell (lvi) (*n.*)	2b. a skirt or outer petticoat
knowledge (xlviii) (*n.*)	9a. the faculty of understanding, the intellect
(without) knowledgyng (of) (xxxvi) (*v.*)	without (someone) having the knowledge of something
knyves (liv) (*n.*)	the blade of a knife, as opposed to the handle

L

lanterne (xxxiii) (*n.*)	2b. something that metaphorically gives light
larger (ix) (*adj.*)	longer
laste shote ancre (xxiv) (*n.*)	the last shot at security or stability (see *OED* anchor 2)
lawdable (xlv) (*adj.*)	deserving of laud
lawde (xliii) (*n.*) **lawdith** (xxviii) (*v.*)	to laud
lay (iv) (*v.*)	5a. to sleep or pass the night; to lodge temporarily
lay (xliii) (*v.*)	26a. to put forward; to allege
lede (xxxi) (*v.*)	1d. to bring a legal action; adduce testimony
lenynge (i) (*v.*)	leaning
lese (i, viii, x, xvi, xxiv, xxvii, liii, lv) **-yng(e)** (xxxvi) (*v.*) (xxi, liii) (*vbl. noun*)	to lose
lesse (xvi) (*conj.*)	lest
lest(e) (xii, xxviii, lv) (*adv.*)	least
lette (hym) (xxxvi) (*v.*)	2b. to forbear to do something

leve her comynge (vii) (*v.*)	to stop commoning. (see common)
leysour (xvii) (*n.*)	leisure
lightely (xxv, xxxix) **lyghtly** (xxxv, xliv, xlviii) (*adv.*)	4viii. for a slight cause; without careful consideration; 4. easily
lignage (xxxi) **lynage** (xix, xlv, xlv, xliii, xlix, li, lxi) (*n.*)	lineage
liquor (xxxix) (*n.*)	1a. a liquid; a fluid
litle and litle (xlv) **lytle and lytle** (iv) (*prep. phrase*)	little by little
luryd (xliv) (*v.*)	lured
lyfte (i) (*adj.*)	left
lyght (xxx) (*adj.*)	13a. of small importance
lyghtened (xiii) (*v.*)	lit
lyke (xlvii, xlix) (*adv.*)	A8. probable, likely
lyst(e) (xi, xxviii, xliii) (*v.*)	to desire
to lyve (lv) (*adj.*)	alive

M

to make rehersall (xlv) (*v.*)	2a. to relate, narrate, or recount
manasheth (v) **-isheth** (ii) **-yshed** (xiii) (*v.*)	to admonish
maner of disposicion (lx) (*n.*)	state of being
mansion (i, lxii) (*n.*)	2a. a dwelling place; an abode
mantel (lvi) (*n.*)	mantle
manyfeste (xlv) **manyfestith** (xxxv) (*v.*)	to manifest
marchyng (xxvii) (*v.*)	to walk
meane (xxix) (*adj.*)	2a. undistinguished in position; often opposed to noble or gentle
medlyd (i) (*v.*)	1. to mix, mingle; to combine
meke (lxii) (*adj.*)	meek
men of armes (xxxvi) (*n.*)	soldiers, warriors
mennys (xxii) (*n.*)	men's
mertites (xxvi) **meryt(es)** (xxxiii) (*n.*)	1. due reward or punishment

mervayl(l) (i, viii, xi, xv, xxi, xxxi, xiv, lix)	a marvel, a wonder, a source of
mervaill (xxv) **mervayle** (xxvii) **mervaylle** (xiv) **marvayll** (xliv) **mervails** (i) **mervayls** (iv) (*n.*)	amazement
mervail (xv) **mervayll** (i) **mervayled** (i) **mervaylynge** (xxxviii) (*v.*)	to marvel, or wonder, at something
mervelous (xxxv) (*adj.*)	Aa. such as to excite wonder
mete (xxxvi, xliv, xliv, xlvii) (*adj.*)	3. suitable, fit, proper
mishap (ii) **myshape** (liii) (*n.*)	1. evil hap; bad luck; misfortune, 2. an unlucky accident; the lack of chance or fortune.
mo (xxxviii, xxxix, xlvii, xlv, lix) (*determiner*)	more
molefye (xxxix) (*v.*)	2. to soften in temper or disposition; to calm or appease
moralite (iii) (*n.*)	4a. a moral allegory
* **black more** (ii) **blacke morion** (i) (*n.*)	1. a very dark-skinned person
moveable (xli) (*adj.*)	2. changeable, fickle, inconstant
murmuracions (xliii) (*n.*)	1. utterance of low continuous sounds; complaining, grumbling
musyk(e) (xliv, lxii) (*n.*)	music
myddes (i, xxxi, xxxviii) (*n.*)	middle
mynysh (x) (*v.*)	diminish
mynystrynge (xxxi) (*v.*)	administering
mysadventure(s) (xxvi, xxxvi, xxxviii) (*n.*)	1. ill-luck, bad fortune; a piece of bad fortune; a mishap or misfortune, 2. an unlucky accident
mysteries (iii, xlv) **mysteryes** (ii) (*n.*)	2. visions

N

nacion Romayne (xlv) (*n.*)	Roman nation
namyd (xliv) (*v.*)	2c. to allege or declare a person to be something
natural (vi, xxii, xxxv, lxi) (*adj.*)	11. native
nedes (xxxii, xlix) (*adv.*)	of necessity, necessarily
newelte (i) (*adj.*)	1. novelty, newness
next (xviii) (*adj.*)	1a. nearest in place or position
none (i, ii, v, xiv, xv, xxiv, xxvii, xxviii, xxxvi, xxx, xxxi, xxxviii, xli, xliv, xlvii, lv, lvii, lviii) (*pron.*)	negation; no; not one; no one
noryshede (xliii) (*v.*)	1. to bring up, rear, nurture
nother (xxii, xlii) (*conj., pron., determiner*)	neither
nourture (i) (*n.*)	1. the breeding, upbringing, training, education received or possessed by one
nyrenesse (prol.) (*adj.*)	nearness

O

obloquie (prol.) (*n.*)	1b. abuse or detraction as it affects the person spoken against; bad repute; reproach
occupyed (xliv) (*v.*)	used
offyce (xlvii) (*n.*)	2b. a duty or charge falling or assigned to one
ones (prol., xliv, lvii) (*conj., adv., n.*)	once
oppressed (i, xxxvi) (*v.*)	2. to affect with a feeling of pressure, constraint, or distress
oppressyd (x) (*v.*)	3. to suppress; to quell, subdue
or (prol, ii, v, viii, ix, x,xviii, xx, xxiii, xxiv, xxv, xxx, xxxv, xxxvi, xlv, xlvii, lxi) (*prep.*)	B1. before
order (xlviii) **-ed** (xlvi) (*v.*)	2a. to arrange, dispose; make ready
ordeyn(e) (ii, x, xxx, xxxi, xli) **-ed** (i) **-yd** (ii, xxiii)	14c. to determine, settle, resolve

ordyned (xxx) (*v.*)	
* ordre of batayl (xviii) (*n.*)	12b. the arrangement or disposition of sections of an army force
ought (lvii) (*v.*)	3a. owed
oute of his wytte (xxiii) **oute of my witte** (lxii)	out of his/my mind
overage (i) (*n.*)	1. work, workmanship
overlate (viii) (*adj.*)	excessively late; too late

P

pacient (i) (*n.*)	B1a. a sufferer; one who suffers patiently, B1b. a sick person
pacyente (xxviii) (*adj.*)	1b. longsuffering, forbearing
for parte (xxiv)	for her part
partaker (xxxii) (*n.*)	one who shares in something
parte takers (xxii) **pertakers** (xliv) (*n.*)	2. a supporter or adherent
passion(e)(s) (i, v, ix, x, xiii, xxi, xxiv, xxvii, xxx, xxxi, xxxix, xlii, xliv, liv, lvii, lxi) **passyon(s)** (ii, v, vii, viii, xv, xviii, xxi, xxxii, xlvi)	3. suffering or affliction generally
passyonyd (xiv) (*adj.*)	full of suffering
payne (vi, xix, xxxv, xxxviii, xliii, lix) (*n.*)	1a. suffering inflicted for a crime or offence; punishment
payne (xxxvi) (n.)	effort
payneful (v) (*adj.*)	being full of pain
payred (lxii) (*v.*)	impaired
peaseable (xliv) (*adj.*)	2. peaceful
peased (xviii) (*v.*)	appeased
all peces (xx)(*n.*)	10a. armed at all points, completely armed
peradventure (ii, iv, v, xxiv, xxxvi, xli, xliii, xliv) (*adv.*)	1. by adventure, chance, fortune
perdurable (xliv) (*adj.*)	everlasting, eternal, as opposed to things of this world and of time
perfight (iii) (*adj.*)	perfect
perforce (xxxvi, xlii) (*adv.*)	1a. by violence; forcibly

personage(s) (v, xxxix, xliv) **personges** (xi) (*n.*)	2. person
perswasions (xxiii) (*n.*)	questions
persyng (i) (*v.*)	piercing
pertye (xvii, xxi) (*n.*)	1. a part
pertye(s) (xxi, xxx) (*n.*)	party
peteyneth (xxxv) (*v.*)	pertains
peyned (xliv) (*v.*)	pained
pite (i) (*n.*)	4a. a pitiable state; sad fate
piteous (i) (*adj.*)	3. deserving pity; moving to compassion; affecting
place (xv) (*n.*)	II.7c. a subject, a topic
place (xi, xvi, lxi) (*n.*)	IV.12b. occasion, opportunity
place (i) (*n.*)	licence, permission
place (xlii) (*n.*)	I.5b. palace
playntes (i) (*n.*)	complaints
pleace (xxxv, xxxix, xliv) (*v.*)	please
pleatyd (xxx) (*v.*)	1b. to contend in debate; to plead
pomell (liv) (*n.*)	3a. the knob terminating the hilt of a sword, dagger, or the like
pompeous (xliv) (*adj.*)	1. characterized by pomp or stately show; magnificent, splendid
porke of Calydonia (xlv) (*n.*)	Calydonian boar
porte (vii) (*n.*)	I.1a. external deportment; mien
power (xxiv) **powre** (xxxiii) (*adj.*)	poor
poysey (xviii) (*n.*)	I.1. a short motto, originally a line or verse of poetry, and usually in patterned language, inscribed on an object
prease (xxvii) (*n.*)	1a. a crowd, a throng
prease (xliii) (*n.*)	praise
* **preasyd** (xxi) (*v.*)	6a. to bear heavily on, to assail with much force; to beset
preuvyll (xxiv) (*v.*)	prevail
prevatyd (xxvi) (*v.*)	prevented

principall of the courte (iv)	3. the courtiers of high degree, importance, or emminence
privasyon (xiv) (*n.*)	deprivation
(made) privy (xxxvi) (*v.*)	4. intimately acquainted with or accessory to some secret, private transaction
proces (xxxi, xxxviii, lxii) (*n.*)	4a. narration; story, tale; discourse or treatise; argument or discussion
properte (xxx) **-ye** (xlv) (*n.*)	quality
propre (xxvi, xxxii, xxxvi) (*adj.*)	1. own
propyse (ix) (*adj.*)	proper, suitable
prove (ii, vii, xxiv, xxvi, xxx, lvii, lix) **-d** (xxix)	I. to make trial of, try, test
provyd(e) (xiii, xxiv, xxxiii, xxxv) (*v.*)	
provyd (xxxvi) (*v.*)	did, accomplished
provydyde (xxxvi) (*adj.*)	prudent, foreseeing, provident
prysonement (xxi) (*n.*)	imprisonment
publishe (xlix) **-isshed** (xxxi) **-yshed** (xv, xlii) **-yshyd** (xvii) (*v.*)	to make public, to publicise
puissance (ii) **pusance** (xxxiii) **puyssance** (xv, xliv) (*n.*)	strength, power
punycion (vi) (*n.*)	punishment
purpose (vii, xiii, xxiii, xxv, xxix, xxxii) (*n.*)	2a. intention, determination
purpose(d) (xxvi, xlv, xlviii) **-yd** (vii, xlviii) (*v.*)	3c. to be resolved or determined
on the purpose (xli)	9b. with the design, in order to do something
pursewt (xi) (*n.*)	pursuit
* **put(te) case** (xxiv, xxx) (*v.*)	1. the act of putting a case; a supposition or hypothesis
put out his voice (x) (*vbl. phrase*)	48g. to utter, pronounce; to vent
* **put them downe** (xxxv) (*vbl. phrase*)	42g. to put to death, kill
to put to (xxxvi) (*vbl. phrase*)	27a. to set someone to do something; to incite or urge

put to payne (xxxviii) (*v.*)	26a. to punish; make to suffer pain
puyssance (xliv) (*n.*)	strength
puyssante (v) (*adj.*)	strong
pynche of deth (xliv) (*n.*)	3. pain caused by the grip of death

Q

quarel(l) (xix, xxvi, lix) (*n.*)	1. a complaint; an accusation
quycke (prol) **quyke** (xliii) (*adj.*)	21a. Mentally active or vigorous prompt to learn, think, invent
quycken (xliv) **-yd** (xviii) **-ykken** (xliv)(*v.*)	to become quycke, see definition of quycke
quite (xxvi) **quyt(e)** (v, ix, xxii, xxvi, xxxi, xli, xlv, xlvii) (*adv., v.*)	I.1a. to set free, release, deliver

R

recover (lv) (*v.*)	9a. restore to life or consciousness
recreacion (xliv) (*n.*)	2b. mental comfort or consolation
*** recreat** (xviii) (*v.*)	2b. to refresh or enliven (the spirits, mind, a person) by some sensuous or purely physical influence
reculynge (xxxvi) (*v.*)	2. to retreat before an enemy
redoundithe (xliv) (*v.*)	6. to have the effect of contributing or turning to some advantage or disadvantage for a person or thing
redy (xliv) (*adj.*)	ready
refrayne (xviii, xxxvi, lx) **refreynynge** (l)	1b. to restrain; to repress any manifestation of emotion
resfrayne (xliv) (*v.*)	
refuce (xxxv) (*v.*)	to refuse
regarde (i, iii, iv, xv, xxxv) **-ed** (liv, lvi, lx) **-yd** (i, iii, xx, xxxvi) (*v.*) **-ing** (i) **-yng(e)** (xvi, lvi) (*vbl. n.*)	1a. to look at, gaze upon, observe
regarded over (xviii) (*v.*)	9a. to consider

regardes (v) (*n.*)	I.1. appearance; habit or manner of looking; air
reherce (xlv, xlv) (*v.*)	2a. to relate, narrate, recount
make rehersall of (xlv) (*vbl. phrase*)	the action of relating or narrating
reised up (xxxviii) (*v.*)	29a. to put an end to (a siege or blockade) by withdrawing the investing forces
relyefe (xxxviii) (n.)	5a. the replacing of a sentinel or watch by a fresh man or body of men
remedy(e)(s) (ii, iii, v, vi, vii, viii, xii, xiii, xv, xvii, xviii, xxiv, xxxii, xxxiv, xxxvi, xxxviii, xxxix, xli, xlii, xliii, xliv, xlvi, xlvii, xlix, lix) (*n.*)	2a. a means of counteracting or removing an outward evil of any kind; reparation, redress, relief
remedy(e) (ii, iii, v, xi, xii, xiii, xviii, xxiv, xxviii, xli, lv. lxi), -ed (xv) (*v.*)	the action of remedying, see remedy above
remember (xxx) (*v.*)	5a. to think or reflect upon
remembrance (prol., i, x, xvii, xviii, xxvi, xxxix, xliii, xlv, xlviii, lix, lx, lxii)	4a. the memory or thought of something or someone
remembraunce (ii) (*n.*)	
remembrynge (lxii) (*v.*)	reminding
rememoracyon (prol) (*n.*)	the action of remembering (or reminding); a recollection
remove (xlvii) (*v.*)	9a. to depart from a place
renome (xvii, xix) (*n.*)	renown
renomyd (viii) (*v.*)	renowned
rentes (xli, xliv) (*n.*)	1a. a separate piece of landed or other property yielding a certain financial return to the owner
reny (xxi) (*v.*)	2a. to deny or disown an utterance
repayre (xxxviii) (*v.*)	4. to reinstate, re-establish
repute (prol., iii, viii, xx, xxxxi, li, liv) -ith (xxviii) -yd (v, vii, xiv, xxiii, xxiv, xxxviii) -yde (xxx, xli) -ed (vi, xliii, xliv) (*v.*)	1. to consider a person or thing to be, or as being, something

requyre (ii, v, vii, x, xiii, xiv, xv, xvii, xvi, xxii, xxviii, xxx, xxxi, xxxv, lv) -**ed** (vii, xxxix) -**ede** (i) -**yd** (xxii) -**ynge** (prol.) **require** (xli) (*v.*)	5b. to beg or request of someone
resite (xlv) **resyted** (xlviii) (*v.*)	recite
reskew (xxxvi) (*v.*)	rescue
resorte (iv) (*v.*)	2b. to return home or to a place
respyre (i) (*v.*)	3. to breathe again after distress; to recover hope or strength
respyte (prol.) (*n.*)	II.7. respect; regard
restyde (xlv) (*v.*)	rested
retayne (xlii) (*v.*)	1a. to restrain; stop; prevent
retrayte (xxxvi) (*n.*)	retreat
revolvyde (i) (*v.*)	4b. to consider, think over, ponder
rote (xliv) (*n.*)	root
rude (xliii, xliv, xliv, xlvii, xlvii, xlvii) (*adj.*)	3a. uncultured, unrefined, 1a. uneducated, unlearned; ignorant
rude (prol., xv, xlv, xlv) (*adj.*)	II.8a. lacking in elegance or polish; deficient in literary merit
rudely (prol., xliv) (*adv.*)	3. in an uncultured, uncivil or discourteous fashion
rudnes (prol., iii) (*n.*)	1. want of learning; ignorance
rumour (xviii, xxiii) (*n.*)	5. noise, 6. uproar, disturbance
russet (lvi) (*n.*)	1a. a coarse woollen cloth
ryband (liv) (*n.*)	ribbon
ryghtwisnes (xxxiii) (*n.*)	righteousness
ryghtwyse (xxi, xxx) (*adj.*)	righteous
ryghtwysly (xliv) (*adv.*)	righteously
rynne (xliv) (*v.*)	run
ryson (xxi) (*v.*)	risen
ryve (vi) (*adj.*)	rife

S

sabilitie (prol.) (*n.*)	civility [?]
saeth (xiv) (*v.*)	to say
saluted (liv) (*v.*)	greeted
salve (xvii) (*v.*)	save
samples (xliii) (*n.*)	examples
savegarde (xxxvi) (*n.*)	1c. safeguard, safety
savyng (vii, viii, xxi, xxix) (*prep.*)	1. excepting, except
sawte (xxxvi) (*v.*)	assault
sayeng(es) (xviii, xix, xxiii, xxxi, lviii)	2. something that is said
sayng (xxiii) (*n.*)	
scape (xxii, lvi) **scapyd** (xxxvi) **skape** (prol., xxiv, xxviii) (*v.*)	to escape
schilde (i) (*n.*)	shield
sclaunder (xxxv, xliv) (*v.*) (xi) (*n.*)	slander
seaced (i) (*v.*)	ceased
season(e) (xvi, xviii, xviii, xxiv, xxxiii, xliii, xlv)	II. a time, period, occasion
secretenes (xlviii) **secretnes** (xlix) (*n.*)	secret
seke (xlv) (*n.*)	sick
seke (xiv) (*v.*)	seek
sekenes (xlii, xlvi) (*n.*)	sickness
semblant (liv, lvi) (*n.*)	semblance
seperate fro us (xliv) (*vbl. phrase*)	1a. to disunite, disconnect us from
Serua de Marenus (i) (*n.*)	Sierra Morena
set by (xliv) (*v.*)	91c. esteem or value highly
sette (xlviii) (*v.*)	sat
seyeng (xxxii) **-ist** (v, lv) (*v.*)	saying
seyng(e) (prol., ii, iv, v, vii, xxii, xxxviii, xlii, xliii, xliv, xlvi, xlix, lviii, lix, lx) **seing(e)** (ii, xxxix, xlix, lxi), -ist (ii) **seyst** (ii, xiv) (*v.*)	to see
shamefastnes (xvi) (*n.*)	1. modesty, ashamedness

sharpe (i) (*adj.)*	10a. tapering to a fine point, without implication of cutting
sharpe (xxviii) (*adj.*)	5c. severe or merciless punishment, persecution, laws, etc.
sharpyd (xlii) (*v.*)	2a. to render the wit more acute
shew (xxi, xxiii) (*v.*)	19b. to profess truly or falsely to be
shew(e) (i, ii, iv, xiii, xviii, xxiv, xxxi, xxxviii, xlv, xlix, liii, lvii, lix) -ed (i, iii, vii, xvi, xviii, xxxi, xxxii, xxxviii, xxxviii, xliv) -est (xiv) -yd (xxxvi, xxxvi, xxxviii, xlvi) -yde (xlii) −yng (v, xxxii) (*v.*)	23a. to communicate, declare, narrate, state, tell
shortyd (xxx) (*v.*)	shortened
sleu (xxxviii) (*v.*)	slew
sleyste (xlvii) (*v.*)	slays
slombere (liv) (*n.*)	slumber
small (v, xxxi, xliii, xliv) (*adj.*)	IV.16a. low in rank; of little importance, or influence; common
small thought (lx) (*n.*)	little care
smocke (lvi) (*n.*)	1a. a woman's undergarment; a shift or chemise
socour(e) (xviii) (*n.*)	succour
solacious (i) (*adj.*)	affording or giving solace
sonde (xviii) (*n.*)	sound
songe (xliv, lxii) (*v.*)	sung
sore (v, vii, ix, xv,xvi, xviii, xxxvi, xliii, xlv, xlviii, l, lii, lviii, lxii) -er (xxxi, xxxiii) (*adj., adv.*)	2a. causing ,involving, or accompanied by mental pain, trouble, or distress
sorow (ii) (*v.*)	to feel sorrow for
soverayne (xliv) (*adj.*)	2. supreme, paramount; greatest
sowne (xxxvi) -yd (xxxvi) (*v.*)	sound
space (i, xxxvi, xxxviii, xlviii) (*n.*)	4a. a period of time
sparkels (iii) (*n.*)	3. a vital or animating principle
spedde of (vii) (*v.*)	1b. to succeed in getting or accomplishing something

speryte (xliii) **spirite(s)** (i, xliv) **sprytes** (xliv) **spyrytes** (xviii) **spirytes** (lviii) (*n.*)	17a. the mind or faculties as the seat of action and feeling, 18b. the faculties of perception or reflection; the senses or intellect
spotte (xxxi) (*v.*)	1a. to stain or tarnish morally
spotte(s) (xxxiii, xliii, xlv) (*n.*)	1a. a moral stain; a disgrace
spotted (xvii) (*adj.*)	2b. morally stained or blemished
square (i) (*adj.*)	cornered
square (i) (*n.*)	corner
stablis(s)hed (xxx, xxxi) **stablysshed** (xliii) (*v.*)	established
still (i) **styll** (xvi) (*adv.*)	3a. continually, always
strake (xlv) (*v.*)	to strike
strange (xlv) (*adj.*)	11a. unfriendly, or 1a. foreign, alien
strange (iii) (*adj.*)	1a. foreign, alien
strength (xxvi) **strenght** (xli) (*v.*)	strengthen
strengthyng (xxiv) (*v.*)	strengthening
streyght (xi) (*adj.*)	II.6a. severe, rigorous
* **streygthly** (xxxvi) (*adv.*)	2. straightway, immediately
stronge (xlv) (*adj.*)	11. fierce, hotly contested
stryves (xxxi) (*n.*)	strifes
studyed (i) (*v.*)	2d. to deliberate, consider
studyng that (lxii) (*v.*)	thinking about that
subbyng (lii) (*v.*)	sobbing
subtile (xliv, xlv) **subtyle** (xxiii, xliv) **subtyll** (xlvii) (*adj.*)	8. characterized by cleverness or ingenuity in conception or execution
subtilly (i) (*adv.*)	see subtile, above
suer (xviii, xxxiii) (*adj.*)	sure
suertie (prol., xxii, xxiv, xxxv) **suretie** (xxx, xxxv, lvii, lviii) (*n.*)	1. safety, security
suet (x, xxii) (*n.*)	suit
suffer (liii, lix) **-ed** (liv) (*v.*) **suffre** (xxii)	12. to put up with, tolerate

sufferance (xliv) (*adj.*)	I.1. patient endurance, forbearance
sufferance (liii) (*n.*)	8. delay; respite
suffisyd me (lix) (*v.*)	was/were sufficient for me
superflew (xxxvii) (*adj.*)	superfluous
superscrypcion (xvi) (*n.*)	1. an inscription upon or above something
surelyer (xxiii) (*adj.*)	surer
surly (lxi) (*adv.*)	surely
suspect(e) (vii, xvii, xviii, xxxv, xxxviii, xlii, xlvii) (*n.*)	1. suspicion
suspect (xxi) (*adj.*)	suspicious
sustentacion (xxxvii, xliii) (*n.*)	2b. the preservation of a condition
suyd (lxi) (*v.*)	14. to petition, appeal to
swarvyd(e) (xxiii, xxv) (*v.*)	3e. to go back on what one has said
symple (v, xxiv, xliv, xliv) (*adj.*)	II.4a. of low rank or position; undistinguished, common, 7a. small, insignificant, weak or feeble, 9. deficient in knowledge or learning
symplenes (i, xlv) (*n.*)	3. ignorance; intellectual weakness, foolishness
syn (ii, xi, xiv, xv, xix, xx, xxii, xxvi, xxviii, xxxiii, xxxv, xxxix, xli, xlii, xliv, xlvii, xlix, li, lv, lvii, lix) **syne** (xxxi, xxxvii) **synne** (xxix, lxii) **sin** (xv) (*prep., conj.,* and *adv.*)	since
syt (xxxviii) (*v.*)	set

T

tabard (lvi) (*n.*)	a garment with short or no sleeves
take avysemente (xxx) (*v.*)	3. to deliberate; to take counsel
taken to wyfe (xlv) (*v.*)	married
tare (xlix) (*v.*)	tore
tast (i) (*v.*)	1. to or explore by touch; to feel
tawny (i, ii, liv, lvi) (*adj.*)	name of a composite colour, consisting of brown with a preponderance of yellow or orange; but formerly applied also to other shades of brown

temerous (vi) (*adj.*)	fearful
tempt (xiii) **-ed** (xxix) (*v.*)	1. to test or try the worth or truth of someone
thredes (lvi) (*n.*)	threads
three square (i) (*adj.*)	having three equal sides; equilaterally triangular
thither (xxxvi) **thyther** (i, xxvii, xxxiii, xxxvi, xlviii) **thyder** (xxvii) (*adv.*)	1. to move to or towards a place
tocheth (xxx, xxxv) **-yd** (xxii) (*v.*)	to touch
toke recreation (xlii) (*v.*)	2a. refreshment or comfort produced by something affecting the senses or body
tong (xiv, xlv) (*n.*)	4a. voice, speech; language
tong (iii) (*n.*)	8a. the speech or language of a people or race
tong(e)(s) (i, vi, xlii, xliii, xx, xlv, xlvi, liii) (*n.*)	tongue
kepe thy tonge (xliii) (*vbl. phrase*)	hold your tongue, cease speaking
torne (xlii) (*v.*)	to alter
torne to thy spirites (ii) (*vbl. phrase*)	turn inwards
tourneis (xliv) (*n.*)	tournaments
trace (ii, xxxix) (*n.*)	I.1a. the way, course or path which anything takes
trance (xviii, xlvi) (*n.*)	2. a faint
traugth (xxx) **trougth** (xviii) **trough** (xx) (*n.*)	truth
travaill (ii, xxvii) **travayll** (iii, xxxvii, liv, lix, lxi) **travayle** (v, xlii) **travels** (iii) **travyls** (iii) (*n.*)	suffering, work and/or travel, often having more than one connotation
travayl(e) (xi, xiv, xliv) **travayll(e)** (i, xxviii)	to suffer, work and/or travel, often
travel(l)yde (xxiii, xxxiv) **traveyleth** (ii) **trawayl** (li) **traveled** (lxii) (*v.*)	having more than one connotation

travelous (i) (*adj.*)	toilsome; laborious
trayn (xliv) (*n.*)	2. a trap or snare
treat (iv) (*v.*)	4. to apply oneself to, work at
trobelous (lv) (*adj.*)	troublesome
troubled (xlv) (*v.*)	to disrupt the impression of something
trymbled (xvi) (*v.*)	trembled
turbacion (i, xxxiv, xxxvi) **turbacyon** (xvi)	confusion, disorder, agitation of mind
turbasyon (xiv) **turbation** (vii) (*n.*)	
turpitud (xliii) (*n.*)	1. baseness; depravity, wickedness

U

unclennis (xlv) (*n.*)	lacking in cleanliness
understanding (xxxix) **understandyng(e)** (xv, xxiv, xxviii, xxxix, xlii, xliv, xlvii) (*n.*)	1a. power or ability to understand; intellect
unhap (viii, lvii) **unhappe** (xxxiii) (*n.*)	1. misfortune, mishap
unhappy (viii, x, xxxv, xxxvii, xxxix, xlvii, liii) (*adj.*)	2. unfortunate, unlucky, ill-fated
unmeasurable (xx) (*adj.*)	2. immoderate, unbounded
unpedyment (xxxi) (*n.*)	impediment
unperfyte (xxxviii) (*adj.*)	imperfect
unvaylable (prol.) (*adj.*)	of no avail; unavailing; useless
unwysedome (xlv) (*n.*)	1. ignorance, folly, stupidity
upse down (xlvii) (*adj. or adv*)	upside down
usyd (ix) (*v.*)	1a. accustomed, usual
utilitie (prol.) (*adj.*)	1a. useful
uttereth (xliv) (*v.*)	3c. to produce or yield; supply

V

vailes (ii) (*n.*)	wings
valewer (prol.) (*n.*)	value
valiantnes (xxvi, xxxvi) (*n.*)	valiant actions
vanquyssith (iii) (*v.*)	vanquishes

velvyt (liv) (*n.*)	velvet
vertuos cardynals (xliv) (*n.*)	cardinal virtues
vertuos theogecals (xliv) (*n.*)	theological virtues
veryfy (xxxvi) (*v.*)	2. to show to be true by demonstration or evidence
vestured (i, ii) (*v.*)	clothed or dressed
visyted (xxxvi) (*v.*)	visited
vysage (xvi) (*n.*)	face

W

wakyng (lvi) (*v.*)	to be awake
warde (xxxvi, xlviii) (*suffix*)	1. to denote direction of movement
warke(s) (xliii, xliv, xlvii, lix, lxi) (*n.*)	work
warkeman (xliii) (*n.*)	workman
watches (i, ii) (*n.*)	10a. a guard
watchyng (ii) (*v.*)	guarding
water of comeforte (xviii) (*n.*)	healing water
waxe (vii) **-yde** (xlv) (*v.*)	II.b. to become, turn
wayes (i, xxxi) (*n.*)	I. road, path
webbe (xlv) (*n.*)	I.1a. a whole piece of cloth in process of being woven or after it comes from the loom
welth(e)(s) (ii, vi, x, xiv, xv, xxi, xxvi, xxxi, xxxix, xlii, xliii, xliv, liii) (*n.*)	1d. An instance or kind of prosperity; a felicity, blessing; the good
wenynge (xlviii) (*v.*)	1. to think, suppose, consider
were (xliv) (*v.*)	to wear
wery (liv) (*adj.*)	weary
werynes (i, lii) (*n.*)	weariness
weryde (li) (*v.*)	worried
wherto (vii) (*prep.*)	II.3a. to which
wist(e) (i, xxxvi, xlviii, lxii) **wyst** (xviii, xlvii, liv) (*v.*)	to know
witte (lxii) **wyt** (xviii) **wytte(s)** (ii, iii, viii, xiii, xiv, xv, xxi, xxiv, xlii, xlv, xlvii, lv) (*n.*)	1. the mind, 2a. understanding, intellect, reason

with one voice (xxxvi) (*prep. phrase*)	7. unanimously
withall (i) (*prep.*)	B. with
without(e) (v, vii, xv, xx, xxxvi, xxviii, xlv, lv) (*prep.*)	C.1c. unless
wold(e) (ii, vi, vii, viii, ix, x, xi, xiii, xiv, xv, xvii, xviii, xix, xxii, xxiii, xxiv, xxv, xxvi, xxviii, xxix, xxxiii, xxxiv, xxxv, xxxvi, xxxviii, xxxix, xli, xlii, xliii, xliv, xlv, xlvii, xlviii, xlix, li, lii, liii, liv, lv, lvi, lix, lx, lxi) **-est** (xi, xli, xliii, li, liii, lv) (*v.*)	would, often also having sense of to wish
woll (xliv) (*v.*)	will
wonte (xxviii, liv) (*v.*)	2. accustomed
worde (liv) (*n.*)	10 c. a significant phrase inscribed upon something; a motto
wowers (xlv) (*n.*)	wooers
wrappyd (xxvii) (*v.*)	II.9. to fold up
wrytyng (xvii, xviii, xix, xxxviii, liv, lvi, lvii, lix) (*n.*)	8a. a written document, note, letter
wylte (xlvii) (*v.*)	will
wynde (xvii) (*v.*)	2a. to proceed, go
wyse (i, ii, xviii, xxiv, xxvi, xxx, xxxvi, xxxviii, xxxix, xlii, xliii, xliv, xlv) (*n.*)	1a. way
wytnes (xxiii, xxxi, xxxvi) (*n.*)	2a. attestation of a fact, event, or statement; testimony, evidence

X

xperience (xviii, lxii) (*n.*)	8. the aptitudes, skill, or judgement acquired through experience

Y

yeolow (liv) (*adj.*)	yellow
yerth (xxxv, xxxvi, xxxix, xlviii) (*n.*)	earth
yes (lxii) (*n.*)	eyes
yough (xlvii) (*n.*)	youth

WORKS CITED

Primary Sources

Alonso, Martin. *Diccionario Medieval Español. Desde las Glosas Emilianenses y Silenses (s. X) hasta el siglo XV.* 2 vols. Salamanca: Universidad Pontifica de Salamanca, 1986.

Aristotle. *The Nicomachean Ethics.* Thomas Aquinas. *Commentary on the Nicomachean Ethics,* trans. C. I. Litzinger. 2 vols. Chicago: Henry Regnery, 1964.

Assy, François. *Prison d'Amour.* Paris: Galiot Du Pré, 1526.

Bacon, Sir Francis. *The Oxford Francis Bacon,* ed. Michael Kiernan. Vol. 15. Oxford: Oxford University Press, 2000.

Báez, Enrique Moreno, ed. Diego de San Pedro, *Cárcel de amor.* Madrid: Cátedra, 1989.

Bale, John. *Index Britanniae scriptorum quos ex variis bibliothecis non parvo labore collegit Ioannes Baleus,* ed. Reginald Lane Poole. Oxford: Clarendon Press, 1902.

Berners, John Bourchier, Lord. *The ancient, honorable, famous, and delight-full historie of Huon of Bourdeaux, one of the peeres of Fraunce, and Duke of Guyenne. Enterlaced with the loue of many ladies, as also the fortunes and aduentures of knights errant, their amorous seruants.* London: Purfoot, 1601.

———. *The Boke of Duke Huon of Burdeux,* ed. S. L. Lee. EETS ES 40, 41, 43, 50. London: Trubner, 1882-1887.

———. *The Castel of loue, translated oute of Spanyshe into Englyssh, by John Bowrchier knyght, lorde Bernes, at the instaunce of the Lady Elizabeth Carewe, late wyfe to syr Nicholas Carewe knight. The which booke treateth of the loue betwene Leriano and Laureola, doughter to the kynge of Macedonia..* London: Kynge, c. 1555.

———. *The castell of loue, translated out of Spanishe in to Englyshe, by Johan Bowrchier Knyght, Lorde Bernis, at the instaunce of the Lady Elizabeth Carew, late wyfe to Syr Nicholas Carew, Knyght. The whiche boke treateth of the loue betwene Leriano and Laureola, doughter to the Kynge of Masedonia.* London: Turke, 1548?.

———. *The Castell of loue, translated out of Spanyshe into Englysshe, by Johan Bowrchier knyght, lorde Bernis, at the instaunce of the Lady Elizabeth Carewe,*

late wyfe to Syr Nicholas Carewe, Knyght. The whiche boke treateth of the loue
betwene Leriano and Laureola, doughter to the kynge of Masedonia. London:
Wyer for Kele, 1552?.

———. *The golden boke of Marcus Aurelius Emperour and eloquent oratour.*
London: Berthelet, 1537.

———. *Here begynneth the first volum of sir Iohan Froyssart of the chronycles of*
Englande, Fraunce, Spayne, Portyngale, Scotlande, Bretayne, Flau[n]ders: and
other places adioynynge. London: Pynson, 1523.

———. *Here begynneth the thirde and fourthe boke of sir Iohn Froissart of the*
chronycles of Englande, Fraunce, Spaygne, Portyngale, Scotlande, Bretayne,
Flaunders: and other places adioynynge. London: Pynson, 1525.

———. *The History of the Valiant Knight Arthur of Little Britain, a romance of*
chivalry originally translated from the French, by Iohn Bourchier, Lord Berners,
ed. Edward Vernon Utterson. London: White Cochrane and Co., 1814.

———. *The hystory of the moost noble and valyaunt knyght Arthur of lytell brytayne.*
London: Copland, 1560.

Boccaccio, Giovanni. *Boccaccio on Poetry: Being the Preface and the Fourteenth*
and Fifteenth Books of Boccaccio's Genealogia decorum gentilium in an English
Version with Introductory Essay and Commentary, ed. and trans. Charles G.
Osgood. Princeton: Princeton University Press, 1930.

———. *Forty-six Lives: Translated from Boccaccio's De claris mulieribus by Henry*
Parker, Lord Morley, ed. Herbert G. Wright. EETS 214. London: Oxford
University Press, 1943.

Boro, Joyce, ed. "*The Castell of Love*: A Critical Edition of Lord Berners's
Translation, with Introduction, Commentary, and Notes." Ph.D. diss.,
Oxford University, 2002.

Brunner, Karl, ed. *The Seven Sages of Rome (Southern Version).* EETS 191.
London: Oxford University Press, 1933.

Bryan, Francis. *A dispraise of the life of a courtier.* London: Grafton, 1548.

Byrne, Muriel St Clare, ed. *The Lisle Letters.* Chicago and London: University
of Chicago Press, 1981.

Calendar of Letters, Despatches, and State Papers, Relating to the Negotiations
between England and Spain: Preserved in the Archives at Simancas and
Elsewhere, ed. G. A. Bergenroth et al., 13 vols. London: Longman, Green,
Longman and Roberts. 1862-1954.

Calendar of Patent Rolls Preserved in the Public Record Office. Henry VII. Vol. II.
A.D. 1494-1509. London: H. M. S. O., 1916.

Calendar of State Papers and Manuscripts, Relating to English Affairs Existing in
the Archives and Collections of Venice, and in Other Libraries of Northern Italy,
1202–1675, ed. Rawdon Brown et al., 38 vols. London: Longman, Green,
Longman, Roberts and Green, 1864-1940.

Chaucer, Geoffrey. *The Riverside Chaucer,* ed. Larry Dean Benson et al. 3rd ed.
Boston: Houghton Mifflin, 1987.

Cicero, Marcus Tullius. *De senectute, De amicitia, De divinatione*, trans. William
    Armistead Falconer. Loeb Classical Library 154. London: Heinemann,
    1923.

——. *Epistolae ad Brutum. The Letters to Brutus*, trans. M. Cary. Loeb
    Classical Library 462. London: Heinemann, 1972.

——. *On Duties*, ed. and trans. M. T. Griffin and E. M. Aitkins. Cambridge:
    Cambridge University Press, 1991.

Cokayne, George Edward. *Complete Peerage of England Scotland Ireland Great
    Britain and the United Kingdom Extant, Extinct, or Dormant*, ed. Vicary
    Gibbs. Vol. 1. London, 1887. 2nd ed. London: St Catherine Press, 1910;
    repr. Gloucester: Alan Sutton, 1987.

Corfis, Ivy A. *Diego de San Pedro's* Cárcel de amor, *A Critical Edition*. London:
    Tamesis, 1987.

——. *Diego de San Pedro's* Tractado de amores de Arnalte y Lucenda: *A
    Critical Edition*. London: Tamesis, 1985.

Cotgrave, Randle. *A Dictionarie of the French and English Tongues*. London:
    Islip, 1611; repr. with introduction by William S. Woods, Columbia, SC:
    University of South Carolina Press, 1950.

Crane, William G. *The Castle of Love, a Translation by John Bourchier*. Facs.
    Gainesville: Scholars Facsimiles and Reprints, 1950.

Crawford, Anne, ed. and intro. *The Household Books of John Howard, Duke of
    Norfolk 1462-1471, 1481-1483*. Gloucestershire: Sutton, 1992.

Dante Alighieri. *The Divine Comedy*, ed. and trans. Charles S. Singleton. 3
    vols. London: Routledge and Paul, 1971.

Dering, Edward. *A briefe & necessary introduction*. London: Awdley, 1572.

Elyot, Sir Thomas. *The Book named The Governor*, ed. S. E. Lehmberg.
    London: Dent, 1962.

——. *The image of gouernance compiled out of the actes of Alexander Seuerus*.
    London: Berthelet, 1541.

——. *Of the knowledeg [sic.] whiche maketh a wise man*. London: Berthelet,
    1533.

——. *Pasquil the Playne*. London: Berthelet, 1533.

Emden, A. B. *A Biographical Register of the University of Oxford to A.D. 1500*.
    London: Oxford University Press, 1957.

Erasmus, Desiderius. *The Education of a Christian Prince*, ed. and trans. Lisa
    Jardine. Cambridge: Cambridge University Press, 1997.

Fortescue, John. *The Governance of England: Otherwise Called the Difference
    between an Absolute and a Limited Monarchy*, ed. Charles Plummer. Oxford:
    Clarendon Press, 1885.

Furnivall, Frederick J. *Captain Cox, his Ballads and Books; or Robert Laneham's
    Letter: Whearin part of the entertaunement untoo the Queen Majesty at
    Killingworth Castl, in Warwik Sheer in this Soomerz Progress. 1575. is signi-*

fied, from a freend officer attendant in the court, unto hiz freend, a citizen and merchaunt of London. London: Taylor for The Ballad Society, 1871.

———. *Complaynte of Scotland.* London: Kegan Paul, Trench, Trübner, 1890.

Gili Gaya, Samuel, ed. *Cárcel de Amor.* Madrid: Espasa-Calpe, 1967.

Grande Dizionario Della Lingua Italiana Moderna. 5 vols. Milan: Garzanti, 1996.

Hodnett, Edward. *English Woodcuts, 1480-1535.* Oxford: Oxford University Press, 1973.

Homer. *The Iliad,* trans. Robert Fagles. London: Penguin, 1991.

Hyginus. "Fabulae." In *The Myths of Hyginus,* ed. and trans. Mary Grant. Lawrence: University of Kansas Press, 1960.

Jayne, Sears Reynolds, and Francis R. Johnson, eds. *The Lumley Library. The Catalogue of 1609.* London: Trustees of the British Museum, 1956.

Kölbing, Eugen, ed. *The Romance of Sir Beues of Hamtoun.* EETS ES 46, 48, 65. London: Trübner, 1885-1894.

Letters and Papers, Foreign and Domestic of the Reign of Henry VIII, Preserved in the Public Record Office, the British Museum, and Elsewhere in England, ed. John S. Brewer, 21 vols. 2nd ed. rev. J. Gairdner and R. H. Brodie. London: Her Majesty's Stationary Office, 1862-1932.

Livy. [*History of Rome.*] *Livy: In Fourteen Volumes,* trans. B. O. Foster. Loeb Classical Library. 14 vols. London: Heinemann, 1919-1959.

Luborsky, Ruth Samson and Elizabeth Morley Ingram. *A Guide to English Illustrated Books, 1536-1603.* Tempe, AZ: Medieval and Renaissance Texts and Studies, 1998.

Malory, Sir Thomas. *Morte Darthur,* ed. Eugène Vinaver. 2nd ed. 3 vols. Oxford: Clarendon Press, 1967.

Manfredi of Ferrara, Lelio. *Carcer damore.* Vinegia: Rusconi, 1514.

Maraffi, Bartolomeo. *Picciol trattato d'Arnalte e di Lucenda intiolato L'amante mal trattato dalla sua amorosa.* Lyon: Balthasar Arnoullet, 1555.

Maximus, Valerius. [*Facta et dicta.*] *Memorable Doings and Sayings,* ed. and trans. D. R. Shackleton-Bailey. Loeb Classical Library 492-93. Cambridge, MA and London: Harvard University Press, 2000.

Menéndez y Pelayo, Marcelino. *Antología de poetas líricos castellanos.* Edición Nacional. Vol. 3. Santander: Aldus S. A. de Artes Gráficas, 1944-1945.

More, Thomas. *Utopia,* ed. and trans. George M. Logan and Robert M. Adams. Cambridge: Cambridge University Press, 1989.

Nicolas, Nicholas Harris. *Testamenta vetusta: Being Illustrations from Wills, of Manners, Customs, &c. as well as of the Descents and Possessions of Many Distinguished Families. From the Reign of Henry the Second to the Accession of Queen Elizabeth.* Vol. 2. London: Nichols & Son, 1826.

Ovid. [*Ars amatoria, Remedia amoris.*] *The Love Poems,* trans. A. D. Melville. World's Classics. Oxford: Oxford University Press, 1990.

———. *Fasti*, trans. James George Frazer. Loeb Classical Library. London: Heinemann, 1931.

———. *Heroides*, trans. Harold Isbell. London: Penguin, 1990.

———. *The Metamorphoses of Ovid*, trans. Mary M. Innes. Harmondsworth: Penguin, 1955.

The Oxford English Dictionary. <http://dictionary.oed.com> (Oxford: Oxford University Press).

Parrilla, Carmen, ed. *Cárcel de amor.* Barcelona: Crítica, 1995.

Plato. *The Platonic Epistles*, trans. J. Harward. Cambridge: Cambridge University Press, 1932.

———. *The Republic*, trans. A. D. Lindsay. London: Everyman's Library, 1906; repr. London: David Campbell, 1992.

Pliny, The Elder. *Naturalis historia. Natural History*, trans. H. Rackham. 10 vols. Loeb Classical Library. London: Heinemann, 1966-1979.

Plutarch. *Alcibiades and Coriolanus. Lysander and Sulla. Plutarch's Lives,* trans. Bernadotte Perrin. Loeb Classical Library. London: Heinemann, 1954-1962.

Rodríguez del Padrón, Juan. "Triunfo de las donas." In *Obras Completas*, ed. César Hernández Alonso, 211–58. Madrid: Editora Nacional, 1982.

Salisbury, John of. *Policraticus. Of the Frivolities of Courtiers and the Footprints of Courtiers and the Footprints of Philosophers*, ed. and trans. Cary J. Nederman. Cambridge: Cambridge University Press, 1990.

Segura, Juan de. *Proceso de cartas de amores: A Critical and Annotated Edition of the First Epistolary Novel (1548) together with an English Translation*, ed. and trans. Edwin B. Place. Evanston: Northwestern University Press, 1950; repr. New York: AMS, 1970.

Seneca, Lucius Annaeus. *Ad Lucilium epistulae morales*, ed. and trans. Richard M. Gummere. Loeb Classical Library 75-77. London: Heinemann, 1917-1925.

Severin, Dorothy Sherman, ed. Fernando de Rojas, *La Celestina*. Madrid: Cátedra, 1988.

Shakespeare, William. *The Riverside Shakespeare*, ed. G. Blakemore Evans. Boston: Houghton Mifflin, 1974.

A Short Title Catalogue of Books Printed in England, Scotland and Ireland, 1475-1640, ed. A.W. Pollard and G. R. Redgrave. 2nd ed. rev. W. A. Jacobs, F. S. Ferguson, and Katherine R. Pantzer. 3 vols. London: Bibliographical Society, 1976-1991.

Skeat, Walter W., ed. *The Tale of Gamelyn*. 2nd ed. Oxford: Clarendon Press, 1893.

Starkey, Thomas. *A Dialogue Between Pole and Lupset*, ed. T. F. Mayer. Camden Fourth Series 37. London: Royal Historical Society, 1989.

Statius, Publius Papinus. *Thebaid*, ed. D. W. T. Vessey, trans. A. D. Melville. World's Classics. Oxford: Oxford University Press, 1995.

Steele, Robert, ed. *Three Prose Versions of the Secretum Secretorum.* EETS ES 74. London: Trübner, 1898.

———— and A.S. Fulton, ed. *Secretum Sectretorum.* Opera hactenus inedita Rogeri Baconi 5. Oxford: Clarendon Press, 1920.

Tilley, Morris Palmer. *A Dictionary of the Proverbs in England in the Sixteenth and Seventeenth Centuries. A Collection of the Proverbs Found in English Literature and the Dictionaries of the Period.* Ann Arbor: University of Michigan Press, 1950.

Utterson, E. V., ed. *Sir John Froissart's Chronicles of England, France [&c.] tr. by J. Bourchier, lord Berners. To which are added, a memoir of the translator, and a copious index.* 2 vols. London: n.p., 1812.

Valera, Diego de. *Epístolas enbiados en diversos tiempos a diversas personas. Con cinco tratados del mismo autor sobre diversas materias,* ed. José Antonio de Balenchana. Madrid: Sociedad de Bibliófilos Española, 1878.

Vallmanyà, Bernardí. *Lo carcer de Amor.* Barcelona: Johann Rosenbach, 1493.

Vickers, Brian, ed. *English Renaissance Literary Criticism.* Oxford: Clarendon Press, 1999.

Virgil. *The Aeneid,* trans. David West. Harmondsworth: Penguin, 1991.

Vives, Juan Luis. *On the Education of A Christian Woman,* ed. and trans. Charles Fantazzi. Chicago and London: University of Chicago Press, 2000.

Waley, Pamela, ed. Juan de Flores, *Grimalte y Gradissa.* London: Tamesis, 1971.

Whinnom, Keith, ed. *Dos opúsculos isabelinos: 'La coronación de la señora Gracisla' (BN Ms. 22020) y Nicolás Núñez, 'Cárcel de amor.'* Exeter: Exeter University Press, 1979.

————, ed. *Obras Completas, II.* Diego de San Pedro, Cárcel de Amor. Madrid: Clásicos Castalia, 1971.

————, and Dorothy Sherman Severin, eds. *Obras Completas, III.* Diego de San Pedro, *Poesías.* Madrid: Clásicos Castalia, 1979.

————, trans. *Prison of Love, c. 1492, Diego de San Pedro, Together with the Continuation, c. 1496 by Nicolas Núñez.* Edinburgh: Edinburgh University Press, 1979.

Whiting, Bartlett Jere. *Proverbs, Sentences, and Proverbial Phrases; from English Writings Mainly Before 1500.* Cambridge: Harvard University Press, 1968.

Wood, Anthony à. *Athenae Oxonienses,* ed. Phillip Bliss 3rd ed. London: Rivington, 1813.

Wright, T., ed. *The Political Songs of England.* London: Camden Society, 1839.

Wyer, Robert. *The boke of Englysshe, and Spanysshe.* London: Wyer, 1554?.

Secondary Sources

Alatorre, Antonio. *Las 'Heroidas' de Ovidio y su huella en las letras españolas.* Mexico City: Universidad Nacional Autónoma de México, 1950.

Amador de los Ríos, José. *Historia crítica de la literatura española.* Vol. 6. Madrid: José Fernández Cancela, 1865.

Armas, Frederick A. de. "Algunas observaciones sobre *La Carcel de amor.*" *Revista de Estudios Hispánicos* 8 (1974): 107-27.

Balteau, J. "Assy, François d'." *Dictionnaire de Biographie Française,* ed. J. Balteau et al., 3: 1330. Paris: Librarie Letouzey, 1939.

Barnes, Geraldine. *Counsel and Strategy in Middle English Romance.* Cambridge: Brewer, 1993.

Baroja, Julio Carlo. *Vidas mágicas e Inquisition.* Vol. 1. Madrid: Taurus, 1967.

Barratt, Alexandra. "Carried Forward: Translations for Women to 1550." Australian and New Zealand Association for Medieval and Early Modern Studies Fifth Biennial Conference. Auckland, New Zealand. 2-5 February 2005. Unpublished conference paper.

Battesti Pelegrin, Jeanne. "Tópica e invención: los lamentos de las madres en la *Cárcel de amor* de Diego de San Pedro." In *La literatura Hispánica Reyes Católicos y Descubrimento. Acta del Congreso Internacional de la literatura hispánica en la época de los reyes Católicos y el Descubrimento,* ed. Manuel Criado del Val, 237-47. Barcelona: PPU, 1989.

Bermejo Hurtado, Haydée, and Dinko Cvitanovic. "El sentido de la aventura espiritual en *Cárcel de amor.*" *Revista de Filología Española* 49 (1966): 289-300.

Bernheimer, R. *Wild Men in the Middle Ages: A Study in Art, Sentiment and Demonology.* Cambridge, MA: Harvard University Press, 1952.

Blake, N. F. "Caxton and Courtly Style." *Essays and Studies* 21 (1968): 29-45.

———. "Lord Berners: A Survey." *Medievalia et Humanistica* 2 (1971): 119-32.

Bohías Balaguer, Pedro. "La novela caballeresca, sentimental y de aventuras." In *Historia general de las literaturas hispánicas,* ed. Guillermo Díaz-Plaja, 2: 189-236. Barcelona: Barna, 1951.

Boro, Joyce. "A Source and Date for the Fragment of *Grisel y Mirabella* Found in the Binding of Emmanuel College 338.5.43." *Transactions of the Cambridge Bibliographical Society* 12 (2003): 422-36.

———. "Lord Berners and His Books: A New Survey." *Huntington Library Quarterly.* Special Issue. Early Tudor Literature in Manuscript and Print. Ed. Alexandra Gillespie. 67 (2004): 236-50.

———. "The Textual History of *Huon of Burdeux*: A Reassessment of the Facts." *Notes and Queries* n.s. 48 (2001): 233-37.

Bourland, C. B. "Boccaccio and the *Decameron* in Castilian and Catalan Literature." *Revue Hispanique* 12 (1905): 1-232.

Bradley, Emily Tennyson. "Edmund Knyvet." *DNB*. CD-ROM. Oxford: Oxford University Press, 1995.

Brownlee, Marina Scordilis. "Medusa's Gaze and the Canonicity of Discourse: Segura's *Proceso*." In *Studies on the Spanish Sentimental Romance (1440-1550): Redefining a Genre*, ed. Joseph J. Gwara and E. Michael Gerli, 21-36. London: Tamesis, 1997.

———. *The Severed Word: Ovid's* Heroides *and the Novela Sentimental*. Princeton: Princeton University Press, 1990.

Buceta, Erasmo. "Cartel de desafío enviado por D. Diego Lopez de Haro al Adelantado de Murcia, Pedro Fajardo, 1480." *Revue Hispanique* 81 (1933): 456-74.

Carley, James P. "Bourchier, John, second Baron Berners (*c.*1467-1533)." In *The Oxford Dictionary of National Biography*, ed. H. C. G. Matthew and Brian Harrison. Oxford: Oxford University Press, 2004.

———, ed. *The Libraries of King Henry VIII*. Corpus of British Medieval Library Catalogues 7. London: British Library in association with British Academy, 2000.

Cátedra, Pedro M. *Amor y Pedagogía en la Edad Media. (Estudios de doctrina amorosa y práctica literaria)*. Salamanca: Universidad de Salamanca Prensa, 1989.

Chambers, R. W. *On the Continuity of English Prose from Alfred to More and his School*. EETS 191. London: Oxford University Press, 1952.

Chorpenning, Joseph F. "Leriano's Consumption of Laureola's Letters in the *Cárcel de amor*." *Modern Language Notes* 95 (1980): 422-25.

———. "The Literary and Theological Method of the *castillo interior*." *Journal of Hispanic Philology* 3 (1979): 121-33.

———. "Rhetoric and Feminism in the *Cárcel de Amor*." *Bulletin of Hispanic Studies* 54 (1977): 1-8.

Collier, J. P. *A Bibliographical and Critical Account of the Rarest Books in the English Language, Alphabetically Arranged*. Vol. 1. London: Joseph Lilly, 1865.

Corfis, Ivy A. "The *Dispositio* of Diego de San Pedro's *Cárcel de Amor*." *Ibero-Romania* 21 (1985): 32-47.

Cornelius, R. D. *The Figurative Castle: A Study in the Medieval Allegory of the Edifice*. Bryn Mawr: Bryn Mawr University Press, 1930.

Cottrell, G. W. "*Cárcel de Amor*." *TLS* 27 (April 1933): 295.

Crane, William G. "*Cárcel de Amor*." *TLS* 1 (June 1933): 380.

———. "Lord Berners's Translation of Diego de San Pedro's *Cárcel de Amor*." *PMLA* 49 (1934): 1032-35.

———. *Wit and Rhetoric in the Renaissance: The Formal Basis of Elizabethan Prose Style*. New York: Columbia University Press, 1937.

Croll, Morris W. "The Sources of the Euphuistic Rhetoric." Ed. R. J. Schoeck and J. Max Patrick. In *Style, Rhetoric, and Rhythm. Essays by Morris W.*

Croll, ed. J. Max Patrick and Robert O. Evans et al., 241-95. Princeton: Princeton University Press, 1966.

Cvitanovic, Dinko. *La novela sentimental española*. Madrid: Prensa Española, 1973.

Dagenais, John. "Juan Rodríguez del Padrón's Translation of the Latin *Bursarii*: New Light on the Meaning of 'Tra(c)tado.'" *Journal of Hispanic Philology* 10 (1985): 117-39.

Damiani, Bruno. 'The Didactic Intention of the *Cárcel de Amor*." *Hispanofíla* 56 (1976): 29-43.

Delaney, Sheila. *Medieval Literary Politics: Shapes of Ideology*. Manchester and New York: Manchester University Press, 1990.

Deyermond, A. D. "El hombre salvaje en la novela sentimental." *Filología* 10 (1964): 97-111.

———. *A Literary History of Spain: The Middle Ages*. London: Ernest Benn, 1971.

———. "The Lost Genre of Medieval Spanish Literature." *Hispanic Review* 43 (1975): 231-59.

———. "The Poetry of Nicolás Núñez." In *The Age of the Catholic Monarchs 1474-1516: Literary Studies in Memory of Keith Whinnom*, ed. idem and Ian Macpherson, 25-36. Liverpool: Liverpool University Press, 1989.

———. *Tradiciones y puntos de vista en la ficción sentimental*. México: Universidad Nacional Autónoma de México, 1993.

Diaz-Plaja, Guillermo, ed. *Historia general de las literaturas hispánicas*. Vol. 3. Barcelona: Editorial Barna, 1953.

Draper, John W. "A Reference to *Huon* in Ben Jonson." *Modern Language Notes* 35 (1920): 439-40.

Dudley, Edward. "The Inquisition of Love: *Tractado* as a Fictional Genre." *Mediaevalia* 55 (1979): 233-43.

Dunn, Peter N. "Narrator as Character in the *Cárcel de amor*." *Modern Language Notes* 94 (1979): 188-99.

Durán, Armando. *Estructura y técnicas de la novela sentimenal y caballeresca*. Madrid: Gredos, 1973.

Edwards, A. S. G. "Lord Berners' Translation of Froissart's *Chronicle*, Fragment of a Manuscript Copy." In *Mostly British: Manuscripts and Early Printed Materials from Classical Rome to Renaissance England in the Collection of Keio University Library*, ed. Takami Matsuda, 172-76. Tokyo: Keio University Press, 2001.

Farinelli, Arturo. *Italia e Spagna*. 2 vols. Turin: Fratelli Bocca, 1929.

Ferster, Judith. *Fictions of Advice. The Literature and Politics of Counsel in Late Medieval England*. Philadelphia: University of Pennsylvania Press, 1996.

Feuillerat, Albert. *John Lyly, Contribution à l'Histoire de la Renaissance en Angleterre*. Cambridge: Cambridge University Press, 1910.

Field, P. J. C. *Romance and Chronicle: A Study of Malory's Prose Style*. London: Barrie & Jenkins, 1971.

Fletcher, Jefferson B. "*Huon of Burdeux* and *The Fairie Queene.*" *JEGP* 2 (1899): 203-12.

Foulché-Delbosc, F., ed. *Cancionero castillano del siglo XV.* Vol. 2. Madrid: Bailly-Ballière, 1915.

Gardiner, James. "Nicholas Carew." *DNB*. CD-ROM. Oxford: Oxford University Press, 1995.

Gascón Vera, Elena. "La ambegüedad en el concepto del amor y de la mujer en la prosa castellana del siglo XV." *Boletín de la Real Academia Española* 59 (1979): 119-55.

———. "Anorexia eucarística: la *Cárcel de amor* como tragedia clássica." *Anuario Medieval* 2 (1990): 64-77.

Gatti, José Francisco. *Contribución al estudio de la Cárcel de Amor: la apología de Leriano*. Buenos Aires: n.p., 1955.

Gayangos, Pascual de. *Libros de Caballerías con un Discurso Preliminar y un Catalogo Razonado*. Biblioteca de Autores Españoles 40. Madrid: Rivadeneyra, 1857; Madrid: Real Academia Española, 1950.

Gerli, E. Michael. "Leriano's Libation: Notes on the Cancionero Lyric, Ars Moriendi, and the Probable Debt to Boccaccio." *Modern Language Notes* 96 (1981): 414-20.

———. "The Old French Source of *Siervo libre de amor:* Guillaume de Deguileville's *Le Rommant des trois pèlerinages.*" In *Studies on the Spanish Sentimental Romance (1440-1550)*, ed. Gwara and idem, 3-20.

———. "La 'religión' de amor' y el antifeminismo en las letras castellanas del siglo XV." *Hispanic Review* 49 (1981): 65-86.

———. "Toward a Poetics of the Spanish Sentimental Romance." *Hispania* 72 (1989): 474-82.

Gilkison, Jean. "Language and Gender in Diego de San Pedro's *Cárcel de Amor.*" *Journal of Hispanic Research* 3 (1994-1995): 113-24.

Gómez, Jesus. "Los libros sentimentales de los siglos XV y XVI: sobre la cuestión del género." *Epos* 6 (1990): 521-32.

Green, Otis H. *España y la tradición occidental. El espíritu castellano el la literatura desde el 'Cid' hasta Calderón*. 4 vols. Madrid: Gredos, 1969.

Greenlaw, Edwin A. "Britomart at the House of Busirane." *Studies in Philology* 26 (1929): 117-30.

Grieve, Patricia E. *Desire and Death in the Spanish Sentimental Romance (1440-1550)*. Newark: Juan de Cuesta, 1987.

Guy, John. "The Henrican Age." In *The Varieties of British Political Thought, 1500-1800*, ed. J. G. A. Pocock, 13-46. Cambridge: Cambridge University Press, 1993.

Gwara, Joseph J. "Another Work by Juan de Flores: *La coronación de la señora Gracisla.*" In *Studies on the Spanish Sentimental Romance (1440-1550)*, ed. idem and Gerli, 75-110.

Hall, Anne Drury. "Tudor Prose Style: English Humanists and the Problem of a Standard." *English Literary Renaissance* 7 (1977): 267-96.

Haywood, Louise M. "Female Voices in Spanish Sentimental Romances." *Journal of the Institute of Romance Studies* 4 (1996): 17-35.

———. "Gradissa: A Fictional Female Reader in/of a Male Author's Text." *Medium Aevum* 64 (1995): 85-99.

Hernández Alonzo, César. *Novela Sentimental Española.* Barcelona: Plaza & Janés, 1987.

Hoffmeister, Gerhart. "Diego de San Pedro und Hans Ludwig von Kufstein: über eine frühbarocke Bearbeitung der spanischen Liebesgeschichte *Cárcel de Amor.*" *Arcadia* 6 (1971): 139-50.

Howe, Elizabeth T. "A Woman Ensnared: Laureola as Victim in the *Cárcel de amor.*" *Revista de Estudios Hispánicos* (USA) 21 (1987): 13-27.

Huguet, Edmond. *Dictionnaire de la Langue Française du Seizième Siècle.* 8 vols. Paris: Didier, 1925-1973.

Husband, Timothy, and Gloria Gilmore-House. *The Wild Man: Medieval Myth and Symbolism.* Exhibition Catalogue. New York: Metropolitan Museum of Art, 1980.

Hutson, Lorna. *The Usurer's Daughter: Male Friendship and Fictions of Women in Sixteenth-Century England.* London: Routledge, 1994.

Hyatte, Reginald. *The Arts of Friendship: The Idealization of Friendship in Medieval and Early Renaissance Literature.* Leiden: Brill, 1994.

Impey, Olga T. "Ovid, Alfonso X, and Juan Rodríguez del Padrón: Two Castilian Translations of the *Heroides* and the Beginnings of Spanish Sentimental Prose." *Bulletin of Hispanic Studies* 57 (1980b): 283-97.

Indini, Maria Luisa. "Nicolás Núñez 'Traditore' di Diego de San Pedro." In *Miscellanea di studi romanzi offerta a Giuliano Gasca Queirazza per il suo 65 compleanno*, ed. Anna Cornagliotti et al., 1: 489-504. Alessandria: Edizioni dell'Orso, 1988.

Kany, Charles E. *The Beginnings of the Epistolary Novel in France, Italy and Spain.* University of California Publications in Modern Philology 21. Berkeley: University of California Press, 1937.

King, Andrew. The Faerie Queene *and Middle English Romance: The Matter of Just Memory.* Oxford: Clarendon Press, 2000.

Kinney, Muriel. "Possible Traces of *Huon de Bordeaux* in the English Ballad of Sir Aldingar." *Romanic Review* 1 (1910): 314-21.

Krause, Anna. "El 'tractado' novelístico de Diego de San Pedro." *Bulletin Hispanique* 54 (1952): 245-75.

Krivatsy, Nati H. and Laetitia Yeandle. "Sir Edward Dering." In *Private Libraries in Renaissance England*, 1: 137-269. Binghampton: MRTS, 1992.

Kurtz, Barbara E. "The Castle Motif and the Medieval Allegory of Love: Diego de San Pedro's *Cárcel de amor.*" *Fifteenth-Century Studies* 11 (1985): 37-99.

———. "Diego de San Pedro's *Cárcel de amor* and the Tradition of the Allegorical Edifice." *Journal of Hispanic Philology* 8 (1984): 123-38.

Lacarra, María Eugenia. "Notes on a Feminist Analysis of Medieval Spanish Literature and History." *La Coronica* 17 (1988-9): 14-22.

———. "Representaciones femininas en la poesía cortesana y en la narativa sentimental del siglo XV." In *Breve historia feminista de la literatura española (en lengua castellana). II. La mujer en la literatura española: modos de representación. Desde la Edad Media hasta el siglo XVII*, ed. Iris M. Zavala. Madrid: Anthropos, 1995. 159-75.

Landmann, Friedrich. "Shakespeare and Euphuism. Euphues an Adaptation from Guevara." *Transactions of the New Shakespeare Society.* Offprint. London, 1882. 241-76.

Lawrance, J. H. H. "On Fifteenth-Century Vernacular Humanism." In *Medieval and Renaissance Studies in Honour of Robert Brian Tate*, ed. Ian Michael and Richard A. Cardwell, 63-79. Oxford: Dolphin, 1986.

Leadam, I. S. "Sir Robert Wingfield." *DNB.* CD-ROM. Oxford: Oxford University Press, 1995.

Lee, S. L. "Bourchier, John." *DNB.* CD-ROM. Oxford: Oxford University Press, 1995.

Lewis, C. S. *English Literature in the Sixteenth Century (Excluding Drama).* Oxford: Oxford University Press, 1954.

Lida de Malkiel, María Rosa. *La originalidad artistica de la Celestina.* Buenos Aires: Eudeba, 1962.

Linage Conde, Antonio. "Los caminos de la imaginación medieval: de la *Fiammetta* à la novela sentimental castellana." *Filología Moderna* 15 (1975): 541-61.

Livermore, Harold. "El caballero salvaje: ensayo de identificatión de un juglar." *Revista de la Fililogía Española* 24 (1950): 166-83.

Luquiers, Frederick Bliss. "The *Roman de la Rose* and Medieval Castilian Literature." *Romanische Forschungen* 20 (1907): 284-324.

MacArthur, John R. "The Influence of *Huon of Burdeux* upon *The Fairie Queene.*" *JEGP* 4 (1902): 215-38.

Mandrell, James. "Author and Authority in *Cárcel de amor*: The Role of El Auctor." *Journal of Hispanic Philology* 8 (1984): 99-122.

Márquez Villanueva, Francisco. "*Cárcel de amor*, novela politica." *Revista de Occidente*, 2nd ser. 14 (1966): 185-200.

———. "Historia cultural e historia literaria: el case de *Cárcel de amor.*" In *The Analysis of Hispanic Texts: Current Trends in Methodology*, ed. Lisa Davis and Isabel Taran, 144-57. New York: Bilingual Press, 1976.

Martin, June Hall. *Love's Fools: Aucassin, Troilus, Calisto and the Parody of the Courtly Lover.* London: Tamesis, 1972.

Matulka, Barbara. *The Novels of Juan de Flores and their European Diffusion.* New York: Columbia University Press, 1931.

Mayer, Thomas F. "Nursery of Resistance: Reginald Pole and his Friends." In *Political Thought and the Tudor Commonwealth: Deep Structure, Discourse and Disguise,* ed. Paul A. Fideler and T. F. Mayer, 50-74. London and New York: Routledge, 1992.

McDill, John. "The Life of Lord Berners." *TLS* (17 April 1930): 336.

Menéndez y Pelayo, Marcelino. *Orígenes de la novela.* 4 vols. Madrid: Bally-Ballière, 1905-1915; repr. Edición Nacional. 4 vols. Santander: C.S.I.C., 1962.

Michie, Sarah. "*The Faerie Queene* and *Arthur of Little Britain.*" *Studies in Philology* 36 (1939): 105-23.

Milares Carlo, Agustín. *Literatura española hasta fines del siglo XV.* Mexico City: Robredo, 1950.

Minnis, A. J. *Medieval Theory of Authorship: Scholastic Literary Attitudes in the Later Middle Ages.* London: Scolar Press, 1984.

Mitchell, G.E. "The Sixteenth Century Editions of *Arthur of Little Britain.*" *Revue Belge de Philologie et d'Histoire* 50 (1972): 793-95.

Nelli, René. *L'Érotique des Troubadours.* Toulouse: E. Privat, 1963.

Neville-Sington, Pamela. "Press, Politics and Religion." In *The Cambridge History of the Book in Britain, Volume III, 1400-1557,* ed. Lotte Hellinga and J. B. Trapp, 576-607. Cambridge: Cambridge University Press, 1999.

Norden, Eduard. *Die antike Kunstprosa vom VI. Jahrhundert vor Christi bis in die Zeit der Renaissance.* 2 vols. Leipzig: Teubner, 1909.

O'Brien, Dennis J. "Lord Berners's 'Huon of Burdeux': Its Cultural Context and its Language." Ph.D. diss., Ohio State University. 1986.

———. "Lord Berners's *Huon of Burdeux*: The Survival of Medieval Ideals in the Reign of Henry VIII." In *Medievalism in England,* ed. Leslie J. Workman, 36-44. Studies in Medievalism 4. Cambridge: Brewer, 1992.

Oberembt, Kenneth J. "Lord Berners's Translation of *Artus de la Petite Bretagne.*" *Mediaevalia et Humanistica* 5 (1974): 191-99.

Ornstein, Jacob. "La misogonia y el profeminismo en la literatura castellana." *Revista de Filología Hispánica* 3 (1942): 219-32.

Parker, Alexander A. *The Philosophy of Love in Spanish Literature, 1480-1680.* Edinburgh: Edinburgh University Press, 1985.

Parrilla, Carmen. "'Acresentar lo que de suyo esta crescido': El cumplimento de Nicolas Núñez." In *Historias y ficciones: Coloquio sobre la litteratura del siglo XV,* ed. R. Beltran et al., 241-56. Valencia: University of Valencia Press, 1992.

Pheeters, D. W. *El humanista español Alonso de Proasa.* Valencia: Castalia, 1961.

Post, Chandler R. *Medieval Spanish Allegory.* Harvard Studies in Comparative Literature 4. Cambridge, MA: Harvard University Press, 1915; repr. Westport: Greenwood Press, 1974.

Prieto, Antonio. *Morfología de la novela (Ensayos de lingüística y crítica literaria).* Barcelona: Planeta, 1975.

Rey, Alfonso. "La primera persona narrativa en Diego de San Pedro." *Bulletin of Hispanic Studies* 58 (1981): 95-102.

Ringler, William. "The Immediate Source of Euphuism." *PMLA* 53 (1938): 678-86.

Riqueur, Martín de. *Historia de la literatura catalana.* Vol. 3. Barcelona: Ariel, 1964.

Rivers, Elias. "A Sixteenth-Century Polish Translation of Flores' *Grisel y Mirabella.*" *Bulletin of Hispanic Studies* 35 (1958): 34-37.

Rodríguez-Puértolas, Julio. "Sentimentalismo 'burgués' y amor cortés: la novela del siglo XV." In *Essays on Narrative Fiction in the Iberian Peninsula in Honour of Frank Pierce,* ed. R. B. Tate, 121-39. Oxford: Dolphin, 1982.

Rohland de Langbehn, Régula. "Fábula trágica y nivel e estilo elevado en la novela sentimental española de los siglos XV y XVI." In *Literatura Hispánica Reyes Católicos y Descubrimento,* ed. Criado del Val, 230-36. Barcelona: PPU, 1989.

———. "El problema de los conversos y la novela sentimental." In *The Age of the Catholic Monarchs 1474-1516: Literary Studies in Memory of Keith Whinnom,* ed. Deyermond and Macpherson, 134-43.

Ronberg, Gert. *A Way With Words: The Language of English Renaissance Literature.* London: Arnold, 1992.

Round, Nicholas G. "The Presence of Mosén Diego e Valera in *Cárcel de amor.*" In *The Age of the Catholic Monarchs 1474-1516: Literary Studies in Memory of Keith Whinnom,* ed. Deyermond and Macpherson, 144-54.

———. "Renaissance Culture and its Opponents in Fifteenth-Century Castile." *Modern Language Review* 57 (1962): 204-15.

Samonà, Carmelo. *Studi sul romanzo sentimentale e cortese nella letteratura spagnola del Quattrocento.* Rome: Carucci, 1960.

Sandeman, George Amelius Crawshay. *Calais under English Rule.* Oxford: Basil Blackwell, 1908.

Sanvisenti, Bernardo. *I primeri influssi di Dante, del Petrarca e del Boccaccio sulla letteratura spagnola.* Milan: Hoepli, 1902.

Schevill, Rudolph. *Ovid and the Renaissance in Spain.* University of California Publications in Modern Philology 4. Berkeley: University of California Press, 1913; repr. Hildesheim: Olms, 1971.

Seaton, Ethel. "Marlowe's Light Reading." In *Elizabethan and Jacobean Studies Presented to Frank Percy Wilson,* ed. Herbert Davis and Helen Gardner, 17-35. Oxford: Clarendon Press, 1959.

Severin, Dorothy Sherman. "From the Lamentations of Diego de San Pedro to Pleberio's Lament." In *The Age of the Catholic Monarchs 1474-1516: Literary Studies in Memory of Keith Whinnom*, ed. Deyermond and Macpherson, 178-84.

———. *Tragicomedy and Novelistic Discourse in* Celestina. Cambridge: Cambridge University Press, 1989.

Sharrer, Harvey L. "La fusión de las novelas artúrica y sentimental a fines de la Edad Media." *El Crotalón* 1 (1984): 147-57.

Solomon, Michael. *The Literature of Misogyny in Medieval Spain: The Arcipreste de Talavera and the Spill.* Cambridge: Cambridge University Press, 1997.

Spinelly, Emily. "Chivalry and its Terminology in the Spanish Sentimental Romance." *La Corónica* 12 (1984): 241-53.

Staines, David. "*Havelok the Dane*: A Thirteenth-Century Handbook for Princes." *Speculum* 51 (1976): 601-23.

Tejerina-Canal, Santiago. "Unidad en *Cárcel de Amor:* el motivo de la tiranía." *Kentucky Romance Quarterly* 31 (1984): 51-59.

Tórrego, Esther. "Convención retórica y ficción narrativa en *Cárcel de amor.*" *Nueva Revista de Filología Hispánica* 32 (1983): 330-39.

Van Beysterveldt, Antony. "El amor caballeresco del *Amadís* y del *Tirante.*" *Hispanic Review* 49 (1981): 407-25.

———. "La nueva teoría del amor en las novelas de Diego de San Pedro." *Cuadernos Hispanoamericanos* 349 (1979): 70-83.

———. *La poesía amatoria del siglo XV y el teatro profano de Juan del Encina.* Madrid: Insula, 1979.

———. "Revisión de los debates feministas del siglo XV y las novelas de Juan de Flores." *Hispania (USA)* 64 (1981): 1-13.

Varela, José Luis. "Revisión de la novela sentimental." *Revista de Filología Española* 48 (1965): 351-82.

Vicente, Luis Miguel. "El lamento de Pleberio: Contraste y parecido con dos lamentos en *Cárcel de Amor.*" *Celestinesca* 12 (1988): 35-43.

Vigier, Françoise. "Fiction epistolaire et *novela sentimental* en Espagne aux XVe et XVIe siècles." *Mélanges de la Casa de Velázquez* 20 (1984): 229-59.

———. "Remèdes à l'amour en Espagne aux XVe XVIe siècles." In *Travaux de l'Institut d'études Hispaniques et Portugaises de l'Université de Tours*, ed. A. Redondo, 2: 151-84. Tours: Tours University Press, 1979.

Waley, Pamela. "*Cárcel de amor* and *Grisel y Mirabella*: A Question of Priority." *Bulletin of Hispanic Studies* 50 (1973): 340-56.

———. "Love and Honour in the *Novelas sentimentales* of Diego de San Pedro and Juan de Flores." *Bulletin of Hispanic Studies* 43 (1966): 253-75.

Walker, Greg. "Cardinal Wolsey and the Satirists: The Case of *Godly Queen Hester* Re-Opened." In *Cardinal Wolsey: Church, State and Art*, ed. S. J. Gunn and P. G. Lindley, 239-407. Cambridge: Cambridge University Press, 1991.

———. *Persuasive Fictions: Faction, Faith and Political Culture in the Reign of Henry VIII.* Aldershot: Scolar Press, 1996.

Wardropper, Bruce. "El mundo sentimental de la *Cárcel de Amor.*" *Revista de la Filología Española* 37 (1953): 168-95.

Warner, J. Christopher. *Henry VIII's Divorce: Literature and the Politics of the Printing Press.* Woodbridge: Boydell Press, 1998.

Weiss, Judith. "Structure and Characterisation in *Havelok the Dane.*" *Speculum* 44 (1969): 247-57.

Weissberger, Barbara. "The Politics of *Cárcel de amor.*" *Revista de Estudios Hispanicos* 26 (1992): 307-26.

———. "Resisting Readers and Writers in the Sentimental Romances and the Problem of Female Literacy." In *Studies on the Spanish Sentimental Romance 1440-1550,* ed. Gwara and Gerli, 173-90.

———. Review of *Tradiciones y puntos de vista en la ficción sentimental,* by Alan Deyermond. *La Corónica* 24 (1996): 211-12.

Whinnom, Keith. "*Autor* and *Tratado* in the Fifteenth Century: Semantic Latinism or Etymological Trap." *Bulletin of Hispanic Studies* 59 (1982): 211-18.

———. "Diego de San Pedro's Stylistic Reform." *Bulletin of Hispanic Studies* 37 (1960): 1-15.

———. "The *Historia de Duobus Amantibus* of Aeneas Sylvus Piccolomini (Pope Pius II) and the Development of Spanish Golden-Age Fiction." In *Essays on Narrative Fiction in the Iberian Peninsula in honour of Frank Pierce,* ed. R. B. Tate, 243-55. Oxford: Dolphin, 1982.

———. "Nicolás Núñez's Continuation of the *Cárcel de Amor* (Burgos, 1496)." In *Studies in Spanish Literature of the Golden Age Presented to Edward M. Wilson,* ed. R. O. Jones, 359-360. London: Tamesis, 1973.

———. *La poesía amatoria de la época de los Reyes Católicos.* Durham: Durham University Press, 1981.

———. *The Spanish Sentimental Romance 1440-1550: A Critical Bibliography.* London: Grant and Cutler, 1983.

Wilson, Edward M. "De l'amour de Leriano a Laureolle." Lot 524. *Biblioteca Phillippica. Medieval Manusacripts: New Series: Part VI. Catalogue of Manuscripts on Papyrus, Vellum and Paper of the 7th Century to the 18th Century from the Celebrated Collection Formed by Sir Thomas Phillipps (1792-1872). Day of Sale Tuesday 30th November at Eleven O'Clock.* London: Sotheby, 1971.

Workman, Samuel K. *Fifteenth Century Translation as an Influence on English Prose.* Princeton: Princeton University Press, 1940; repr. New York: Octagon, 1972.

Yoon, Sun-Me. "La continuación de Nicolás Núñez a *Cárcel de amor.*" *Dicenda* 10 (1991-2): 327-43.

Zandvoort, R. W. "What is Euphuism?" In *Mélanges de Linguistique et de Philologie. Fernand Mossé In Memoriam,* 509-17. Paris: Didier, 1959.